Italian

Without the Fuss

Want to take your Italian further?

Living Language® makes it easy with a wide range of programs that will suit your particular needs.

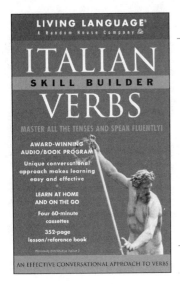

SKILL BUILDER: ITALIAN VERBS

ISBN: 0-609-60441-4 • $29.95/C$42.00

An award-winning program that will help you master verbs—the key to fluency. This is not just a book full of verb charts, but a program that teaches you how to USE verbs. There's also a handy grammar summary for easy reference. There are 40 lessons on four 60-minute cassettes, plus a 352-page coursebook.

Also available in French, Spanish, and German.
Coursebooks are also sold separately for $6.95/C$9.50.

THE FEARLESS INTERNATIONAL FOODIE CONQUERS THE CUISINE OF FRANCE, ITALY, SPAIN & LATIN AMERICA

ISBN: 0-609-81113-4 • $11.00/C$17.00

The ultimate guide to help you conquer the fine art of international dining, whether abroad or in your own neighborhood! Each section begins with an overview of the cuisine followed by typical ingredients and dishes, from appetizers through desserts. There is an easy-to-follow pronunciation key, loads of fascinating culture notes, and a helpful glossary on spices, sauces, and more!

Also available: *The Fearless International Foodie Conquers Pan-Asian Cuisine*

AVAILABLE AT YOUR LOCAL BOOKSTORE OR BY CALLING 1-800-726-0600
For a complete list of Living Language titles, please visit our Web site at
www.livinglanguage.com

Italian

Without the Fuss

BY

Ana Stojanović, M.A.

EDITED BY Zvjezdana Vrzić, Ph.D.

LIVING LANGUAGE®
A Random House Company

Published by Living Language, A Random House Company, New York, New York.
Living Language is a member of the Random House Information Group.

Random House, Inc. New York, Toronto, London, Sydney, Auckland
www.livinglanguage.com

Living Language and colophon are registered trademarks of Random House, Inc.
Manufactured in the United States.

Layout and graphics by Barbara M. Bachman

Illustrations by Norman Bendell

ISBN 0-609-81062-6

10 9 8 7 6 5 4 3 2 1

FIRST EDITION

To my friends

AUTHOR'S ACKNOWLEDGMENTS

Many thanks to Alba Forzoni and Helen Langone for their help

during the writing of this book.

Special thanks to Zvjezdana Vrzić, friend, editor, and

endless source of patience, encouragement, and inspiration,

without whom this book would never

have been completed.

PUBLISHER'S ACKNOWLEDGMENTS

Special thanks to the Living Language team: Lisa Alpert, Elizabeth Bennett,

Christopher Warnasch, Suzanne McQuade, Helen Tang, Fernando Galeano, Sophie Chin,

Mary Lee, Denise DeGennaro, Linda Schmidt, Marina Padakis,

Pat Ehresmann, Lisa Montebello, and Barbara M. Bachman.

Many thanks also to the dedicated reviewers, Antonella Ansani and Giuseppe Manca.

CONTENTS

WHAT'S GOING ON IN THE DIALOGUES	WHAT WORDS YOU'LL LEARN	WHAT STRUCTURES YOU'LL KNOW

WHAT'S GOING ON IN THE DIALOGUES	WHAT WORDS YOU'LL LEARN	WHAT STRUCTURES YOU'LL KNOW

WHAT'S GOING ON IN THE DIALOGUES	WHAT WORDS YOU'LL LEARN	WHAT STRUCTURES YOU'LL KNOW

WHAT'S GOING ON IN THE DIALOGUES	WHAT WORDS YOU'LL LEARN	WHAT STRUCTURES YOU'LL KNOW

Lesson 15: WHEN PIGS FLY . . . • 307

WHAT'S GOING ON IN THE DIALOGUES	WHAT WORDS YOU'LL LEARN	WHAT STRUCTURES YOU'LL KNOW
Quando voleranno gli asini . . . Sibling rivalry and watching TV.	• **Come on down!:** The joys of pop culture • **You fool!:** Insults and comebacks	• **Watch it!:** How to give commands and order people around • **Ne, ne, ne:** The pronoun *ne* and its many uses • **Watch it!:** More commands • **Strut your stuff!:** A review

Italian

Without the Fuss

WELCOME!

So you want to learn some *italiano?* But you don't want to do it by just memorizing long verb conjugation charts or ever-handy stock phrases like "Jeeves, please serve the mutton to the ambassador at eight." If that's the case, then you've come to the right place! *Benvenuti!* Welcome!

Italian Without the Fuss will help you learn as quickly and easily as possible, and the best part is that you'll have fun along the way. You'll have a chance to hear real conversations, the kind you might actually hear on the street and not just read in textbooks. And you won't need a crash course in grammar jargon before you start. We've tried to make this book as accessible and user-friendly as possible. Of course, this doesn't mean you'll just wake up one morning fluent in Italian. The bad news is: you **will** have to do some studying, but the good news is: it **won't** by dry and boring. That, you can count on.

So, what's *Italian Without the Fuss* all about? Well, you'll start off with an introduction to the sounds of the language. Italian is fairly easy that way—what you see is pretty much what you get, so you should be able to start speaking right off the bat. Then we really get down to business with 15 lessons, and an hour-long audio CD to give you plenty of listening and speaking practice. There are appendices, too, for quick reference if you get stuck, and a two-way glossary where you can look up any word in the book.

To make things easy, all the lessons have the same structure, and it's not just any structure—it's been scientifically designed to help you learn most effectively. Yes, we have the technology! Here's the basic layout of each lesson:

COMING UP...
Get a quick overview of what you'll learn in the lesson.

LOOKING AHEAD
Get ready to listen to the lesson's dialogues and get some advanced tips to help you follow along.

LET'S WARM UP
Think ahead about the topic of the dialogue and learn a few new words so you can get more out of it.

HEAR...SAY
Listen to a dialogue, try to understand as much as you can, then **read along** and **learn to speak** by repeating the phrases from the audio CD.

HOW'S THAT AGAIN?
Make sure you got the gist of the dialogue.

WORKSHOP
Discover the secrets of the Italian language; learn about its words and structure.

WORDS TO LIVE BY
Stock up on new words and phrases and get to use them, too.

THE NITTY-GRITTY
Overcome your fear of grammar with simple explanations and plenty of practice.

TAKE IT FOR A SPIN
Practice makes perfect! Try out all the good stuff you've just learned.

LET'S PUT IT IN WRITING
Read all about it! Fun texts help you learn to maneuver through the written word.

TAKE IT UP A NOTCH
Challenge yourself with additional practice that'll really make you think!

STRUT YOUR STUFF
Put it all together and review what you've learned by practicing a bit more.

CRIB NOTES
Get answers to all your questions, and check the translations of the dialogues.

But that's not all! You'll also get loads of good stuff that will spice up your learning, teach you **how** best to learn a new language, how to avoid particular pitfalls, and tell you about the culture and habits of the place. All at no extra cost!

TAKE A TIP FROM ME!
Be smart and get the most out of your efforts—you'll get tips on how to study, shortcuts, and memory tricks.

HEADS UP!
Avoid the pitfalls and common mistakes typically made by new learners!

THE FINE PRINT
Get ambitious and learn more about grammar or vocabulary.

WORD ON THE STREET

Talk like a real Italian: learn common expressions, idioms, and even slang terms, so you won't sound like an out-of-date textbook.

DID YOU KNOW?

Get in the know by learning about Italy, its culture, and the everyday life of its people. This is a great place to start not just talking like an Italian, but feeling like one, too.

So, that's it! You're ready to start. *In bocca al lupo!* Good luck, or "in the mouth of the wolf," as the Italians would say!

GETTING STARTED IN ITALIAN

BEFORE WE START...

Let's talk a little bit about language learning in general. The first thing you need to know is: **You know more than you think!** You don't believe me? Check out some of these words: *banana, idea, gala, hotel, pasta, radio, cinema.* So? What's the big deal, right? You already know English! Well, as it turns out, this means that you also already know some Italian, because these words are spelled exactly the same and have the same meaning in both languages. They're just pronounced a little differently. There are also many words that look only a little different, and you should be able to recognize them pretty easily. See for yourself:

ITALIAN	ENGLISH	ITALIAN	ENGLISH
banca	bank	*elegante*	elegant
centro	center	*possibile*	possible
parco	park	*professione*	profession
museo	museum	*dottore*	doctor
città	city	*studente*	student
difficile	difficult	*agente*	agent
differente	different	*idiota*	idiot

You get the idea. For the curious among you, the reason that so many English words look like Italian words is that they have Latin roots, and Italian is a Romance language. Yeah, so? Well, in this case, *Romance* refers not to the pleasures of courtship, but to the Italians' Roman roots. And which language did they speak in Ancient Rome? Latin. There you have it! That's why you can recognize so many of them. But Italian and English don't have just word roots in common. They also share similar word endings (suffixes, grammatically speaking). Take a look:

COMMON ITALIAN WORD ENDINGS AND THEIR ENGLISH COUNTERPARTS		
ITALIAN	ENGLISH	EXAMPLE
–tà	*–ty*	*realtà* = reality *università* = university *città* = city
–ione	*–ion*	*conversazione* = conversation *informazione* = information *professione* = profession

ITALIAN	ENGLISH	EXAMPLE
–ente/–ante	–ent/–ant	*differente* = different *elegante* = elegant *studente* = student
–ale	–al	*generale* = general *ideale* = ideal *normale* = normal
–bile	–ble	*possibile* = possible *memorabile* = memorable

And there's an ending that looks different in Italian and English, but serves the same function:

–mente	–ly	*probabilmente* = probably *generalmente* = generally

And if you're feeling confident now, just wait! There's a lot more to *comunicazione* (communication, of course) than just words and grammar. It's amazing how much you can glean from a conversation just by looking at facial expressions and body language. And the Italians do body language bigger and better than anyone else! Try this sometime: watch a movie or a sitcom and mute the sound. You'll be surprised by how well you'll be in tune with what's going on without hearing a single word spoken.

And there's also *la cultura* (You guessed it!). Communication happens in context, and the more you know about the context of Italian daily life and its rich history, the more easily you'll be able to read between the lines, get the point, and get your own message across. And don't worry, you're not on your own here either—there'll be plenty of cultural tidbits and information to help you impress (or fool!) even the most discerning locals.

Okay, so now that your head is probably bigger than your doorway and you're wondering why you need to study another language in the first place, let's get serious for a moment. The truth is (you might want to sit down for this) that despite how much you already know, you still have a lot to learn. The good news is that, as with everything else, I'll be there to help, not just by telling you **what** you need to learn but by giving you some tips on **how** to do it easily and well.

Take a Tip from Me!

Here comes my first tip: Pace yourself. Try to come up with a working schedule and set goals. Ideally, you will spend a little bit of time on your Italian every day—sometimes thirty minutes a day will go a lot further than two hours in one sitting. But if you can't manage to find time every day, don't despair: Just try to work regularly, and grab a free moment here and there to remind yourself of what you've learned. Take advantage of your free time—maybe you can rent an Italian movie on movie night or pop in the latest Eros Ramazotti CD while you're cooking dinner. You should try to get as much and as varied an exposure to the language as possible. Words and expressions have a way of just creeping into your memory. The most important thing is to have fun. As I said, Italian is a lot more than just a language. It's an easy culture to fall in love with. It happened to me, and I'm hoping the same happens to you. Once it does, the words will come easily . . .

Allora, siete pronti? So, are you ready? *Cominciamo!* Let's get started! Let's talk about Italian pronunciation.

SOUND IT OUT IN ITALIAN

Did your English teacher ever write *ghoti* on the board and tell you that it spelled "fish"? It makes perfect sense, argued George Bernard Shaw: just take the "gh" sound in *tough,* the "o" in *women* and the "ti" in *education,* and you get a perfectly acceptable way of spelling "fish." Well, guess what! Italian is **nothing** like English. When it comes to Italian pronunciation, *siete fortunati*—you're in luck—because what you see is what you get. Unlike the often bizarre spelling in English, Italian words sound pretty much the way they look—their spelling is virtually phonetic. As long you remember a few simple rules, you should start sounding like an Italian in no time!

OOHS AND AAHS: VOWEL SOUNDS

One of the easiest ways for an Italian to spot an American is by the way we pronounce vowels. First of all, Italian vowels are always pronounced—there's no such thing as a "silent *e*" in Italian. Secondly, they're always pronounced the same way. An "a" always sounds like *ah* in "father," "e" always sounds like *eh* in get, "i" is pronounced *ee* as in "feet," "o" is *oh* as in "caught," and "u" is always *oo,* as in *ooo, baby, baby.* Nothing simpler! Finally—and this is where our Anglo-Saxon accent tends to show up the most—Italian vowels are "crisper" than our vowels. The Fonz is not cool in Italy! Don't turn your *eh* into an *eh-eeeee.* Short and sweet, that's the rule.

ITALIAN VOWEL SOUNDS		
LETTER	SOUND	EXAMPLE
a	*ah*	*banca* (BAHN-kah)*, "bank"
e	*eh*	*elegante* (eh-leh-GAHN-teh), "elegant"
i	*ee*	*idiota* (ee-dee-OH-tah), "idiot"
o	*oh*	*dottore* (doh-TTOH-reh), "doctor"
u	*oo*	*studente* (stoo-DEHN-teh), "student"

*Notice that capital letters will be used to mark the pronunciation of stressed syllables.

Take a Tip from Me!

When you first begin to speak, do some warm-up exercises to loosen up your mouth. Say all of the vowels in order (a-e-i-o-u), going from one vowel right into the next. Stretch your mouth as much as possible on each sound. Do this <u>loudly</u>! Stand in front of a mirror and watch your mouth as you make each sound. When you're speaking, try to imitate an Italian— try to feel the language, its melodic intonation. Exaggerate the sounds a little. Yes, it'll probably feel silly, but silly can be fun, too, and it will help you loosen up and get over the embarrassment of speaking—Aaaaaaaaaah!!!—a foreign language! Also, try to get as much listening practice as you can. Hearing the sounds pronounced by a native speaker will help you develop an ear for the language, which will in turn improve the way you speak. *Piano piano* (slowly), you'll be able to tell if something "just sounds right" or not, and that's your goal.

Take a Tip from Me!

Okay, so now that we have our oohs and aahs in order, what happens when you have two vowels in a row? In Italian, each vowel in a vowel combination is pronounced, but sometimes they naturally flow one into the other, forming a single sound. Try your hand at these common combinations:

COMMON TWO-VOWEL COMBINATIONS		
VOWEL COMBINATIONS	PRONUNCIATION	EXAMPLE
ai	*ahy*	*mai* (MAHY), "never; ever"
au	*ow*	*auto* (OW-toh), "car"
ei	*ay*	*sei* (SAY), "six"
ia	*yah*	*italiano* (ee-tah-LYAH-noh), "Italian"
io	*yoh*	*fiore* (FYOH-reh), "flower"
iu	*yoo*	*fiume* (FYOO-meh), "river"
oi	*oy*	*poi* (POY), "then; later"
ua	*wah*	*quando* (KWAHN-doh), "when"
ue	*weh*	*questo* (KWEH-stoh), "this"
uo	*woh*	*buono* (BWOH-noh), "good"
ui	*wee*	*guida* (GWEE-dah), "guide"

Heads Up!

Sometimes, the "i" in the "ia" combination is stressed, in which case each vowel is pronounced separately, as in *farmacia* (fahr-mah-CHEE-ah), "pharmacy." In fact, there are vowel combinations where each vowel is always individually pronounced: "ae" as in *maestro* (mah-

Now that you know what to do when you see two vowels in a row, let's look at combinations of three vowels. They don't quite form one sound, but the transition from one vowel to the next is *smooooooooth.*

COMMON THREE-VOWEL COMBINATIONS		
VOWEL COMBINATIONS	PRONUNCIATION	EXAMPLE
aia	*ahyah*	*calzolaia* (kahl-tsoh-LAH-yah), "female shoemaker"
aio	*ahyoh*	*calzolaio* (kahl-tsoh-LAH-yoh), "male shoemaker"
iei	*yehee*	*miei* (MYEH-ee), "mine; my"
uio	*ooyoh*	*buio* (BOO-yoh), "dark"
uoi	*wohee*	*tuoi* (TWOH-ee), "yours; your"

Well, that does it for vowels. Now let's take a look at *le consonanti.*

PETER PIPER PICKED...: CONSONANT SOUNDS

The good news about consonants is that most of them sound just like they do in English. A *b* is a "b," a *d* is a "d." No problem! But here, too, there are a few important rules to remember.

We're on a Roll: The "r" Sound in Italian

The Italian "r" sound is trilled. But if you don't know how to purr like a kitten naturally, don't worry. You don't need to rrrrrrrrroll your "r"s until the cows come home. It's a single sound, and it actually sounds a lot like the "dd" sound in "u*dd*er." Try this: Tap the tip of your tongue against the ridge behind your top front teeth as you push air out. In case you're wondering, the technical, linguistic term for this is—are you ready?—a "flap." So, flap away, and keep practicing until you get it. It will come eventually. Here are a few words to practice with:

radio (RAH-dyoh)	radio	**realtà (reh-ahl-TAH)**	reality
rampante (rahm-PAHN-teh)	rampant	**regolare (reh-goh-LAH-reh)**	regular
rapido (RAH-*pee*-doh)	fast, rapid	**ritorno (ree-TOHR-noh)**	return
raro (RAH-roh)	rare	**russo (ROO-ssoh)**	Russian

Twice as Long: Double Consonants

When you see a double consonant in Italian, as in the last word you just pronounced, hold the sound a little longer than you would a single consonant. The syllable before a double consonant is often stressed and its vowel sound is **very** short and crisp, which naturally makes you stress the consonant more. (To help you remember this, double consonants will be doubled in the pronunciation of words in the glossary. It doesn't mean you should pronounce them twice, just hold them longer.) Compare:

sete (SEH-*teh*)	thirst	**sette** (SEH-*tteh*)	seven
casa (KAH-*zah*)	house	**cassa** (KAH-*ssah*)	cash register
sono (SOH-*noh*)	I am; they are	**sonno** (SOH-*nnoh*)	sleep
dopo (DOH-*poh*)	after	**doppio** (DOH-*ppyoh*)	double
pena (PEH-*nah*)	pity; pain; punishment	**penna** (PEH-*nnah*)	pen

Some Sounds Simply Sound Strange: More Special Sounds in Italian

There are a few Italian sounds that are difficult for non-native speakers, but a lot of that is just because of the way they look on paper:

"gli" is pronounced (lyee), a lot like the "lli" in mi*lli*on.
"gno" is pronounced (nyoh), a lot like the "ni" in o*ni*on.

As you practice these sounds, try reducing the space between the "n" and the "y" (or the "l" and the "y") as much as possible until they blend into one sound. The middle of your tongue should be touching the ridge of the roof of your mouth. Master this, and the next time you're in an Italian restaurant (where you should dine as often as possible from now on), you can impress your date by confidently ordering *gnocchi* by saying "NYOH-kkee" instead of "ga-KNOCK-kkey." Let's practice:

signore (*see*-NYOH-*reh*)	Mr.
signora (*see*-NYOH-*rah*)	Mrs.
signorina (*see*-*nyoh*-REE-*nah*)	Miss
spagnolo (*spah*-NYOH-*loh*)	Spanish
gnocchi (NYOH-*kkee*)	potato dumplings
bagagli (*bah*-GAH-*lyee*)	luggage, bags
figlio (FEE-*lyoh*)	son
biglietto (*bee*-LYEH-*ttoh*)	ticket
meglio (MEH-*lyoh*)	better
famiglia (*fah*-MEE-*lyah*)	family

Some Letters Do Double Duty

A few letters are pronounced differently, depending on what comes before or after them. The letters "c" and "g" have both a "hard" and a "soft" pronunciation:

- "C" is pronounced *k*, like the "c" in "*c*ar," unless it's followed by an "e" or "i," in which case it's pronounced *ch*, as in "*ch*eese" or "*ch*icken."
- "G" is pronounced *g*, like the "g" in "*g*old," unless it's followed by an "e" or "i," in which case it's pronounced *j*, like the "g"s in "*g*in*g*er."

Take a Tip from Me!

If you have trouble remembering when "c" is pronounced *ch* and not *k*, and when "g" is pronounced *j* not *g*, pick a word that will remind you. For example, remember *ciao* and *centro* for the soft "c" sound, and *gelato* and *giro* for the soft "g" sound. When you see a new word, and you're not sure how to pronounce it, just follow your examples!

Take a Tip from Me!

Can you think of another letter that has two possible pronunciations in English? If you came up with "s," you're on the right track. In English, "s" is sometimes pronounced *s*, as in "*s*on," and sometimes *z*, as in "wa*s*." Well, the same thing happens in Italian:

- "S" is usually pronounced *s*, except when it appears between two vowels or before the letters b, d, g, l, m, n, v, or r, in which case it's pronounced *z*, as in *casa* (KAH-zah), "house" or *sbaglio* (ZBAH-lyoh), "mistake."
- The combination "sc" is pronounced *sh* before an "e" or an "i."

stadio (STAH-dyoh)	stadium	**mese (MEH-zeh)**	month
solo (SOH-loh)	only; alone	**sci (SHEE)**	ski
Basta! (BAH-stah)	Enough!	**scuola (SKWOH-lah)**	school
cosa (KOH-zah)	thing; what	**fresche (FREHS-keh)**	fresh (plural)

Heads Up!

Whenever you see the combinations "ch" and "gh," they're always pronounced as *k* and *g*. The "h" is inserted to keep the "hard" sound of the "c" and "g," even when they're followed by an "e" or "i." Let's practice:

cosa (KOH-zah)	what; thing	**arancia (ah-RAHN-chah)**	orange
caffè (kah-FFEH)	coffee; café	**Chi? (KEE)**	Who?
Ciao! (CHAH-oh)	Hi!; Bye!	**Grazie. (GRAH-tsyeh)**	Thanks.
centro (CHEN-troh)	center	**gelato (jeh-LAH-toh)**	ice cream
Piacere. (pyah-CHEH-reh)	Nice to meet you.	**giro (JEE-roh)**	ride; tour
perché (pehr-KEH)	why; because	**Mangia! (MAHN-jah)**	Eat!

Heads Up!

Heads Up!

Notice that when "ci" or "gi" is followed by another vowel, the "i" is not pronounced. It's as if it's "absorbed" by the "c" or "g" to give it the soft sound. For example, the name *Giorgio* (George,) is pronounced (JOHR-joh) and not (JEEOHR-jeeoh).

Heads Up!

Some Letters Just Sound Different in Italian

- The letter "h" is always silent in Italian. It usually appears only in words of foreign origin or after the letters "c" and "g" to help them retain their hard sound.
- The letter "z" is pronounced *ts*, like in "pu*ts*." However, depending on where you're traveling in Italy, you may also hear it pronounced *ds*, like in "bu*ds*."

hotel (oh-TEHL)	*hotel*
zoo (TSOH-oh or **DZOH-oh)**	*zoo*
zucchero (TSOO-keh-roh or **DZOO-keh-roh)**	*sugar*

Some Letters Aren't Really Italian

The following letters appear only in words that the Italians adopted from another language, usually English. They're pronounced the way they would be in the original language.

LETTER	PRONUNCIATION	EXAMPLE
j	"j" as in *jazz*	*jazz* (JEHDZ)
	"y" as in yes	*Jugoslavia* (yoo-goh-ZLAH-vee-ah)
k	"k" as in English	*ketchup* (KEH-chahp)
w	"w" as in English	*weekend* (wee-KEHND)
x	"x" in extra	*ex-* (EHKS)
y	"y" in yes	*yoga* (YOH-gah)

Okay, so we've talked about the sounds that make up the Italian language. But what about how those sounds are combined into words?

CAN YOU HANDLE STRESS?

Word stress, that is. Sure you can! Italian words are generally stressed on the second to last syllable, as in: *colore* (koh-LOH-reh), *fortuna* (fohr-TOO-nah), *idea* (ee-DEH-ah), *persona* (pehr-SOH-nah). When the last syllable is stressed, it is always marked with an accent mark, as in *città* (chee-TAH) or *università* (oo-nee-vehr-see-TAH). There are also some exceptions that you'll just have to memorize as you come across them, like *telefono* (teh-LEH-foh-noh), but there aren't too many of them. Don't worry about this too much. Even if you get the stress wrong, you'll be easily understood, and that should be your main goal in learning any language.

Take a Tip from Me!

One of the best ways to improve your pronunciation is to hear yourself speak. University language classes require students to visit the language lab. A language lab would allow you to record yourself pronouncing assigned words or phrases and then compare your pronunciation with a native speaker's. Now, there's no need to invest thousands of dollars in a personal language lab, but you might want to consider spending a few bucks on a cassette voice recorder or a microphone for your computer. As you work through the lessons, record yourself reading the dialogues in this book, after you've listened to them on the CD. You can also record yourself reading individual words from this book, liner notes to an Italian CD, a recipe from an Italian cookbook, a menu you swiped from an Italian restaurant, or anything else you can get your hands on, as long as it's in Italian. Just listen to yourself speak. You'll be surprised by how easy it is for you to spot (and correct!) your typical mistakes.

Here are my final thoughts about speaking Italian: Never let the fear of saying something less than perfectly (whether it be due to a pronunciation or grammar or vocabulary mistake) stop you from talking to someone. Think of all the people you encounter who speak English with an accent, and yet you can still do business with them, discuss politics with them, and get to know them. The only way to learn to speak a foreign language is to actually speak it. Painfully obvious, I know, but you'd be surprised how many people seem to lose sight of this simple fact. Don't let that be you.

Take a Tip from Me!

I've said my piece, so now we can move on and get down to business. *Andiamo!* Let's go! Lesson 1 awaits . . .

In bocca al lupo!

LIKE OIL AND WATER

Come il diavolo e l'acqua santa
(*Lit.* Like the devil and holy water)

Yes, the animals are intelligent, cute. . . . They're . . . delicious.

COMING UP . . .

- *Hello, my name is . . .* : **How to meet and greet people in Italian**
- **Saying** *good-bye*
- *What do you do?*: **Talking about professions**
- *Whodunit?*: **The pronouns** *I, you, he, she, it,* **etc., in Italian**
- *Is that so?*: **Asking simple questions**
- *To be or not to be?*: **Introducing and talking about yourself with** *essere* **(to be)**
- **Saying** *no*

LOOKING AHEAD

Ciao! Come va? Hi! How's it going? *Bene*, I hope. *Siete pronti?* Are you ready? In this lesson, you'll learn how to take your first steps toward making *le conoscenze* (friends and acquaintances) in Italian. For a long time, Giovanni and Gabriella have been trying to find a girlfriend for their *amico* (friend), Pietro—committed bachelor and consummate *macellaio* (butcher). Somehow Pietro manages to strike out with everyone he meets the moment he opens his mouth. Tonight they want to introduce him to Gabriella's *amica*, Marina. Let's see if he has more luck this time . . .

ACTIVITY 1: LET'S WARM UP

What do you think the following phrases mean? Match the Italian phrases on the left with their English counterparts on the right.

1.	*Ciao!*	a.	Fine, thanks.
2.	*Come stai?*	b.	Hi!
3.	*Bene, grazie.*	c.	How are you?
4.	*Dov'è lei?*	d.	Pleased to meet you.
5.	*Piacere.*	e.	Where is she?

Take a Tip from Me!

As I said in the introduction, it is impossible to overstate the importance of listening to a new language as much as possible. In the beginning, anewlanguagesoundslikeajumbleof soundsandit'sveryhardtotelllonewordfromanother. Listening as often as possible will help train your ear. At first, you should just be listening for the sounds and melody of the language. Eventually, individual words will start to emerge. Whenever possible, you should listen to all of the dialogues a few times before you read along or look at the translation.

Now you're ready to listen. Pop in that CD and hit "play." *Andiamo!* Let's go!

HEAR . . . SAY 1

Giovanni and Gabriella have known Pietro for a long time, ever since he tried hitting on Gabriella by giving her the best cuts of meat, only to find out she was married! Giovanni went to settle the score, but when Pietro handed him a thick *bistecca* (steak) to treat the black eye he had just given him, a friendship was born. Since then, Giovanni and Gabriella have been on the lookout for a good match for Pietro. But it hasn't been an easy job. Ever the optimists, however, they decide to try again with Marina, a new co-worker and a friend of Gabriella's who seems to have a good sense of humor. When Giovanni and Gabriella arrive at *il ristorante* (the restaurant), they find Pietro already waiting for them . . .

Giovanni: Ciao, Pietro! Come stai?

Pietro: Ciao, Giovanni. Ciao, Gabriella. Bene, grazie. E voi?

Gabriella: Non c'è male. . . . Siamo in ritardo?

Pietro: Ma, no! Non siete in ritardo. (*looking around*) E Marina? Dov'è?

Gabriella: (*notices Marina walking in*) Eccola! Ciao, Marina!

Giovanni: Guarda chi si vede!

Marina: Ciao, ciao! (*and kiss, kiss*)

Giovanni: Marina, ti presento il mio amico—

Pietro: (*cutting him off, a little too eager to introduce himself, and a little too formal for the occasion*) Buona sera. Mi permetta di presentarmi. Mi chiamo Pietro. Pietro Rossetti.

Marina: (*playing along, amused, being very proper and formal*) Molto lieta. Io sono Marina Mellini.

Pietro: Piacere.

ACTIVITY 2:   **HOW'S THAT AGAIN?**

Let's see how much of the dialogue you were able to understand. You can answer in English or just try using a single word or simple phrase in Italian.

1. Do Gabriella and Giovanni arrive *in ritardo* (late) at the *ristorante?*

2. How is Pietro doing this evening? (*Come sta Pietro stasera?*)

3. *Chi* (who) spots Marina first?

4. What is Pietro's *cognome* (last name)?

5. What is Marina's *cognome?*

You can find answers to these and other burning questions in this week's *Enquirer.* Just kidding. But you **can** find them at the end of this lesson in the Crib Notes section, along with the translation of the dialogue you just heard.

Take a Tip from Me!

Remember: Don't worry about understanding every single word. If you were able to understand the gist of the conversation, you're way ahead of the game. If not, don't despair. We're just beginning! Read and listen to the dialogue one more time now and try to get as comfortable as you can with the phrases. When you're done, let's get down to some of the nitty-gritty stuff!

Take a Tip from Me!

Per piacere, step into the workshop . . .

WORKSHOP 1

Take a Tip from Me!

One of the best ways to learn new vocabulary is to use flash cards. Buy a pack of 3″ × 5″ index cards, and start writing out the words and phrases you're learning. Write the Italian on one side and the English on the other. When you use your flash cards, begin with the Italian side first and always say the words out loud (or sound them out in your head if you're in a public place and don't want to look like you're talking to yourself). Try to go through them as fast as you can. You're aiming for instant recognition. Remember to shuffle your cards regularly to avoid remembering a word just because of the card that came before it.

Once you have the Italian side down, start practicing with the English side first. You'll probably find that it's much easier to recognize the meaning of an Italian word than to come up with a word in Italian based on its English translation, but you want to be able to do both. As you work through the cards, you can eliminate the ones that you recognize instantly, and focus on the ones that are more difficult. If you get stuck on a word, try to come up with an association, then get rid of your crutch when you no longer need it.

Once in a while, put them all together again and review. The great thing about flash cards is that they're portable and easy to use so you can take advantage of even a few free moments. Pop a few of them in your pocket and go through them as you're eating lunch, waiting for the bus, or even waiting in line in the supermarket. Now, here's some material to put on those cards!

Take a Tip from Me!

WORDS TO LIVE BY

HELLO, MY NAME IS . . .: HOW TO MEET AND GREET PEOPLE IN ITALIAN

Could you notice a difference in the way that Gabriella and Giovanni spoke with Pietro and Marina, and the way that Pietro and Marina spoke with each other? Giovanni and

Gabriella are pretty comfortable and casual with both Pietro and Marina, while Pietro and Marina are formal with each other. That makes sense—they've only just met (although in this case it was a little exaggerated since Pietro was trying very hard to play the gentleman). The same would be true in any language. So, let's review some common greetings you can use with your friends and others you can use in more formal situations.

The Meet and Greet

USE	WITH FRIENDS	WITH ANYONE AT ALL	WITH PEOPLE YOU DON'T KNOW WELL OR WITH ELDERS
Hello.	Ciao. Salve.		Buon giorno. Buona sera. (PM only)
How are you?	Come stai?	Come va?	Come sta?
Very well.		Molto bene. Benissimo.	
Fine, thanks.		Bene, grazie.	
Not bad.		Non c'è male.	
So so.		Così così.	
Meet . . . / This is . . .	Ti presento . . .	Questo è . . .	Le presento . . .
I'm . . .		Sono . . .	
My name is . . .		Mi chiamo . . .	
Nice to meet you.		Piacere.	Molto lieto / Molto lieta. (m. / f.)*

Did You Know?

KISS OR SHAKE?: WHAT YOUR BODY SHOULD BE DOING WHEN YOUR MOUTH IS SAYING *CIAO!*

Italians usually greet each other with a handshake, which is also expected when meeting someone for the first time. A kiss on both cheeks is common among friends and acquaintances. While Italians also hug as a greeting, this is less common than a handshake and/or a kiss.

Now, do you want to try some of this stuff out? Let's do it!

---

*M. stands for *masculine* and *f.* stands for *feminine*.

Marina wanted to look good for her evening out, so she decided to spring for an expensive haircut at a new *salone di bellezza*. Take Marina's role in the following dialogue and meet her fabulous new *parrucchiere* (no, it's not a strange kind of bird, it's a hairdresser)!

Marina:	_____
Bruno:	Buon giorno.
Marina:	_____
Bruno:	Ah, sì! Marina Mellini. Piacere. Io mi chiamo Bruno.
Marina:	_____

If you can coerce someone to help you in your endeavor, practice this simple exchange with one of your friends. Or, the next time you meet someone, try to think about what you would say to them in Italian in the same situation.

And now for the mechanics of it all. The G-word! Grammar! Don't be afraid. We'll start off nice and easy . . .

THE NITTY-GRITTY

WHODUNIT?: THE PRONOUNS *I, YOU, HE, SHE, IT*, ETC., IN ITALIAN

For those of you who slept through grade school English, a pronoun is a word that takes the place of a noun. For example, when, in the next dialogue, Marina tells her vegetarian friends about her disastrous night out with a butcher, she'll talk about Pietro, but she doesn't have to use his name all the time. Marina can say "he" instead of Pietro. "He" is a pronoun. *Chiaro?* Get it? And pronouns like "I, you, he, they . . ." take the place of the subject of the sentence. They tell you who or what is performing the action in question.

Now that we've got that out of the way, the subject pronouns in Italian are:

PRONOUNS REPLACING SUBJECTS			
SINGULAR		**PLURAL**	
io	I	*noi*	we
tu	you (informal)	**voi**	you
Lei	you (formal)	**voi**	you
lui	he	*loro*	they
lei	she	**loro**	they

Did You Know?

The first thing you're probably wondering is "What's this informal and formal business again?" Well, that's a very good question, my astute friends! In Italian, you address people differently, depending on how well you know them or how much respect you want to show them. You would use *tu* when speaking to your family, your friends, to a child, or to a pet, but you'd use *Lei* for people you've just met, your boss, your elders, and in most of your daily encounters: at the store, at the newsstand, on the bus or train. Young people use *tu* with each other right off the bat. It would sound silly for two fourteen-year-olds to call each other *Lei* (it would be like calling each other "Sir" or "Madam" in English). If you really want to see Italians laugh, use *Lei* with a pet sometime! On the other hand, it might come off as rude or presumptuous if you address an adult with *tu*. Just to be on the safe side, stick with *Lei* whenever you're not sure about what's appropriate.

Did You Know?

Take a Tip from Me!

Notice that *Lei,* meaning "you (formal, singular)" and *lei,* meaning "she," is basically the same pronoun, but the one meaning "you" is capitalized—to distinguish it from "she" and, of course, to be polite. Talk about killing two birds with one stone!

Take a Tip from Me!

The Fine Print

The "true" grammatical plural for *Lei* is *Loro* (makes sense, doesn't it?). However, nowadays this usage is *fuori moda* (out of style), as they say. In everyday conversation, *voi* is the plural form, whether you're being polite or incredibly rude. However, you might hear *Loro* in some very formal or "snooty" situations.

ACTIVITY 4: **TAKE IT FOR A SPIN**

Tu or *Lei?* What would you use in the following situations (assuming you're an adult yourself)?

1. With your mother?
2. With a new colleague?
3. With the newspaper vendor you see every day?

4. With your boss's dog?
5. With the man you've just bumped into on the bus?
6. With your weird uncle Guglielmo?
7. With a boy who comes up to you on the street asking for money?
8. With your good friend Paola?
9. With the clerk at the grocery store?
10. With your mother's old school friend?

IS THAT SO?: ASKING SIMPLE QUESTIONS

As we all know, communication is not a one-way street, so let's take a quick look at how you can ask a simple question. Really, it couldn't be easier. Just as in English, you can simply raise your voice at the end of the sentence.

Siamo in ritardo?

Are we late?

Sei sicura?

Are you sure?

Take a Tip from Me!

If someone asks you a question, the best way to keep the conversation going is to show interest with a simple *E Lei?* or *E voi?* (And you?) Hey, it's also considered polite. This is one situation where subject pronouns will come in very handy. At least, *I* think so. *E voi?*

Take a Tip from Me!

Now let's get back to the *ristorante* and see how Pietro's doing.

HEAR . . . SAY 2

Well, they got past the introductions, and Marina is still talking to Pietro. That's a good sign, right? Maybe Gabriella and Giovanni can start a matchmaking business after this . . . or maybe not. Let's see. Remember, listen to the dialogue first, without looking at the text, then listen again and read along.

Pietro:	"Marina Mellini . . ." Che bel nome! È molto . . . elegante.
Marina:	Grazie. È molto gentile. È venditore per caso?
Gabriella:	Sì! Un venditore di fumo!
Pietro:	Ha, ha! No, non sono venditore. Sono macellaio. E Lei?

Marina:	Che coincidenza! Io sono vegetariana.
Pietro:	Beh . . . . Sì, gli animali sono intelligenti, carini . . . sono . . . deliziosi.
Gabriella:	*(to Giovanni)* Oh, Dio! Non va bene.
Giovanni:	*(to Gabriella)* No. Non sono d'accordo—è molto interessante.
Marina:	Mi dispiace. Devo andare. Arrivederci!
Gabriella:	Sei sicura? . . . Va bene. Ciao, Marina. Ci vediamo domani.
Giovanni:	Ciao, ciao!
Pietro:	*(Marina's already outta there.)* ArrivederLa. . . . "Deliziosi!" Che idiota!

ACTIVITY 5: HOW'S THAT AGAIN?

Well, how do you think Pietro fared?

1. What does Pietro do (what's his profession)? *(Che mestiere fa Pietro?)*
2. How does Marina react to it?
3. What does Gabriella think about *il futuro* (the future) of this budding relationship?
4. What do you think *coincidenza, vegetariana, animali, intelligenti, deliziosi,* and *interessante* mean?

As always, if you really need to, you can peek at the answers and the translation at the end of the chapter.

Word on the Street

Beh! is something you'll hear Italians say all the time. It's their equivalent of "well" but it can mean a variety of things, depending on how it's said or what body language accompanies it. It might mean "I don't know" or "Maybe" or it might just be a pause before starting a new sentence.

WORKSHOP 2

WORDS TO LIVE BY

SAYING *GOOD-BYE*

Now that you know how to say hello and introduce yourself, you'll also need to know how to say good-bye.

PARTING IS SUCH SWEET SORROW...

USE	WITH FRIENDS	WITH ANYONE AT ALL	WITH PEOPLE YOU DON'T KNOW WELL OR TO SHOW RESPECT
Bye.	Ciao.	Arrivederci.	ArrivederLa.
See you!	Ci vediamo!		
See you soon.		A presto.	
See you later.		A più tardi.	
See you tomorrow.		A domani.	

For some reason, people in Italy are seldom satisfied with a single *Ciao!* You'll often hear them say it two, three, or more times in a row. So if you really want to live the part, next time you're saying good-bye to your friends, give them a *Ciao, ciao!*

Also, you wouldn't want to sound impolite in your new language. Here are a few phrases everyone should know:

Per piacere. / Per favore.	Please.
Grazie.	Thank you.
Prego.	You're welcome. / Here you are.
Mi dispiace.	I'm sorry.
Scusi / Scusa. (formal / informal)	Excuse me; Sorry.
Sono d'accordo.	I agree.
Non sono d'accordo.	I don't agree.

Word on the Street

Italian, like English and any other language, has a rich store of quirky, interesting, and funny expressions that you can use to spice up your conversation. There were two in this dialogue: **venditore di fumo** literally means "a salesman of smoke," and it's used to mean "a fake, a poseur." Gabriella was just teasing, of course, and making a pun among friends. **Guarda chi si vede** literally means "look who can be seen" and you can use it as a greeting to mean "Look who's here!", "Well, if it isn't . . .", or "Long time no see."

Now it's your turn.

ACTIVITY 6: TAKE IT FOR A SPIN

What would you say in the following situations?

1. Someone offers you a seat on the bus. _____

2. You need to get past someone on the street. _____

3.   "May I have another glass of wine, _____?"

4.   You're leaving the newsstand where you buy your paper every morning and say:

    _____

5.   Someone thanks you for passing the salt. _____

I hope you're gettin' over your fear of grammar because it's getting to be that time again . . .

THE NITTY-GRITTY

TO BE OR NOT TO BE?: INTRODUCING AND TALKING ABOUT YOURSELF WITH *ESSERE* (TO BE)

Now that you know how to say *io, tu, Lei, lui, lei, noi, voi,* and *loro*, let's learn how to actually say something about all of the people you've met so far. You can do it with one of the most important verbs in any language: *essere* (to be). *Eccolo!* Here it is!

ESSERE (TO BE) IN THE PRESENT TENSE			
(io) **sono**	I am	*(noi)* **siamo**	we are
(tu) **sei**	you are (infml. sing.)*	*(voi)* **siete**	you are (pl.)
(Lei) **è**	you are (fml. sing.)	*(voi)* **siete**	you are (pl.)
(lui) **è**	he is	*(loro)* **sono**	they are
(lei) **è**	she is	*(loro)* **sono**	they are

Notice that the verb forms change depending on the subject. In fact, in this case, the same is true in English: *I am, you are, he is.* The changes are usually simpler in English because there are generally only two forms of a verb, e.g., "meet" and "meets." What this means is that in Italian you can usually tell who the subject is from the verb form used. And this means that subject pronouns can be **omitted** in Italian; in fact, they usually are. For example, in English you would say *I'm Marco,* but you can't say just *am Marco.* In Italian, on the other hand, that's precisely what you'd say: *Sono Marco.* You would say *Io sono Marco* only if you want to stress that you (and not some other guy) are Marco. Don't think that the subject pronouns are useless, though. Believe me, you'll be grateful you know them when you want to emphasize who's doing what or avoid confusion.

---

*Abbreviations are used as follows: *sing.* "singular," *pl.* "plural," *fml.* "formal," and *infml.* "informal."

The Fine Print

One of the most important "side effects" of the fact that Italian verbs show who is performing an action is that Italian, unlike English, has free word order. In general, Italian follows the same basic word order as English: subject—verb—object, but you are also free to move things around to emphasize one thing over another. This is especially evident in questions, where you generally put the word you want to emphasize at the front of the sentence. So, for example, *È Marco un meccànico?* and *È un meccànico Marco?* are both legitimate ways to phrase the question "Is Marco a mechanic?" The former example simply seeks confirmation of Marco's profession (the emphasis is on Marco), while the latter stresses "mechanic" as opposed to another profession.

ACTIVITY 7: TAKE IT FOR A SPIN

Okay, now it's your turn to show your stuff. Fill in the blanks with the correct form of *essere* (to be) or the missing pronoun.

1. *Mi permetta di presentarmi. _____ Pietro Rossetti.*
2. *Gli animali _____ carini.*
3. *Voi _____ in ritardo.*
4. *E Lei? _____ vegetariano?*
5. *_____ siamo americani.*
6. *Tu _____ d'accordo?*
7. *Il ristorante _____ molto quieto.*
8. *_____ siete molto intelligenti.*
9. *Giovanni _____ taxista.*
10. *Tu _____ un idiota!*

ACTIVITY 8: TAKE IT FOR A SPIN

Do you remember how *essere* (to be) was used in the dialogues? Write down all the sentences from the dialogues that include *essere*.

The Uses of Essere (To Be)

So, what can you say using *essere?* All sorts of things!

- First of all, as you heard in the dialogues, you can introduce yourself or someone else:

  Sono Marina Mellini.

  I'm Marina Mellini.

  Questo è Pietro.

  This is Pietro.

- You can describe someone:

  Pietro è un idiota.

  Pietro is an idiot.

  Marina è vegetariana.

  Marina is a vegetarian.

- You can state what someone does for a living:

  Sono un macellaio.

  I'm a butcher.

  Siete studenti?

  Are you students?

- You can also use *essere* to talk about nationality, and we'll spend more time on this in the next lesson.

  Sono di Parigi. Sono francese.

  I'm from Paris. I'm French.

Heads Up!

One thing you should <u>not</u> use *essere* for is to ask how someone is doing or to respond if someone asks you. In Italian, they use the verb *stare* (to stay) for this purpose, as in: *Come sta/stai?* (How are you?) and *Sto bene, grazie* (I'm fine, thank you).

WHAT DO YOU DO?: TALKING ABOUT PROFESSIONS

Now let's take a closer look at using *essere* with the names of professions. In Italian, most professions have a masculine and feminine form, just like *actor* and *actress* in English. However, some words for professions, especially those ending in *-ista* or *-ente* are used for either a man or a woman. Here are some common professions you can use with *essere* (to be):

	MASCULINE		FEMININE	MEANING
		agente		agent
	attore		attrice	actor / actress
	direttore		direttrice	director, boss
	dottore		dottoressa	doctor
Sono . . .		medico		doctor
Sei . . .	macellaio		macellaia	butcher
È . . .		meccànico		mechanic
	presidente		presidentessa	president
	professore		professoressa	professor
	studente		studentessa	student
		taxista		taxi driver
		turista		tourist
	venditore		venditrice	salesperson

Take a Tip from Me!

Notice that there are patterns in the masculine and feminine endings:

MASCULINE	FEMININE
–o	–a
–tore	–trice
–ore	–oressa

In fact, whenever you're talking about people, the words you use to describe them will generally match their gender:

MASCULINE	FEMININE
vegetariano	vegetariana
italiano	italiana
idiota	

But we'll spend more time on this in the next lesson . . .

Take a Tip from Me!

Now let's try out what you've just learned.

TAKE IT FOR A SPIN

Fill in the blanks.

1. *Pietro è un* (butcher) _____.

2. *Marina è* (vegetarian) _____.

3. *Maria è un'* (actress) _____?

4. *Sono un* (taxi driver) _____.

5. *Sei un* (tourist) _____?

6. *Anna è una* (saleswoman) _____.

7. *Lidia è una* (doctor) _____.

8. *Enzo è uno* (student) _____.

9. *È un* (mechanic) _____ *Marco?*

Word on the Street

There are a few expressions that are really easy to use but convey a lot of meaning. I call them linguistic "shortcuts" and you can use them to keep a conversation going when you're stuck or just to sound less like a textbook and more like a real person. **Che** (what) is one of them. You can stick pretty much any noun with it to come up with a fine exclamation: **Che coincidenza!** (What a coincidence!) or **Che idiota!** (What an idiot!), for example.

SAYING *NO*

So what **do** you say if someone calls you an *idiota*? Here's a simple, if not creative, response: *Non sono idiota!* (Well, what do you expect for Lesson 1? Don't worry. There's good stuff coming up!) But this brings us to an interesting question: How do you say that something is **not** so in Italian? Take a look:

Ma no! Non siete in ritardo.

But no! You're not late.

Non sono venditore.

I'm not a salesman.

Non va bene.

It's not going well.

Io non sono d'accordo.

I don't agree.

Non parlo italiano.

I don't speak Italian. (Well, not yet, but just wait!)

No means "no." (Could this get **any** easier?) *Non* means "not" and it goes before the verb.

TAKE IT FOR A SPIN

Say the opposite of the following statements.

1. *Pietro è molto gentile.*_____
2. *Gli animali sono deliziosi.*_____
3. *Pietro vede Marina.*_____
4. *Giovanni è un attore.*_____
5. *Sono d'accordo.*_____
6. *Va bene.*_____
7. *Pietro è un venditore.*_____
8. *Voi siete turisti.*_____
9. *Loro sono in ritardo.*_____
10. *Io non sono un idiota.*_____

That's it for now. It's time for you to see what this lesson was really about.

Take a Tip from Me!

Now that you've worked through the whole lesson, listen to the dialogues on your CD one more time. This will be the best indicator of your progress. Do this after each lesson. If you still have trouble understanding the dialogues, you should spend a little time reviewing. But I'm willing to bet you'll understand just about everything, and you're ready to move on. Again, don't worry about every word, but if there's something specific you still don't understand and you're curious about it, write it down. Keep a record of your questions. They'll probably be answered as you move through later lessons. And if you ever have a chance to ask an Italian speaker or teacher a question, take advantage of it.

Take a Tip from Me!

CRIB NOTES

Giovanni:	Hi, Pietro! How are you?	Marina:	Hey, hey!
Pietro:	Hi, Giovanni. Hi, Gabriella. Fine, thanks. And you?	Giovanni:	Marina, meet my friend . . .
Gabriella:	Not bad . . . Are we late?	Pietro:	Good evening. Allow me to introduce myself. My name is Pietro. Pietro Rossetti.
Pietro:	No! You're not late. And Marina? Where is she?	Marina:	Pleased to meet you. I'm Marina Mellini.
Gabriella:	Here she is! Hi, Marina!	Pietro:	Nice to meet you.
Giovanni:	Look who's here! / Long time no see.		

Pietro:	"Marina Mellini . . ." What a beautiful name! It's very . . . elegant.	Pietro:	Well. . . . Yes, animals are intelligent, cute. . . . They're . . . delicious.
Marina:	Thank you. You're very kind. Are you a salesman by chance?	Gabriella:	Oh, no! It's not going well.
Gabriella:	Yes, a *poseur*! (*Lit.* A salesman of smoke.)	Giovanni:	No. I don't agree—it's very interesting.
Pietro:	Ha, ha! No, I'm not a salesman. I'm a butcher. And you?	Marina:	I'm sorry. I have to go. Good-bye.
Marina:	What a coincidence! I'm a vegetarian.	Gabriella:	Are you sure? . . . Okay. Bye, Marina. See you tomorrow.
		Giovanni:	Bye, bye!
		Pietro:	Good-bye! . . . "Delicious!" What an idiot!

ANSWER KEY

ACTIVITY 1

1. b; 2. c; 3. a; 4. e; 5. d

ACTIVITY 2

1. No, Gabriella and Giovanni aren't late in arriving at the *ristorante*.
2. Pietro is doing *bene*—fine!
3. Gabriella spots Marina first.
4. Pietro's *cognome* is Rossetti.
5. Marina's *cognome* is Mellini.

ACTIVITY 3

Marina:	*Buon giorno.*
Bruno:	*Buon giorno.*
Marina:	*Sono Marina Mellini. / Mi chiamo Marina Mellini.*
Bruno:	*Ah, sì! Marina Mellini. Piacere. Io mi chiamo Bruno.*
Marina:	*Molto lieta. / Piacere.*

ACTIVITY 4

1. *tu;* 2. *Lei;* 3. *Lei;* 4. *tu;* 5. *Lei;*
6. *tu;* 7. *tu;* 8. *tu;* 9. *Lei;*
10. *Lei* (unless she gave you permission to use *tu*)

ACTIVITY 5

1. Pietro is a butcher
2. Marina says she is a vegetarian.
3. Gabriella thinks this budding relationship is doomed.
4.

coincidenza	coincidence
vegetariana	vegetarian
animali	animals
intelligenti	intelligent
deliziosi	delicious
interessante	interesting

ACTIVITY 6

1. *Grazie.;* 2. *Scusi.;* 3. *per favore / per piacere;* 4. *A domani.;* 5. *Prego.*

ACTIVITY 7

1. *Sono;* 2. *sono;* 3. *siete;* 4. *È;* 5. *Noi;*
6. *sei;* 7. *è;* 8. *Voi;* 9. *è;* 10. *sei.*

ACTIVITY 8

Siamo in ritardo?
Are we late?
No, non siete in ritardo.
No, you're not late.
Dov'è lei?

Where is she?
Io sono Marina Mellini.
I'm Marina Mellini.
È molto gentile.
You're very nice.
Sono macellaio.
I'm a butcher.
Io sono vegetariana.
I'm a vegetarian.
Gli animali sono intelligenti, carini.
Animals are intelligent, cute.
Sono deliziosi.
They're delicious.

ACTIVITY 9

1. *Pietro è un macellaio.*
2. *Marina è vegetariana.*
3. *Maria è un'attrice?*
4. *Sono un taxista.*
5. *Sei un turista?*
6. *Anna è una venditrice.*
7. *Lidia è una dottoressa.*
8. *Enzo è uno studente.*
9. *È un meccànico Marco?*

ACTIVITY 10

1. *Pietro non è molto gentile.*
2. *Gli animali non sono deliziosi.*
3. *Pietro non vede Marina.*
4. *Giovanni non è un attore.*
5. *Non sono d'accordo.*
6. *Non va bene.*
7. *Pietro non è un venditore.*
8. *Voi non siete turisti.*
9. *Loro non sono in ritardo.*
10. *Io sono un idiota.* (Gotcha!)

2.

SHOOTING THE BREEZE

Parlare del più e del meno
(*Lit.* Talking about more and less)

svizzera?!

Where are you from?

Buon giorno. Have you made any new *conoscenze* (acquaintances) since we last spoke? No? Well, what are you waiting for? Get out there and meet people! Can you remember some of what we learned in the last *lezione*? *Non siete sicuri?* You're not sure? Remember that you can use *essere* (to be) to talk about yourself or people you know—you can introduce people, talk about what they do, what they're like. . . . *Per esempio* (for example), *io sono Ana e sono una professoressa.* Did you understand that I'm Ana and I'm a professor? Okay, now you tell me a few things about yourself . . . .

Bene. So, now you're *in Italia* and what's the first thing you do? Whether you're thinking of going straight to a *museo* or just roaming about the streets and soaking up the *atmosfera*, you're sure to pass by a small place with a *Bar/Tabacchi* sign on it—the perfect place to begin your Italian adventure. Walk in, order *un caffè*, and you'll start to feel Italian roots you never knew you had. Maybe you're even a little hungry, *avete fame*, and you're in the mood for *un panino* (a sandwich) or *una pasta* (a pastry). Either way, *entriamo!* Let's go inside!

ACTIVITY 1: LET'S WARM UP

To eat or not to eat, that is the question! In a *bar*, you can order *qualcosa da bere* (something to drink), or *qualcosa da mangiare* (something to eat). What do you think you would be getting if you ordered the items listed below? Guess their meanings and check off the appropriate column.

		QUALCOSA DA BERE	QUALCOSA DA MANGIARE
1.	*un dolce con crema*		
2.	*un cappucino*		
3.	*un pizzetta*		
4.	*un caffè*		
5.	*un'acqua minerale*		
6.	*un panino con prosciutto*		

Take a Tip from Me!

Remember: Listen to the conversation once or twice on the CD, and see if you can guess what's going on. Get used to the sound of the language, and don't worry about being able to make out every word. Then listen again as you read along.

Take a Tip from Me!

Now you're ready to listen to our next dialogue, which takes place in a . . . well, I'll let you guess.

HEAR . . . SAY 1

Barbara is from Switzerland, and this year she's vacationing in Florence with her old college friend, Delphine, who lives in France. They've just arrived from *la stazione* (the train station), dropped off their bags at the *albergo* (hotel), and they're already back on the street, ready to start exploring. Next to their hotel is a small *bar*, and they decide to go in for a cup of coffee and a quick *spuntino* (snack).

Barbara: Buon giorno.
Il barista: Mi dica?
Barbara: Un caffè e un bicchiere d'acqua minerale, per favore.
Il barista: Frizzante o naturale?
Barbara: Frizzante.
Il barista: Ecco il caffè. (*turning to Delphine*) E per Lei?
Delphine: Un cappuccino.
Il barista: Altro?
Delphine: Sì . . . qualcosa da mangiare.
Il barista: Ci sono paste, panini, pizzette. . . . Cosa vuole?
Delphine: Una pasta con crema per me.
Barbara: E io vorrei un panino con il prosciutto.
Il barista: Una pasta e un panino!
Barbara: Grazie. Quanto Le devo?
Il barista: Cinque euro.
Barbara: Ecco.
Delphine: Scusi, signore. C'è una toilette?
Il barista: Sì. Ecco la chiave.

So, Barbara takes care of *il conto* (the bill), as Delphine attends to more pressing matters. While Delphine is in *la toilette* (twah-LEHT), an overly friendly Italian approaches Barbara.

Lorenzo: Hai da accendere?
Barbara: Sì. Prego.

Lorenzo:	Sei una turista?
Barbara:	Sì.
Lorenzo:	Di dove sei?
Barbara:	Sono svizzera.
Lorenzo:	Anch'io sono svizzero! Sei sola?
Barbara:	No. Ho un'amica qui . . . Ah, eccola!
Lorenzo:	Un altro caffè?
Barbara:	No, grazie. Non abbiamo tempo.

Take a Tip from Me!

Notice that the *barista* and Barbara address each other with *Lei,* while Lorenzo starts in right away with *tu.* That's because Barbara and Lorenzo are both young, and he wants to establish an immediate familiarity with her.

Take a Tip from Me!

Let's see how good a *barista* you would make. Did you get their order?

ACTIVITY 2: HOW'S THAT AGAIN?

1. Which phrases does the *barista* use to ask for their order?_____
    _____

2. What does Barbara order? *(Cosa prende Barbara?)*_____
    _____

3. What does Delphine order? *(Cosa prende Delphine?)*_____
    _____

4. How much is their *conto?*_____

5. What does Delphine ask for at the end of the dialogue? What does the *barista*
    give her?_____

6. Where is Barbara from? *(Di dov'è Barbara?)*_____
    _____

7. What does Lorenzo suggest? Do they accept?_____
    _____

Check your answers in the Crib Notes section at the end of the lesson. When you've finished, let's practice some vocabulary that'll come in handy at an Italian *caffè.*

WORKSHOP 1

***WHAT WOULD YOU LIKE?*: ORDERING AT A CAFÉ**

As you may know, Italians are wild about coffee, and you can take your pick of one of the following types:

un caffè	*refers to a single shot of espresso*
un caffè ristretto / basso	*"short" cup of espresso, meaning one where less water passes through the grinds, making the coffee extra strong*
un caffè lungo / alto	*"long" cup of espresso, one with more water in the cup, giving you weaker coffee but a few more sips to drink*
un cappuccino	*shot of espresso with a shot of steamed milk and foam*
un caffèlatte	*shot of espresso with hot milk*
un caffè corretto	*shot of espresso laced with a liqueur*
un caffè americano	*American coffee with milk*

Did You Know?

Italians are very particular about the way they consume their coffee—they take milk with their coffee only in the morning. So, if you want to fit in, don't be caught dead ordering a *cappuccino* or a *caffèlatte* after you hear that twelfth peal of the church bell! Opt for *un espresso* instead.

And if you're really not the coffee-drinking type, you can opt for *un bicchiere* (a glass) of:

un'acqua minerale	*mineral water*
frizzante / gassata	*carbonated*
naturale / non-gassata	*natural, non-carbonated*

Or you might prefer:

una spremuta d'arancia	*freshly squeezed orange juice*
un succo	*juice*
una coca (KOH-kah)	*cola*
un tè	*tea*

As I mentioned, the bar is also a great place for a quick *spuntino* (snack). Here are some of the things you can order:

una pizzetta	personal-size pizza
una pizzetta margherita	plain pizza, with tomatoes and cheese
un panino	sandwich
un tramezzino	type of sandwich, shaped like a triangle
una pasta	pastry
un cornetto	croissant

Heads Up!

If you're thinking, "Hey, wait a minute, doesn't *pasta* mean "pasta," you're absolutely right—it does. But it can also mean "pastry." Usually, the food you're referring to will be clear from the context.

Heads Up!

Did You Know?

Italians usually have a light breakfast consisting of coffee and *un cornetto*. Sometimes they might have a *panino* instead, but you won't see them eating anything as elaborate as bacon and eggs or waffles. If breakfast is included in your hotel room rate, it will usually be a Continental breakfast, although pricier hotels and those catering to an American clientele often adjust their menus to their clients' tastes.

Did You Know?

Okay, so now that you know **what** you can order, **how** do you do it? Well, first, the *barista* is likely to prompt you with:

Mi dica.	Tell me.
Per Lei? / Per te?	For you? (formal / informal)
Cosa vuole?	What would you like?
Desidera?	What would you like?
Altro? / Qualcos'altro?	Something else?

You can order by simply saying the name of the item and / or pointing to it, or if you want to get fancy, you can say:

Vorrei . . .	I'd like . . .
Ha . . . ?	Do you have . . . ?
Per me . . .	For me . . .

Word on the Street

And when you're ready to pay, ask:

Quanto Le devo?	*How much do I owe you?*
Quanto viene?	*How much does it come to?*

To get the *barista*'s (or anyone else's) attention, say:

Scusi. / Scusa.	*Excuse me. (formal / informal)*

To address someone you don't know, you can say:

Signore	*Mr.*
Signora	*Mrs.*
Signorina	*Miss / Ms.*

Heads Up!

But when you're talking <u>about</u> someone, rather than addressing the person directly, you'd say: *il signor Lentini, la signora Rossi*, or *la signorina Tomasi*. More about *il* and *la*, the definite articles, to come later in this lesson.

Did You Know?

Surprising though it may be, considering the Italians' love of food and their talent for lingering and savoring every bite, in most cafés in Northern Italy, you'll see Italians drink their *caffè* in one quick swig standing at the bar, then quickly return to work. It is customary to first pay for what you want at the *cassa* (register), and then hand your receipt (together with some change, for speedier service) to the *barista* when placing your order. However, in touristy areas, you can usually enjoy your order first and then pay either directly at the bar or at the *cassa*. If you have your heart set on people-watching at a café, be prepared to pay a higher price for food and drinks consumed at a table.

Finally, after a long day of sightseeing, the thing you might appreciate most in a café is its *toilette* (twah-LEHT) or *bagno* (bathroom), for which you'll often need to ask for *la chiave* (the key).

Let's see what you've learned. Make a dialogue using the following phrases:

—*Altro?*
—*Tre euro.*
—*Mi dica.*
—*Quanto Le devo?*
—*Un caffè basso.*
—*Un cornetto, per piacere.*

Did You Know?

If you're looking for a way to strike up a conversation with a stranger at a bar, you can always rely on: *Ha da accendere?* (Do you have a light?). Many Italians are avid smokers, and smoking is permitted in virtually all restaurants and in many public places where it is forbidden in the United States. That said, the global anti-smoking campaign seems *piano piano* to be taking effect in Italy. The latest surveys show that approximately twenty-five percent of Italians are smokers. In addition, there now exist many smoke-free offices and restaurants with non-smoking sections.

Did You Know?

As I said, a *bar / tabacchi* is a good place to strike up a conversation with strangers, and there's a good chance they'll be tourists just like you. For all you non-smokers out there, an easy way to make contact is to ask about someone's nationality:

Di dov'è?	Where are you from? (formal)
Di dove sei?	Where are you from? (informal)

To respond to this question, you could say:

Sono americana. Sono di New York.

I'm American. I'm from New York.

Sono italiano. Sono di Palermo.

I'm Italian. I'm from Palermo.

So, the rule is:

Sono . . .	+ a nationality
Sono di . . .	+ a city

Did you notice that, just like with professions, the word for nationality matches the gender of the person? The nationality of a man typically ends in −o, and that of a woman in −a. Nationalities ending in −e can refer to a man **or** a woman.

	MALE NATIONALITY	FEMALE NATIONALITY	CITY OF ORIGIN
	americano	americana	di Miami
	brasiliano	brasiliana	di Rio de Janeiro
		canadese	di Toronto
		cinese	di Pechino
Sono . . .		francese	di Parigi
Sei . . .	giamaicano	giamaicana	di Kingston
È . . .		giapponese	di Tokyo
		inglese	di Londra
	italiano	italiana	di Roma
	russo	russa	di Mosca
		ugandese	di Kampala

João è di Rio de Janeiro. Lui è brasiliano.

João is from Rio de Janeiro. He's Brazilian.

Anche Marisa è brasiliana. Lei è di Ipanema.

Marisa is Brazilian, too. She's from Ipanema.

Heads Up!

Notice that nationalities are not capitalized in Italian. Neither are the names of languages, the days of the week, or the months of the year. But you'll hear more about that later.

Heads Up!

ACTIVITY 4:   **TAKE IT FOR A SPIN**

What nationality are they?

1. Barbara è di Zurigo. È _____.

2. Delphine è di Parigi. È _____.

3. Il barista è di Firenze. È _____.

4. Megumi è di Kyoto. È _____.

5. *Tony Blair è di Londra. È* _____.

6. *Katarina è di Mosca. È* _____.

7. *Joshua è di Chicago. È* _____.

8. *Ming è di Pechino. È* _____.

9. *Jessica è di Toronto. È* _____.

10. *Bob Marley è di Kingston. È* _____.

As you're about to find out, this whole masculine/feminine business will prove to be very important in Italian.

THE NITTY-GRITTY

LET'S TALK ABOUT SEX: ALL ABOUT THE GENDER OF NOUNS

Okay, so professions (which are nouns) and nationalities (which are modifiers or adjectives) match the gender of the person you're talking about. Well, brace yourselves, because as it turns out, **all** Italian nouns and adjectives have a gender, even those that refer to inanimate objects and abstract concepts, not just those that refer to men and women. Now, before you start developing a grand social theory based on the gender of nouns in Italian—e.g., why a sandwich is masculine but a pastry is feminine—it's important to realize that gender in Italian is just a grammatical convention and nothing more. Now that we have that straight, let's spend some time on nouns. How can you tell if a noun is masculine or feminine? Well, if you've been paying attention thus far, you'll find that it's actually pretty easy: most feminine nouns end in *–a*, as in *pasta*, and most masculine nouns end in *–o*, as in *panino*.

Piece of *torta* (cake), right? Almost, but not quite. You may have noticed that some nouns, like *bicchiere*, end in *–e*. With these nouns, you can't tell their gender just by looking at them—you'll simply have to memorize the gender when you learn the noun. Still, I can give you a couple of rules to help you out: nouns ending in *–ione*, like *stazione*, are usually feminine, and those ending in *–ore*, like *signore*, are usually masculine. Nouns that end in a consonant (and these are usually borrowed from another language), like *bar* or *computer*, also tend to be masculine. And, don't forget the typical endings for professions you learned in Lesson 1.

COMMON NOUN ENDINGS	
MASCULINE	FEMININE
–o	–a
–e	
–ore	–ione

Heads Up!

Remember that there is a group of nouns ending in *–ista*, like *barista* and *taxista*? These nouns usually refer to people, and they can be either masculine or feminine, even though they end in *–a*. In this lesson, our *turista* happens to be female, but a *turista* can just as easily be male. By the way, *idiota* is another noun that ends in *–a* but which can be either masculine or feminine. In fact, all nouns ending in *–iota* can be either masculine or feminine, like *patriota*, for example.

Heads Up!

ACTIVITY 5:   TAKE IT FOR A SPIN

Circle the correct gender and try to remember or guess the meaning of the following nouns. Remember that some nouns can be used for either gender. (Hint: If a word doesn't immediately look familiar, sound it out):

MEANING

1.	*telefono*	M	F	_____
2.	*pianta*	M	F	_____
3.	*stazione*	M	F	_____
4.	*hotel*	M	F	_____
5.	*attrice*	M	F	_____
6.	*ottimista*	M	F	_____
7.	*sigaretta*	M	F	_____
8.	*bar*	M	F	_____
9.	*amica*	M	F	_____
10.	*venditore*	M	F	_____

TWO'S COMPANY, THREE'S A CROWD: THE PLURAL FORM OF NOUNS

So, what happens if you have more than one of something? You make it plural, *vero (correct)*? In English, we do this by adding *–s* or *–es* to a word, as in: *map → maps*. In Italian, they do it like this: *panino → panini; pasta → paste; bicchiere → bicchieri*. In other words, the last letter of the word changes: *–a* becomes *–e*; *–o* and *–e* become *–i*.

PLURAL NOUN ENDINGS		
	SINGULAR	PLURAL
FEMININE	*–a*	*–e*
MASCULINE	*–o*	*–i*
FEM. OR MASC.	*–e*	*–i*

Nouns that end in an accented vowel, like *caffè,* or in a consonant, like *bar,* stay the same whether they're singular or plural.

Heads Up!

Ora tocca a voi. Now it's your turn.

ACTIVITY 6: TAKE IT FOR A SPIN

In addition to food and drink, you can buy all sorts of useful items at a *bar / tabacchi.* Tell your friend all about it by making the following words plural and using *ci sono,* as in the example.

1. *panino* _Ci sono panini._____
2. *pasta* _____
3. *caffè* _____
4. *pizza* _____
5. *cornetto* _____
6. *sigaretta* _____
7. *tramezzino* _____
8. *spremuta* _____

If you're still worried about this whole gender thing, there is something else to help you remember whether a noun is masculine or feminine, singular or plural: the word that accompanies it.

LITTLE WORDS MEAN A LOT: A, AN, AND THE IN ITALIAN

An article is what you read in the paper, but it's also a type of a word. It's what stands in front of a noun when you say "**a** house" or "**the** house" or *una casa* or *la casa* in Italian. In Italian, articles match the noun in gender and number, just like the adjectives do. Indefinite articles (*a* and *an* in English and *una* and *un* in Italian) are used only with singular nouns.

THE ARTICLE *A / AN* IN ITALIAN		
	SINGULAR	EXAMPLE
FEMININE	*una*	*una pizza*
MASCULINE	*un*	*un panino, un americano*

The Fine Print

To make pronunciation easier, the article *una* is abbreviated to *un'* when it comes before a vowel, as in *un'acqua*. On the other hand, the article *un* adds a vowel and becomes *uno* when it comes before a word that starts with the letter "z." *Uno* is also used with words that start with "s" followed by another consonant, as in *uno svizzero*.

The definite article in English is *the.* In Italian, it has the following forms:

THE ARTICLE *THE* IN ITALIAN			
	SINGULAR	PLURAL	EXAMPLE
FEMININE			
before a consonant	*la*	*le*	*la pizza* → *le pizze*
before a vowel	*l'*	*le*	*l'acqua* → *le acque*
MASCULINE			
before a consonant	*il*	*i*	*il panino* → *i panini*
before a vowel	*l'*	*gli*	*l'americano* → *gli americani*

The Fine Print

To make pronunciation easier, the article *il* becomes *lo* when it comes before a word that starts with the letter "z" or with "s" followed by another consonant, as in *uno svizzero*. In the plural, it's *gli,* as in *gli svizzeri*.

In general, articles are used in Italian in much the same way as in English: the article *a/an* is used when introducing a concept for the first time or when talking about a general instance of something. The article *the* is used when referring to something that's already been mentioned or when you have a specific item in mind. So, for example, when Barbara is ordering she uses the article *un* to ask for a coffee, a glass of mineral water, and a sandwich:

Un caffè e un bicchiere d'acqua minerale, per piacere.

A coffee and a glass of mineral water, please.

Io vorrei un panino con prosciutto.

I would like a ham sandwich.

But when her order is ready, the *barista* uses the article *il* because he's referring to a specific item that's already been mentioned.

| *Ecco il caffè.* | Here's the coffee. |
| *Ecco la chiave.* | Here's the key. |

Take a Tip from Me!

You should always try to remember new nouns together with their articles. That way, you'll easily remember their gender. When you look at *il bicchiere,* for example, you can immediately tell from the article that it's masculine, even though the word itself ends in *–e.*

Take a Tip from Me!

ACTIVITY 7: TAKE IT FOR A SPIN

Write each word listed, with the appropriate article meaning "the," first in the singular, then in the plural. I've done the first one for you.

1.   *un panino*   _____*il panino*_____   _____*i panini*_____

2.   *una pasta*   _____   _____

3.   *una pizza*   _____   _____

4.   *un caffè*   _____   _____

5.   *un cornetto*   _____   _____

6.   *una sigaretta*   _____   _____

7.   *un tramezzino*   _____   _____

8.   *una spremuta*   _____   _____

9.   *un'acqua*   _____   _____

10. *un americano*   _____   _____

Let's get back to the bar and see what's happening . . . right after this quick exercise:

ACTIVITY 8: LET'S WARM UP

To the best of your ability, fill in the blanks choosing from the following words:

strade   *un biglietto per l'autobus*   *francobolli*
una pianta della città   *una carta telefonica*   *cartoline*   *piazze*

1. _____ shows you where all the _____

   and _____ in the city are.

2. You have to stick _____ on your _____ before you mail them.

3. You can make a telephone call from a public pay phone using _____.

4. To ride the bus, you need _____.

And now back to our program . . .

HEAR . . . SAY 2

Barbara, having politely evaded the advances of the self-proclaimed *svizzero*, and Delphine, having successfully returned from you-know-where, are about to leave. Suddenly Barbara remembers that they need *una pianta della città* (a city map) and a few other things.

Barbara:	Scusi, signore. Ho bisogno di una pianta della città . . .
Il barista:	Non ho una pianta, però ci sono molti venditori per strada in piazza Duomo.
Barbara:	Ha biglietti dell'autobus?
Il barista:	Sì, certo. Quanti ne vuole?
Barbara:	Due, grazie.
Il barista:	Qualcos'altro?
Delphine:	Sì. Dieci cartoline. Ha francobolli per l'Europa?
Il barista:	Sì. Ecco. Altro?
Delphine:	Vorrei anche una carta telefonica.
Il barista:	Ne abbiamo da cinque, dieci o venti euro.
Delphine:	Da dieci.
Il barista:	Allora—due euro per i biglietti, sette per le cartoline e dieci per la scheda. Diciannove. Grazie.
Lorenzo:	Buon divertimento a Firenze!

Did You Know?

The piazza Duomo is the square surrounding Florence's most famous church: *la Cattedrale di Santa Maria del Fiore*. Also called *il Duomo,* the church is known for its impressive octagonal dome designed by Filippo Brunelleschi (1377–1446). Next to the church is the Baptistery with its famous bronze doors decorated with relief panels depicting the life of Christ. *Il Duomo* is a term used in many towns to refer to the main church, so you'll hear people talking about the *Duomo* not just in Florence, but in Milano, Siena, Pisa, and elsewhere, as well.

Did You Know?

1. Did the *barista* have *una pianta della città*? Where does he suggest Barbara buy one?
2. How many *biglietti dell'autobus* does she buy?
3. What does Delphine buy? Where is she mailing them?
4. Can you find another word for *carta telefonica* in the dialogue?

Siete pronti per lavorare? Are you ready to do some work? Let's get to it.

WORKSHOP 2

WORDS TO LIVE BY

THE BARE NECESSITIES: ASKING FOR WHAT A TOURIST NEEDS

Amazing what you can get while sipping a good *caffè* . . .

una pianta della città	*city map*
un biglietto dell'autobus	*bus ticket*
una carta / scheda telefonica	*pre-paid telephone card*
una cartolina	*postcard*
un francobollo	*stamp*

and my favorite:

una gomma (americana)	*chewing gum (Lit. American rubber)*

Did You Know?

One of the most popular items sold at a *bar / tabacchi* is *la schedina* (lottery ticket), which you need to fill out in order to participate in the *Totocalcio* lottery. If you successfully predict the outcome of thirteen soccer games, you win a lot of *denaro* (money). *Totocalcio* is a favorite Italian pastime, so popular, in fact, that it's made its way into colloquial usage. If someone you know is spending money like it's water, you can say: *Ha fatto tredici?* (Did (s)he make a 13?), implying (s)he's won the lottery.

Wherever you decide to do your shopping, *Buon divertimento!* Have fun! Here's how to ask for what you want:

Vorrei . . .	*I would like . . .*
Ho bisogno di . . .	*I need . . .*
Ha . . . ?	*Do you have . . . ?*

The salesperson might ask:

Quanti ne vuole?   *How many would you like?*

The Fine Print

Ne is a word that you'll hear thrown around all over the place. It's used most frequently to mean "some / any of them," as in *Quanti ne vuole?* (How many of them do you want?), when you're talking about quantities. Don't worry about using it yet, just don't be freaked out when you hear it or see it.

THE COUNTDOWN: NUMBERS FROM 1 TO 20

Another thing that will come in handy if you plan to go shopping is knowing your numbers. Let's start with one through twenty.

1	**uno**	11	**undici**
2	**due**	12	**dodici**
3	**tre**	13	**tredici**
4	**quattro**	14	**quattordici**
5	**cinque**	15	**quindici**
6	**sei**	16	**sedici**
7	**sette**	17	**diciassette**
8	**otto**	18	**diciotto**
9	**nove**	19	**diciannove**
10	**dieci**	20	**venti**

Here's a bonus question. You get *dieci* extra points if you can guess what *zero* means. If you have no idea, you get a big fat *zero* (hey, that's [TSEH-roh] *in italiano*).

ACTIVITY 10:   TAKE IT FOR A SPIN

Give the answer:

1. *due + due =* _____

2. *nove – quattro =* _____

3. *dieci + nove – tre =* _____

4. *cinque + dieci =* _____

5. *quindici – sei =* _____

6. *sei + sette =* _____

7. *otto – sette – uno =* _____

8. *diciassette – tre* = _____

9. *due × sei* = _____

10. *quattro × cinque* = _____

THE NITTY-GRITTY

LET'S TALK ABOUT SEX AGAIN . . . AND NUMBER: THE GENDER AND NUMBER OF ADJECTIVES

As you know, Italian nouns have a gender, and any word that describes a noun has to match its gender. You've already seen how that works with articles. Now let's take a look at adjectives. You heard Barbara say she was *svizzera* but Lorenzo said he was *svizzero*, even though in English they're both just Swiss. Have you noticed a pattern here? When describing singular nouns, many adjectives end in *–o* when they're masculine and *–a* when they're feminine. In the plural, *–o* becomes *–i*, and *–a* becomes *–e*.

Barbara è svizzer<u>a</u> e Lorenzo è svizzer<u>o</u>. Sono svizzer<u>i</u>.

Barbara is Swiss and Lorenzo is Swiss. They're Swiss.

Marina è vegetarian<u>a</u> e Chiara è vegetarian<u>a</u>. Sono vegetarian<u>e</u>.

Marina is vegetarian and Chiara is vegetarian. They're vegetarian.

Heads Up!

When you're talking about a group of men and women, the adjective describing them will be masculine and plural.

Another group of adjectives ends in *–e* when they're singular and *–i* when they're plural, and these adjectives do "double duty"—they can be used together with both masculine and feminine nouns..

l'animale intelligent<u>e</u> →   **gli animali intelligent<u>i</u>**

the smart animal   the smart animals

l'acqua mineral<u>e</u> →   **le acque mineral<u>i</u>**

the mineral water   the mineral waters

As you can see, adjective endings are exactly the same as noun endings:

ADJECTIVE ENDINGS		
	SINGULAR	PLURAL
FEMININE	*–a*	*–e*
MASCULINE	*–o*	*–i*
FEM. OR MASC.	*–e*	*–i*

Heads Up!

What's nice about the agreement of adjectives is that the noun and the adjective often end in the same letter, as in *carta telefonica*, so you will naturally tend to make the agreement simply because it sounds better that way. However, because words ending in *–e* can be either gender, it's possible to have a noun ending in *–e* and an adjective ending in *–a* or *–o*, and vice versa, as is the case with *caffè ristretto* and *acqua minerale*. This is where you need to be careful and make sure that you have your vowels in order.

Finally, did you notice something strange about Italian adjectives? They tend to come after the noun, not before: *un caffè ristretto, un'acqua minerale, una carta telefonica.*

Okay, enough talk. It's time for some action . . .

ACTIVITY 11: TAKE IT FOR A SPIN

Select from the adjectives listed below to complete the sentences. Make sure they match the gender of the nouns they're describing.

alto   telefonico   italiano   vegetariano   francese

1. Barbara ha un'amica _____.

2. Marina è _____.

3. Un caffè _____, per piacere.

4. Ho bisogno di una carta _____.

5. Firenze è una città _____.

TO HAVE AND HAVE NOT: TALKING ABOUT WHAT YOU HAVE WITH THE VERB *AVERE* (TO HAVE)

The verb *avere* means "to have." *Eccolo!* Here it is!

AVERE (TO HAVE) IN THE PRESENT TENSE			
I have	*io ho*	*noi abbiamo*	we have
you have	*tu hai*	*voi avete*	you all have
you have	*Lei ha*	*voi avete*	you all have
he has	*lui ha*	*loro hanno*	they have
she has	*lei ha*	*loro hanno*	they have

Take a Tip from Me!

Here's something to help you remember this conjugation. *Avere* **is what you might call a "shoe" verb: You can draw a shoe around the forms that are similar, i.e., all but the** *noi* **and** *voi* **forms. Many Italian verbs are similar to** *avere* **in this way.**

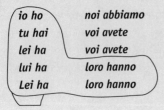

Take a Tip from Me!

The verb *avere* is used much like its English counterpart:

Ha biglietti dell'autobus?

Do you have bus tickets?

Ne abbiamo da cinque, dieci o venti euro.

We have them (in denominations) of five, ten, or twenty euros.

Ho un'amica qui.

I have a friend here.

But it's also used in many common idiomatic expressions:

* *avere bisogno di* (to need)

    Ho bisogno di una pianta della città.

    I need a city map. (*Lit.* I have a need for a map of the city.)

* *avere ragione* (to be right)

    Hai ragione.

    You're right. (*Lit.* You have reason.)

- *avere tempo* (to have time)

  Non abbiamo tempo.

  We don't have time.

You'll see a lot more expressions with *avere* in upcoming lessons. Now, let's practice.

ACTIVITY 12: **TAKE IT FOR A SPIN**

Fill in the blanks with the appropriate form of *avere*.

1. Barbara, (tu) _____ tempo per uno spuntino?

2. Scusi, _____ da accendere?

3. I turisti _____ bisogno di una pianta della città.

4. Sei solo? —No, _____ un amico qui.

5. Ecco un telefono! (tu) _____ una carta telefonica?

6. Cosa c'è da mangiare? (noi) _____ panini, paste, pizze . . .

7. (voi) _____ francobolli per le cartoline?

8. I venditori di strada _____ piante e cartoline.

9. Delphine _____ un'amica svizzera.

10. (io) _____ bisogno di un caffè!

See you in *lezione tre*!

HEAR...SAY 1

Barbara:	Hello
Bartender:	Your order? (*Lit.* Tell me?)
Barbara:	A coffee and a glass of mineral water, please.
Bartender:	Carbonated or non-carbonated?
Barbara:	Carbonated.
Bartender:	Here's the coffee. And for you?
Delphine:	A cappuccino.
Bartender:	Anything else?
Delphine:	Yes . . . something to eat.
Bartender:	There are pastries, sandwiches, mini pizzas . . . What would you like?
Delphine:	A pastry with custard for me.
Barbara:	And I'd like a sandwich with ham.
Bartender:	One pastry and one sandwich!
Barbara:	Thank you. How much do I owe you?

Bartender:	Five euros.
Barbara:	Here you go.
Delphine:	Excuse me, sir. Is there a bathroom here?
Bartender:	Yes. Here's the key.
Lorenzo:	Do you have a light?
Barbara:	Yes. Here you go.
Lorenzo:	Are you a tourist?
Barbara:	Yes.
Lorenzo:	Where are you from?
Barbara:	I'm Swiss.
Lorenzo:	I'm Swiss, too! Are you alone?
Barbara:	No. I have a friend here . . . Here she is.
Lorenzo:	Another coffee?
Barbara:	No, thank you. We don't have time.

HEAR...SAY 2

Barbara:	Excuse me, sir. I need a city map.
Bartender:	I don't have a map, but there are a lot of street vendors in piazza Duomo.
Barbara:	Do you have bus tickets?
Bartender:	Yes, of course. How many would you like?
Barbara:	Two, thanks.
Bartender:	Anything else?
Delphine:	Yes. Ten postcards. Do you have stamps for Europe?

Bartender:	Yes. Here you are. Anything else?
Delphine:	I'd also like a telephone card.
Bartender:	We have them in denominations of five, ten, and twenty euros.
Delphine:	Ten.
Bartender:	So, two euros for the tickets, seven for the post cards, and ten for the phone card. Nineteen. Thank you.
Lorenzo:	Have fun in Florence!

ANSWER KEY

ACTIVITY 1

	Qualcosa da bere	Qualcosa da mangiare
1. *una pasta con crema*		a custard-filled pastry
2. *un cappuccino*	a cappuccino	
3. *una pizzetta*		a small pizza
4. *un caffè*	a coffee	
5. *un'acqua minerale*	a mineral water	
6. *un panino con il prosciutto*		a ham sandwich

2. Barbara orders *un caffè, un bicchiere d'acqua minerale e un panino con il prosciutto* (an espresso, a glass of mineral water, and a ham sandwich).
3. Delphine orders *un cappuccino e una pasta con crema* (a cappuccino and a custard-filled pastry).
4. Their *conto* is five euros.
5. Delphine asks if there's a bathroom, and the *barista* gives her the key.
6. Barbara is *svizzera* (Swiss).
7. Lorenzo offers them another coffee, but Barbara declines saying they don't have time.

ACTIVITY 2

1. The *barista* says: *Mi dica?, E per Lei?, Cosa vuole?* and *Altro?*

ACTIVITY 3

Mi dica.
Un caffè basso. / Un cornetto, per piacere.
Altro?
Un cornetto, per piacere. / Un caffè basso.
Quanto Le devo?
Tre euro.

ACTIVITY 4

1. *svizzera;*   2. *francese;*   3. *italiano;*
4. *giapponese;*   5. *inglese;*   6. *russa;*
7. *americano;*   8. *cinese;*   9. *canadese;*
10. *giamaicano.*

ACTIVITY 5

1. M—telephone;   2. F—map;   3. F—station;
4. M—hotel;   5. F—actress;   6. M / F—
optimist;   7. F—cigarette;   8. M—bar;
9. F—friend;   10. M—vendor / salesman.

ACTIVITY 6

1. *Ci sono panini.*
2. *Ci sono paste.*
3. *Ci sono caffè.*
4. *Ci sono pizze.*
5. *Ci sono cornetti.*
6. *Ci sono sigarette.*
7. *Ci sono tramezzini.*
8. *Ci sono spremute.*

ACTIVITY 7

1. *il panino, i panini;*   2. *la pasta, le paste;*
3. *la pizza, le pizze;*   4. *il caffè, i caffè;*   5. *il cornetto, i cornetti;*   6. *la sigaretta, le sigarette;*
7. *il tramezzino, i tramezzini;*   8. *la spremuta, le spremute;*   9. *l'acqua, le acque;*
10. *l'americano, gli americani*

ACTIVITY 8

1. *Una pianta della città; strade; piazze*
2. *francobolli; cartoline.*
3. *una carta telefonica*
4. *un biglietto dell'autobus*

ACTIVITY 9

1. No, the *barista* didn't have a *pianta della città,* but he suggests that Barbara buy one from a street vendor in piazza Duomo.
2. She buys *due* (two) *biglietti dell'autobus.*
3. Delphine buys ten *cartoline* (postcards) with stamps to mail them to Europe.
4. A synonym for *carta telefonica* is *scheda telefonica.*

ACTIVITY 10

1. *quattro;*   2. *cinque;*   3. *sedici;*
4. *quindici;*   5. *nove;*   6. *tredici;*   7. *zero;*
8. *quattordici;*   9. *dodici;*   10. *venti*

ACTIVITY 11

1. *francese;*   2. *vegetariana;*   3. *alto;*
4. *telefonica;*   5. *italiana*

ACTIVITY 12

1. *hai;*   2. *ha;*   3. *hanno;*   4. *ho;*   5. *Hai;*
6. *Abbiamo;*   7. *Avete;*   8. *hanno;*   9. *ha;*
10. *Ho.*

3.

SLOW AND STEADY WINS THE RACE

Chi va piano, va lontano
(*Lit.* He who goes slowly goes far)

Are you free?

COMING UP...

- *Take me to the dance on time*: How to get a taxi and tell them where to go
- *You don't look a day over 30*: Talking about age
- *The countdown*: Numbers from 21 to 100
- *Living in the moment*: Talking about the present with *–are* verbs
- *Talking about this and that*: Questo (this) and quello (that)
- *I'll be in and out*: Some basic prepositions

LOOKING AHEAD

Avete un momento? Do you have a moment? Great! Tell me, did you have your *caffè* and *cornetto* yet? Or perhaps you opted for *un panino* and *un bicchiere d'acqua minerale?* Or are you still just *o*hing and *a*hing from all those gender differences in the last lesson? Hey, if *o* and *a* don't ring a bell at this point, you might want to consider giving Lesson 2 another *o*, I mean, go. What was that? You say, now is not the time for lectures? *Avete ragione!* You're right! Just breathe deeply and count to ten: *uno, due, tre, quattro . . .* Make that twenty! . . . *venti!* Okay, good. Now let's talk about what awaits . . . a fabulous soirée, I mean *una festa favolosa,* at a centuries-old *castello* outside of Rome. I certainly hope you have something *elegante* to wear! *Andiamo! Il treno* is about to leave the *stazione.*

ACTIVITY 1: **LET'S WARM UP**

Before you listen to the dialogue, match the word or phrase in the first column with what you think it means from the second column.

1.	*Ma guarda un po'!*	a.	stadium
2.	*la maturità*	b.	more or less
3.	*giovane*	c.	high school graduation
4.	*più o meno*	d.	shopping mall; commercial center
5.	*libero*	e.	building; edifice
6.	*l'edificio*	f.	meeting place
7.	*il centro commerciale*	g.	I wish!
8.	*lo stadio*	h.	young
9.	*il luogo di riunione*	i.	Fancy that!
10.	*Magari!*	j.	free

Find out how you fared by checking the answers in the Crib Notes section, then listen to the dialogue.

Did You Know?

CASTLES IN THE AIR: THE TOWN OF BRACCIANO

Bracciano lies about twenty-five miles north of Rome and is home to an impressive castle dating back to the fifteenth century. It's the main town on Lake Bracciano, a lake formed in old volcanic craters, and it offers beautiful views, in addition to great water sports facilities.

Did You Know?

Having just arrived in Bracciano from Rome all decked out for a special *festa* (party, celebration), Paola leaves *la stazione* to look for a taxi.

Paola: Taxi! È libero?

Taxista: Sì.

Paola: Al castello, per piacere. A quest'indirizzo. (*showing him the address*)

Taxista: Subito . . . (*noticing her outfit*) C'è una festa stasera?

Paola: Sì. Festeggiamo venticinque anni dalla maturità.

Taxista: Festeggiate al castello?

Paola: No. Quello è il luogo di riunione.

Taxista: Mah . . . Venticinque anni? Non è possibile! Sembra molto giovane . . .

Paola: Magari!

Taxista: Davvero ha . . . quarantaquattro anni?

Paola: Più o meno . . . (*eager to get off the subject of her age and on to something else*) Cos'è quest'edificio?

Taxista: Questo è il nuovo centro commerciale.

Paola: Ma guarda un po'!

Taxista: Sì. E quello è un nuovo ipermercato.

Paola: Che orrore! . . . E questo qui è il castello?

Taxista: No, questo qui è lo stadio. Quello lì è il castello.

Paola: Grazie. Arriviamo proprio in orario.

Did You Know?

THIS OLD THING?: HOW TO TAKE A COMPLIMENT

A major cultural difference between the U.S. and Italy is that the Italians are much more reserved when it comes to compliments. If someone pays you a compliment, saying *grazie* implies that you agree and you could come off a little . . . *gassato* (full of yourself). So, if someone compliments you on your outfit, say something like "this old thing?" Now you know why Paola responds with *Magari!* (Don't I wish!) when she's told she looks very young.

ACTIVITY 2: HOW'S THAT AGAIN?

How well did you do with the new words you heard in the dialogue? I bet you remembered some of them from the Looking Ahead section and our warm-up activity. Before we review them in our *officina*, let's talk about the dialogue.

1. Where (*dove*) is Paola going?
2. What (*cosa*) are they celebrating?
3. How old is Paola? (*Quanti anni ha Paola?*)
4. What do they pass on the way to the *castello*?
5. Do they arrive *in orario* (on time)?

Now let's see how much you really understood. Step into the workshop . . .

WORKSHOP 1

WORDS TO LIVE BY

TAKE ME TO THE DANCE ON TIME: **HOW TO GET A TAXI AND TELL THEM WHERE TO GO**

A *taxi* (now, do you really need a translation for that one?) is a great way to get around if you can afford it. To tell the *taxista* (taxi driver) where to take you, just say:

> **A** . . . + *the name of a well-known location* . . . + ***per piacere.***
> + the **indirizzo** (address)

If you have trouble pronouncing the address, just show it to the driver and say:

> **A quest'indirizzo, per piacere.**   To this address, please.

Heads Up!

When *il, la, i, le, etc.,* follow the preposition *a,* the two words "blend together" and are combined into one word, like this:

a + *il* = *al*	*a* + *i* = *ai*
a + *la* = *alla*	*a* + *le* = *alle*
a + *l'* = *all'*	*a* + *gli* = *agli*

as in: *al castello* (to the castle)

  The same thing happens with the preposition *da,* which means "from, since":

da + *il* = *dal*	*da* + *i* = *dai*
da + *la* = *dalla*	*da* + *le* = *dalle*
da + *l'* = *dall'*	*da* + *gli* = *dagli*

as in: *vent'anni dalla maturità* (twenty years since high-school graduation)

Heads Up!

And look at the new words you can add to your store of "places around town":

il centro commerciale	*shopping mall; commercial center*
l'ipermercato	*mega-supermarket*
il castello	*castle*
lo stadio	*stadium*

Heads Up!

Remember to use *lo,* and not *il,* and *gli* and not *i,* with masculine nouns that begin with an "*s*" + another consonant or with "*z.*"

Heads Up!

If you're traveling with a group, it's not a bad idea to choose *un luogo di riunione* (a meeting place) should you split up or get lost.

Finally, the following descriptive words often say just enough to stand as expressions on their own:

subito	*right away*
davvero	*really; truly*
sempre	*always*
più o meno	*more or less*

Before we get to the nitty-gritty, I have a question for you. Tell me: What do these verbs have in common?

festeggiare	*to celebrate*
sembrare	*to seem*
arrivare	*to arrive*

Word on the Street

This dialogue was full of little expressions that go a long way. *Mah!* is an expression similar to *Beh!* You'll hear it a lot. It's used to show disbelief or annoyance. *Magari!* is a quintessential Italian expression. It means something like "Don't I wish!" Another one is *Guarda cosa c'è!* meaning "Fancy that!" And *Che orrore!* (How horrible!) is another great example of *che*'s usefulness in forming exclamations. Finally, another word you can get a lot of mileage out of is *proprio* (just, really, indeed). It's one of those words you can throw in just about anywhere as an intensifier. So, *arriviamo proprio in orario* means "we're arriving just in time." *Sono proprio un idiota* means "I really am an idiot." Just be careful: you **can't** use *proprio* to mean "Really? Is that so?" In that case, use *Davvero?*

While you're kicking that about your head, let's do another little activity.

TAKE IT FOR A SPIN

Here's one to make you feel *proprio* smart: If I tell you that all of the following words are opposites, and I give you the meaning of one, can you guess what its counterpart means? Yeah, I thought so . . .

più	more	*meno*	_____
qui	here	*lì*	_____
questo	this	*quello*	_____
libero	free	*occupato*	_____
giovane	young	*vecchio*	_____
nuovo	new	*anziano*	_____

As promised, we thus arrive at the nitty-gritty.

THE NITTY-GRITTY

LIVING IN THE MOMENT: TALKING ABOUT THE PRESENT WITH *–ARE* VERBS

Okay, so did you figure out what all those verbs have in common? Don't be a wise guy! Telling me that they're all actions won't score you any points because that's what verbs are! *Come?* What was that? They all end in *–are?* Bingo! You're absolutely right! Your prize is that you will soon find out what's so special about verbs ending in *–are*. Here's the deal: Italian verbs end in *–are*, *–ere*, or *–ire* in their infinitive form.[1]

Verbs that share the same ending in the infinitive also take the same endings when they change according to who's speaking (person) and when the action is happening (tense). We call these regular verbs. You know what this means, don't you? You should be a **big** fan of regular verbs because once you learn the basic pattern, you'll be able to say all sorts of things. So, without further ado (drum roll, please . . .), I present to you the regular *–are* verbs in the present tense. To use it properly just drop the *–are* ending from the infinitive and replace it with the appropriate endings.

–ARE VERB ENDINGS IN THE PRESENT TENSE			
IO	*–o*	**NOI**	*–iamo*
TU	*–i*	**VOI**	*–ate*
LEI	*–a*	**VOI**	*–ate*
LUI / LEI	*–a*	**LORO**	*–ano*

[1] The infinitive is the basic form of a verb, the one you'll find listed in a dictionary. If you come across any grammatical term whose meaning you don't know, just look it up in the Appendix F.

Here's how it works with an actual verb:

ARRIVARE (TO ARRIVE) IN THE PRESENT TENSE			
IO	arrivo	NOI	arriviamo
TU	arrivi	VOI	arrivate
LEI	arriva	VOI	arrivate
LUI / LEI	arriva	LORO	arrivano

You heard both Paola and the *taxista* use some regular *–are* verbs in our dialogue:

Arriviamo proprio in orario.

We're arriving just on time.

Festeggiamo venticinque anni dalla maturità.

We're celebrating twenty-five years since our high school graduation.

Festeggiate al castello?

Are you celebrating at the castle?

Sembra molto giovane.

You seem very young.

Take a Tip from Me!

Notice that even the irregular verbs you know also often end in a similar way:

IO	sono	ho	arrivo
TU	sei	hai	arrivi
NOI	siamo	abbiamo	arriviamo
VOI	siete	avete	arrivate
LORO	sono	hanno	arrivano

So, when you're talking about yourself, the verb will always end in *–o*, when you're addressing someone with *tu*, the verb will end in *–i*, etc. This should make it easier for you to understand what someone's saying, and you should be able to make a pretty quick and accurate guess about the different forms of most verbs. In fact, the underlined endings are the same across all the regular verb groups. So, relax, practice, and be surprised at how quickly you develop an ear for these things.

Guess what! Some of the best things in life are expressed with *–are* verbs: *mangiare* (to eat), *amare* (to love), *sposare* (to marry), *pensare* (to think). But, as we all know, all good things come at a price: *costare* (to cost), *pagare* (to pay) . . . You can now use these and any other regular verb ending in *–are*, and there are a lot! Just look!

Guess the meaning of these verbs, which are all regular *—are* verbs, then give the form of the verb that's asked for. The first one is done for you.

1.	*parlare*	to speak	*lui*	*parla*
2.	*arrivare*		*noi*	
3.	*entrare*		*tu*	
4.	*invitare*		*loro*	
5.	*preparare*		*noi*	
6.	*studiare*		*voi*	
7.	*telefonare*		*lei*	

TALKING ABOUT THIS AND THAT: *QUESTO* (THIS) AND *QUELLO* (THAT)

At this point, you might be able to guess that any word that describes a noun will agree with it in gender and number. The same is true, of course, for *questo* (this) and *quello* (that). Let's look at *questo* first. The forms are:

QUESTO (THIS)		
	SINGULAR	**PLURAL**
MASCULINE	*questo*	*questi*
FEMININE	*questa*	*queste*

Heads Up!

Questo and *questa* are shortened to *quest'* when they come before a word beginning with a vowel.

When *questo* is used together with a noun, it means "this". When it's used alone, it means "this one" (or just "this" when you're pointing to something).

Cos'è quest'edificio?

What's this building?

Questa festa è favolosa!

This party is fabulous!

If you want to stress proximity, you can add *qui / qua* (here) following *questo*.

Questo qui è lo stadio.

This (one) over here is the stadium. (pointing)

Quello (that) works the same way, but the forms are a little more complicated when it's used together with a noun:

QUELLO (THAT), BEFORE A NOUN		
	SINGULAR	PLURAL
MASCULINE before a consonant before a vowel before "s" + consonant	*quel* *quell'* *quello*	*quei* *quegli* *quegli*
FEMININE before a consonant before a vowel	*quella* *quell'*	*quelle* *quelle*

Quel treno arriva sempre in ritardo.

That train always arrives late.

Quei panini sono con prosciutto.

Those sandwiches are with ham.

Vorrei quella pasta.

I would like that pastry.

Take a Tip from Me!

Notice that the endings of the different forms of *quello* are directly based on the definite to articles (meaning "the"), which you already know. This should make them easier to remember. Compare the relationship between articles and *quello*: *quel treno / il treno; quello stadio / lo stadio; quella festa / la festa, quei treni / i treni; quegli indirizzi / gli indirizzi; quelle feste / le feste.*

Take a Tip from Me!

When *quello* is used alone to mean "that one," the forms are:

	SINGULAR	PLURAL
QUELLO (THAT ONE) USED ALONE		
MASCULINE	quello	quelli
FEMININE	quella	quelle

Quello è il nuovo ipermercato.

That's (*Lit.* That one is) the new mega-supermarket.

To emphasize distance, you can use *lì/la* (there) following *quello*:

Quello lì è il castello.

That (one) over there is the castle.

ACTIVITY 5: **TAKE IT FOR A SPIN**

Fill in the form of *questo* or *quello* that makes sense in each sentence.

1.   (This) _____ tassì è occupato, ma (that one) _____ è libero.
2.   (That) _____ treno arriva sempre in orario.
3.   (This) _____ signora è americana. (That one) _____ è ugandese.
4.   A (this) _____ indirizzo, per piacere.
5.   (That) _____ bar ha una toletta.

Had enough grammar? For a change of pace, turn on the CD player and listen to the next dialogue . . .

HEAR...SAY 2

La festa è finita (the party's over), for Paola at least. She wants to take the last train back to Rome. She calls for a cab to take her to *la stazione*.

Impiegata: Radio Taxi. Buona sera.
Paola: Buona sera. Chiamo per un taxi.
Impiegata: A che indirizzo?
Paola: Sono in via Mazzini, numero settantanove.

Impiegata:	Il taxi numero ventitrè arriva fra cinque minuti.
Paola:	Grazie. Aspetto fuori.

Il taxi arriva and Paola gets in. The driver is a little intense-looking and seems thrilled to learn she's in a hurry.

Paola:	Buona sera. Alla stazione, per favore . . . Ho fretta.
Taxista:	Ha fretta?
Paola:	Sì. C'è un treno per Roma tra dieci minuti. E quello è l'ultimo treno.
Taxista:	(*peeling out*) Abita a Roma?
Paola:	Sì.
Taxista:	(*screeching around a corner*) A Roma, i taxisti guidano come pazzi, vero?
Paola:	Hmm. Proprio come qui . . . Oddio! Il treno non c'è!
Taxista:	Che peccato! (*hopefully*) La porto a Roma?
Paola:	No, grazie. Torno alla festa . . . a piedi.

ACTIVITY 6: HOW'S THAT AGAIN?

Poor Paola! What a ride! Answer the questions and try to use any Italian words or phrases you remember from the dialogue.

1. How long did she have to wait for the taxi?
2. How did the *taxista* drive?
3. Did she make her *treno*?
4. Where did she go from *la stazione*?
5. How do you think she got there?

Did You Know?

TAXI!: GOING FOR A RIDE IN ROME

Roman *taxisti* are to Italy what New York cabbies are to the United States: *PAZZI!* (CRAZY!). So, just get in, close your eyes, and hold on! For the armchair travelers among you, catch a glimpse of what I mean in the movie *Night on Earth,* directed by Jim Jarmusch. It features five separate stories taking place at the same moment in time in five taxis in five cities around the world. One of the stories was filmed in Rome and stars Roberto Benigni (of *Life is Beautiful* fame) as the taxi driver. His passenger is a priest, and he takes advantage of the opportunity to confess his sins.

Did You Know?

WORKSHOP 2

Look at all the new —*are* verbs you can start using!

chiamare	to call
aspettare	to wait
abitare	to live
guidare	to drive
portare	to bring; to take; to carry
tornare	to return; to go back; to turn

Word on the Street

You can never know too many interjections! ***Oddio!*** means "Oh, God!" and it expresses great concern or great surprise. ***Che peccato!*** means "What a pity!" or "That's too bad!" (it literally means "What a sin!"). It's generally used to express disappointment or compassion (although it can just as easily be used sarcastically to express "Yeah, like I really care!"). It's opposite would be ***Che fortuna!*** (How lucky!).

YOU DON'T LOOK A DAY OVER 30: TALKING ABOUT AGE

There's another verb in there that you already know, but with a couple of new twists. Do you remember that the verb *avere* (to have) is used in some very useful idiomatic expressions, like *avete ragione* (you're right) and *avete fortuna* (you're lucky)? Well, you heard two more today. In the last dialogue you heard Paola say:

Ho fretta.

I'm in a hurry.

In the first dialogue, the *taxista* concluded:

Ha quarantaquattro anni?

You're forty-four years old?

So, *avere fretta* means "to be in a hurry" (*Lit.* to have hurry). But let's spend a little more time on that second one. In Italian, age is expressed with *avere . . . anni*, i.e., you **have** a certain number of years.

To ask how old someone is, say:

Quanti anni ha / hai?   How old are you? (formal / informal)

What you're literally asking is "how many years do you have?" This is an important distinction to remember: *avere* is used in a lot of common expressions for which we use "to be" in English: "to be in a hurry, to be right, to be lucky," etc. So, you would answer with:

Ho vent'anni.   *I'm twenty years old. (Lit. I have twenty years.)*

Magari! More likely, if you're like Paola or me, you won't get much use out of the last expression knowing only the numbers from *zero* to *venti*. So, let's learn to count a little higher. They predict that the life expectancy of children born in the year 2000 will reach *cento* (a hundred), so let's count from 21 to 100.

THE COUNTDOWN: NUMBERS FROM 21 TO 100

The units of ten from 30 to 100 are:

30	**trenta**	70	**settanta**
40	**quaranta**	80	**ottanta**
50	**cinquanta**	90	**novanta**
60	**sessanta**	100	**cento**

To add the single digits, you do just that: tag on the single digit to the tens unit, and write the whole thing as one word. For example:

venti + **quattro** = **ventiquattro (24)**

quaranta + **sette** = **quarantasette (47)**

Remember to drop the last letter from numbers that end in a vowel, before adding *uno* or *otto*:

ottanta + **uno** = **ottantuno (81)**

sessanta + **otto** = **sessantotto (68)**

21	**ventuno**
32	**trentadue**
43	**quarantatrè**
54	**cinquantaquattro**
65	**sessantacinque**
76	**settantasei**
87	**ottantasette**
98	**novantotto**
29	**ventinove**

So, now you can tell people how old you really are, or you can choose to stay at that eternal age:

Ho ventinove anni . . . Davvero!

I'm twenty-nine . . . Really!

Should you choose not to discuss your age with anyone, you can still use these numbers on other occasions, such as to give an address.

Sono in via Mazzini, numero settantanove.

I'm at 79 Mazzini Street.

The Fine Print

To give an address in Italian, state the street first and then give the number. Words commonly used in addresses, like *via* (street), *strada / viale* (avenue), and *piazza* (square) are not capitalized unless they begin a sentence.

Now let's see how well you've absorbed all this number stuff.

ACTIVITY 7: TAKE IT FOR A SPIN

Let's learn a thing or two about Rome using numbers. Write out the relevant numbers:

1. Legend has it that Rome was founded on this day of April 753 BC by twin brothers who had been raised by a wolf. The brothers, named Romolo and Remo (or Romulus and Remus, as we call them) set out to found a new city, but they were very competitive about the question of who would be ruler. In a violent clash, Romolo killed Remo and named the new city Roma: 23 _____

2. Length in kilometers of the Tiber, the river that flows through Rome:
   25 _____

3. Average height in meters of Rome's famous seven hills: 50 _____

4. Year A.D. in which construction of Rome's Colosseum began:
   72 _____

5. Year B.C. in which Rome's first emperor, Augustus, was crowned:
   27 _____

6. Number of entrances and stairways needed for the 50,000 visitors that Rome's Colosseum could hold: 80 _____

7. Size in hectares (100 m^2) of the Vatican, the world's smallest state, located in Rome: 44 _____

Now let's take another quick look at grammar. It'll be short and sweet.

THE NITTY-GRITTY

I'LL BE IN AND OUT: SOME BASIC PREPOSITIONS

Prepositions are short words that often convey a great deal of information. You've already encountered *di,* when you learned how to say which city you're from, as in *sono di Roma.* But let's take a look at two more prepositions, which are often used when talking about places and movement. The prepositions *a* and *in* can both mean "to, at, by," depending on the context. Let's look at some possibilities:

1. Use *a* to tell someone (like *un taxista*) where you're going, but use *in* when you're talking about where something is located.

   Al castello, per favore.

   To the castle, please.

   A quest'indirizzo.

   To this address.

   Sono in via Mazzini, numero settantanove.

   I'm at 79 Mazzini Street.

   Abitano in piazza Buonarotti, numero sei.

   They live at 6 Buonarotti Square.

2. Use *a* when you talk about a city you're in or going to, but use *in* when you're talking about a country.

   Abito a Roma, in Italia.

   I live in Rome, in Italy.

   Andiamo a Madrid, in Spagna.

   Let's go to Madrid, in Spain.

   Dove sono? —Sono in Canada, a Toronto.

   Where are they? —They're in Canada, in Toronto.

3. Use *in* to talk about the type of place where you work, but *a* to specify the name of the company.

   Manuela lavora in una farmacia.

   Manuela works in a pharmacy.

Paola lavora alla Olivetti.

Paola works at Olivetti.

Barbara lavora in una banca.

Barbara works at a bank.

Delphine lavora alla Crédit Lyonnaise.

Delphine works at Credit Lyonnaise.

4. Use *in* to specify a means of transportation, but if you go on foot, you go *a piedi*.

Torniamo in treno.

We'll come back by train.

Vanno in macchina.

They're going by car.

Arriviamo in autobus.

We're arriving by bus.

Viaggio in aereo.

I'm travelling by plane.

Heads Up!

Just like *a* and *da,* the preposition *in* combines with the definite article:

in + **il** = **nel**	**in** + **i** = **nei**
in + **la** = **nella**	**in** + **le** = **nelle**
in + **l'** = **nell'**	**in** + **gli** = **negli**
in + **lo** = **nello**	

Heads Up!

Take a Tip from Me!

Prepositions are among the least "translatable" words in a language. Their meaning can change radically depending on the context. Don't let this frighten you. Do your best to remember the rules (and apply them!), but realize that you will probably make mistakes and that this is okay.

Take a Tip from Me!

Ready to try your hand at it?

Fill in the right preposition.

1. *Paola abita _____ Roma, _____ Italia.*

2. *Sono _____ via Condotti.*

3. *Andiamo _____ macchina? — No, _____ piedi.*

4. *Lorenzo lavora _____ una banca, _____ Banca Nazionale di Lavoro.*

5. *Dove? — _____ stadio, per favore.*

Word on the Street

The Italian spoken in different regions of Italy can vary quite a bit from the standard (but don't worry—everyone can understand and speak "standard" Italian, as well). The dialect they speak in Rome is known as **romanesco,** and here are a few tips on how it sounds. In *romanesco,* the *l* is often replaced by an *r,* so for example, the article *il* becomes *er.* There are other changes, too. The articles *uno, una,* and *un* often come out as *no, na, n;* the *gli* sound comes out as a *j* sound; the preposition *di* changes to *de,* and *per* becomes *pe'.*

What's this? *La festa è finita?* The party's over? Oh, well. *Ci vediamo alla lezione quattro!*

CRIB NOTES

HEAR . . . SAY 1

Paola:	Taxi! Are you free?
Taxi Driver:	Yes.
Paola:	To the castle, please. To this address.
Taxi Driver:	Right away. Is there a party tonight?
Paola:	Yes. We're celebrating twenty-five years since high school graduation.
Taxi Driver:	You're celebrating at the castle?
Paola:	No, that's the meeting place.
Taxi Driver:	But! . . . Twenty-five years? That's impossible! You seem so young . . .
Paola:	Don't I wish!
Taxi Driver:	You're really . . . forty-four years old?
Paola:	More or less . . . What's this building?
Taxi Driver:	This is the new shopping mall.
Paola:	Fancy that! (*Lit.* But look a little!)
Taxi Driver:	Yes. And that's a new mega-supermarket.
Paola:	How horrible! . . . And this here is the castle?
Taxi Driver:	No, this over here is the stadium. That over there is the castle.
Paola:	Thank you. We're arriving just in time.

Dispatcher:	Radio Taxi. Good evening.
Paola:	Good evening. I'm calling for a cab.
Dispatcher:	To which address?
Paola:	I'm at 79 Mazzini Street.
Dispatcher:	Car number twenty-three is arriving in five minutes.
Paola:	Thanks. I'm waiting outside.
Paola:	Good evening. To the train station, please . . . I'm in a hurry.
Taxi Driver:	You're in a hurry?
Paola:	Yes. There's a train for Rome in ten minutes. And that's the last train.
Taxi Driver:	You live in Rome?
Paola:	Yes.
Taxi Driver:	In Rome the taxi drivers drive like mad, don't they?
Paola:	Hmm. Just like they do here . . . Oh, no! The train's not there!
Taxi Driver:	What a pity! Shall I take you to Rome?
Paola:	No, thanks. I'm going back to party . . . on foot.

ANSWER KEY

ACTIVITY 1

1. i; 2. c; 3. h; 4. b; 5. j; 6. e;
7. d; 8. a; 9. f; 10. g.

ACTIVITY 2

1. Paola is going to the *castello* in Bracciano. Then she's going to *una festa* (a party).
2. They're celebrating twenty-five years since their *maturità* (high school graduation).
3. Paola is forty-four years old, *più o meno* (more or less).
4. They pass *il centro commerciale* (the shopping mall), *un ipermercato* (a mega-supermarket), and *lo stadio* (the stadium) on the way to the castle.
5. Yes, they arrive on time.

ACTIVITY 3

più	more	*meno*	less
qui	here	*lì*	there
questo	this	*quello*	that
libero	free	*occupato*	occupied
giovane	young	*vecchio*	old
nuovo	new	*anziano*	old

ACTIVITY 4

1. *parlare*	to speak	io	*parlo*
2. *arrivare*	to arrive	noi	*arriviamo*
3. *entrare*	to enter	tu	*entri*
4. *invitare*	to invite	loro	*invitano*
5. *preparare*	to prepare	noi	*prepariamo*
6. *studiare*	to study	voi	*studiate*
7. *telefonare*	to call	lei	*telefona*

ACTIVITY 5

1. *Questo; quello;* 2. *Quel;* 3. *Questa; Quella;* 4. *quest';* 5. *Quel*

ACTIVITY 6

1. *Cinque minuti* (five minutes).
2. *Come un pazzo* (like a madman)!
3. She didn't make the train; it wasn't there when they arrived.
4. *Alla festa* (to the party).
5. *A piedi* (on foot).

ACTIVITY 7

1. *ventitrè;* 2. *venticinque;* 3. *cinquanta;*
4. *settantadue;* 5. *ventisette;* 6. *ottanta;*
7. *quarantaquattro*

ACTIVITY 8

1. *a; in;* 2. *in;* 3. *in; a;* 4. *in; alla;*
5. *Allo*

4.

DON'T AIR YOUR DIRTY LAUNDRY IN PUBLIC

I panni sporchi si lavano in casa

(*Lit.* Dirty clothes are washed at home)

A good catch!

Che peccato that Paola missed her *treno* after such a great *festa* and had to deal with one nosy *taxista* and one who was *pazzo!* Next time, instead of saying *Alla stazione, per favore* and going *in taxi*, she'll probably choose to go *a piedi* right off the bat. But let's not dwell on the past, when we have so much to talk about! Antonella, the person we'll meet in the next dialogue, is a young girl (*una ragazza giovane*) with a very hip *nonna* (grandmother). *Ascoltiamo!* Let's listen!

ACTIVITY 1: LET'S WARM UP

Before you hear Antonella's somewhat surprising story, see if you can guess your way to the answers to the following questions:

1.   *Fare pettegolezzi* means:
     a. to fire up the stove
     b. to fare poorly
     c. to gossip

2.   Who is *più giovane?*
     a. *la madre*
     b. *la nonna*

3.   Who is *meno giovane?*
     a. *il padre*
     b. *il nonno*

4.   *Fare l'avvocato* means:
     a. to practice law
     b. to roll logs
     c. to play with Legos

5.   *Dare contro a* means:
     a. to date an Iran contra
     b. to contradict someone
     c. to dare a coward to do something

HEAR...SAY 1

Antonella is sitting at *La Lanterna,* her favorite *caffè,* with her best *amica,* Gioia, when Massimo, their friend from *l'università,* passes by. He sees the two of them huddled together and giggling.

Massimo:	Ciao, ragazze! Fate pettegolezzi?
Gioia:	(*caught in the act, looking at Antonella*) Mah, no!
Antonella:	(*it's O.K.—she wants to tell Massimo, too*) Sì . . . Mia nonna ha un nuovo ragazzo.
Gioia:	Ed è veramente un ragazzo!
Massimo:	Cavolo! Quanti anni ha?
Antonella:	Sessantacinque!
Massimo:	E tua nonna?
Antonella:	È vecchia come la Grecia! Lui ha vent'anni meno di lei.
Massimo:	Cosa ne pensano i tuoi?
Antonella:	I miei sono fuori di sè. Mio padre non parla con lei.
Gioia:	E tua madre?
Antonella:	Lei è meno dura . . . Fa finta di niente.
Massimo:	E tua nonna?
Antonella:	Mia nonna dà contro a tutti, come sempre.
Gioia:	Da quanto tempo sono insieme?
Antonella:	Da sei mesi. Vanno d'accordo . . .
Massimo:	"Finché la va, la va."
Gioia:	E che lavoro fa questo tipo?
Antonella:	Fa l'avvocato.
Gioia:	Un avvocato!
Massimo:	Un buon partito!

ACTIVITY 2:   HOW'S THAT AGAIN?

Let's see if you got the scoop, too.

1. Antonella's *nonna* has a new . . .
    a. ragtime album
    b. crazy neighbor
    c. boyfriend

2. The new *ragazzo* is . . .
    a. twenty years old
    b. twenty years younger than the *nonna*
    c. twenty years older than the *nonna*

3. He's . . .
    a. a lawyer
    b. an avocado lover
    c. a street vendor

4. Antonella's *genitori* (parents) are *fuori di sè:*
   a. outside on the lawn
   b. flower children
   c. beside themselves

5. Her *padre* is . . .
   a. not talking to *la nonna*
   b. talking gibberish
   c. not talking to anyone

6. Her *madre* is . . .
   a. finding it funny
   b. pretending it's nothing
   c. baking cakes

WORKSHOP 1

Word on the Street

Ragazzo means "boy" and *ragazza* "girl," but that's also how you would refer to your boyfriend or girlfriend. Plus, you'll often hear young people greeting a group of their friends with *Ciao ragazzi / ragazze!* (Hi, guys! Hi, gang!). Another word for boyfriend / girlfriend is *il fidanzato / la fidanzata,* which also means "fiancé(e)."

WORDS TO LIVE BY

ALL IN THE FAMILY: TALKING ABOUT YOUR FAMILY

Speaking of boyfriends and girlfriends, meeting the folks has to be one of the more nerve-wracking experiences in a budding relationship. Well, I hope we know each other well enough by now that you feel comfortable meeting *la famiglia.*

il nonno	*grandfather*
la nonna	*grandmother*
i nonni	*grandparents*
il padre	*father*
la madre	*mother*
i genitori	*parents*
il marito	*husband*
la moglie	*wife*
il figlio	*son*
la figlia	*daughter*

i figli	children
il fratello	brother
la sorella	sister
il cugino	male cousin
la cugina	female cousin
lo zio	uncle
la zia	aunt
il / la nipote	grandchild (m / f); nephew / niece
i parenti	relatives

Take a Tip from Me!

Notice that a good number of words referring to family members are simply masculine and feminine versions of the same word: *nonno / a, figlio / a, cugino / a, zio / a.* Remember, too, that when you're referring to a mixed group of people, i.e., a mix of males and females, words referring to the group will be masculine plural. So, "grandparents" is *i nonni,* and "children" would be *i figli,* whether you're talking about sons or a son and a daughter. But if you're talking about daughters only, you'd say *le figlie.*

Take a Tip from Me!

Heads Up!

I parenti is what we call a "false friend"; it sounds like it should mean "parents" but it really means "relatives."

Heads Up!

Word on the Street

This dialogue abounds in colorful expressions to spice up your conversation.

Cavolo!	Literally, it means "cabbage," but on the street it means "Wow!" or "Shoot!"
Cosa ne pensi / pensano?	What do you / they think (about it)?
essere fuori di sè	to be beside (Lit. outside) oneself
un buon partito	a good catch
andare d'accordo	to get along well
un tipo	guy (Lit. type)
fare finta (di niente)	to pretend (it's nothing)
dare contro a	to counter; to contradict

If Antonella's grandmother is this wacky, I'm curious about the rest of the family! Here's Antonella's family tree. Note: *di* (of) is the Italian equivalent of our "'s." It shows who (or what) belongs to whom, so *la sorella di Ada* is "Ada's sister."

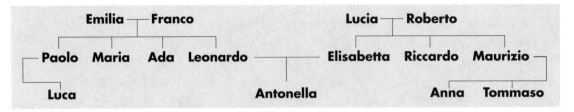

Who's who? Fill in the relationship . . .

1. *Maria è _____ di Ada, Leonardo e Paolo.*

2. *Lucia è _____ di Anna e Tommaso.*

3. *Tommaso è _____ di Anna.*

4. *Elisabetta è _____ di Leonardo.*

5. *Elisabetta, Riccardo, Maurizio sono _____ di Lucia e Roberto.*

6. *Luca è _____ di Antonella.*

7. *Emilia e Franco sono _____ di Paolo, Maria, Ada e Leonardo.*

8. *Maria è _____ di Antonella.*

9. *Maurizio è _____ di Antonella e _____ di Anna.*

10. *Anna è _____ di Elisabetta.*

Did You Know?

LA FAMIGLIA: A PORTRAIT OF AN ITALIAN FAMILY

The stereotype about the large Italian family is truly a thing of the past. Italy has one of the lowest birth rates in Europe, averaging 1.2 children per woman. According to a survey conducted in the year 2000, Italians on average, have their first child around age 30, although women in the south of Italy tend to have their children at a younger age. In addition, Italy itself is getting older, which means there are more and more *nonni* out there. Nevertheless, while Italian families may be shrinking, they still tend to be very close, even with more distant relatives.

Did You Know?

THE NITTY-GRITTY

WHAT'S MINE IS YOURS: WORDS SHOWING OWNERSHIP

As you already learned in Activity 3, the basic way of showing belonging, ownership, or possession in Italian is using the preposition *di* (of).

È la nonna di Antonella.

She's Antonella's grandmother.

When it's obvious who you're referring to (as the possessor), you can also use possessive adjectives, like *my*, *your*, *her*, and *their* to keep things brief:

È sua nonna.

She's her grandmother.

Here's another example:

Elisabetta, Riccardo e Maurizio sono i figli di Lucia e Roberto.

Elisabetta, Riccardo, and Maurizio are Lucia and Roberto's children.

Elisabetta, Riccardo e Maurizio sono i loro figli.

Elisabetta, Riccardo, and Maurizio are their children.

Now take a look at all the possessive adjectives in Italian:

	MASCULINE		FEMININE	
	SINGULAR	PLURAL	SINGULAR	PLURAL
MY	*mio*	*miei*	*mia*	*mie*
YOUR (INFML.)	*tuo*	*tuoi*	*tua*	*tue*
YOUR (FML.)	*Suo*	*Suoi*	*Sua*	*Sue*
HIS / HER	*suo*	*suoi*	*sua*	*sue*
OUR	*nostro*	*nostri*	*nostra*	*nostre*
YOUR (PL.)	*vostro*	*vostri*	*vostra*	*vostre*
THEIR	*loro*			

WORDS SHOWING OWNERSHIP

Take a Tip from Me!

Notice that the possessives have the familiar masculine and feminine endings: *o / i* and *a / e*. *Loro* (their) is the only form that doesn't change at all, regardless of the gender or the number of the noun that follows it, but that should only make it easier to remember.

When it comes to showing belonging, there are three basic rules you have to remember about possessive adjectives:

1. Unlike most adjectives, possessive adjectives come **before** the noun, as in *mia nonna*.

2. Possessive adjectives agree with the object or person possessed, **not** the possessor (this one is really important!). Therefore, you use forms that match the noun that **follows** the possessive adjective, not the possessor of that noun. For example, *il suo amico* can mean "his friend" or "her friend". The possessive *suo* agrees with *amico*.

If it's not clear from the context who the possessor is, Italians will follow up with the question *suo di chi?* (whose 'his / her'?) You can clear things up by specifying *suo di lui* or *suo di lei*.

3. Normally, you should use a definite article (*il / la*) together with the possessive, as in:

> **la macchina di Massimo** → **la sua macchina**

> Massimo's car → his car

> **Barbara è la nostra amica.**

> Barbara is our friend.

> **Paola arriva in ritardo. Il suo treno non c'è.**

> Paola arrives late. Her train isn't there.

However, when you're talking about a single family member, use the possessive word alone.

> **la cugina di Gioa** → **sua cugina**

> Gioia's cousin → her cousin

> **il padre di Antonella** → **suo padre**

> Antonella's father → her father

When you're talking about more than one family member, you need the article again. And with *loro*, you always have to use the article.

> **i cugini di Gioia** → **i suoi cugini**

> Gioia's cousin → her cousins

> **la madre di Elisabetta, Riccardo e Maurizio** → **la loro madre**

> Elisabetta, Riccardo, and Maurizio's mother → their mother

> **Marina parla a un amico di Giovanni e Gabriella. Il loro amico è Pietro.**

> Marina is talking to Giovanni and Gabriella's friend. Their friend is Pietro.

Word on the Street

I miei (*Lit.* "mine") is a colloquial way of referring to your parents, like "my folks" in English. Naturally, if you're referring to someone else's parents, you would say *i tuoi*, *i suoi*, etc. Or, if you prefer something that's a bit more slang and less flattering, you can say *i vecchi*, which literally means "the old ones." This is similar to the English expression "my old man." There's your memory association!

Note that the **article + possessive** can also stand in for a noun, meaning "mine, yours, hers, ours, theirs, etc." (The noun that is replaced by the possessive is underlined.)

> ***Questo è <u>la mia macchina.</u> → La sua è dal meccanico.***
>
> This is my car. His / Hers is at the mechanic's.
>
> ***Barbara ha bisogno di <u>un'altra pianta della città.</u> → La sua è a casa.***
>
> Barbara needs another city map. Hers is at home.

The Fine Print

When the possessive functions as a pronoun (that is, when it replaces a noun), you should always use the definite article, even when talking about a single family member.

> ***<u>Mio padre</u> è vecchio. Il suo è giovane.***
>
> My father is old. His / Hers is young.
>
> ***<u>Mia sorella</u> è vegetariana. —Anche la mia!***
>
> My sister is vegetarian. —So is mine!

Now let's see if we can keep all these rules straight.

ACTIVITY 4: **TAKE IT FOR A SPIN**

Fill in the blank with the appropriate possessive word. Remember, the possessive should agree with the person or object that belongs to someone, rather than the person to whom it belongs.

1. *Gioia è l'amica d'Antonella. Anche Massimo è (her)_____ amico.*

2. *(My)_____ madre non parla a (my)_____ padre.*

3. *(Her)* _____ *famiglia è di Roma. (His)* _____ *è*
    di Napoli.

4. *È Pietro (your, pl.)* _____ *macellaio? (Ours)* _____ *è*
    Vincenzo.

5. *Invitiamo tutta la famiglia! (yours, sing. infml.)* _____ *cugini e*
    (mine) _____ .

6. *Il mio dizionario è qui. Dov'è (yours, sing. infml.)* _____ ?

7. *Guido io? —No. (my)* _____ *macchina è proprio lì.*

8. *(Their)* _____ *famiglia è favolosa! Sono tutti pazzi!*

9. *(Her)* _____ *sorella arriva sempre in ritardo.*
    (Her folks) _____ *sono fuori di sè!*

10. *Abbiamo bisogno di una pianta della città. —Ecco (mine)* _____ !

Did You Know?

Now that we have this question of ownership all straightened out, let's do a little more work with adjectives . . .

MORE OR LESS THE SAME: MAKING COMPARISONS

The expression *più o meno* is your key to making comparisons in Italian. Just add *di* (of), which in this case means "than," and you're good to go.

più . . . di	more . . . than
meno . . . di	less . . . than

Ha vent'anni meno di lei.

He's twenty years younger than she is. (*Lit.* He has twenty years less than she.)

Mia madre è meno dura di mio padre.

My mother is less harsh than my father.

Heads Up!

Don't forget that, like *a* (to), *da* (from), and *in* (in), the preposition *di* (of) combines with the definite articles:

di + il = del   **di + i = dei**

di + la = della   **di + le = delle**

di + l' = dell'

di + lo = dello   **di + gli = degli**

Mia sorella è più generosa della tua.

My sister is more generous than yours.

When you're talking about equality, just use *come* (like; as). In the dialogue, you heard this (not-so-nice) comment about the *nonna:*

È vecchia come la Grecia!

She's as old as Greece!

Let's see if you know *più* or *meno* than when we started.

ACTIVITY 5:   TAKE IT FOR A SPIN

Più or *meno?* Make sentences according to the example, and remember that adjectives agree with the nouns they describe.

Luca / + / giovane / Antonella → Luca è più giovane di Antonella.

1.   *mio padre / + / vecchio / mia madre* _____

2.   *mia nonna / – / generoso / mio nonno* _____

3.   *Paola / + / elegante / Annalisa* _____

4.   *i taxisti a Roma / + / pazzo / i taxisti a New York* _____

5.   *quel tipo / = / pazzo / un taxista a Roma* _____

I don't know about you, but I'm really curious to see what happened with Antonella's *nonna.* But first, what are you doing this weekend? *Cosa fate voi questo week-end?*

Match the Italian with the English. *In bocca al lupo!*

1. *dare una festa*
2. *Non esiste!*
3. *Porta bene gli anni!*
4. *essere in gamba*
5. *divertente*
6. *Ma, dai!*
7. *Non fare così!*
8. *fare una passeggiata*
9. *Che buon'idea!*

a. amusing; fun
b. What a good idea!
c. Don't be like that!
d. No way!
e. (S)he carries her years well!
f. to be on the ball; to be smart
g. to give a party
h. Come on!
i. to go for a walk

HEAR . . . SAY 2

A few months later, Antonella and Gioia are once again at the *caffè*, watching the world go by.

Gioia: Cosa fai questo week-end?

Antonella: Diamo una festa per mia nonna e suo marito.

Gioia: Suo marito?

Antonella: Sì!

Gioia: Non esiste! Quel tipo giovane? L'avvocato?

Antonella: Sì!

Gioia: Porta bene gli anni, tua nonna?

Antonella: È più in gamba di noi! E tu? Cosa fai questo week-end?

Gioia: Vado al cinema con Massimo e un suo cugino.

Antonella: Che cosa danno?

Gioia: Un film.

Antonella: Uffa! Le tue risposte non sono molto divertenti!

Gioia: Ma, dai! Non fare così. Un film di Fellini.

Antonella: I suoi film sono un po' difficili da capire . . .

Gioia: Sì, un po' . . . però le sue idee sono molto interessanti.

Antonella: È vero . . . Senti, perché non fate una passeggiata dopo il cinema, passate da noi e fate la conoscenza dell'avvocato?

Gioia: Che buon'idea!

Can you believe it? *La nonna* went and tied the knot!

1. The *ragazzo* has now become her . . ._____

2. What is *la famiglia* doing to celebrate the occasion?_____
    _____

3. Has Gioia met the *ragazzo*, oops, *marito*, yet?_____
    _____

4. What are Gioia's plans for the weekend?_____
    _____

5. What does Antonella think of *i film di Fellini?*_____
    _____

Now let's make sure you understood everything.

WORKSHOP 2

WORDS TO LIVE BY

Well, as we saw, people with spirit tend to *portare bene gli anni* (carry their years well; age well). In fact, my own *nonna* sometimes seemed to be more *in gamba* (on the ball; capable) than I was. I always found the time I spent with her to be *molto divertente* (very amusing; fun). *Strano ma vero.* Strange but true.

WEEKEND PLANS: DISCUSSING PLANS AND ACTIVITIES

So, what do you like to do on the weekend? What's your favorite *passatempo* (pastime)?

andare al cinema	to go to the movies
andare a una festa	to go to a party
fare una passeggiata	to go for a walk
fare un giro	to go for a walk / drive / ride
restare a casa	to stay at home
fare la conoscenza di	to meet someone; make the acquaintance of

Here's a great way to suggest doing something:

perché non + action	why don't + action

Word on the Street

Perché non facciamo un po' di pratica? Why don't we do a little practice? *Che buon'idea!* What a good idea!

ACTIVITY 8: TAKE IT FOR A SPIN

How would you respond to the following situations, using the vocabulary you've just learned?

1. You just found out that your *zia* won the lottery.

    _____

2. Your *amico* suggests going to see a film you've been wanting to see.

    _____

3. Your friend gets mad at you for an innocent joke and wants to leave.

    _____

4. You can't find your remote control and hate to get up.

    _____

5. Your friend tells you about her new man—a bodybuilder with a doctorate in Romantic poetry who made a fortune on the stock market.

    _____

Here's a bonus question: Your Italian instructor says, *Perché non parliamo di tre verbi irregolari? Uffa!* Hey, you're catching on! And sorry to disappoint you, but, we are in fact going to talk about three irregular verbs. But, believe me, you'll get a lot of mileage out of them.

THE NITTY-GRITTY

I SCREAM, YOU SCREAM...: THE VERBS *ANDARE* (TO GO), *DARE* (TO GIVE), AND *FARE* (TO DO; TO MAKE)

Siete pronti? Here are the verbs, just ready and waiting to be memorized (get out those flash cards!).

ANDARE, DARE, AND FARE IN THE PRESENT TENSE

	ANDARE (TO GO)	DARE (TO GIVE)	FARE (TO DO; TO MAKE)
IO	vado	do	faccio
TU	vai	dai	fai
LUI / LEI	va	dà	fa
NOI	andiamo	diamo	facciamo
VOI	andate	date	fate
LORO	vanno	danno	fanno

Take a Tip from Me!

Notice how similar these three verbs are in the present tense. For *tu, lui / lei / Lei*, and *loro*, only the first letter is different: *vai—dai—fai; va—dà—fa; vanno—danno—fanno.*

Take a Tip from Me!

These verbs are used often in conversation because people tend to do a lot of going, giving, making, and, well, doing.

Cosa fai questo week-end?

What are you doing this weekend?

Vado al cinema.

I'm going to the movies.

Diamo una festa per mia nonna e suo marito.

We're throwing (*Lit.* giving) a party for my grandmother and her husband.

Fare, dare, and *andare* also make appearances in some great idiomatic expressions:

* with *andare:*

andare d'accordo	to get along well
Come va?	How's it going?
Me ne vado.	I'm leaving. I'm outta here!

Andare also shows up in the saying *Finché la va, la va* (As long as it lasts, it lasts).

Take a Tip from Me!

Notice that *andare* is also often used together with the prepositions *a* (to; at) and *in* (in), as in *andare al cinema* (to go to the movies), *andare a scuola* (to go to school), *andare a piedi* (to go by foot), *andare in macchina* (to go by car), *andare in treno* (to go by train), and *andare in autobus* (to go by bus).

Take a Tip from Me!

- with *dare:*

dare contro a	to counter; to go against the grain
Ma dai!	Come on! Come off it!

- with *fare:*

You already know *fare pettegolezzi* (to gossip), and *fare finta di niente* (to pretend it's nothing), but here are a couple of new ones:

fare una passeggiata	to take a walk
fare la conoscenza di	to meet
Non fare cosi!	Don't be like that!

Fare is also used in the most popular cocktail party question in America:

Che lavoro fa?

What do you do?

When responding, you'd use *fare* + the name of the profession.

Fa l'avvocato.

He practices law.

Faccio l'architetto.

I'm an architect.

Facciamo una prova! Let's test this out and see how well you've mastered your new irregular verbs.

ACTIVITY 9: TAKE IT FOR A SPIN

Answer the questions in complete sentences using the information in parentheses.

1.   *Dove andate? (al cinema)* _____

2. *Che lavoro fa, signorina? (avvocato)* _____

3. *E tua sorella, cosa fa? (dare contro a suo marito)* _____

_____

4. *Massimo va alla festa questo week-end? (Sì, con suo cugino)* _____

_____

5. *I tuoi genitori vanno d'accordo? (Sì)* _____

Bene. Here's one more expression with *fare* for the road: *fare una domanda*, which means "to ask a question," which is exactly what we're going to learn about now.

Q & A: ASKING QUESTIONS WITH QUESTION WORDS

When you want to ask more than a simple yes / no question, you have to use a question word, like *who, what, when, where, why,* or *how.* You've already encountered some of the basic question words in Italian. Here they are all together:

chi	who
che / cosa / che cosa	what; which
quando	when
dove	where
perché	why
come	how
quanto	how much

Chi sei?

Who are you?

Cosa ne pensano i tuoi?

What do your parents think about it?

Quando andate al cinema?

When are you going to the movies?

Dov'è lei?

Where is she?

Perché non passate da noi?

Why don't you stop by our house?

Come stai?

How are you?

Quanto costa?

How much does it cost?

Note that *che*, *cosa*, and *che cosa* are pretty much interchangeable when they mean "what." The only thing you need to remember is that you can only use *che* together with a noun, i.e., when you mean "which."

Che / Cosa / Che cosa fai?

What are you doing?

Che lavoro fa?

What do you do? (*Lit.* Which work do you do?)

Let's see just how good a conversationalist you can be.

ACTIVITY 10:   TAKE IT FOR A SPIN

Ask questions based on the statements.

1. <u>Gioia</u> va alla festa.

   _____

2. <u>Diamo</u> una festa per mia nonna.

   _____

3. Il ragazzo di mia nonna fa <u>l'avvocato</u>.

   _____

4. Paola va <u>alla stazione</u>.

   _____

5. La turista cerca <u>una pianta della città</u>.

   _____

6. Pietro è <u>un amico di Giovanni e Gabriella</u>.

   _____

7. Massimo e suo cugino non vanno al cinema <u>perché sono in ritardo</u>.

   _____

8. Ci vediamo <u>domani</u>.

   _____

Before I send you off to relax and prepare for lesson 5, let's take a brief look at two small but significant words.

FROM ME TO YOU: THE PREPOSITIONS *DI* (OF) AND *DA* (FROM; TO; AT; BY)

- *di*

As you've already seen, the preposition *di* means "of" most of the time, and its main uses are to show ownership and origin.

È la nipote di Lucia.

She's Lucia's granddaughter / niece.

Sono di Madrid.

I'm / They're from Madrid. (*Lit.* I'm / They're of Madrid.)

And, in case you've already forgotten, it's also used in comparisons to mean "than."

Il suo ragazzo è più giovane di lei.

Her boyfriend is younger than she is.

- *da*

The preposition *da* is interesting as it has many meanings. Its main, literal, meaning is "from" as in:

Vengo dalla stazione.

I'm coming from the station.

Da is also used with the name of a person, a store, a restaurant or with an occupation to mean "to," "at," or "by."

Perché non passate da noi?

Why don't you pass by our house?

La nonna va dal dottore.

Grandmother is going to the doctor.

But it's also used to express how long something has been going on or how much time has passed since something happened.

Sono insieme da sei mesi.

They've been together for six months.

Studio italiano da due settimane.

I've been studying Italian for two weeks.

Festeggiamo vent' anni dalla maturità.

We're celebrating twenty years since our high school graduation.

Notice that when *da* is used to express the duration of an action in Italian, you use a verb in the present tense.

The Fine Print

Da can also be used to describe the purpose or nature of something. This usage is difficult to explain with steadfast rules, so at this point focus more on recognizing it than using it.

I suoi film sono un po' difficili da capire.

His movies are a little difficult to understand.

Una scheda telefonica da cinque, dieci o venti euro.

A telephone card for five, ten, or twenty euros.

Ready for your last activity?

ACTIVITY 11:   TAKE IT FOR A SPIN

Di or *da?* You know what to do.

1. *Antonella è la figlia* _____ *Elisabetta e Leonardo.*

2. *La nonna* _____ *Antonella ha un ragazzo giovane.*

3. *Sono insieme* _____ *sei mesi.*

4. *I genitori* _____ *Antonella sono fuori* _____ *sè.*

5. *Gioia e Massimo vanno* _____ *Antonella per fare la conoscenza* _____ *avvocato.*

That was that. *Quando ci vediamo? Ci vediamo alla lezione cinque!*

CRIB NOTES

Massimo:	Hi, guys! Gossiping?
Gioia:	No!
Antonella:	Yes . . . My grandmother has a new boyfriend.
Gioia:	And he really is a boy!
Massimo:	No way! (*Lit.* Cabbage!) How old is he?
Antonella:	Sixty-five.
Massimo:	And your grandmother?
Antonella:	She's as old as Greece! He's twenty years younger than she is.
Massimo:	What do your parents think about all this?
Antonella:	My parents are beside themselves. My father isn't speaking to her.
Gioia:	And your mother?
Antonella:	She's less harsh . . . She's pretending everything's fine.
Massimo:	And your grandmother?
Antonella:	My grandmother is going against the grain (*Lit.* is giving "con" to everyone), as always.
Gioia:	How long have they been together?
Antonella:	Six months. They get along well . . .
Massimo:	"As long as it lasts, it lasts."
Gioia:	And what does this guy do?
Antonella:	He practices law.
Gioia:	A lawyer!
Massimo:	A good catch!

Gioia:	What are you doing this weekend?
Antonella:	We're throwing (*Lit.* giving) a party for my grandmother and her husband.
Gioia:	Her husband?
Antonella:	Yes!
Gioia:	No way! (*Lit.* It doesn't exist) That young guy? The lawyer?
Antonella:	Yes!
Gioia:	Your grandmother carries her years well?
Antonella:	She's more on the ball (*Lit.* in leg) than we are. And you? What are you doing this weekend?
Gioia:	I'm going to the movies with Massimo and one of his cousins.
Antonella:	What are they showing (*Lit.* giving)?
Gioia:	A movie.
Antonella:	Ugh! Your answers are not very amusing.
Gioia:	Come on! Don't be like that. One of Fellini's films.
Antonella:	His movies are a little hard to understand . . .
Gioia:	Yes, a bit . . . but his ideas are very interesting.
Antonella:	True . . . Listen, why don't you guys take a walk after the movie, come by our house, and meet the lawyer?
Gioia:	What a good idea!

ANSWER KEY

ACTIVITY 1

1. c;   2. a;   3. b;   4. a;   5. b

ACTIVITY 2

1. c;   2. b;   3. a;   4. c;   5. a;   6. b.

ACTIVITY 3

1. *la sorella;*   2. *la nonna;*   3. *il fratello;*
4. *la moglie;*   5. *i figli;*   6. *il cugino;*
7. *i genitori;*   8. *la zia;*   9. *lo zio; il padre;*
10. *la nipote.*

ACTIVITY 4

1. *il suo;*   2. *Mia; mio;*   3. *La sua; La sua;*
4. *il vostro; Il nostro;*   5. *I tuoi; i miei;*
6. *il tuo;*   7. *la mia;*   8. *La loro;*   9. *Sua; I suoi;*   10. *la mia*

ACTIVITY 5

1. *Mio padre è più vecchio di mia madre.*
2. *Mia nonna è meno generosa di mio nonno.*
3. *Paola è più elegante di Annalisa.*
4. *I taxisti a Roma sono più pazzi dei taxisti a New York.*
5. *Quel tipo è pazzo come un taxista a Roma.*

ACTIVITY 6

1. g; 2. d; 3. e; 4. f; 5. a; 6. h;
7. c; 8. i; 9. b

ACTIVITY 7

1. *suo marito* (her husband).
2. They're throwing a party (*danno una festa*)!
3. No, Gioia hasn't met the *marito* yet, but hopes to this weekend.
4. She's going to the movies with Massimo and one of his cousins.
5. They're a little *difficili da capire* (difficult to understand).

ACTIVITY 8

1. *Cavolo!* or *Ma dai!*   2. *Che buon idea!*
3. *Ma dai! Non fare così!*   4. *Uffa!* or *Cavolo!*
5. *Non esiste!* (and in this case, perhaps the literal translation might be more appropriate!) or *Che buon partito!*

ACTIVITY 9

1. *Andiamo al cinema.*
2. *Faccio l'avvocato.*
3. *Mia sorella dà contro a suo marito.*
4. *Sì, questo week-end Massimo va alla festa con suo cugino.*
5. *Sì, i miei genitori vanno d'accordo.*

ACTIVITY 10

1. *Chi va alla festa?*
2. *Chi dà una festa per vostra nonna? / Cosa / Che / Che cosa fate per vostra nonna?*
3. *Che lavoro fa il ragazzo di tua / Sua nonna?*
4. *Dove va Paola?*
5. *Cosa / Che cosa / Che cerca la turista?*
6. *Chi è Pietro?*
7. *Perché non vanno al cinema Massimo e suo cugino?*
8. *Quando ci vediamo?*

ACTIVITY 11

1. *di;* 2. *di;* 3. *da;* 4. *di; di;* 5. *da; dell'*

5.

YOU'VE GOT MAIL!

C'è posta per te!

Who's your favorite actor?

COMING UP...

- *Let's log on*: Talking about computers and the Internet
- *What's happening?*: Talking about your favorite pastimes
- *All about me!*: How to tell people about yourself
- *Like it or not*: Talking about likes and dislikes using *mi piace* (I like)
- *What do you enjoy doing?*: Talking about actions using infinitives
- *Q & A*: More on questions
- *Strut your stuff!*: A review

Cavolo! I wonder how Antonella's *nonna* landed such a *buon partito! Un avvocato giovane* (well, relatively speaking anyway), and from what I hear he dances up a storm. To top it all off, apparently, *la sua famiglia* is ecstatic about his new *moglie*. Go figure. I wonder how they met. Maybe it's a truly modern love story and *la nonna*, who's so *in gamba*, likes to *fare la chat* (chat online), and met him *nella rete* (on the Web). Hmm. Excuse me for a minute. I have something important to do. *Il mio computer* (kohm-PYOO-tehr) awaits. Take a few minutes and try your hand at the following exercise while I go *navigare in Internet* (surf the Net).

<table>
<tr><td>ACTIVITY 1:</td><td>**LOOKING AHEAD**</td></tr>
</table>

What's your favorite *hobby* (OH-bee) or *passatempo?* Do any of the ones listed below sound exciting? (First you have to figure out what they mean by matching the words on the left with the translations on the right.)

1.	*fare le spese*	a.	to chat
2.	*fare due chiacchiere*	b.	to dance
3.	*fare giardinaggio*	c.	to listen to music
4.	*ascoltare la musica*	d.	to garden
5.	*ballare*	e.	to shop

O.K., I'm back. Unfortunately I didn't find *un buon partito nella rete*—but I did realize that it's a great place to meet people and learn about all sorts of things. Here are just a few of the people I found who were looking to *fare le conoscenze*. Who knows, you might have *fortuna* and find your own *principe azzurro* (knight in shining armor) (*Lit.* blue prince) or *principessa* (princess). And if not, at least I'm sure you'll find *un sito* (a site) that will interest you . . .

HEAR . . . SAY 1

Mi chiamo Maurizio Severi. Ho ventidue anni e vado all'università a Perugia. Faccio lingue. Studio molto, ma quando ho tempo libero vado al cinema. Il mio regista preferito è Stanley Kubrick. Ti piacciono i suoi film? Quali? Forse abbiamo interessi simili . . .

Ciao a tutti! Sono io . . . Sandra. Questa è la mia prima volta nella rete. Non sono sicura cosa fare . . . Perché non parliamo un po' del mio tesoro, il Signor Holmes? È un gatto proprio straordinario. Ama le carezze più del cibo! Ma il mio fratello pazzo tortura il povero Signor Holmes e i miei non fanno niente! Che ingiustizia! Voi avete un gatto? Com'è? Mi piacciono molto gli animali...Aspetto le vostre risposte. A più tardi!

Buon giorno. Mi chiamo Laura e studio l'italiano da sei mesi. Cerco un amico o un'amica per fare due chiacchiere in italiano. Abito a Columbus, Ohio negli Stati Uniti e sono italo-americana. Ho una grande famiglia! Siamo sei figli. Ho tre sorelle e due fratelli. Quanti fratelli e sorelle avete voi? Il mio fratello maggiore è sposato e ha due figli gemelli. Hanno cinque anni. Anch'io sono sposata e aspetto un bambino. Lavoro come insegnante e mio marito è meccanico. Il week-end, mi piace fare giardinaggio, ma andare a fare le spese è il mio hobby preferito. Qual'è il vostro passatempo preferito?

Ciao, ragazzi! Sono Andres e sono brasiliano. Adesso abito a Bologna. Sono celibe e lavoro in una ditta commerciale. Ci sono altri brasiliani qui in Italia? Dove siete? Mi piace molto ascoltare la musica latina e ballare la salsa. Perché non cliccate sul mio sito? Facciamo una stanza di chat per i brasiliani in Italia... tutti i dettagli sono sulla mia pagina web.

ACTIVITY 2: HOW'S THAT AGAIN?

So, who did you like best? First, let's see how much you learned about them. See if you can answer these questions about the four people you've just met. Try to do it in Italian if you can.

	PERSONA 1	PERSONA 2	PERSONA 3	PERSONA 4
Come si chiama?				
Dove abita?				
Quanti anni ha?				
Che lavoro fa?				
Qual'è il suo passatempo preferito?				
Ha fratelli o sorelle?				

What else can you tell me about them?

1. Who is the aunt of twin boys? _____

2. Who studies languages? _____

3. Who is Mr. Holmes? _____

4. Who is the Latin lover? _____

If you got all that, we are in *very* good shape! Do you realize all the different things you can now say about yourself and others? I don't know about you, but I'm impressed!

WORKSHOP 1

WORDS TO LIVE BY

LET'S LOG ON: TALKING ABOUT COMPUTERS AND THE INTERNET

Well, as we've already discussed, *la rete* (the Web) is a great place to spend some *tempo libero* (free time) and meet people. It shouldn't be difficult for you to *surfare / navigare in Internet* because so much Italian computer lingo is taken directly from English. So, when you go online, you can *cliccare* (click) *su un sito* (on a site) in order to:

fare la chat / chattare (cheh-TTAH-reh)	to chat on-line
mandare una e-mail	to send an e-mail
aspettare una risposta	to wait for a response

Did You Know?

THE INFORMATION AGE: INTERNET CAFÉS IN ITALY

There are Internet cafés throughout all of the major cities in Italy. You'll always find directions in English. Many of these businesses also offer mailbox rentals and shipping services. They're a great resource if you're lucky enough to spend an extended period of time in *una città italiana*.

If it's your *prima volta* (first time) on-line, and you're not sure what to say, you can start by introducing yourself and talking about your *hobby / passatempo preferito* (favorite hobby). You're bound to find someone with *interessi simili* (similar interests).

WHAT'S HAPPENING?: TALKING ABOUT YOUR FAVORITE PASTIMES

So, what do you like to do in your *tempo libero*?

fare le spese	to shop
fare due chiacchiere	to chat (in the general sense)
fare giardinaggio	to garden
ascoltare la musica	to listen to music
ballare	to dance
guardare la tv (tee-VOO)	to watch TV

Or you can always talk about *la famiglia*. Here are some words you may not already know:

minore	younger (referring to a sibling or child)
maggiore	older (referring to a sibling or child)
il bambino / la bambina	baby (m. / f.)
i gemelli	twins (m. pl.)
sposato / sposata	married (m. / f.)
celibe	single man
nubile	single woman
single [SEEN-guhl] (Yes, an English word is used here.)	single (m. / f.)
il gatto	cat
il cane	dog

If you're wondering what this dog and cat business is, then you probably don't have any *animali domestici* (pets). If you did, I'm sure you'd consider them part of *la famiglia*. In fact, they're probably your *tesoro* (treasure), and you couldn't imagine *la vita* (life) without them. You can tell by the way they say *miao* (meow) or *bau* (woof) if they want *una carezza* (a caress) or *il cibo* (food). And, if you don't have *una pagina web* (a Web page) devoted solely to them, then I'm sure you have a veritable gallery in your wallet. O.K., now it's your turn to say a few things.

ACTIVITY 3: TAKE IT FOR A SPIN

Let's play the opposites game. Match the words in the left column with their closest opposites from the right column.

1.	sposato	a.	nubile
2.	minore	b.	genitori
3.	bambini	c.	guardare la tv
4.	sposata	d.	maggiore
5.	ballare	e.	celibe

One of the first things we talk about when getting to know people is our likes and dislikes. Let's see how you can do that *in italiano. È uno zuccherino!* (It's a cinch!)

LIKE IT OR NOT: TALKING ABOUT LIKES AND DISLIKES USING *MI PIACE* (I LIKE)

When you want to say you like something in Italian, you say:

- *Mi piace* if you're talking about a single thing, a place, a person, or activities
- *Mi piacciono* if you're talking about more than one thing, place, or person

Do you remember what Andres said in his Web posting?

Mi piace ascoltare la musica latina.

I like listening to Latino music.

And what about Sandra?

Mi piacciono gli animali.

I like animals.

As always, being a good conversationalist means asking questions, too, not just talking about yourself. So, you can ask:

- *Ti piace / Ti piacciono . . . ?* to someone you'd address with *tu*
- *Le piace / Le piacciono . . . ?* to someone you'd address with *Lei*

Ti piacciono i suoi film?

Do you (sing.infml.) like his films?

Le piace fare giardinaggio?

Do you (sing.fml.) like gardening?

Heads Up!

Remember that nouns ending in a consonant, like *film* or *computer,* have the same form in the singular or plural: *il film → i film, il computer → i computer*. The same is true for all nouns ending in an accented letter: *la città → le città.*

Like I said: *uno zuccherino, vero?* Here's another one.

WHAT DO YOU ENJOY DOING?: TALKING ABOUT ACTIONS USING INFINITIVES

In English, when we want to talk about the concept of doing something, we use the *−ing* form of a verb, like *shopping, skiing,* or *studying*. In Italian, they just use the infinitive form of the verb, the one ending in *–are*, *–ere*, and *–ire*. For example, when you talk about things you enjoy doing, you'd use an infinitive. Remember when Andres says:

> **Mi piace ballare.**
>
> I like dancing.

And Laura says:

> **Mi piace fare giardinaggio.**
>
> I like gardening.
>
> **Andare a fare le spese è il mio hobby preferito.**
>
> Going shopping is my favorite hobby.

Notice that the infinitive is treated as a singular noun, i.e., the verb you use with it should be singular.

> **Parlare l'italiano è uno zuccherino!**
>
> Speaking Italian is a cinch!

Let's see if that's true!

ACTIVITY 4: TAKE IT FOR A SPIN

Mi piace molto andare al cinema, ma non mi piacciono i film doppiati (dubbed). There, I just told you something about myself. Now, you tell me a little bit about yourself. Make sentences with all of the following items, using *mi piace / non mi piace* if they're singular nouns or if they're actions, or *mi piacciono / non mi piacciono* if they're plural nouns:

1. *fare pettegolezzi* _____
2. *gli animali* _____
3. *navigare in Internet* _____
4. *andare al cinema* _____
5. *i musei* _____
6. *la mia famiglia* _____
7. *parlare l'italiano* _____
8. *fare la chat* _____
9. *i computer* _____
10. *viaggiare in treno* _____

Great! Now let's get back to our dialogue.

HEAR . . . SAY 2

Laura is very eager to practice her Italian, so she joined an Italian *stanza di chat* on celebrities. With the time difference (Italy is six hours ahead of the United States), she's often online with just one or two people. This time she finds someone who shares her affection for Brad Pitt.

Teresa: Qual'è il tuo attore preferito?

Laura: Il mio è Brad Pitt.

Teresa: Anche il mio. Ti piace il suo ultimo film?

Laura: Non sono sicura . . . Sembra un po' pazzo.

Teresa: È vero. È sposato?

Laura: No. È celibe, credo.

Teresa: Ma Jennifer Aniston non è sua moglie?

Laura: Hai ragione. Hanno figli?

Teresa: Credo di no.

Laura: Allora, non abbiamo fortuna! Chi dorme non pecca, ma non piglia pesci.

Teresa: Quanti anni ha?

Laura: Trenta, credo.

Teresa: È un po' vecchio per me, ma non importa . . . È super bono!

Laura: Vecchio? Ma quanti anni hai?

Teresa: Sedici. E tu?

Laura: Trentacinque.

Teresa: Cavolo! Mia madre ha trentasei anni.

ACTIVITY 5: HOW'S THAT AGAIN?

At this point, a little embarrassed to have been talking to a sixteen-year-old about Brad Pitt, Laura says good-bye. But this is the great thing about the Internet, *vero*? It brings together people of all ages and backgrounds. Then again, chat rooms usually have profiles, if you care to look. Anyway, what happened here? Try to give all your answers in Italian.

1. *Qual è il loro attore preferito?* _____

2. *Quell'attore è sposato?* _____

3. *Come si chiama sua moglie?* _____

4. *Hanno figli?* _____

5. *Cosa dice Teresa di Brad Pitt?* _____

Did You Know?

LIGHTS, CAMERA, ACTION!: THE MOVIE *IL POSTINO*

Yes, we live in the information age, but nothing beats getting a bonafide, old-fashioned letter. In fact, part of me has always wanted to be *un postino* (a mailman), (don't laugh!) just because of the joy I could spread by delivering letters. Anyway, a wonderful movie that attests to the transformative power of the written word is *Il postino*. A labor of love for leading actor Massimo Troisi (who died the day after production finished), the film tells the story of a simple-minded mailman in a small Sicilian fishing village who develops an unlikely friendship with exiled Chilean poet, Pablo Neruda.

Did You Know?

WORKSHOP 2

WORD ON THE STREET

Chi dorme non pecca, ma non piglia pesci is an old saying that means "The early bird catches the worm." Literally it means "He who sleeps doesn't sin, but neither does he catch any fish."

WORDS TO LIVE BY

ALL ABOUT ME!: HOW TO TELL PEOPLE ABOUT YOURSELF

Let's briefly review some of the things you've learned how to do *in italiano* in these five lessons. You know how to:

STATEMENT OR QUESTION	RESPONSE
• Introduce yourself: *Sono . . .* *Mi chiamo . . .*	*Piacere.*
• Introduce someone else: *Le presento . . .* *Ti presento . . .* *Questo è . . .*	*Molto lieto / lieta.* *Ciao!*

STATEMENT OR QUESTION	RESPONSE
• Ask where someone is from: *Di dov'è Lei?* *Di dove sei?*	*Sono di* + city *Sono* + nationality
• Ask where someone lives: *Dove abita?* *Dove abiti?*	*A* + city *In* + country *A / In* + address
• Ask someone what they do: *Che lavoro fa?* *Che lavoro fai?* *Cosa fa?* *Cosa fai?*	*Sono / faccio* + occupation *Faccio / studio* + field of study *Lavoro in* + place of work
• Ask someone's age (but only if you think it's appropriate!): *Quanti anni ha?* *Quanti anni hai?*	*Ho . . . anni.*
• Return a question: *E Lei?* *E tu?*	
• Make a suggestion: *Perché non* + an action, as in: *Perché non andiamo a ballare?* Why don't we go dancing?	

Heads Up!

You use *fare* + a field of study to talk about what you're studying. Compare: *faccio legge* means "I'm studying law," but *faccio l'avvocato* means "I'm a lawyer / I practice law."

Little words say so much. Here are a few you encountered in this lesson:

mentre	*while*
ultimo	*last, latest (note that it goes <u>before</u> the noun)*
allora	*so; then; well*
ed	*and (when it comes before a word beginning with **e** or **i**; otherwise, **e**)*

Word on the Street

Super bono / Super bona is an expression meaning "really hot." But don't use it when you're talking about food or coffee—it's reserved solely for talking about people.

Finally, let's look at how you can mitigate your statements a little. When you're giving an answer you're not too sure about, just tag *credo* (I think) on the end. Laura did this when she said *è celibe, credo*. Two more useful expressions are: *credo di sì* (I think so) or *credo di no* (I don't think so).

La nonna di Antonella ha un nuovo marito, vero? —Credo di sì.

Antonella's grandmother has a new husband, right? —I think so.

Lorenzo è svizzero? —Credo di no. È italiano, credo.

Lorenzo's Swiss? —I don't think so. He's Italian, I think.

Now, let's practice one more time.

ACTIVITY 6:   TAKE IT FOR A SPIN

Ciao, ragazzi! Questo è il mio amico, Antonio. Io devo andare, ma torno subito. Perché non fate due chiacchiere con lui? (Fill in the correct responses.)

Io:	*Antonio, ti presento il mio studente / la mia studentessa. È americano / a ed è in Italia per studiare la lingua.*
Antonio:	*Piacere.*
Tu:	_____
Antonio:	*Sono calabrese, ma abito a Roma.*
Tu:	_____
Antonio:	*Sono studente. Faccio economia. E tu?*
Tu:	_____
Antonio:	*Io ho venticinque anni. Ti piace l'Italia?*
Tu:	_____
Antonio:	*Allora, perché non andiamo a prendere un caffè mentre aspettiamo Ana? C'è un bar qui vicino. Va bene?*
Tu:	_____

Ah, siete qui, amici miei! Va bene. I'm back. I hope you enjoyed your coffee break with Antonio, but now it's time to get back to work. Let's review some of the major grammar points we have covered so far.

Q & A: MORE ON QUESTIONS

You've already learned all the major question words: *chi, che / cosa / che cosa, come, dove, quando, perché.* But let's spend a little time on *quanto* (how much / many) and *quale* (which). You may have already noticed that they agree with the noun they refer to:

	QUANTO (HOW MUCH / MANY)		QUALE (WHICH)	
	SINGULAR	PLURAL	SINGULAR	PLURAL
MASCULINE	*quanto*	*quanti*	*quale*	*quali*
FEMININE	*quanta*	*quante*	*quale*	*quali*

Qual è il tuo attore preferito?

Which is your favorite actor?

Quanti anni hai?

How old are you? (*Lit.* How many years do you have?)

Quanti fratelli e sorelle avete voi?

How many brothers and sisters do you (all) have?

Whenever there is a relatively limited choice involved, i.e., one name among many or one actor among many, you should use *quale.* Let's look at a few more examples that will help you remember this rule:

Quale pasta prendi?

Which pastry are you having (*Lit.* taking)?

Quali film ti piacciono?

Which movies do you like?

The Fine Print

Note that just like *dove* and *come,* the singular form *quale* loses its final –e before a vowel, but with *quale* you don't need an apostrophe at the end. (Don't ask me why!) Compare: *qual è il suo nome?* but *dov'è lo stadio?*

Finally, just like *questo* and *quello, quanto* and *quale* can stand on their own to replace a noun:

Ti piacciono i suoi film? —Quali?

Do you like his movies? —Which ones?

Vuole dei panini? Quanti?

You want some sandwiches? How many?

Let's practice.

ACTIVITY 7:	**TAKE IT FOR A SPIN**

Fill in the blanks with the appropriate form of *quale* or *quanto*.

1. _____ *sito ti piace di più?*

2. *Da* _____ *giorni aspetti la loro risposta?*

3. _____ *è la tua attrice preferita?*

4. (Which)_____ *cartoline compri?*

5. *Ho bisogno di francobolli.* —(How many)_____

STRUT YOUR STUFF!

Pronti? Ready for a review? This will be your Guido Sarducci version of the last five units; the big stuff and nothing but the big stuff. Here's what you have to remember:

- All nouns in Italian have gender. They can be either masculine (typically ending in *–o*) or feminine (typically ending in *–a*). Nouns ending in *–e* can be either masculine or feminine, and you simply have to memorize the gender when you learn the noun. Articles can also help you figure out the gender of a noun.

- Most (but not all) adjectives go **after** the noun, and they have to match the gender and number of the noun.

- *Questo* (this), *quello* (that) and all the possessive adjectives come **before** the noun.

ACTIVITY 8:	**TAKE IT FOR A SPIN**

For each noun listed below, give the appropriate indefinite article (*un / uno / una*, etc.), demonstrative adjective (*questo* and *quello*), and form of the possessive (don't forget the article where necessary!). The first letter is provided. I've done the first one for you as an example.

	UN . . .	QUESTO . . .	QUELLO . . .	IL MIO . . .
1. amica	un'amica	quest'amica	quell'amica	n . . . la nostra amica
2. treno	_____	_____	_____	t . . . _____
3. computer	_____	_____	_____	l . . . _____
4. macellaio	_____	_____	_____	m . . . _____
5. sorelle	_____	_____	_____	s . . . _____
6. studente	_____	_____	_____	s . . . _____
7. bicchiere	_____	_____	_____	t . . . _____
8. zio	_____	_____	_____	n . . . _____
9. città	_____	_____	_____	v . . . _____
10. cane	_____	_____	_____	m . . . _____

Now, let's spend a little more time on possessives. First of all, remember that they match the gender and number of the object / person possessed, **not** the possessor. And they're always accompanied by a definite article (*il, la,* etc.), unless you're referring to an individual family member, and *loro* **always** takes a definite article. But here's an exception to the exception: if the individual family member is modified in any way (i.e., has an adjective describing it), then you need the article again, as when Sandra says:

<u>Il</u> mio fratello <u>pazzo</u> tortura il povero signor Holmes.

My crazy brother tortures poor Mr. Holmes.

The same is true when Laura says:

Il mio fratello maggiore è sposato.

My older brother is married.

If they had just said "my brother" then they would have said *mio fratello,* but the adjectives *pazzo* and *maggiore* mean that you have to use the article. Another thing to watch out for with possessive adjectives is that when it's clear from the context whom something belongs to, you can omit the possessive. It's not wrong to use it, you just don't need to. This is especially true when you're talking about articles of clothing or parts of the body, as in:

Prendo la (mia) giacca.

I'm taking my jacket.

Prendo la (mia) macchina.

I'm taking my car.

Word on the Street

ACTIVITY 9: TAKE IT FOR A SPIN

Translate into Italian.

1. Her husband is a professor. _____

2. Here's my taxi! _____

3. Where are your (sing. infml.) cousins going? _____

4. This is my crazy sister, Paola. _____

5. Our favorite hobby is chatting online. _____

6. I speak Italian with my friends. _____

7. Are you (sing. fml.) taking your computer to the café? _____
   _____

8. Their restaurant is more elegant than yours (pl.). _____
   _____

9. Why don't you (pl.) write an e-mail to Andres? _____
   _____

10. Where's my appetizer? _____

Now that we've reviewed how to talk about people and things, let's take a look at what these people might be doing.

Verbs in Italian change to show who's speaking, being spoken to, or spoken about. Therefore, subject pronouns (*io, tu, lui, lei, noi, voi, loro*) are usually not used, except for emphasis or clarity. So far, you've learned how to conjugate regular –*are* verbs and a few irregular verbs in the present tense. So, what can you say using the present tense?

• Give or ask for general information or make a statement of fact or opinion:

Luigi è un taxista.

Luigi is a taxi driver.

Abitano a Torino.

They live in Torino.

Paola porta bene gli anni.

Paola is aging well.

- Indicate what's happening:

  Parlo con il mio amico.

  I'm talking to my friend.

  Vanno al cinema. They're going to the movies.

- Talk about future plans. A time is usually specified:

  Questo fine-settimana, diamo una festa.

  This weekend, we're having a party.

  Il treno arriva fra cinque minuti.

  The train is arriving in five minutes.

- Make a suggestion, using *perché non*

  Perché non facciamo una stanza di chat?

  Why don't we start a chat room?

  Perché non andiamo al cinema con Massimo?

  Why don't we go to the movies with Massimo?

- Indicate how long something has been going on, with *da*

  Studio l'Italiano da sei mesi.

  I've been studying Italian for six months.

  Laura è insegnante da dieci anni.

  Laura's been a teacher for ten years.

- Give a group command (e.g., *Let's do it!*), using the *noi* and *voi* forms:

  Parliamo italiano!

  Let's speak Italian!

  Provate gli gnocchi!

  Try (pl.) the gnocchi!

TAKE IT FOR A SPIN

Complete the dialogues based on the information provided.

1. —_____ ?

   —Mi chiamo Marina. _____ ?

   —Andrea.

2. — Signor Tadeucci, _____ la mia amica, Claudia.

   _____ .

3. _____ ?

   —Faccio medicina. _____ ?

   — _____ ingegnere.

4. _____ tua cugina?

   —Ventotto.

   —Allora, _____ giovane di mio fratello!

   — _____ ?

   —Trentadue.

   —Un buon partito!

5. — _____ Lei?

   —A Milano.

   — _____ ?

   —No, _____ svizzero, ma _____ a
   Milano.

   — _____ ?

   — _____ professore.

ACTIVITY 11: **TAKE IT FOR A SPIN**

Now say something about these people: their name, occupation, where they live, etc.
Check out the example first.

madre / Yoko / medico / New York / giapponese
→ *Mia madre si chiama Yoko. È medico. Abita a New York, ma è giapponese.*

1. *zio / Werner / in banca / Berlino / tedesco*
2. *amico / Pietro / macellaio / Roma / trentadue anni*

3.   *genitori / Roberto e Giulia / insieme da cinquant'anni*
4.   *fratello / Lorenzo / lingue / parlare inglese, russo, tedesco, giapponese*
5.   *nipote / Maria / sposata / due figli / Vincenzo e Silvia / diciassette, otto / Napoli*

Well, now that you know how to tell the world all about yourself, let's move on to some of the things you'll probably find yourself doing on a trip to Italy.

CRIB NOTES

HEAR...SAY 1

My name is Maurizio Severi. I'm twenty-two years old and I go to university in Perugia. I study languages. I study a lot, but when I have free time I go to the movies. My favorite director is Stanley Kubrick. Do you like his films? Which ones? Maybe we have similar interests . . .

Hi everyone! It's me . . . Sandra. This is my first time on the Web. I'm not sure what to do. Why don't we talk a bit about my treasure, Mr. Holmes. He is a truly extraordinary cat. He loves petting (*Lit.* caresses) more than food. But my crazy brother tortures poor Mr. Holmes and my folks don't do anything. What injustice! Do you have a cat? What's its name? I like animals a lot . . . I'm waiting for your replies. Later!

Hello. My name is Laura and I've been studying Italian for six months. I'm looking for a friend to chat with in Italian. I live in Columbus, Ohio, in the United States and I'm Italian-American. I have a big family! There are six children. I have three sisters and two brothers. How many brothers and sisters do you have? My older brother is married and he has two twin boys. They're five years old. I'm married, too, and I'm expecting a baby. I work as a teacher and my husband is a mechanic. On weekends, I like to do some gardening, but shopping is my favorite hobby! What's your favorite hobby?

Hi, guys! I'm Andres and I'm from Brazil. Now I live in Bologna. I'm single and I work in a sales firm. Are there other Brazilians here in Italy? Where are you? I really like to listen to Latino music and dance salsa. Why don't you click onto my Web site? Let's make a chat room for Brazilians in Italy . . . all the details are on my Web page.

HEAR...SAY 2

Teresa: Which is your favorite actor?
Laura: Mine is Brad Pitt.
Teresa: Mine, too. Do you like his latest movie?
Laura: I'm not sure. He seems a little crazy.
Teresa: It's true. Is he married?
Laura: No. He's single, I think.
Teresa: But isn't Jennifer Aniston his wife?
Laura: You're right. Do they have children?
Teresa: I don't think so.

Laura: So, we're out of luck. The early bird gets the worm. (*Lit.* He who sleeps doesn't catch any fish.)
Teresa: How old is he?
Laura: Thirty, I think.
Teresa: He's a little too old for me. But it doesn't matter . . . He's really hot!
Laura: Old? But how old are you?
Teresa: Sixteen. And you?
Laura: Thirty-five.
Teresa: Wow! My mother is thirty-six . . .

ACTIVITY 1

1. e; 2. a; 3. d; 4. c; 5. b

ACTIVITY 2

	Persona 1	Persona 2	Persona 3	Persona 4
Come si chiama?	Maurizio	Sandra	Laura	Andres
Dove abita?	a Perugia		a Columbus, Ohio	a Bologna
Quanti anni ha?	più di 19 (perché è all'università)	meno di 18	più di 22 (perché è insegnante)	più di 18 (perché lavora)
Che lavoro fa?	studente	studente	insegnante	lavora in una ditta commerciale
Qual'è il suo passatempo preferito?	andare al cinema	il suo gatto, il Signor Holmes	fare le spese	ascoltare la musica latina e ballare salsa
Ha fratelli o sorelle?		sì—un fratello pazzo	sì—tre sorelle e due fratelli	

1. *Laura è la zia dei gemelli.*
2. *Maurizio fa lingue all'università.*
3. *Mr. Holmes è il gatto di Sandra.*
4. *Andres è l'amante latino.*

ACTIVITY 3

1. e; 2. d; 3. b; 4. a; 5. c

ACTIVITY 4

1. *(Non) mi piace fare pettegolezzi.*
2. *(Non) mi piacciono gli animali.*
3. *(Non) mi piace navigare in Internet.*
4. *(Non) mi piace andare al cinema.*
5. *(Non) mi piacciono i musei.*
6. *(Non) mi piace la mia famiglia.*
7. *(Non) mi piace parlare l'italiano.*
8. *(Non) mi piace fare la chat.*
9. *(Non) mi piacciono i computer.*
10. *(Non) mi piace viaggiare in treno.*

ACTIVITY 5

1. *Il loro attore preferito è Brad Pitt.*
2. *Sì, è sposato.*
3. *Sua moglie si chiama Jennifer Aniston.*
4. *No, non hanno figli.*
5. *Non importa se Brad Pitt è un po' vecchio per Teresa perché è super bono.*

ACTIVITY 6

Io:	*Antonio, ti presento il mio studente / la mia studentessa. È americano / a ed è in Italia per studiare la lingua.*
Antonio:	*Piacere.*
Tu:	*Ciao. / Piacere. E tu? Di dove sei? / Dove abiti?*
Antonio:	*Sono calabrese, ma abito a Roma.*
Tu:	*Che lavoro fai?*
Antonio:	*Sono studente. Faccio economia. E tu?*
Tu:	*Sono . . . / Faccio . . . / Lavoro in . . . Quanti anni hai?*
Antonio:	*Io ho venticinque anni. Ti piace l'Italia?*
Tu:	*Sì, molto. / Mi piace molto.*
Antonio:	*Allora, perché non andiamo a prendere un caffè mentre aspettiamo Ana? C'è un bar qui vicino. Va bene?*
Tu:	*Va bene. Andiamo!*

ACTIVITY 7

1. *Quale;* 2. *Quanti;* 3. *Qual;* 4. *Quale;* 5. *Quanti?*

ACTIVITY 8

1. *un . . . un'amica*	*questo . . . quest' amica*	*quello . . . quell' amica*	*il mio . . . la nostra amica*	
2. *un treno*	*questo treno*	*quel treno*	*il tuo treno*	
3. *un computer / —*	*questo computer / questi computer*	*quel computer / quei computer*	*il loro computer / i loro computer*	
4. *un macellaio*	*questo macellaio*	*quel macellaio*	*il mio macellaio*	
5. *—*	*queste sorelle*	*quelle sorelle*	*le sue sorelle*	
6. *uno studente*	*questo studente*	*quello studente*	*il Suo studente*	
7. *un bicchiere*	*questo bicchiere*	*quel bicchiere*	*il tuo bicchiere*	
8. *uno zio*	*questo zio*	*quello zio*	*nostro zio*	
9. *una città / —*	*questa città / queste città*	*quella città / quelle città*	*la vostra città / le vostre città*	
10. *un cane*	*questo cane*	*quel cane*	*il mio cane*	

ACTIVITY 9

1. *Suo marito è un professore.*
2. *Ecco il (mio) taxi!*
3. *Dove vanno i tuoi cugini?*
4. *Questo è la mia sorella pazza, Paola.*
5. *Il nostro hobby / passatempo preferito è fare la chat / chattare.*

6. *Parlo l'italiano con i miei amici.*
7. *Porta il (suo) computer al bar / caffè?*
8. *Il loro ristorante è più elegante del vostro.*
9. *Perché non mandate una e-mail a Andres?*
10. *Dov'è il mio antipasto?*

ACTIVITY 10

1. —*Come ti chiami? / —Come si chiama?*
   —*Mi chiamo Marina. E tu? E Lei?*
   —*Andrea.*
2. —*Signor Tadeucci, Le presento la mia amica, Claudia. / —Questa è la mia amica, Claudia.*
   —*Piacere.*
3. —*Che lavoro fa? / Che lavoro fai? / Cosa fa? / Cosa fai? / Che cosa studi?*
   —*Faccio medicina. E tu? / E Lei?*
   —*Sono ingegnere.*
4. *Quanti anni ha tua cugina?*
   —*Ventotto.*
   —*Allora, è più giovane di mio fratello!*
   —*Quanti anni ha (lui / tuo fratello)?*

—*Trentadue.*
—*Un buon partito!*
5. *Dove abita Lei?*
   —*A Milano.*
   —*È italiano?*
   —*No, sono svizzero, ma lavoro / habito a Milano.*
   —*Che lavoro fa?*
   —*Sono professore. / Faccio il professore.*

ACTIVITY 11

1. *Mio zio si chiama Werner. Lavora in banca. Abita a Berlino. È tedesco.*
2. *Il mio amico Pietro è macellaio. Abita a Roma e ha trentadue anni.*
3. *I miei genitori, Roberto e Giulia, sono insieme da cinquant'anni.*
4. *Mio fratello si chiama Lorenzo. Fa lingue. Parla inglese, russo, tedesco e giapponese.*
5. *Mia nipote si chiama Maria. È sposata, ha due figli. Vincenzo ha diciassette anni e Silvia ha otto anni. Abitano a Napoli.*

6.

IT'S JUST WHAT I NEED!

È arrivato come il cacio sui maccheroni!
(*Lit.* It came like cheese on macaroni!)

I'm so hungry, I could eat a horse!

COMING UP...

- *Can I order, please?*: How to order in a restaurant
- *Enjoy your meal!*: A typical Italian meal
- *I could eat a horse*: More on food and restaurant talk
- *Living in the moment*: Talking about the present with –*ere* verbs
- *I'll have some of that*: How to say "some" in Italian
- *Too much of a good thing*: Words expressing quantity
- *–issimo!*: Very, very, very
- *Saluti! Cheers!*: The verb *bere* (to drink)

LOOKING AHEAD

Let's leave the sometimes cold world of *i computer, le stanze di chat, le pagine web,* and *la e-mail* behind for a bit and turn to something more basic—the very Italian pleasure of *andare al ristorante* (dining out). After all, while *fare la chat* is a fine way to communicate, *fare due chiacchiere* (chatting) face-to-face, over a nice glass of *Chianti* is something altogether different. Come to think of it, just about anything you do for fun—*ascoltare la musica, guardare la tv, fare le spese*—is usually more fun *insieme.*

ACTIVITY 1: **LET'S WARM UP**

Associations: Which pairs make the most sense to you?

1.	rush hour	a.	*una fame da lupo / una fame da morire*
2.	Sandra Bullock	b.	*troppo turistica*
3.	👍	c.	*molto simpatica*
4.	Las Vegas	d.	*tanta gente*
5.	All you can eat!	e.	*un segno*

I hope you enjoyed that little psychological experiment. At the end of the lesson, I'll tell you what your answers mean. *Scherzi a parte,* all joking aside, let's listen to our dialogue.

HEAR...SAY 1

Fatima and Lotte are *compagne di scuola* (school buddies). They've both been in Italy for a few months now, studying at the same language school. Fatima prides herself on feeling like a native, and today she's dragged Lotte to see some frescoes in a little-known Tuscan village. They arrive at the bus station after a full day of sightseeing, and Lotte *ha molta fame* (is very hungry), as you might imagine. But Fatima is always in search of a place that's just right.

Lotte: Una trattoria! Meno male—ho una fame da lupo!

Fatima: È troppo turistica. C'è un'osteria molto carina qui vicino, credo.

Lotte: Se insisti . . .

After a walk that wouldn't quite qualify the *osteria* as *vicino* (close), Fatima finds the place she's looking for.

Fatima: Vedi? C'è tanta gente—segno che è un buon ristorante.

Lotte: Oppure segno che facciamo la coda per un tavolo.

Fatima:	Chiediamo . . .
Il cameriere:	Buona sera.
Fatima:	C'è un tavolo per due?
Il cameriere:	Quaranta minuti. Va bene?
Lotte:	(*shocked*) Quaranta minuti!!
Fatima:	(*oblivious to Lotte's reaction*) Sì, grazie . . . Allora, prendiamo un aperitivo?
Lotte:	(*annoyed*) Io non bevo prima di mangiare.
Fatima:	Ma cosa ti prende? Perché non cerchi di divertirti un po'?
Lotte:	Perché ho una fame da morire!

After a *lunghissimo* wait, they're finally seated *a tavola*, and the waiter arrives.

Il cameriere:	Buona sera, signore. Desiderano?
Fatima:	Vediamo il menù . . . Cosa prendi?
Lotte:	Cominciamo con un antipasto. Un po' di prosciutto crudo e un po' di formaggio.
Il cameriere:	E per primo?
Fatima:	Per me una pasta . . . degli gnocchi alla romana.
Lotte:	E per me la ribollita.
Il cameriere:	Come secondo?
Lotte:	Io prendo la bistecca alla fiorentina. Com'è oggi?
Il cameriere:	È molto buona.
Lotte:	Va bene.
Fatima:	E io prendo il coniglio alla cacciatora.
Il cameriere:	E per contorno?
Fatima:	Dei fagiolini, per piacere.
Lotte:	Delle patate arrosto.
Il cameriere:	Porto subito l'antipasto.

Well, food is finally on the way! *Meno male!*

ACTIVITY 2: HOW'S THAT AGAIN?

1. Why doesn't Fatima want to eat at the *trattoria?* _____

   _____

2. What does Fatima think is proof that the *osteria* is *un buon ristorante?* _____

   _____

3. What does Fatima suggest they start with? Why does Lotte refuse?_____

_____

4. Why is Lotte in a bad mood?_____

5. What do they order? _____

Now let's take a closer look at some of the phrases you heard in the dialogue.

WORKSHOP 1

WORDS TO LIVE BY

CAN I ORDER, PLEASE?: HOW TO ORDER IN A RESTAURANT

Let's start with the really important stuff, like how to say you're hungry. You can simply say:

Ho fame.   I'm hungry.

Or you can be a little more emphatic:

Ho molta fame.   I'm very hungry.
Ho una fame da lupo!   I could eat a horse! (Lit. I have the hunger of a wolf!)
Ho una fame da morire!   I'm starving. (Lit. I have a hunger to die from!)

Word on the Street

The expression **da morire** (to die for; to die from) is one of the most popular intensifiers in everyday speech. You'll probably also hear it from an excited young man declaring to the world that he's just seen *una ragazza* and she was **bella da morire!**

If you're hungry, then you'll be able to find satisfaction at one of the following types of establishments:

il ristorante   restaurant
l'osteria   officially, it's a wine bar, but often it's just a trendy way of saying
                        "restaurant"
la trattoria   simple, homestyle restaurant
la rosticceria   an on-the-go establishment selling roasted meat and other food

But be careful, because if the place is really *carino / carina* (nice; cute), *turistico* (touristy), or *famoso* (famous), and you see *tanta gente* (a lot of people) waiting out front, it's usually *un segno* (a sign) that you'll have to *fare la coda* (wait in line) for *un tavolo* (a table). Of course, you can always relax and have *un aperitivo* (an aperitif) while you wait.

Heads Up!

The noun *la gente* is singular in Italian. So while we would say "there <u>are</u> a lot of people" the Italians say *c'è tanta gente*.

Heads Up!

Once you're seated *a tavola*, *il cameriere* (the waiter) or *la cameriera* (the waitress) will come to take your order.

Word on the Street

Waiters in more formal establishments will often ask for your order with ***Desiderano?*** which is the *Loro* form of *desiderare*. You'll seldom be addressed this formally otherwise. What you're likely to hear in most places is: ***Pronti?*** (Ready?) or ***Mi dica?*** (Tell me?).

ENJOY YOUR MEAL!: A TYPICAL ITALIAN MEAL

A typical Italian meal features at least three courses:

l'antipasto	*appetizer*
il primo piatto	*first dish*
il secondo piatto	*second or main dish (So when you hear **Come secondo?** the waiter isn't asking if you want seconds.)*

Plus:

il contorno	*side dish*

Did You Know?

An *antipasto* usually consists of a plate of cold cuts, including *prosciutto crudo,* the famous Italian cured ham, and *formaggio* (cheese). *Crostini,* pieces of thin toasted bread spread with a liver paté, and *bruschetta,* thick slices of toasted bread with olive oil, chopped tomatoes, and spices, are other popular choices. Typical *primi* include *pasta, risotto,* or a hearty *minestra* (soup). *I secondi* are the main dish, and *la carne* (meat), or *il pesce* (fish), are the order of the day. Note that the main dish doesn't include anything on the side, so you'll have to order *il contorno* separately: *i fagioli* (beans), *le patate* (potatoes), or *un'insalata* (a salad). *Buon appetito!* (Enjoy your meal!)

Did You Know?

Did You Know?

Did You Know?

CHEERS: TYPICAL ITALIAN APERITIFS

People often think an *aperitivo* is an appetizer, but it's really an aperitif—a drink to open your appetite (*aperto* means "open"). Popular Italian *aperitivi* include Campari, Cinzano, Martini, Cynar, and the Venetian sparkling wine *prosecco*. But be careful what you ask for: If you order "a Campari" you'll probably get a Campari and soda. For a straight Campari, say *un bitter Campari,* instead.

Here's what Fatima and Lotte order:

gli gnocchi alla romana	*potato dumplings (note the pronunciation) in a red sauce*
la ribollita	*hearty bean soup (once made with leftover, hence "re-boiled" beans)*
la bistecca alla fiorentina	***bistecca** means "steak" and **bistecca alla fiorentina** is a thick slab of meat marinated in olive oil, pepper, and other spices, then grilled rare*
il coniglio alla cacciatora	*rabbit in a hunter's sauce*
i fagiolini	*green beans*
le patate arrosto	*roasted potatoes*

Take a Tip from Me!

Take a Tip from Me!

You now know how many courses to order, but there's a good chance you'll still have a panic attack when faced with a bona fide Italian menu. Well, <u>don't</u> panic. It's perfectly normal. The best thing to do is have a phrase book or dictionary handy to look up the items you don't understand. Or simply ask the waiter about the item you're interested in with: *Cos'è . . .* or *Cosa sono . . .* And if pronunciation is what has you worried, just point to the item on the *menù* and say *Vorrei questo . . .* or *Prendo questo . . .*

Did You Know?

Did You Know?

LIGHTS, CAMERA, ACTION!: THE MOVIE *BIG NIGHT*

For a warm and entertaining look at Italian-American culture, as well as the joy of dining, rent *Big Night,* starring Stanley Tucci, Minnie Driver, and Isabella Rossellini. You'll meet two brothers, Primo and Secondo (guess who's older), who run a failing restaurant on the Jersey Shore. Primo is the front man and Secondo the inspired chef, who refuses on principle to serve a guest *pasta* with *risotto,* even if it means losing the business they desperately need. The movie culminates with a grand dinner prepared in honor of a special guest—Louis Prima. To see if he actually turns up, you'll have to rent the movie.

Let's look at some of the new verbs you heard:

bere	to drink
chiedere	to ask
credere	to believe
divertirsi	to have fun
insistere	to insist
prendere	to take
vedere	to see

Word on the Street

Here are two more good expressions to keep handy:

Meno male!	Thank goodness!
Cosa ti prende?	What's gotten into you? (Lit. What's taking you?)

Heads Up!

Cercare means "to look for" but *cercare di* + infinitive means "to try to do something." Also, note that verbs ending in *–care*, like *cercare,* or those ending in *–gare,* like *pagare,* take an *h* before endings beginning with *–e* or *–i* to retain the hard *k* or *g* sounds: *cerchi, cerchiamo, paghi, paghiamo.*

Finally, a few of those little words that say so much . . .

se	if
oppure	otherwise; or
prima di	before

As in:

Prima di tornare al lavoro, facciamo due esercizi. (Before returning to work, let's do two exercises!)

ACTIVITY 3: TAKE IT FOR A SPIN

1. You walk by *una rosticceria* and the smell of the food makes your mouth water. You
   think: _____

2. You're telling your friend about your *cugina* who's got a great personality. _____

_____

3. You've just sat down at *un tavolo* in a chic *osteria,* when your friend looks over your shoulder and suddenly decides he has to leave immediately. You say: _____

_____

4. It's the only English-language movie showing in town. You show up a few minutes before show time, thinking "Hey, I'm in Italy. There won't be many people waiting to see a movie in English." Boy, are you wrong! You see _____ And what are they doing? _____

5. You rushed out of the house this morning without even a Pop Tart. You had to work through lunch, and just as you were ready to go home, your boss asked you to join her for a drink after work. You get home around 10 P.M., and tell your husband / wife: _____

ACTIVITY 4: TAKE IT FOR A SPIN

Match the dish (in the left column) with the course (in the right column), and put them all in the right order using the sample:

Per _____ (course) _____ , *prendo* _____ (dish) _____ .

i fagioli	l'antipasto
un Cinzano	il secondo
un risotto	il contorno
il pesce	il primo
i crostini	l'aperitivo

You know, all this talk about hunger is making **me** hungry. How about you? Here's something to kill your appetite: **Grammar! Yuck!** Right? Nah. It's not so bad. In any case, that's what we're doing now, so listen up!

THE NITTY-GRITTY

LIVING IN THE MOMENT: TALKING ABOUT THE PRESENT WITH *—ERE* VERBS

You already know that there are three types of verbs in Italian: *—are, —ere,* and *—ire.* Well, the forms of *—ere* verbs in the present tense are just as simple as those of *—are* verbs: Drop the *—ere* ending and replace it with *—o, —i, —e, —iamo, —ete,* or *—ono.*

VEDERE (TO SEE) IN THE PRESENT TENSE		
	–ERE ENDINGS	VEDERE
IO	–o	ved–o
TU	–i	ved–i
LUI / LEI	–e	ved–e
NOI	–iamo	ved–iamo
VOI	–ete	ved–ete
LORO	–ono	ved–ono

So, when Fatima says:

Vedi?

Do you see?

Chiediamo . . .

We'll ask . . .

Cosa prendi?

What are you getting (*Lit.* taking)?

Or when Lotte says:

Se insisti . . .

If you insist . . .

they're both using regular *–ere* verbs. So now you can say lots of things.

Take a Tip from Me!

Did you notice that the *io, tu,* and *noi* endings (i.e., *–o, –i,* and *–iamo*) are exactly the same for *–are* and *–ere* verbs? And do you know what that means? It means that you already know half of the *–ere* verb forms! So, stop complaining! The rest should be a piece of cake.

Take a Tip from Me!

ACTIVITY 5:   **TAKE IT FOR A SPIN**

Read through the dialogue again, and find ten verbs in the present tense. Then decide whether they're regular *–are* or *–ere* verbs, irregular verbs you know, or something you've never seen before. Write the infinitive of each verb in the appropriate column. I've already given you a few above.

REGULAR –ARE	REGULAR –ERE	IRREGULAR	?!?!?!?!?!
1.			
2.			
3.			
4.			
5.			
6.			
7.			
8.			
9.			
10.			

I hope there aren't too many verbs on your ?!?!?!? list. And if there are, stay tuned—it will all become clear very soon. First, let's take a look at the types of things you can say with –ere verbs. Here are some of the most common.

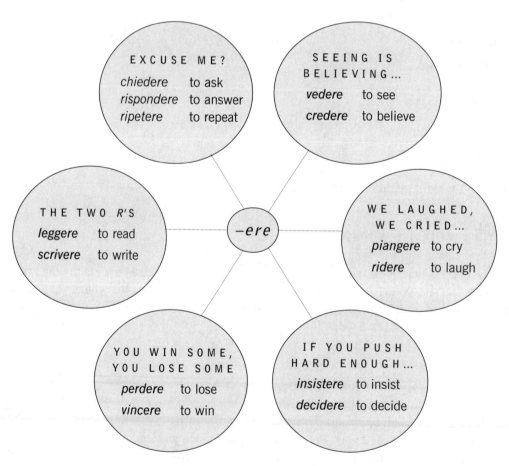

ITALIAN WITHOUT THE FUSS

Why don't you show off what you know . . .

It's your turn to dine out with a friend. Fill in the correct form of the verb, and *buon appetito*!

You: *Cosa (prendere, noi)* _____?

A Friend: *(vedere, noi)* _____ *cosa c'è e (decidere, noi)*_____

_____.

You: *Io (prendere)* _____ *il risotto. E tu?*

A Friend: *Io (prendere)* _____ *una minestra.*

You: *Perché non (prendere, tu)* _____ *gli gnocchi se hai fame?*

A Friend: *Cosa sono gli gnocchi?*

You: *Un tipo di pasta, (credere, io)* _____, *ma (chiedere, noi)*

_____.

A Friend: *Se (insistere, tu)* _____.

When ordering food, you'll need to know how to say "some."

I'LL HAVE SOME OF THAT! HOW TO SAY "SOME" IN ITALIAN

The easiest way to say "some" is with the expression *un po' di* (a little bit of) and a singular noun.

Cominciamo con un antipasto: un po' di prosciutto crudo e un po' di formaggio.

Let's start with an appetizer: some prosciutto and some cheese.

Un po' di pane . . .

Some bread . . .

Or you can use the preposition *di* + the definite article (*il, la,* etc.). And don't forget the combined forms: *del, della, dello, dell', dei, delle, degli.*

Per me dei fagiolini.

Some green beans for me.

Per me delle patate arrosto.

Some roasted potatoes for me.

If you're talking about items that are countable, you can also use:

- *alcuni / alcune* (some; a few; several) + a plural noun (masc. / fem.)
- *qualche* (some) + a singular noun

For example:

Vorrei comprare qualche cartolina.

I want to buy some postcards.

Vado al cinema con alcuni amici.

I'm going to the movies with some friends.

Ready to try your hand at this?

<table>
<tr><td>ACTIVITY 7:</td><td>**TAKE IT FOR A SPIN**</td></tr>
</table>

Say you'd like some of the following by using *di* followed by the definite article and the words or phrases provided and *per piacere*. (For example: *formaggio → Del / un po' di formaggio, per favore.*)

1. vino_____

2. antipasti_____

3. pane_____

4. patate_____

5. bottiglia di vino per la tavola_____

6. crostini_____

7. pasta_____

8. minestra_____

9. bicchieri_____

10. aperitivo_____

Well, if you were to head out to an Italian *trattoria* right now, you'd be in pretty good shape, but there's still some work to be done! Meanwhile, let's see how Fatima and Lotte's evening is progressing . . .

HEAR . . . SAY 2

Throughout the meal, the only words spoken are Fatima's *Signore, mi porta una forchetta?* (Sir, can you bring me a fork?). Fatima takes advantage of an interruption by the *cameriere* to make conversation with Lotte, who is concentrating on her food.

Il cameriere: Un altro quartino di vino rosso?

Lotte: *(shakes her head no, chewing avidly)*

Fatima:	No, grazie . . . (*looking over at Lotte eating away*) la mia amica non beve molto. Ti piace la bistecca?
Lotte:	Sì, molto. È buonissima, però è troppo piccola.
Fatima:	Troppo piccola?! Sei pazza!
Lotte:	Sì—proprio piccolissima! (*finishing her huge steak and finally looking up with a contented smile*) Prendiamo anche un dolce?
Fatima:	Sì, certo. Ci sono alcune pasticcerie fantastiche in questa zona . . . Ma tu piangi?
Lotte:	Tu sei impossibile! Vai via, io resto qui.
Fatima:	Va bene . . . vinci tu. Restiamo qui . . .
Lotte:	No, vinci tu, come sempre. Paghiamo il conto . . . e andiamo a trovare una pasticceria famosa!
Fatima:	Una decisione buonissima!

ACTIVITY 8:   HOW'S THAT AGAIN?

Choose the best answer.

1. Lotte says her *bistecca* is . . .
   a. too big.
   b. too small.
   c. just right.

2. Lotte wants to order . . .
   a. more *vino*.
   b. a side dish.
   c. dessert.

3. Fatima suggests . . .
   a. a fantastic pastry shop in the neighborhood.
   b. a fantastic pastry for which the restaurant is famous.
   c. a fantastico vacation for two in the Cayman Islands.

4. At Fatima's suggestion, Lotte . . .
   a. asks for the bill *(il conto)*.
   b. has a pang for *tiramisù*.
   c. starts to cry.

5. Fatima offers . . .
   a. to pay for dinner.
   b. to stay and have *un dolce* at the *trattoria*.
   c. a tissue to Lotte.

6.   In the end . . .
      a. Fatima wins and they set out in search of a hip *pasticceria* (pastry shop).
      b. Lotte wins, and they stay where they are.
      c. They're both thrown out for arguing.

How about you? Room for *un dolce*? Let's do some more work, but a reward awaits at the end, I promise!

WORKSHOP 2

WORDS TO LIVE BY

I COULD EAT A HORSE: MORE ON FOOD AND RESTAURANT TALK

No meal in Italy would be complete without *un po' di vino*. You can choose:

vino rosso	*red wine*
vino bianco	*white wine*
vino della casa	*house wine*

If you opt for the house wine, you can sometimes ask for *un bicchiere*, but more often you'll have to choose:

un quartino	*quarter of a liter*
un mezzo litro	*half a liter*
un litro	*liter*

If you need something brought to the table, say:

Mi porta . . .	*Can you bring me . . .*
• **una forchetta**	• *a fork*
• **un coltello**	• *a knife*
• **un cucchiaio**	• *a spoon*
• **un tovagliolo**	• *a napkin*
• **del sale**	• *some salt*
• **del pepe**	• *some pepper*

Or, as in Activity 7, just say what you need with *per piacere*.

After you've enjoyed a typical Italian meal, take your pick of the best way to top it all off:

il dolce	*dessert*
la frutta	*fruit*
il digestivo	*after dinner drink*

And don't forget *un caffè* to keep you going! Hopefully, here's what you'll be saying about your meals in Italy, even those at a *piccolissima* (very small) hole in the wall.

Fantastico!	*Fantastic!*
Buonissimo!	*Really good!*

At least until you get *il conto* (the bill), that is.

Heads Up!

The adjective *buono* can come either before or after the noun. When it follows the noun, it has the typical forms: *buono / buoni, buona / buone.* But when it comes before a singular noun, *buono* is shortened to *buon* before most masculine nouns (but *buono* is used with those that start with a "z" or an "s" + consonant combination), and *buona* takes an apostrophe before nouns starting with a vowel. You've already seen this in the expressions *un buon partito* and *che buon'idea.*

Did You Know?

KEEP THE CHANGE: TIPPING IN ITALY

A service charge is usually included in the bill in Italy (the menu or bill will indicate *servizio compreso*), so you don't have to leave a tip. However, if you're satisfied with the service, it's customary to round off the bill. If the service is not included (as is sometimes the case in very touristy restaurants) leave ten to fifteen percent. Also, don't be surprised to see a cover charge of a few euros, listed as *coperto,* on your bill. It's to cover the bread and anything else you might have enjoyed that isn't on the menu.

Label everything you see on the table.

Take a Tip from Me!

O.K., this may sound strange, but with certain topics that are particularly vocabulary-heavy, if you really want to remember everything, the best way is to label as many things as you can around the house. This way, when you open the drawer to get a spoon, you'll see the word *cucchiaio*, one of my favorite words to pronounce, by the way: (koo-KYAH-yoh), and pretty soon it'll lodge in your memory. You can do the same with furniture or the rooms in your house. But if you're too worried about what the neighbors will think, then just try to think of the words in Italian as you come across the objects they represent in daily life.

Okay, *basta con le chiacchiere. Facciamo un po' di grammatica.*

THE NITTY-GRITTY

TOO MUCH OF A GOOD THING: WORDS EXPRESSING QUANTITY

You just learned the partitive and how to say you want *some* of something, but how can you express whether this quantity is sufficient? Or what if you want to say just how much you like something, or how much it annoys you, or how well you speak Italian? You get the picture. Well, you'd use one of the following words:

	poco	abbastanza	molto / tanto	troppo
0				➝
	few	enough	a lot of / so many	too many
	a little	enough	very / a lot	too (much)

Simple enough, right? Well, there's a "but." Each of these words can be used to describe a noun, an adjective, or a verb. When they're used in front of an adjective or a verb, things are simple enough—the form of the words does not change at all. For example:

È molto buona.

It's very good.

È troppo piccola.

It's too small.

Mi piacciono tanto i dolci . . .

I like dessert a lot . . .

But (I told you there was one), when these words are used as adjectives, they have to do what all adjectives do. What was that? You got it—they match the gender and number of the noun. These adjectives come **before** the noun.

Here are the forms:

	SINGULAR	PLURAL
MASCULINE	poco	pochi
	molto	molti
	tanto	tanti
	troppo	troppi
FEMININE	poca	poche
	molta	molte
	tanta	tante
	troppa	troppe

Notice that they all have the typical adjective endings, except that you need the "h" before the "i" and "e" with *poco* to keep the hard *k* sound.

C'è tanta gente.

There are so many people.

Mi piacciono pochi vini.

I like few wines.

Tante grazie.

Thank you so much. (*Lit.* Many thanks.)

Word on the Street

Now for the fun part! Another way of saying *molto* is by adding the suffix *–issimo / a* to any adjective (but only after you take off its final vowel). **Bellissimo! Semplicissimo! Bravissimo! Giovanissimo!**

SALUTI! CHEERS! THE VERB BERE (TO DRINK)

Before we all get carried away, let's look at one more irregular verb: *bere* (to drink). It's an important one, I'm sure you'll agree.

BERE (TO DRINK) IN THE PRESENT TENSE			
IO	bevo	NOI	beviamo
TU	bevi	VOI	bevete
LUI / LEI	beve	LORO	bevono

And before you get all bent out of shape, notice that the only irregular thing about *bere* is that its stem is *bev–* (instead of just *b–*). The endings are all perfectly regular. *Bene.* Now let's practice.

ACTIVITY 10: TAKE IT FOR A SPIN

Try your hand at translating the following dialogue between two . . . ahem . . . friends, who have possibly already had one too many to drink . . .

Friend 1:   What are you getting?
Friend 2:   Another bottle of wine.
Friend 1:   You drink too much.
Friend 2:   Come on! You drink a lot, too.
Friend 1:   No, I only drink a little wine.
Friend 2:   Yeah, but you drink a lot of aperitifs!
Friend 1:   Yeah, but you cry like a baby!
Friend 2:   That's because I drink too much.
Friend 1:   Nah. You don't drink too much . . .

Okay, you've made it to the end, and now you get to see how well you fared. But before I let you go, I promised you a reward at the end of the lesson . . .

Word on the Street

If you want to be a wise guy on your very first outing to an Italian *ristorante,* when *il cameriere* asks if you'd like more water, a little olive oil, or suggests a salad from the menu, you can answer the way my Florentine friends do:

L'acqua per le piante.
L'erba per la mucca.
L'olio per la macchina.

In other words, "Water for the plants, grass for the cow, and oil for the car."

Basta! Ciao!

CRIB NOTES

HEAR...SAY 1

Lotte:	A trattoria! Thank goodness! I could eat a horse (*Lit.* I am as hungry as a wolf)!
Fatima:	It's too touristy. There's a really cute wine bar nearby, I think.
Lotte:	If you insist . . .
Fatima:	See? There are so many people—a sign of a good restaurant!
Lotte:	Or sign that we'll be standing in line for a table.
Fatima:	Let's ask . . .
Waiter:	Good evening.
Fatima:	Is there a table for two?
Waiter:	Forty minutes. Okay?
Lotte:	Forty minutes!!
Fatima:	Yes, thank you . . . So, should we get an aperitif?
Lotte:	I don't drink before eating.
Fatima:	But what's gotten into you? Why don't you try to have some fun?
Lotte:	Because I'm starving!

Waiter:	Good evening, ladies. What would you like?
Fatima:	Let's look at the menu . . . . What are you having?
Lotte:	We'll start with an appetizer: some prosciutto and some cheese.
Waiter:	And as a first course?
Fatima:	For me a pasta . . . some gnocchi Roman style.
Lotte:	And for me the bean soup.
Waiter:	And as a second course?
Lotte:	I'll have the Florentine steak. Is it good today?
Waiter:	It's very good.
Lotte:	Okay.
Fatima:	And I'll have the rabbit in hunter's sauce.
Waiter:	And on the side?
Fatima:	Some green beans, please.
Lotte:	Some roasted potatoes.
Waiter:	I'll bring out the appetizer right away.

HEAR...SAY 2

Waiter:	Another quarter liter of red wine?
Lotte:	(shakes her head no, chewing avidly)
Fatima:	No, thank you . . . (looking over at Lotte wolfing down her food). My friend doesn't drink much.
Fatima:	Do you like the steak?
Lotte:	Yes, very much. It's very good. But it's too small.
Fatima:	Too small?! You're crazy!

Lotte:	Yes, truly very small! (finishing her huge steak and finally looking up) Are we going to have some dessert?
Fatima:	Yes, of course. There are some fantastic pastry shops in this area . . . . But, are you crying?
Lotte:	You're impossible. You go; I'm staying here.
Fatima:	Okay . . . you win . . . . We're staying here.

Lotte: No, you win, like always. Let's pay the bill and go and find a famous pastry shop.

Fatima: An excellent decision!

ACTIVITY 1:

1. d; 2. c; 3. e; 4. b; 5. a

ACTIVITY 2:

1. Fatima thinks it's *tropo turistica,* too touristy.
2. Fatima thinks a lot of people waiting out front is a sign of *un buon ristorante,* "a good restaurant."
3. Fatima suggests they have *un aperitivo,* "a drink," at the bar. Lotte says she doesn't drink before eating, but she's probably just angry.
4. Because she's starving!
5. They order some *prosciutto* and *formaggio, degli gnocchi, la ribollita, la bistecca alla fiorentina, il coniglio alla cacciatora, dei fagiolini,* and *le patate arroste.*

ACTIVITY 3:

1. *Ho fame.*
2. *È molto simpatica.*
3. *Cosa ti prende?*
4. *tanta gente. La gente fa la coda (per comprare i biglietti).*
5. *Ho una fame da lupo/da morire!*

ACTIVITY 4:

Per aperitivo prendo un Cinzano.
Per antipasto prendo i crostini.
Per primo prendo il risotto.
Per secondo prendo il pesce.
Per contorno prendo i fagioli.

ACTIVITY 5:

	REGULAR –ARE	REGULAR –ERE	IRREGULAR
ho			*avere*
è (multiple instances)			*essere*
insisti		*insistere*	
vedi		*vedere*	

	REGULAR –ARE	REGULAR –ERE	IRREGULAR
facciamo			*fare*
chiediamo		*chiedere*	
va (multiple intances)	*andare*		
prendiamo		*prendere*	
bevo			*bere*
prende		*prendere*	
cerchi	*cercare*		
ho			*avere*
desiderano	*desiderare*		
vediamo		*vedere*	
prendi		*prendere*	
cominciamo	*cominciare*		
prendo		*prendere*	

ACTIVITY 6:

Cosa prendiamo?
Vediamo cosa c'è e decidiamo.
Io prendo il risotto. E tu?
Io prendo una minestra.
Perché non prendi gli gnocchi se hai fame?
Cosa sono gli gnocchi?
Un tipo di pasta credo, ma chiediamo.
Se insisti.

ACTIVITY 7:

1. *Del/Un po' di vino, per piacere.*
2. *Dei/Alcuni antipasti, per piacere.*
3. *Del/Un po di' pane, per piacere.*
4. *Delle patate, per piacere.*
5. *Qualche bottiglia di vino per la tavola, per piacere.*
6. *Dei/Alcuni crostini, per piacere.*
7. *Della/Un po' di pasta, per piacere.*
8. *Della/Un po' di minestra, per piacere.*
9. *Dei/Alcuni bicchieri, per piacere.*
10. *Qualche aperitivo, per piacere.*

ACTIVITY 8:

1. b; 2. c; 3. a; 4. c; 5. b; 6. a.

ACTIVITY 9:

la caraffa di vino
the carafe of wine

il coltello
the knife

il piatto
the plate

il bicciere
the glass

il cucchiaio
the spoon

il conto
the check

la tazza di caffè
the cup of coffee

la tavola
the table

il dolce
the dessert

la forchetta
the fork

ACTIVITY 10:

- Cosa prendi?
- Un'altra bottiglia di vino.
- Bevi troppo.
- Ma, dai! Anche tu bevi molto.
- No. Io bevo solo un po' di vino.

- Sì, ma bevi tanti apperitivi!
- Sì, ma tu piangi come un bambino!
- Perchè bevo troppo.
- Ma, no! Non bevi troppo . . .

WHERE THERE'S A WILL, THERE'S A WAY

Volere è potere

(*Lit.* To want is to be able)

Is there a problem?

COMING UP...

- *Do you have a reservation?*: **Checking into a hotel**
- *Front desk, please*: **Different ways of saying what you need in a hotel**
- *Quanti ne abbiamo oggi?* **What's today's date?**
- *First things first*: **Saying** *first, second,* **etc., in Italian**
- *Where there's a will, there's a way*: **The verbs** *volere* **(to want),** *potere* **(can; to be able to), and** *dovere* **(must; to have to)**
- *To Whom It May Concern*: **Pronouns like** *to me, to you, to us,* **etc.**
- *Between like and need*: *Piacere* **and other verbs used with pronouns like** *to me, to you, to us,* **etc.**

LOOKING AHEAD

So, I don't know what you've been doing since we last spoke, but I had a *fame da morire*, and I treated myself to some *bruschetta* and a big *bistecca* with a nice *quartino di vino rosso*. What did you choose as your *primo* and *secondo*? Oh, and did I mention that I topped it all off with a small *bicchiere di limoncello?* (*Limoncello* is a very popular after-dinner liqueur with a taste of, you've got it, lemon.) Mmmmm. *Buonissimo!* Although I will admit the *digestivo* went to my head a little, and I headed straight to bed . . . There's nothing like the comfort of home . . . or the hotel, if you're traveling. But just imagine this: You've traveled across an ocean, making three *coincidenze* (connecting flights), and you're dreaming of the big queen-size bed in your *camera matrimoniale* (double room). You're ready to check in, only to learn there's been some sort of mix-up, and your *prenotazione* (reservation) doesn't seem to mean all that much. *Roba da pazzi!* Crazy stuff! But stranger things have happened . . . Just ask Mr. Johnson.

ACTIVITY 1: **LET'S WARM UP**

Match the Italian phrase with what you think it means.

1. *le valigie*   a. hotel
2. *cambiare camera*   b. full
3. *al completo*   c. to share the bill
4. *l'albergo*   d. luggage
5. *dividere il conto*   e. to change rooms

And now let's see what happened to Mr. Johnson . . .

HEAR . . . SAY 1

Il primo giorno: mercoledì, 18 luglio, 2002

So, it's *luglio a Venezia* (July in Venice) and Mr. John Johnson, an importer of fine glass from the United States, has just arrived for some business meetings and a tour of the famous Murano glass works. It's been a long trip, and all he can think about is getting some rest and sprawling out on the big bed he's reserved at the *Palazzo Bellini*. As it turns out, the name *Palazzo* is a little misleading. The hotel is a little strange, especially its perpetually confused *portiere* (concierge), Gianfranco, who greets Mr. Johnson as he approaches *la reception*.

Gianfranco: Benvenuto al Palazzo Bellini. Mi chiamo Gianfranco. Desidera?

Johnson 1:   Ho una prenotazione . . . al nome di Johnson.

Gianfranco: Il signor Johnson . . . Vediamo . . . Sì, ecco—una camera matrimoniale con doccia, da mercoledì, il 18 (diciotto) luglio, a sabato, 21 (ventuno) luglio, vero?

Johnson 1:   Sì, esatto.

Gianfranco: Quanti ne abbiamo oggi?

Johnson 1:   Oggi è il 18 (diciotto) luglio.

Gianfranco: In questo caso, va bene. Le do la camera numero quarantasei, al terzo piano.

Johnson 1:   Grazie.

Mr. Johnson seems to be well on his way to reaching his bed. But don't be fooled by appearances. He goes to *camera quarantasei,* only to return a few moments later.

Gianfranco: Sì, Signor Johnson. C'è qualcosa che non va?

Johnson 1:   Devo cambiare camera.

Gianfranco: Non Le piace la camera?

Johnson 1:   No, mi piace, ma c'è già qualcuno nella camera quarantasei.

Gianfranco: Roba da pazzi!

At that moment, another gentleman approaches the desk.

Johnson 2:   Scusi.

Gianfranco: Sì, Signor Johnson. C'è qualcosa che non va?

Johnson 2:   Ci sono delle valigie nella mia camera e non sono le mie.

Gianfranco: Roba da pazzi!

Johnson 1:   Scusi signore, posso farLe una domanda?

Johnson 2:   Sì, certo.

Johnson 1:   Come ha detto che si chiama?

Johnson 2:   Johnson.

Johnson 1:   In camera quarantasei? Al terzo piano?

Johnson 2:   Sì. Ma perché mi fa tutte queste domande?

Johnson 1:   Perché anch'io sono Johnson e quelle sono le mie valigie.

Gianfranco: Roba da pazzi! Ecco il problema!

Johnson 1:   Allora, adesso posso cambiare camera?

Gianfranco: Roba da pazzi!

Johnson 1:   Come "roba da pazzi"?

Gianfranco: Mi dispiace, signori, ma l'albergo è al completo. Dovete condividere la camera.

Johnson 1:	Io voglio trovare un altro albergo.
Gianfranco:	Signore, a luglio a Venezia, tutti gli alberghi sono al completo.
Johnson 1:	Uffa!
Gianfranco:	Ma almeno potete dividere anche il conto.

Poor Mr. and Mr. Johnson! Did you understand what *il problema* was?

ACTIVITY 2: HOW'S THAT AGAIN?

1. *Quanti giorni resta il Signor Johnson 1 al Palazzo Bellini?* _____

    _____

2. *Il Signor Johnson 1 ha una prenotazione?* _____

    _____

3. *A quale piano (floor) è la sua camera?* _____

    _____

4. *Chi è già nella camera numero quarantasei?* _____

    _____

5. *Ci sono delle camere libere in un altro albergo?* _____

    _____

6. *Qual è la soluzione di Gianfranco?* _____

    _____

Did You Know?

LA SERENISSIMA: THE CHARMS OF VENICE

Birthplace of Marco Polo, Venice, or Venezia, is also called *la Serenissima* (the most serene). While this name is more than appropriate for this romantic city—where all transportation occurs *a piedi* or on the *vaporetti* (ferries), *traghetti* (traditional gondola ferries), and *gondole* that service its myriad of canals—it belies a long history as Europe's greatest power in trade with the Far East. Venice is a truly magical city! It's so unique, in fact, that the Venetians decided to call their *piazze campi* and their streets *calli* rather than *vie*. Legend has it that Venezia's famous *gondolieri* have *i piedi palmati* (webbed feet). If a gondolier allows anyone to see his feet, he dies. I once asked a gondolier if this was true. He laughed out loud and assured me it wasn't, but he refused to show me his feet. Judge for yourselves.

Did You Know?

WORKSHOP 1

WORDS TO LIVE BY

DO YOU HAVE A RESERVATION?: CHECKING INTO A HOTEL

Which type of establishment do you prefer?

l'hotel / l'albergo	hotel (m.)
la pensione	small, family-run hotel similar to a bed and breakfast

Or maybe you see yourself in a *palazzo*, which literally means "palace," but is often used in the names of grand hotels in Venice. Either way, if you're traveling to Italy during the high season, you should always *fare una prenotazione* (make a reservation), as many hotels will be *al completo* (full; booked solid).

Vorrei fare una prenotazione.	I'd like to make a reservation.
Per una notte / settimana.	For one night / week.
Per due notti / settimane.	For two nights / weeks.

When you arrive at *la reception* (yep—it's the same word as in English. In fact, it **is** the English word), say:

Ho una prenotazione.	I have a reservation.

Be sure to specify the type of *stanza* or *camera* (room) you need because a single room in Italy is just that, single, and in it you'll find a small twin bed.

singola	single
doppia	double, with two twin beds
matrimoniale	double, with one double bed

Also be sure to mention if you'd like a room *con doccia* (with shower) or *con bagno* (with bath) because many of the smaller hotels offer rooms with shared bathrooms. Be sure to ask if breakfast is included in the price, although you should be aware that *la colazione* in most Italian hotels consists of a simple continental breakfast with coffee and pastries. If breakfast is extra, you're probably better off heading to a local *bar* for your morning meal.

La colazione è inclusa nel prezzo?	Is breakfast included in the price?

If you haven't made *una prenotazione* and you're shopping around for a hotel on the spot, hotels that are full will usually display a sign saying "*completo.*" If, on the other hand, rooms are still available, the sign will read *"camere"* or *"stanze."* It's always a good idea to ask to see the room first.

Posso *vedere la camera?*   *Can I see the room?*

If you're not pleased with the room you've been given, reserved or not, you can ask to change it:

Posso *cambiare camera?*	*Can I change rooms?*
Vorrei *una camera* . . .	*I'd like a room that's . . .*
• **più grande.**	• *bigger.*
• **più silenziosa.**	• *quieter.*

Word on the Street

If you want to confirm something you've just heard, you can repeat the information and tag ***vero?*** (is that true?) or ***giusto?*** (is that right?) to the end of the statement. Alternatively, you can ask a question by interjecting ***ha detto / hai detto,*** as when Mr. Johnson 1 says ***Come ha detto che si chiama?*** (What did you say your name was?).

Did You Know?

FOUR STARS: HOTELS IN ITALY

What happened to Mr. Johnson is an exception rather than the rule: hoteliers in Italy keep to world standards. What you should be prepared for, however, in all but the finest hotels, is smaller rooms, smaller bathrooms, and . . . well, smaller everything. Note, too, that some hotels in Italy occupy only one or two floors of a building. So, you could come across a single building that houses a few different hotels, each with a different quality rating (from *una* to *cinque stelle,* "stars") and prices to match. In many family-run hotels, you're likely to get a good taste of local color from your proprietor *gratis* (free of charge)!

Ora tocca a voi. Now, it's your turn.

ACTIVITY 3:   TAKE IT FOR A SPIN

Unscramble the following dialogue.

—*Sì.*
—*Con doccia?*
—*La prendo.*

—*Quanto costa?*
—*Sì, certo.*
—*La prima colazione è inclusa?*
—*Novanta euro per notte.*
—*Vorrei una stanza singola per due notti.*

QUANTI NE ABBIAMO OGGI?: WHAT'S TODAY'S DATE?

If you're making a reservation, or making plans of any kind for that matter, knowing how to specify the day and the date will help. *I giorni della settimana* (the days of the week) in Italian are:

DAYS OF THE WEEK	
lunedì	Monday (m.)
martedì	Tuesday (m.)
mercoledì	Wednesday (m.)
giovedì	Thursday (m.)
venerdì	Friday (m.)
sabato	Saturday (m.)
domenica	Sunday

I mesi dell'anno (the months of the year) are:

MONTHS OF THE YEAR	
gennaio	January
febbraio	February
marzo	March
aprile	April (m.)
maggio	May
giugno	June
luglio	July
agosto	August
settembre	September (m.)
ottobre	October (m.)
novembre	November (m.)
dicembre	December (m.)

Take a Tip from Me!

Note that the days and the months in Italian are not capitalized (unless they begin a sentence, of course), and that they are all masculine, except for *la domenica*.

Take a Tip from Me!

Unlike in English, the date in Italian is given in the following order: day / month / year. The date is accompanied by the definite article, and it's given using cardinal (one, two, three . . . , or in Italian, *uno, due, tre . . .*), not ordinal (first, second, third . . .), numbers.

il diciotto luglio

July 18th

Dal diciotto al ventun luglio.

From the 18th to the 21st of July.

The only exception is the first of the month, for which you use the ordinal number: *il primo* (the first).

Word on the Street

I bet you thought only English had that clever little rhyme: "Thirty days has September, April, June, and November. All the rest have thirty-one, except February which has twenty-eight, and in leap years twenty-nine." Well, the Italians have it, too, only theirs actually rhymes.

Trenta giorni ha novembre	Thirty days has November
con aprile, giugno e settembre.	with April, June, and September.
Di ventotto ce n'è uno.	Of twenty-eight there's only one.
Tutti gli altri ne han trentuno.	All the others have thirty-one.

ACTIVITY 4: TAKE IT FOR A SPIN

Fill in the months with the correct number of days:

1. *I mesi con trenta giorni:* _____

    _____

2. *I mesi con trentun giorni:* _____

    _____

3. *Il mese con ventotto giorni:* _____

    _____

TAKE IT FOR A SPIN

Fill in the date in Italian.

1. *Cerco una stanza doppia per* (October 20) _____.

2. *La signora Mellini arriva* (Monday, December 3) _____.

3. *Mi dispiace, l'hotel è al completo* (from August 15 to August 22) _____.

4. *Partiamo per Roma* (Saturday, May 10) _____.

5. *Restiamo in Italia* (from September 5 to October 15) _____.

Speaking of dates, we have one with Mr. Grammar.

THE NITTY-GRITTY

***WHERE THERE'S A WILL, THERE'S A WAY:* THE VERBS *VOLERE* (TO WANT), *POTERE* (CAN), AND *DOVERE* (MUST)**

The verbs *volere*, *potere*, and *dovere* are—you guessed it!—irregular, so you'll just have to sit down and memorize them.

	VOLERE (WANT)	*POTERE* (CAN)	*DOVERE* (MUST)
IO	voglio	posso	devo / debbo
TU	vuoi	puoi	devi
LUI / LEI	vuole	può	deve
NOI	vogliamo	possiamo	dobbiamo
VOI	volete	potete	dovete
LORO	vogliono	possono	devono / debbono

VOLERE, POTERE, AND *DOVERE* IN THE PRESENT TENSE

Fortunately, they're not all that irregular. Did you notice that the endings are the same as those of regular *–ere* verbs (except for *può*)? It's just the middle that changes a little.

Take a Tip from Me!

Dovere is another "shoe" verb. You can draw a shoe around the forms that share the same stem, *dev–*.

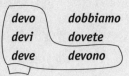

devo	dobbiamo
devi	dovete
deve	devono

Volere, *potere*, and *dovere* express will or desire, ability, and obligation. You use them much the same way as you would in English: they're usually followed by another verb in the infinitive.

> **Dovete condividere la camera.**
>
> You have to share the room.
>
> **Voglio trovare un altro albergo.**
>
> I want to find another hotel.
>
> **Posso cambiare camera?**
>
> Can I change rooms?

As in English, *volere* can also be followed by an object.

> **Voglio una stanza più silenziosa.**
>
> I want a quieter room.

Heads Up!

When *dovere* is used with a noun or an amount, it means "to owe:"

> **Quanto Le devo? —Dieci euro.**
>
> How much do I owe you? —Ten euros.

Remember, too, that *potere* means "to be able" with reference to circumstances or permission. When you're talking about ability in the sense of know-how, you should use *sapere* (to know), which we'll talk about in Lesson 9.

Heads Up!

ACTIVITY 6: TAKE IT FOR A SPIN

You know the drill: Fill in the blanks with the appropriate form of *potere*, *dovere*, or *volere*.

1. *Vai a Venezia in luglio?* _____ *fare una prenotazione per l'hotel.*

2. *(io)* _____ *cambiare camera?* _____ *una camera più grande.*

3. *Per andare in autobus, (Lei)* _____ *comprare un biglietto.*

4. Yoko _____ fare la chat per imparare l'italiano, ma non ha un computer.

5. (io) _____ farLe una domanda?

And now let's get back to the *Palazzo Bellini* and see how things are going for the Johnsons. But before that . . .

ACTIVITY 7: **LOOKING AHEAD**

Connect the phrases that have the same meaning or that are related in some way.

la coperta	dare una cosa per un'altra
ci vuole	il cuscino
fare uno scambio	abbiamo bisogno di

Now where were we? Ah, yes. The *Palazzo Bellini*.

HEAR . . . SAY 2

It seems things haven't improved much. Not only that, but the guests have all started muttering *roba da pazzi* under their breath. On the upside, they seem to have developed a strange camaraderie and propensity for creative problem solving.

Il secondo giorno: giovedì, 19 (diciannove) luglio, 2002 (duemiladue)

Johnson 1:	Aspetta Gianfranco?
Cliente:	Sì, ma non c'è. Ha bisogno di lui?
Johnson 1:	Ci serve una coperta . . .
Cliente:	Vi do io una coperta . . . Ha per caso un cuscino in più?
Johnson 1:	Sì—abbiamo sei cuscini! Le diamo un cuscino.
Cliente:	Roba da pazzi! (*both laugh*)
Johnson 1:	Allora, possiamo fare uno scambio: un cuscino per una coperta.
Cliente:	Che idea!

Il terzo giorno: venerdì, 20 (venti) luglio, 2002.

Gianfranco:	Room service.
Johnson 1:	Gianfranco?! (*praying he's wrong*)
Gianfranco:	Signor Johnson! Buona sera.

Johnson 1:	(*under his breath*) Roba da pazzi! (*to Gianfranco*) Come mai è in cucina stasera?
Gianfranco:	Il venerdì Gianluca non c'è.
Johnson 1:	Ah!
Gianfranco:	Le posso portare qualcosa in camera?
Johnson 1:	No, no, grazie. Non si disturbi. Vado al ristorante, grazie.

ACTIVITY 8: HOW'S THAT AGAIN?

Giovedì:

1. *Perché il signor Johnson ha bisogno di Gianfranco?*_____

_____

2. *Chi dà una coperta al signor Johnson?*_____

_____

Venerdì:

3. *Chi risponde al telefono quando il signor Johnson chiama il room service?*_____

_____

4. *Di solito* (usually; normally) *chi lavora in cucina?*_____

_____

5. *Il signor Johnson ordina qualcosa dal Room Service? Perchè?*_____

_____

I'd be willing to bet that *i signori Johnson non vedono l'ora di partire* (can't wait to leave), although I'm sure they'll at least have plenty of amusing *ricordi* (memories) for the future. Let's leave them to their fate for now and do some more work.

The Fine Print

In Italian, you don't use an article with the *giorni della settimana*, unless you want to indicate that something happens regularly on a given day. So, when Gianfranco says *il venerdì, Gianluca non c'è*, it means that Gianluca is never there on Fridays. Likewise, you might say *il mercoledì e la domenica vado in palestra* meaning "I go to the gym on Wednesdays and Sundays," i.e., every Wednesday and every Sunday.

WORKSHOP 2

FRONT DESK, PLEASE: **DIFFERENT WAYS OF SAYING WHAT YOU NEED IN A HOTEL**

If it's your *prima volta* going to a hotel, you might want to find out what amenities it has to offer:

L'hotel ha . . .	Does the hotel have . . .
• **il ristorante?**	• *a restaurant?*
• **la piscina?**	• *a pool?*
• **la palestra?**	• *a gym?*
• **il garage? (gah-RAHZH)**	• *a garage?*
• **la cassaforte?**	• *a safe-deposit box?*

And you can ask specifics about the room:

C'è . . . in camera?	Is there . . . in the room?
• **un frigo-bar**	• *a minibar*
• **l'aria condizionata**	• *air-conditioning (fem.)*
• **un televisore**	• *a television set*
• **un fön / asciugacappelli**	• *a hair dryer*
• **un ferro**	• *an iron*

If something's missing from your room, tell the *portiere*:

Ho bisogno di . . .	I need . . .
Mi serve . . .	I could use . . .
Mi manca . . .	I'm missing . . .
• **una coperta**	• *a blanket*
• **un cuscino**	• *a pillow*
• **un asciugamano**	• *a towel*
• **del sapone**	• *some soap (masc.)*

And if that doesn't work, you can always *fare uno scambio* (make an exchange) with one of the other guests (just kidding, of course).

FIRST THINGS FIRST: **SAYING *FIRST, SECOND,* ETC., IN ITALIAN**

Finally, if you'd like a *camera con vista* (a room with a view), you might want to specify which *piano* (floor) you'd like to be on. To do so, you need to know your ordinal numbers:

primo	*first*
secondo	*second*
terzo	*third*
quarto	*fourth*
quinto	*fifth*
sesto	*sixth*
settimo	*seventh*
ottavo	*eighth*
nono	*ninth*
decimo	*tenth*

The Fine Print

The symbol Italians use to indicate an ordinal number is the degree symbol (°). So, 1° = first, 2° = second, etc.

Did You Know?

LIGHTS, CAMERA, ACTION!: THE MOVIES *THE COMFORT OF STRANGERS* AND *BREAD AND TULIPS*

There are two movies which will afford you two very different views of Venice. *The Comfort of Strangers,* starring Christopher Walken and Helen Mirren, offers some spectacular, moody views of the city (and a rather disturbing, dark story). *Pane e tulipani* (*Bread and Tulips*), starring Bruno Ganz, looks at regular life in such an "irregular" city. The latter is the story of a *casalinga* (homemaker), whose day trip to Venice ends up lasting much longer, as she rediscovers long-forgotten parts of herself.

Ora tocca a voi! Now it's your turn.

ACTIVITY 9: TAKE IT FOR A SPIN

Who's the odd man out? Cross out the item that doesn't belong.

1.	*il fön*	*il cuscino*	*il sapone*	*l'asciugamano*
2.	*il ferro*	*il televisore*	*la coperta*	*l'asciugacappelli*
3.	*il frigo-bar*	*la palestra*	*la piscina*	*il garage*

Time to make the donuts!

TO WHOM IT MAY CONCERN: PRONOUNS LIKE *TO ME, TO YOU, TO US,* ETC.

In the sentence "I'm writing a postcard to Marco," the phrase "a postcard" is the direct object and "Marco" is the indirect object, normally introduced by a preposition, "to." Today we'll focus on indirect objects. In English, they are often introduced by the prepositions "to" or "for." In Italian, they're introduced by *a* (to) or *per* (per) (*scrivo una cartolina a Marco*). Like other nouns, indirect objects can be replaced by pronouns. For example:

Do la camera numero quarantasei al signor Johnson.

I'm giving room number forty-six to Mr. Johnson.

Gli do la camera numero quarantasei.

I'm giving (to) him room number forty-six.

The indirect object pronouns are:

PRONOUNS MEANING *TO ME, TO YOU, TO US,* ETC.			
TO ME	*mi*	TO US	*ci*
TO YOU (SING. INFML.)	*ti*	TO YOU (PL.INFL.)	*vi*
TO YOU (SING. FML.)	*Le*	TO YOU (PL. FML.)	*vi*
TO HIM	*gli*	TO THEM	*gli*
TO HER	*le*	TO THEM	*gli*

Heads Up!

Notice that, as with the pronouns *Lei* and *lei*, the indirect object pronoun *Le*, meaning "to you (sing. formal)," is capitalized in writing to distinguish it from *le*, meaning "to her."

Indirect object pronouns are often used with verbs like *parlare* (to speak), *dare* (to give), *mandare* (to send), *scrivere* (to write), *chiedere* (to ask), and *rispondere* (to answer), which are typically followed by the preposition *a*.

Domani do il messaggio al signor Johnson. → **Domani gli do il messaggio.**

I'll give the message to Mr. Johnson tomorrow. → I'll give the message to him tomorrow.

Parlo <u>ai miei bambini</u> ogni giorno. → ***<u>Gli</u> parlo ogni giorno.***

I talk <u>to my kids</u> every day. → I talk <u>to them</u> every day.

Scrivi <u>a nostra famiglia</u> dall'Italia? → ***<u>Ci</u> scrivi dall'Italia?***

Will you write <u>to our family</u> from Italy? → Will you write <u>to us</u> from Italy?

An important additional point about indirect object pronouns is that they always precede the verb:

Perchè <u>mi</u> fa tutte queste domande?

Why are you asking me all these questions?

<u>Vi</u> do una coperta.

I'll give you a blanket.

<u>Le</u> diamo un cuscino.

We'll give you a pillow.

The Fine Print

The "correct" indirect object pronoun for "to them" is *loro,* but *gli* is what's commonly used in everyday speech. *Loro* has a very formal tone, and you're most likely to see it only in formal writing. However, should you find yourself at an ambassador's party and choose to use it, you should know that, unlike all the other indirect object pronouns, *loro* goes after the verb, not before.

Heads Up!

When used with the verb *potere* (can), *volere* (to want), or *dovere* (must), indirect object pronouns can either precede these verbs or be attached to the end of the infinitive which follows. In this case, drop the final *–e* from the infinitive before attaching the pronoun, as in:

<u>Le</u> posso portare qualcosa in camera? = ***Posso portar<u>Le</u> qualcosa in camera?***

Can I bring something to your room for you? (*Lit.* Can I bring something to you in your room?)

<u>Ci</u> devi mandare una cartolina! = ***Devi mandar<u>ci</u> una cartolina!***

You have to send us a postcard!

Posso chiedervi qualcosa? Volete fare un esercizio?

TAKE IT FOR A SPIN

Replace the underlined phrases with an indirect object pronoun.

1. *Parlo <u>al portiere</u>.* _____

2. *Diamo la camera numero cinquantacinque <u>alla signora Baldini</u>, va bene?* _____

   _____

3. *Facciamo una prenotazione <u>per loro</u>.* _____

   _____

4. *Barbara scrive una cartolina <u>a me e alla mia famiglia</u>.* _____

   _____

5. *La cliente da una coperta <u>ai signori Johnson</u>.* _____

   _____

6. *Perché non rispondi <u>a me</u>?* _____

   _____

7. *Il barista serve un cappuccino <u>a Delphine</u>.* _____

   _____

8. *Domani mando una e-mail <u>a voi</u>.* _____

   _____

BETWEEN LIKE AND NEED: THE VERB PIACERE AND OTHER VERBS USED WITH PRONOUNS LIKE TO ME, TO YOU, TO US, ETC.

One of the most useful verbs that's always used with an indirect object is *piacere* (to like). You've already used it in Lesson 5 in the expressions *mi piace* "I like + singular noun" and *mi piacciono* "I like + plural noun." Well, now you know that *mi* is an indirect object pronoun, and you can use *piace* and *piacciono* with all the other indirect object pronouns, too. For example, if you want to ask if someone likes something, you would use *ti piace / piacciono?* (do you (sing. infml.) like?) if you address them with *tu*. Use *Le piace / piacciono* (do you (sing. fml.) like?) if you address them with *Lei*, and use *vi piace / piacciono* (do you (pl.) like?) if you're talking to a group of people, etc.

Non Le piace la camera?

You don't like the room?

Vi piacciono i canali di Venezia?

Do you like the canals of Venice?

Gli piace andare a piedi?

Do they / does he like going on foot?

Two more useful verbs that are used just like *piacere* (i.e., with indirect object pronouns) are: *mancare* (to miss) and *servire* (to need).

Ci manca una coperta.

We're missing a blanket.

Mi servono dei cuscini.

I need some pillows.

Gli manca un ferro.

They're / he's missing an iron.

Vi serve un ferro?

Do you need an iron?

The Fine Print

The expression *mi piace qualcosa / qualcuno,* literally translated, means "something / someone is pleasing to me." So, things are turned somewhat upside down in Italian with respect to the English expression "I like something / someone." The same is true for the expressions with *mancare* and *servire: Ci manca una coperta,* literally means "a blanket is missing to us." *Mancare* and *servire* are most commonly used in the *lei / lui* and *loro* form, but their other forms are used on occasion, as well. For example, if you want to say "I miss you," say *mi manchi,* i.e. "you're missing to me."

ACTIVITY 11:   **TAKE IT FOR A SPIN**

1. You've checked into your hotel and you find that the room has not been made up properly. Tell the *portiere* that you're missing the following items using *mi manca* (I miss + singular noun) if it's a single object or *mi mancano* (I miss + plural noun) if there's more than one:

   1.   *delle coperte* _____

   2.   *un cuscino* _____

   3.   *degli asciugamani* _____

   4.   *un fön* _____

   5.   *un ferro* _____

2. You're asking a travel agent to book a hotel for you and your partner, and you tell her you need the following amenities using *ci serve:*

   1. *un garage* _____
   2. *una palestra* _____
   3. *una piscina* _____
   4. *un cassaforte* _____
   5. *un frigo-bar* _____

LET'S PUT IT IN WRITING

Check out these hotel listings for *la città di Venezia:*

	STANZE	TV	FRIGO-BAR	ROOM SERVICE	RISTORANTE	PISCINA	PALESTRA
Palazzo Bellini ★★★	12	•	•	•	•		
Pensione Vecchia ★★	6		•				
Albergo Marco Polo ★★★	24	•	•	•	•		•
Hotel Canaletto ★★★	15	•	•	•			
Hotel Fiore ★★★★	30	•	•	•	•	•	•

ACTIVITY 12:   **TAKE IT FOR A SPIN**

1. *Quale hotel non ha una tv nelle stanze?* _____

   _____

2. *Quale hotel ha una piscina?* _____

   _____

3. *Quali hotel hanno un ristorante?* _____

   _____

4. *Quali hotel hanno una palestra?* _____

   _____

5. *Quali sono gli hotel a tre stelle?* _____

_____

6. *Qual è l'hotel a quattro stelle?* _____

_____

7. *Hanno tutti un frigo-bar?* _____

_____

CRIB NOTES

HEAR...SAY 1

The first day: Wednesday, July 18, 2002

Gianfranco: Welcome to the Palazzo Bellini. My name is Gianfranco. How can I help you?

Johnson 1: I have a reservation . . . for the name Johnson.

Gianfranco: Mr. Johnson . . . Let's see . . . Yes, here it is—a double room with shower, from Wednesday, July 18, to Saturday, July 21, right?

Johnson 1: Yes, exactly.

Gianfranco: What's today's date?

Johnson 1: Today is July 18.

Gianfranco: In that case, it's O.K. I'm giving you room number forty-six, on the third floor.

Johnson 1: Thanks.

Gianfranco: Yes, Mr. Johnson. Is there a problem?

Johnson 1: I have to change rooms.

Gianfranco: You don't like the room?

Johnson 1: No, I like it, but there's already someone in room forty-six.

Gianfranco: Crazy stuff!

Johnson 2: Excuse me.

Gianfranco: Yes, Mr. Johnson. Is there something wrong?

Johnson 2: There are bags in my room, and they're not mine.

Gianfranco: Crazy stuff!

Johnson 1: Excuse me, sir. Can I ask you a question?

Johnson 2: Yes, of course.

Johnson 1: What did you say your name was?

Johnson 2: Johnson.

Johnson 1: In room forty-six. On the third floor?

Johnson 2: Yes, but why are you asking me all these questions?

Johnson 1: Because I'm Johnson, too, and those are my bags.

Gianfranco: That's crazy! That's the problem.

Johnson 1: So, now can I change rooms?

Gianfranco: Crazy stuff!

Johnson 1: What do you mean "Crazy stuff"?

Gianfranco: I'm sorry, gentlemen, but the hotel is full. You'll have to share the room.

Johnson 1: I want to find another hotel.

Gianfranco: Sir, in July in Venice, all the hotels are booked solid.

Johnson 1: Damn!

Gianfranco: But at least you can share the bill, too!

HEAR...SAY 2

The second day: Thursday, July 19, 2002

Johnson 1: You're waiting for Gianfranco?

Client: Yes, but he's not here. Are you in need of him?

Johnson 1: We need a blanket . . .

Client: I'll give you a blanket. . . . Do you by chance have an extra pillow?

Johnson 1: Yes—we have six pillows! We'll give you a pillow.

Client: Crazy stuff!

Johnson 1: So, we can make an exchange: one pillow for one blanket.

Client: What an idea!

The third day: Friday, July 20, 2002
Gianfranco: Room service.
Johnson 1: Gianfranco?
Gianfranco: Mr. Johnson! Good evening.
Johnson 1: Crazy stuff! How come you're in the kitchen tonight?
Gianfranco: Gianluca's not here on Fridays.

Johnson 1: Oh!
Gianfranco: Can I bring something to your room for you?
Johnson 1: No, no, thanks. I'm going to the restaurant. Thanks. Don't worry. (*Lit.* Don't get disturbed.)

ANSWER KEY

ACTIVITY 1

1. d;   2. e;   3. b;   4. a;   5. c

ACTIVITY 2

1. *Il Signor Johnson 1 resta al Palazzo Bellini quattro giorni.*
2. *Sì, il Signor Johnson 1 ha una prenotazione.*
3. *La sua camera è al terzo piano.*
4. *Il Signor Johnson 2 è già nella camera numero quarantasei.*
5. *No. Non ci sono delle camere libere in un altro albergo.*
6. *La soluzione di Gianfranco è di condividere la camera.*

ACTIVITY 3

You: *Vorrei una stanza singola per due notti.*
A Friend: *Con doccia?*
You: *Sì. / Sì, certo.*
A Friend: *Va bene. Ne ho una al terzo piano.*
You: *Quanto costa?*
A Friend: *Novanta euro per notte.*
You: *La prima colazione è inclusa?*
A Friend: *Sì, certo. / Sì.*
You: *La prendo.*

ACTIVITY 4

1. *I mesi con trenta giorni: aprile, giugno, settembre, novembre*
2. *I mesi con trentun giorni: gennaio, marzo, maggio, luglio, agosto, ottobre, dicembre*
3. *Il mese con ventotto giorni: febbraio*

ACTIVITY 5

1. *Cerco una stanza doppia per* <u>*il venti ottobre.*</u>
2. *La signora Mellini arriva* <u>*lunedì, tre dicembre.*</u>
3. *Mi dispiace, l'hotel è al completo* <u>*dal quindici agosto al ventidue agosto.*</u>
4. *Partiamo per Roma* <u>*sabato, dieci maggio.*</u>
5. *Restiamo in Italia* <u>*dal cinque settembre al quindici ottobre.*</u>

ACTIVITY 6

1. *Vai a Venezia a luglio?* <u>*Devi*</u> *fare una prenotazione per l'hotel.*
2. <u>*Posso*</u> *cambiare camera?* <u>*Voglio*</u> *una camera più grande.*
3. *Per andare in autobus,* <u>*deve*</u> *comprare un biglietto.*
4. *Yoko* <u>*vuole*</u> *fare la chat per imparare l'italiano, ma non ha un computer.*
5. <u>*Posso*</u> *farLe una domanda?*

ACTIVITY 7

la coperta — dare una cosa per un'altra
ci vuole — il cuscino
fare uno scambio — abbiamo bisogno di

ACTIVITY 8

Giovedì:
1. *Il signor Johnson ha bisogno di Gianfranco perché gli manca una coperta.*
2. *La cliente dà una coperta al signor Johnson.*

Venerdì:
3. *Gianfranco risponde al telefono quando il signor Johnson chiama il Room Service.*
4. *Di solito Gianluca lavora in cucina.*
5. *Il signor Johnson non ordina dal Room Service perché va al ristorante.*

ACTIVITY 9

1. *il cuscino*—it's the only item that doesn't belong in the bathroom
2. *la coperta*—it's the only item that isn't an appliance
   Alternatively: *il fön*—the only item that's usually found in the bathroom, not in the room.
3. *il frigo-bar*—it's the only amenity that is in the room; the rest are part of the whole hotel

1. *Gli parlo.*
2. *Le diamo la camera numero cinquantacinque, va bene?*
3. *Gli facciamo una prenotazione.*
4. *Barbara ci scrive una cartolina.*
5. *La cliente gli dà una coperta.*
6. *Perché non mi rispondi?*
7. *Il barista le serve un cappuccino.*
8. *Domani vi mando una e-mail.*

ACTIVITY 11

1. *Mi mancano delle coperte.*
   Mi manca un cuscino.
   Mi mancano degli asciugamani.
   Mi manca un fön.
   Mi manca un ferro.

2. *Ci serve un garage.*
   Ci serve una palestra.
   Ci serve una piscina.
   Ci serve un cassaforte.
   Ci serve un frigo-bar.

ACTIVITY 12

1. *La Pensione Vecchia non ha una tv nelle stanze.*
2. *L'Hotel Fiore ha una piscina.*
3. *Il Palazzo Bellini, l'Albergo Marco Polo e l'Hotel Fiore hanno un ristorante.*
4. *L'Albergo Marco Polo e l'Hotel Fiore hanno una palestra.*
5. *Il Palazzo Bellini, l'Albergo Marco Polo e l'Hotel Canaletto sono gli hotel a tre stelle.*
6. *L'Hotel Fiore è l'hotel a quattro stelle.*
7. *Sì, hanno tutti un frigo-bar.*

8.

IT COSTS AN ARM AND A LEG

Costa un occhio della testa

(*Lit*. It costs an eye of your head)

Don't get lost! Follow the red flag . . .

COMING UP...

- *Monuments, fountains, and piazzas, oh, my!*: Enjoying a city tour
- *'Tis the season*: Seasons of the year
- *It's a beautiful day*: Talking about the weather
- *I don't feel well*: Talking about your health
- *Living in the moment*: The present tense of regular *–ire* verbs
- *Never in a million years*: Negative words, like *never, no one, nothing,* etc.
- *You're it!*: Pronouns like *me, him, us, them,* etc.
- *Oh, yeah? Come over here and say that!*: The irregular verbs *dire* (to say) and *venire* (to come)

LOOKING AHEAD

If I had a hotel experience like Mr. Johnson's, I know I'd head right for the streets! Imagine having to *condividere la camera* with a stranger, be missing *una coperta* or *un cuscino*, and not even be able to order room service in peace. *Roba da pazzi! A Palazzo Bellini serve un portiere normale!* (What they need at the Palazzo Bellini is a normal concierge!) When all is said and done, however, I think Mr. Johnson was a pretty good sport. After all, there are people who are never satisfied. Like Mr. del Vecchio, for example, whom you're about to meet. Not even the beautiful *fontane* (fountains), *piazze* (squares), and *cose da vedere* (sights) of Rome can make him happy. How about you? Are you a *bastian contrario* (curmudgeon) or a good sport? *Seguite la bandiera rossa* (follow the red flag) and we'll see . . .

Take a Tip from Me!

In the dialogue you're about to hear, the tone of the *guida* is a bit more formal than what you'd hear in normal conversation. Her sentences are a little more complex, but don't be daunted. While the sentences might be longer, most of the new vocabulary consists of words whose meaning you should be able to guess pretty easily from ones that sound similar in English. Just look:

Take a Tip from Me!

ACTIVITY 1: LET'S WARM UP

Sound out the following words, and match them with similar sounding words we use in English:

1.	*una foto*	a.	legend
2.	*la colonna*	b.	battle
3.	*le illustrazioni*	c.	fountain
4.	*la battaglia*	d.	photo
5.	*i Barbari*	e.	finish
6.	*la leggenda*	f.	center
7.	*la fontana*	g.	prefer
8.	*finire*	h.	barbarians
9.	*preferire*	i.	illustrations
10.	*il centro*	j.	column

Allora, siete pronti per il giro?

Mr. del Vecchio and his longtime friend, Chiara, are going on a wonderful *giro* (tour) of Rome, lead by our friendly *guida*, Elisabetta. While Chiara is excited by everything she sees, nothing seems to make Mr. del Vecchio *contento* (happy), and he sees in everything a scheme to part him from his *soldi*. Let's see how it goes . . .

Elisabetta:	Benvenuti a Roma, signori e signore. Sono Elisabetta. Un attimo e partiamo, ma prima: non voglio perdere nessuno. Allora, vi prego di stare sempre insieme. Se mi seguite, non c'è nessun problema. Se mi perdete di vista, cercate la bandiera rossa. Va bene?
Tutti:	Sì. Va bene . . .
Elisabetta:	Il giro comincia qui, in Piazza Navona, e finisce in Piazza di Spagna. Piazza Navona è un posto molto popolare. Quando fa bel tempo, come oggi, vengono tanti turisti, ma anche molti romani, per prendere un caffè o un aperitivo e guardare la gente . . . Nel centro, c'è la Fontana dei Quattro Fiumi di Lorenzo Bernini.
Chiara:	Elisabetta, facciamo una foto davanti alla fontana?
Elisabetta:	Sì. Perché no? Chiediamo a quel signore . . . Scusi, signore. Ci fa una foto?

After a great deal of shuffling, arranging, and re-arranging in front of the *Fontana dei Quattro Fiumi*, the man finally takes a photo of the group. A little frustrated, Elisabetta suggests a short break.

Elisabetta:	Allora, cosa preferite: prendere un tartufo al caffè Tre Scalini o continuare?
Tutti:	Tartufo!!
Del Vecchio:	Io preferisco continuare. Il tartufo sicuramente costa un occhio della testa.
Chiara:	Offro io. Va bene?

Embarrassed by Chiara's offer to pay, del Vecchio decides to splurge on a *tartufo* and treat Chiara. Once he learns that the famous ice cream was actually **invented** at Tre Scalini, he feels a little bit better about the money he's just spent. Soon the red flag starts bobbing down the streets of Rome again, twenty *turisti* in tow . . .

Elisabetta:	Alla vostra sinistra c'è la Colonna di Marco Aurelio con tante illustrazioni delle sue battaglie contro i Barbari . . . Psst! Lo sentite?

Tutti:	Cosa?
Elisabetta:	Il rumore delle urla dei Barbari . . .
Del Vecchio:	Ma cosa dice? Io non sento niente. Non sento neanche lei . . .
Chiara:	Io posso sentirLa benissimo. Tu non senti mai niente.

Did You Know?

AROUND ROME: PIAZZA NAVONA

Built in the seventeenth century, Piazza Navona is one of Rome's most popular and beautiful sights; everyone from tourists to fashion photographers to native Romans turns out in droves for a leisurely evening *passeggiata*. At Christmas a fair for children is also held here. In addition to Bernini's famous Fountain of the Four Rivers (built in 1651) whose rivers—the Nile, the Ganges, the Danube, and the Rio della Plata—represent the four corners of the world, the *piazza* is home to the Church of St. Agnes in Agony, a prototypical example of Baroque architecture.

A couple of curiosities about the fountain: *la statua* (the statue) representing the Nile is hiding its head because the source of the Nile was unknown at the time (although some insist that it's because the ornate façade of the nearby church is simply unbearable to look at). Also, in 1997, three vandals broke the tail of the dragon on *la statua del Danubio* into three pieces. The attack lead to stiffer fines for *il vandalismo* (vandalism) and more rigorous patrolling of Italy's *monumenti storici* (historical monuments). The bottom line: no more swimming *nella fontana!*

ACTIVITY 2:   HOW'S THAT AGAIN?

1. *Dove comincia il giro?*_____

2. *Dove finisce?*_____

3. *Cosa devono fare i turisti per non perdere Elisabetta?*_____

4. *Come si chiama la fontana in Piazza Navona? Di chi è?*_____

5. *Perché non vuole prendere un tartufo, il signor del Vecchio?*_____

6. *Che monumento famoso vedono i turisti dopo Piazza Navona?*_____

7. *Cosa vedono i turisti sulla Colonna?*_____

_____

8. *Qual è il problema del signor del Vecchio?*_____

_____

How well did you fare? If you had trouble, don't worry. You'll find plenty of help in the next section.

WORKSHOP 1

WORDS TO LIVE BY

MONUMENTS, FOUNTAINS, AND PIAZZAS, OH MY!: ENJOYING A CITY TOUR

Un giro organizzato (a guided tour) is a great way to get to know a city. Here are some of the *cose da vedere* you might pass:

la chiesa	church
la cattedrale	cathedral
la sinagoga	synagogue
la piazza	square
la fontana	fountain
il monumento	monument
le rovine	ruins
la tomba	tomb
la statua	statue
la colonna	column
la torre	tower

Here are some phrases the *guida* is likely to use:

Il giro comincia in / a . . .	The tour begins in / at . . .
Il giro finisce in / a . . .	The tour ends in / at . . .
Vi prego di stare sempre insieme.	I'd like to ask you to stay together at all times.
Seguite la bandiera.	Follow the flag.
A sinistra . . .	To the left . . .
A destra . . .	To the right . . .
Davanti a . . .	In front of . . .
Dietro a . . .	Behind . . .
Sopra . . .	On top . . .

| Sotto . . . | Below; underneath |
| **In fondo** . . . | At the bottom . . . |

As you know, Italy is pretty much a living *museo*. Before going, you should probably decide what type of *arte* [art (fem.)] you're most interested in seeing, so you can plan to see all the important *posti* or *luoghi* (places).

la pittura	*painting*
la scultura	*sculpture*
l'arte classica	*classical art*
l'arte medievale	*medieval art*
l'arte rinascimentale	*Renaissance art*
l'arte moderna	*modern art*

Word on the Street

Mr. del Vecchio may be a *bastian contrario* (curmudgeon), but it's true that doing the tourist thing can often be quite pricey. So don't be surprised if you find yourself inclined to use the very vivid expression: **Costa un occhio della testa!** (It costs an arm and a leg!) which literally means "It costs an eye of your head!" If, on the other hand, you've just found out that your stocks are soaring, you may feel inspired to treat everyone. Just say: **Offro io!** (It's on me!) and you could very well become the most popular tourist in the bunch.

Finally: *Sorridete!* (Smile!) Don't forget to capture the moment for posterity (and to show the Joneses). You can ask a passerby to take your picture:

| **Ci fa una foto?** | *Will you take a picture of us?* |

Now it's your turn to show your stuff!

ACTIVITY 3: TAKE IT FOR A SPIN

Say that you'd like to see the following sights. Begin each sentence with *Voglio vedere* . . .

1. the museum of modern art _____

2. the monuments _____

3. the synagogue _____

4. the fountains _____

5. the ruins _____

Now explain what you're interested in. Begin each sentence with *M'interessa* if what interests you is singular and *M'interessano* if it's plural . . .

6. medieval art _____

7. painting _____

8. Renaissance art _____

9. sculpture _____

10. churches _____

Still smiling? Good—it's time for some *grammatica.*

THE NITTY-GRITTY

LIVING IN THE MOMENT: THE PRESENT OF REGULAR *–IRE* VERBS

Since you already know how to form the present tense of regular *–are* and *–ere* verbs, regular *–ire* verbs should be *un gioco da ragazzi* (child's play). Remember how it works? Just drop the *–ire* ending and replace it with *–o, –i, –e, –iamo, –ite,* or *–ono.*

Take a Tip from Me!

Psst! Did you notice that the *–ere* and *–ire* conjugations are virtually identical? The only difference is in the *voi* ending. For *–ere* verbs it's *–ete,* and for *–ire* it's *–ite.* Doesn't get easier than that, right? Well, I have a trick up my sleeve, so stand by . . .

You may be wondering what you can say using *–ire* verbs. All sorts of things! For example, when Elisabetta says:

Un attimo e partiamo.

One moment and we're leaving.

Se mi seguite, non c'è nessun problema.

If you follow me, there's no problem.

Lo sentite?

Do you hear it?

Elisabetta is using the verbs *partire* (to leave), *seguire* (to follow), and *sentire* (to hear), all of which are regular *–ire* verbs. *Aprire* (to open) and *servire* (to serve) are also regular *–ire* verbs, as is *offrire* (to offer), which, as we've discussed, will probably come in handy when you're feeling generous:

Offro io!

My treat! (*Lit.* I'm offering.)

I know what you're thinking: Where's the catch? Well, as it turns out, there is one. Just to keep things interesting, the Italians decided to have two types of regular *–ire* verbs: the type you just learned and another one where you insert an *–isc–* before the ending in all but the *noi* and *voi* forms (which, incidentally, makes for a whole group of "shoe verbs!").

	–IRE	PARTIRE (TO LEAVE)	FINIRE (TO FINISH)
IO	–o / –isco	part–o	fin–isco
TU	–i / –isci	part–i	fin–isci
LUI / LEI	–e / –isce	part–e	fin–isce
NOI	–iamo	part–iamo	fin–iamo
VOI	–ite	part–ite	fin–ite
LORO	–ono / –iscono	part–ono	fin–iscono

PRESENT TENSE OF –IRE VERBS

Some common verbs in this second group include: *capire* (to understand), *preferire* (to prefer), *suggerire* (to suggest), and *trasferire* (to transfer). You've already heard a few of them in action. Do you remember them?

Il giro finisce in Piazza di Spagna.

The tour finishes in Piazza di Spagna.

Io preferisco continuare.

I prefer to continue.

The Fine Print

So, how can you tell if a verb is an *–isc–* verb or not? One way is to look in the glossary and check to see if there's an (*isc*) next to it. But if you want to figure it out on your own, here's the rule: When there are two or more consonants in a row before the *–ire* ending, you don't need the *–isc–*; otherwise you do. *Per esempio, pa<u>rt</u>ire, se<u>nt</u>ire,* and *o<u>ffr</u>ire* don't need the *–isc–* but *prefe<u>r</u>ire, ca<u>p</u>ire,* and *sugge<u>r</u>ire* do. The only exception you need to worry about is *seguire*, which doesn't take an *–isc–* even though the *–ire* ending is preceded by only one consonant.

Ora tocca a voi.

1.   *Vuoi vedere una chiesa?* —*(preferire)* _____ *vedere le rovine.*

2.   *Dove (finire)* _____ *il giro?*

3.   *Quando (aprire)* _____ *il museo?*

4.   *(voi, sentire)* _____ *la guida così da lontano?*

5.   *Vi (io, suggerire)* _____ *di andare a vedere la sinagoga sabato.*

6.   *Vuoi fare un giro della città? (noi, partire)* _____ *insieme.*

7.   *(voi, capire)* _____ *la guida?*

8.   *I turisti (preferire)* _____ *prendere un tartufo.*

9.   *Cosa (loro, servire)* _____ *all'albergo per colazione?*

10.   *Chi paga?* —*(offrire)* _____ *io!*

Well, that's very kind of you. You must be in a good mood! I hope all the negativity coming up doesn't bring you down . . .

NEVER IN A MILLION YEARS!: NEGATIVE WORDS, LIKE *NEVER*, *NO ONE*, *NOTHING*, ETC.

Simple negation in Italian is easy: just stick a *non* (not) before the verb, and you're done. But what if you want to be more specific and say things like *never, no one, nothing, not even,* etc.? Well, that's not too difficult, either. The most important thing to remember is that you keep the *non* before the verb even when you add the more specific negative word after it. The negative words in Italian are:

NEGATIVE WORDS IN ITALIAN	
niente	nothing
nessuno	no one
mai	never (*also* ever)
più	no longer; no more
ancora	not yet (*also* yet)
neanche	not even
affatto	not at all (*also* entirely)
né . . . né	neither . . . nor . . .

This is pretty straightforward, and who better to show us how it works than the ever-negative Mr. del Vecchio:

> ### Non sento niente.
>
> I don't hear anything. (*Lit.* I don't hear nothing.)

So, if you can remember that double negatives are the rule in Italian, you're in pretty good shape. Might I point out, by the way, that in this instance, "proper" Italian works a lot like colloquial English. I hear people using double negatives in English all the time in casual conversation—but, hey, I don't want you never tellin' no one that I'm promoting "bad" English. Hey, wasn't that a **triple** negative? Well, guess what! Triple or even quadruple negation is perfectly correct in Italian, too. In fact, you can use as many specific negative words as make sense in a sentence.

> ### Tu non senti mai niente.
>
> You never hear anything. (*Lit.* You don't never hear nothing.)

Heads Up!

The Fine Print

When *nessuno* begins a sentence, the *non* is omitted. For example:

Nessuno vuole venire al museo con me.

No one wants to come to the museum with me.

Nessuno can also be used as an adjective to mean "not any; not a single one," in which case it comes before the noun:

Non c'è nessun problema.

There isn't any problem.

Non ho nessun'idea.

I have no idea.

Take a Tip from Me!

A good way to remember negative words is in pairs with their opposites:

nessuno	←→	**qualcuno / tutti** (somebody / everybody)
mai	←→	**sempre** (always)
niente	←→	**qualcosa / tutto** (something / everything)
non . . . ancora	←→	**già** (already)
non . . . affatto	←→	**molto / tanto** (many / a lot)

Think you can handle all that? Let's see.

ACTIVITY 5:   TAKE IT FOR A SPIN

Answer the questions using a double negative.

1. *Elisabetta vuole perdere qualcuno?* _____

    _____

2. *Cosa ordina il signor del Vecchio all'Antico Caffè Greco?* _____

    _____

3. *Il signor del Vecchio può sentire le urla dei barbari?* _____

    _____

4. *Il signor del Vecchio sente Elisabetta, vero? (neanche)* _____
    _____

5. *Al signor del Vecchio piace prendere un tartufo e spendere dei soldi?* _____
    _____

6. *Lotte beve sempre prima di mangiare, giusto?* _____
    _____

7. *Pietro, il macellaio, ha tanto successo con le donne, vero?* _____
    _____

8. *Gianfranco, il portiere al Palazzo Bellini, capisce tutto, giusto?* _____
    _____

Good news! *Non facciamo più la grammatica . . . per il momento.* Let's re-connect with Mr. del Vecchio and Chiara instead, but first try your hand at deciphering the meaning of these new words.

ACTIVITY 6: **LET'S WARM UP**

Time to play the association game again. Pick the phrase that best suits each concept.

1. AH-CHOO!   a. *la città eterna*
2. Make a wish . . .   b. *la leggenda*
3. Rome   c. *l'allergia al polline*
4. shopping spree   d. *lanciare spiccioli nella fontana*
5. Sleepy Hollow   e. *avere le vertigini*
6. vertigo   f. *spendere soldi*

HEAR . . . SAY 2

Well, *il giro* seems to be going well, despite Mr. del Vecchio's grumbling and Chiara's slight annoyance with him. We'll catch up to them as they reach the *Fontana di Trevi*. Who knows, maybe some of the tourists will be so moved by the sight of it that they'll run right into the fountain and attempt an impromptu recreation of Anita Ekberg and Marcello Mastroianni's passionate (and wet!) nocturnal encounter from Fellini's *La Dolce Vita*! One can always hope . . .

Elisabetta: Fra qualche minuto arriviamo alla Fontana di Trevi. Se credete alla leggenda e volete tornare a Roma, vi suggerisco di lanciare alcuni spiccioli nella fontana.

Del Vecchio: Io non credo alla leggenda!

Chiara: Tu non sei mai contento!

Oh, well. So much for recreating a passionate encounter. The tour continues, and they reach the finale, exhausted . . .

Elisabetta: Ecco Piazza di Spagna e la sua famosa Scalinata. Possiamo salire—sopra c'è una bellissima vista della città eterna. E in fondo abbiamo un'altra fontana del Bernini: la Fontana della Barcaccia.

Chiara: Che bella giornata! C'è il sole, tira vento e tutte queste azalee . . . La primavera a Roma è proprio bellissima!

Del Vecchio: Non mi sento bene. Sono allergico al polline e non mi piace né il sole né il vento.

At the top of the *Scalinata di Piazza di Spagna* (the Spanish Steps) . . .

Chiara: Non capisco. Perché non guardi il panorama?

Del Vecchio: Non mi sento bene. Ho le vertigini.

Elisabetta: E se vi piace la letteratura, anche la Fondazione Keats-Shelley è qui.

Chiara: Possiamo entrare?

Elisabetta: Purtroppo il museo è chiuso. Ma invece di andare al museo, possiamo fare uno spuntino all'Antico Caffè Greco, frequentato da Byron, Goethe e anche da Buffalo Bill. Oppure, chi non vuole pranzare con gli scrittori può fare un po' di shopping in Via Condotti . . .

Del Vecchio: Io preferisco stare qui a guardare la gente . . .

Chiara: . . . e non spendere troppi soldi. Capisco.

Some things (or people) *non cambiano mai*, do they?

ACTIVITY 7: HOW'S THAT AGAIN?

1. *Secondo la leggenda, cosa devono fare i turisti per tornare a Roma?*_____

   _____

2. *Come si chiama la fontana in Piazza di Spagna? Di chi è?*_____

   _____

3. *C'è un museo in Piazza di Spagna? Come si chiama?*_____

   _____

4. *Perché è famoso l'Antico Caffè Greco?* _____

_____

5. *Cosa possono vedere i turisti dalla Scalinata in Piazza di Spagna?* _____

_____

If you got all that, you're probably ready to lead a tour of Rome yourself.

Did You Know?

PEOPLE WATCHING: ROME'S PIAZZA DI SPAGNA

La Scalinata di Piazza di Spagna, or The Spanish Steps, is one of the liveliest locales in Rome. In *primavera* (spring), the steps and its three landings are flanked with blooming azaleas, but the place makes for great people-watching in any season. Park yourself on the steps and watch lovers accosted by pushy rose peddlers, tourists taking tons of pictures, and groups of young people playing guitar and singing old Beatles songs. At the bottom of the steps lies Bernini's *Fontana della Barcaccia,* the Fountain of the Old Boat, and at the top awaits a magnificent view of Rome—the Eternal City. Last, but certainly not least, the nearby *Via Condotti* is home to some of Rome's ritziest shops.

Now that we've enjoyed some sightseeing, let's head back inside the workshop . . .

WORKSHOP 2

WORDS TO LIVE BY

'TIS THE SEASON: SEASONS OF THE YEAR

Springtime may be the best time to see Rome, but the truth is—it looks pretty spectacular whatever the *stagione* (season).

la primavera	*spring*
l'estate	*summer (f.)*
l'autunno	*fall*
l'inverno	*winter*

IT'S A BEAUTIFUL DAY: TALKING ABOUT THE WEATHER

Still, *il tempo* (the weather) can play a sizable role in your appreciation of a place. Here are some phrases to help you comment on what nature throws your way. Notice that many weather-related expressions use the verb *fare*.

Che tempo fa?	*What's the weather like?*
Fa bel tempo.	*It's nice out.*
Fa caldo.	*It's hot.*
Fa freddo.	*It's cold.*
Fa fresco.	*It's cool out.*
C'è il sole.	*It's sunny.*
Tira vento.	*It's windy.*
Piove.	*It's raining.*
Nevica.	*It's snowing.*

Or you can sum it all up with:

Che bella giornata!	*What a beautiful day!*
Che brutta giornata!	*What a miserable (Lit. ugly) day!*

I DON'T FEEL WELL: TALKING ABOUT YOUR HEALTH

Speaking of miserable, that's the state our *signor del Vecchio* seems to be in perpetually. Let's take a look at some of his favorite expressions:

Non mi sento bene.	*I don't feel well.*
Sono allergico / allergica al polline.	*I'm allergic to pollen.*
Ho le vertigini.	*I'm dizzy (from heights).*
Mi gira la testa.	*I'm dizzy (Lit. My head is turning.)*
Ho mal di testa.	*I have a headache.*
Ho mal di gola.	*My throat hurts.*
Ho mal di stomaco.	*I have a stomach ache.*

In case you're wondering what the Italian word for "hypochondriac" is, it's *ipocondriaco*.

The Fine Print

This one's for the really picky ones among you: Did you notice that in the first dialogue Elisabetta said "la Fontana dei Quattro Fiumi **di** Lorenzo Bernini" and in the second she said "La Barcaccia **del** Bernini"? That's because when you're talking about someone really famous—so famous that you don't need to specify his or her first name—you use *di* + the definite article because he's not just any Bernini, he's *the* Bernini.

Before we get back to grammar, let's take a look at some words that will help your conversation flow more smoothly by connecting or contrasting one thought with the next.

in questo caso	in this case
allora	so, then
invece di	instead of
oppure	otherwise, else, or

Allora, invece di parlare, facciamo un po' di pratica!

ACTIVITY 8: TAKE IT FOR A SPIN

What season is it?

1. *Fa fresco e tira vento:* _____
2. *Nevica e fa freddo:* _____
3. *Piove tanto:* _____
4. *C'è sempre il sole e fa caldo:* _____

Now tell me what you might typically do, depending on the circumstances. Choose from the following options:

fa bel tempo   *non mi sento*   *bene piove*   *in primavera*

5. *Quando _____, mi piace navigare in Internet.*
6. *_____, mi piace fare giardinaggio.*
7. *Quando _____, preferisco stare a letto.*
8. *Quando _____, mi piace fare una passeggiata.*

'Tis that time again, *amico / a mio / a* . . .

THE NITTY-GRITTY

YOU'RE IT!: PRONOUNS LIKE ME, HIM, US, THEM, ETC.

If you remember, in the sentence *I'm writing a postcard to Marco*, "a postcard" is the direct object. In *scrivo una cartolina a Marco*, it's "*una cartolina.*" Notice that direct objects are not introduced by a preposition, i.e., they **directly** follow the verb. A direct object pronoun replaces the direct object. *Un gioco da ragazzi!* The direct object pronouns in Italian are:

PRONOUNS LIKE *ME, HIM, US, THEM*, ETC.			
ME	*mi*	US	*ci*
YOU (SING. INFML.)	*ti*	YOU (PL.)	*vi*
YOU (SING. FML.)	*La*	YOU (PL.)	*vi*
HIM / IT	*lo*	THEM (M.)	*li*
HER / IT	*la*	THEM (F.)	*le*

Take a Tip from Me!

Notice that the direct object pronouns for the *io, tu, noi,* and *voi* forms are identical to the indirect object pronouns, so it's hard to go wrong. Also notice that the direct object pronouns meaning "him," "her," and "them (fem.)" are identical to the definite articles (*lo, la, le*).

Like indirect object pronouns, direct object pronouns go before the verb.

> **Scrivo <u>una cartolina</u> a Marco.** → **<u>La</u> scrivo a Marco.**

> I'm writing <u>a postcard</u> to Marco. → I'm writing <u>it</u> to Marco.

Do you remember how they were used during *il giro?* Chiara uses a direct object pronoun when she says:

> **Io <u>la</u> sento benissimo.**

> I hear <u>her</u> very well.

Elisabetta also used it:

> **Se <u>mi</u> seguite, non c'è nessun problema.**

> If you follow <u>me</u>, there's no problem.

> **<u>Lo</u> sentite?**

> Do you hear <u>it</u>?

Finally, remember that, like indirect object pronouns, when direct object pronouns are used with *potere, volere,* or *dovere,* the pronoun can be attached to the end of the infinitive:

> **Io posso sentir<u>la</u> benissimo. = Io <u>la</u> posso sentire benissimo.**

> I can hear her very well.

Okay, now let's practice!

Replace the underlined phrase with a direct object pronoun.

1.   *I turisti seguono <u>Elisabetta</u>.* _____

2.   *Vedi <u>la Fontana dei Quattro Fiumi</u>?* _____

3.   *Potete seguire <u>la bandiera rossa</u>.* _____

4.   *Sentite <u>le urla dei Barbari</u>?* _____

5.   *Ci fa una foto? Può vedere <u>noi tutti</u>?* _____

6.   *Mandiamo <u>una e-mail</u> a mia sorella.* _____

7.   *Bevo <u>il cappuccino</u> solo prima di mezzagiorno.* _____

     _____

8.   *Puoi prendere <u>un taxi</u> fino alla stazione.* _____

     _____

9.   *Non voglio <u>il coniglio</u>. Non mangio carne.* _____

     _____

10. *Mi dispiace. Non può cambiare <u>camera</u>. L'albergo è al completo.* _____

     _____

Before we say *ciao, ciao,* life just wouldn't be interesting without . . .

OH, YEAH? COME OVER HERE AND SAY THAT!: THE VERBS *DIRE* (TO SAY) AND *VENIRE* (TO COME)

Two verbs for the road. The first one is pretty easy: all you have to remember is to use the irregular stem, *dic–*, in all but the *voi* form (which, by the way, happens to be completely regular). The endings are all simple *–ire* endings.

DIRE (TO SAY) IN THE PRESENT TENSE			
IO	dico	NOI	diciamo
TU	dici	VOI	dite
LEI / LUI	dice	LORO	dicono

Ma cosa dici?

But what are you saying?

Dicono che non è difficile imparare l'italiano.

They say that it's not difficult to learn Italian.

That was the easy part. *Purtroppo*, however, there's no such luck with *venire*. It's as if they took three different conjugations and combined them into one.

VENIRE (TO COME) IN THE PRESENT TENSE			
IO	*vengo*	**NOI**	*veniamo*
TU	*vieni*	**VOI**	*venite*
LEI / LUI	*viene*	**LORO**	*vengono*

Just remember the characteristic *io* form and repeat after me: *vengo, vieni, viene; veniamo, venite, vengono. Vengo, vieni, viene; veniamo, venite, vengono.* It has a certain beat to it, if you think about it.

Vengono tanti turisti.

Many tourists come.

The Fine Print

Just so you don't feel like you're memorizing *venire* for nothing, you get a couple of freebies: the verbe *tenere* (to hold; to keep) follows the same pattern: *tengo, tieni, tiene; teniamo, tenete, tengono.* Only the *voi* form ends in *–ete* instead of *–ite* and that's simply because *tenere* is an *–ere* verb. *Rimanere* (to remain; to stay) is another useful verb with a similar pattern: *rimango, rimani, rimane; rimaniamo, rimanete, rimangono.*

ACTIVITY 10:	**TAKE IT FOR A SPIN**

Fill in the correct form of *venire* or *dire*.

1. *(Tu)* _____ *a Piazza Navona per il giro della città?*

2. *Se (voi)_____ in ritardo, non possiamo fare il giro.*

3. *Cosa _____ questa guida? Non sento niente!*

4. *Non ti piace fare lo shopping? Ma perché non _____ mai niente?*

5. *Perché non fate più la festa questa settimana? —Perchè non _____ nessuno!*

Non volete fare più la grammatica? Ma perché non dite niente? Va bene. Ci vediamo fra poco . . .

CRIB NOTES

Elisabetta:	Welcome to Rome, ladies and gentlemen. I'm Elisabetta. One moment, and we're leaving, but first: I don't want to lose anyone. So, I'd like to ask you to always stay together. If you follow me, there's no problem. If you lose sight of me, just look for the red flag. Okay?
All:	Yes. Okay . . .
Elisabetta:	The tour begins here, in Piazza Navona, and ends in Piazza di Spagna. Piazza Navona is a very popular spot. When the weather is nice, as it is today, many tourists, but also many Romans, come here to have a cup of coffee or an aperitif and do some people-watching . . . In the center, there's the Fountain of the Four Rivers by Lorenzo Bernini.
Chiara:	Elisabetta, shall we take a picture in front of the fountain?

Elisabetta:	Yes. Why not? Let's ask that gentleman . . . Excuse me, sir. Will you take a picture of us?
Elisabetta:	So, what do you prefer: having an ice cream at the Tre Scalini café or continuing on?
All:	Tartufo!!
Del Vecchio:	I prefer continuing. The tartufo surely costs an arm and a leg (*Lit.* an eye of the head).
Chiara:	It's on me (*Lit.* I'm offering). Okay?
Elisabetta:	On your left is the Column of Marcus Aurelius with many illustrations of his battles against the barbarians. . . . Psst! Do you hear it?
All:	What?
Elisabetta:	The sound of the screams of the barbarians . . .
Del Vecchio:	But what is she saying? I don't hear anything. I don't even hear her . . .
Chiara:	I can hear her very well. You never hear anything.

Elisabetta:	In a few minutes, we'll be arriving at the Fontana di Trevi. If you believe in the legend and want to return to Rome, I suggest that you throw a few coins in the fountain.
Del Vecchio:	I don't believe it!
Chiara:	You're never happy.
Elisabetta:	Here's the Piazza di Spagna and its famous Spanish Steps. We can climb them—on top there's a wonderful view of the Eternal City. And at the bottom we have another fountain by Bernini: The Fountain of the Old Boat.
Chiara:	What a beautiful day! It's sunny, the wind is blowing and all these azaleas! . . . Spring in Rome is just beautiful!
Del Vecchio:	I don't feel well. I'm allergic to pollen, and I don't like the sun or the wind.

Chiara:	I don't understand. Why aren't you looking at the view?
Del Vecchio:	I don't feel well. I'm dizzy.
Elisabetta:	And if you like literature, the Keats-Shelley Memorial Foundation is also here.
Chiara:	Can we go in?
Elisabetta:	Unfortunately the museum is closed. But instead of going to the museum, we can have a snack at the Antico Caffè Greco, frequented by Byron, Goethe, and also by Buffalo Bill. Or, whoever doesn't want to have lunch with the writers can do some shopping in Via Condotti . . .
Del Vecchio:	I prefer to stay here and watch the people . . .
Chiara:	. . . and not spend too much money. I understand.

ACTIVITY 1

1. d;   2. j;   3. i;   4. b;   5. h;   6. a;
7. c;   8. e;   9. g;   10. f

ACTIVITY 2

1. *Il giro comincia in Piazza Navona.*
2. *Finisce in Piazza di Spagna.*
3. *I turisti devono stare sempre insieme e seguire Elisabetta e la bandiera rossa.*
4. *La fontana in Piazza Navona si chiama La Fontana dei Quattro Fiumi, di Lorenzo Bernini.*
5. *Il signor del Vecchio non vuole prendere un tartufo perché "sicuramente costa un occhio della testa"—è troppo caro.*
6. *Dopo Piazza Navona i turisti vedono la Colonna di Marco Aurelio.*
7. *Sulla Colonna vedono illustrazioni delle sue battaglie contro i Barbari.*
8. *Non può sentire la guida, non vuole spendere dei soldi—non è mai contento.*

ACTIVITY 3

1. *Voglio vedere il museo d'arte moderna.*
2. *Voglio vedere i monumenti.*
3. *Voglio vedere la sinagoga.*
4. *Voglio vedere le fontane.*
5. *Voglio vedere le rovine.*
6. *M'interessa l'arte medievale.*
7. *M'interessa la pittura.*
8. *M'interessa l'arte rinascimentale.*
9. *M'interessa la scultura.*
10. *M'interessano le chiese.*

ACTIVITY 4

1. *Preferisco;*   2. *finisce;*   3. *apre;*
4. *Sentite;*   5. *suggerisco;*   6. *Partiamo;*
7. *Capite;*   8. *preferiscono;*   9. *servono;*
10. *Offro*

ACTIVITY 5

1. *No, Elisabetta non vuole perdere nessuno.*
2. *No, il signor del Vecchio non ordina niente all'Antico Caffè Greco.*
3. *No, il signor del Vecchio non può sentire niente.*
4. *No, il signor del Vecchio non sente neanche Elisabetta.*
5. *No, al signor del Vecchio non piace né prendere un tartufo né spendere dei soldi.*

6. *No, Lotte non beve mai prima di mangiare.*
7. *No, Pietro, il macellaio, non ha affatto successo con le donne.*
8. *No, Gianfranco, il portiere al Palazzo Medici, non capisce niente.*

ACTIVITY 6

1. c;   2. d;   3. a;   4. f;   5. b;   6. e

ACTIVITY 7

1. *Secondo la leggenda, per tornare a Roma i turisti devono lanciare degli spiccioli nella Fontana di Trevi.*
2. *La fontana in Piazza di Spagna si chiama La Barcaccia, di Bernini.*
3. *C'è un museo in Piazza di Spagna. Si chiama Fondazione Keats-Shelley.*
4. *L'Antico Caffè Greco è famoso per i suoi clienti famosi, come Keats, Byron, Shelley e anche Buffalo Bill.*
5. *Sopra la Scalinata c'è una bellissima vista di Roma.*

ACTIVITY 8

1. *autunno;*   2. *inverno;*   3. *primavera;*
4. *estate;*   5. *piove;*   6. *In primavera;*   7. *non mi sento bene;*   8. *fa bel tempo*

ACTIVITY 9

1. *I turisti la seguono.*
2. *La vedi?*
3. *Potete seguirla. / La potete seguire.*
4. *Le sentite?*
5. *Ci fa una foto? Può vederci? / Ci può vedere?*
6. *Lo mandiamo a mia sorella.*
7. *Lo bevo solo prima di mezzogiomo.*
8. *Puoi prenderlo fino alla stazione. / Lo puoi prendere fino alla stazione.*
9. *Non lo voglio. Non mangio carne.*
10. *Mi dispiace. Non può cambiarla. / Non la può cambiare. L'albergo è al completo.*

ACTIVITY 10

1. *Vieni;*   2. *venite;*   3. *dice;*   4. *dici;*
5. *viene*

183

LESSON 8 • IT COSTS AN ARM AND A LEG

9.

ONCE IN A BLUE MOON

Ogni morte di papa

(*Lit.* Every death of a pope)

You have to come with us!

- *What do you want to do tonight?*: Making plans
- *As time goes by*: Adverbs of time, like *often, seldom,* etc.
- *I won't take no for an answer*: How to convince and resist being convinced
- *Know thyself*: The difference between *sapere* (to know) and *conoscere* (to be acquainted with)
- *Get outta here!*: The irregular verb *uscire* (to go out)
- *What time is it?*: Telling time

So, what was your favorite part of *il giro?* I have to admit that *la leggenda*, which says: *per tornare a Roma, lanciate degli spiccioli nella Fontana di Trevi*, always puts me in a hopeful mood. Then again, *il panorama* from the top of *La Scalinata di Piazza di Spagna* is also *incantevole* (enchanting). *Guardare la gente* in Piazza di Spagna and Piazza Navona isn't too bad, either. Hmm. I guess when it comes to tourism, I lean more toward Chiara's side—I'm usually *felice* (happy) doing just about anything, and I'm willing to *spendere tanti soldi* to experience everything I can. How about you? Are you a *bastian contrario* like Mr. del Vecchio or an *ottimista* like Chiara? Well, anyway, *un giro* is a great way to see all the *cose da vedere*, but it's also fun to do some "regular" stuff, the kinds of things people do every day. *A volte* (sometimes) it's fun just to *stare a casa e guardare la tv* (and let me tell you, you'll get an interesting slice of Italian culture. *Non vi prendo in giro.* "I'm not kidding."). But there are usually more exciting options for getting to see how Italians have fun. Just pick up *un giornale* (a newspaper) and check out the local listings.
Pronti per il primo esercizio?

LET'S WARM UP

Insert a "=" if you think the following phrases are similar in meaning and a "≠" if they're not.

1. *prendere in giro* _____ *dire sul serio*

2. *ho voglia di . . .* _____ *vorrei . . .*

3. *stare a casa* _____ *uscire*

4. *mi piace . . .* _____ *non sopporto . . .*

5. *a volte* _____ *ogni tanto*

HEAR . . . SAY 1

Livia and Alba are students at the *Università di Bologna*. They're hanging out outside, after class, discussing their evening plans. Livia plans to stay in—she's a serious student who usually goes out only on weekends. But Alba, who's always ready to go out, tries to work her magic on Livia . . .

Alba: Cosa fai stasera?
Livia: Non so. C'è un film alla tv alle nove e venti. E tu?
Alba: Ho voglia di uscire . . .

Livia: Di solito io esco solo il fine-settimana.

Alba: Dai! Perché non usciamo insieme? Vediamo cosa c'è. Ecco il giornale.

Livia: Ah! L'oroscopo! Sai cosa mi consiglia?

Alba: Cosa?

Livia: "Meglio stare a casa e mettere tutto in ordine."

Alba: Mi prendi in giro?

Livia: Dico sul serio.

Alba: Allora, vediamo . . . C'è il nuovo film di Tornatore all'Odeon alle nove e un quarto.

Livia: Non sopporto l'attrice . . . come si chiama?

Alba: Non lo so, ma non importa. Allora, cosa ne dici di un po' di jazz?

Livia: Chi c'è?

Alba: "Quattro gatti e un topo" al Cabiria alle dieci e mezzo. Li conosci?

Livia: No. E tu?

Alba: No. Okay . . . Sai giocare a biliardo?

Livia: No.

Alba: Allora, c'è una nuova enoteca molto popolare.

Livia: Okay. Andiamo lì. Ma come? Il mio motorino è dal meccanico.

Alba: Possiamo prendere l'autobus. Ci vediamo alla fermata alle otto.

Livia: Alle otto non posso. Facciamo alle nove, nove e un quarto.

Alba: Perchè?

Livia: Vorrei guardare la mia telenovela.

Alba: Incredibile! D'accordo . . . Sai, viene anche Enzo.

Livia: Chi è? Non lo conosco.

Alba: Ma, sì! Lo conosci—abbiamo il corso di marketing con lui . . .

Livia: Ah, sì—Enzo! È molto simpatico . . . Come mai lo conosci?

Alba: Studiamo insieme ogni tanto . . .

ACTIVITY 2:   **HOW'S THAT AGAIN?**

1. *Cosa vuol fare Livia stasera?* _____

2. *Cosa vuol fare Alba?* _____

3. *Perché Livia non vuole guardare il nuovo film di Tornatore?* _____

4. *Chi sono "Quattro gatti e un topo"?* _____

5. *Cosa fa Livia alle otto?* _____

6. *Chi è Enzo?* _____

The Fine Print

Notice that a final *–e* is often "swallowed" in pronunciation as in *cosa vuol(e) fare Alba* or in the famous Italian expression: *il dolce far niente* (and not *fare*), "the joy of doing nothing."

Did You Know?

LA DOTTA: THE CITY OF BOLOGNA AND ITS ANCIENT UNIVERSITY

Founded circa 1050, the University of Bologna is Europe's oldest university. By the thirteenth century, it boasted more than 10,000 students, and its faculty included female professors! Today it is home to one of the finest business and medical schools in the country. Bologna's university is probably what earned the city its nickname of *la Dotta* (the Learned). It owes its other famous nickname, *la Grassa* (the Fat), to its inhabitants' renowned appreciation of fine cuisine. Bologna has a third nickname, *la Turrita* (the Towered), going back to the Middle Ages when it had more than 100 towers (*la torre* means "the tower"). Only two of those remain today, *la torre degli Asinelli* and *la torre Garisenda,* which stand in the center of the city.

Enough chatting, let's get to work!

WORKSHOP 1

WORDS TO LIVE BY

WHAT DO YOU WANT TO DO TONIGHT?: MAKING PLANS

If you want to suggest doing something, whether it's *il fine-settimana* or any other *giorno,* you can say:

Hai voglia di . . . ?	*Do you feel like . . . ?*
Cosa ne dici di . . . ?	*What do you say to . . . ?*

Here are some things you might enjoy:

giocare a . . .	*to play . . .*
• **biliardo**	• *billiards, pool*
• **tennis**	• *tennis (m.)*
• **pallavolo**	• *volleyball (f.)*
• **carte**	• *cards (f. pl.)*
guardare una telenovela	*to watch a soap opera*
leggere l'oroscopo	*to read the horoscope*

If you ask me, I'd choose a fine glass of *vino* at a nice *enoteca* (wine bar) over all of those things.

When you want to *uscire* (go out), do you prefer to *andare in macchina, prendere l'autobus* or *andare a piedi*? Most Italians will hop on their *motorino* (a small motorcycle or scooter), which is undisputably the fastest way to get around Italy's narrow city streets.

Did You Know?

VROOM!: THE UBIQUITOUS *MOTORINO*

The *motorino* is truly an integral part of the Italian citydweller's lifestyle. To give you an idea of just how popular they are, Florence, with its population of circa 400,000 inhabitants has around 150,000 *motorini*. And there's no particular "profile" of a motorcycle rider—businessmen, professional women, even grandmothers will zip by you in any *stagione*. I once saw a guy walk out of his building with his dog, who immediately ran to his master's Vespa, hopped on, and the two zipped away together. *Dico sul serio!* I'm serious! And there are special parking lots for motorcycles—you'll see streets lined with dozens of them in a row. If you're feeling confident, you can rent a *motorino* of your own and take your chances with the crazy traffic. If, on the other hand, you're more the "armchair traveler" type, rent *Caro Diario,* Nanni Moretti's comical video diary, which includes a great segment where we get to follow him as he takes his *motorino* through Rome's lesser-known neighborhoods and explains his strange obsession with Jennifer Beals.

Did You Know?

Maybe you're the serious type and think it's *meglio* (better) to *stare a casa* and *mettere tutto in ordine* (to put everything in order).

Word on the Street

A few expressions that will probably get a lot of mileage, on or off *un motorino* . . .

Non sopporto . . .	I can't stand . . .
Mi prendi in giro?	Are you pulling my leg? (Lit. Are you taking me for a ride?)
Dico sul serio.	I'm serious. I mean it. (Lit. I'm saying it seriously.)

If you don't want to be egotistical about it, you can just conjugate *sopportare, prendere,* and *dire* and apply the expressions to anyone at all!

Now let's loosen those lips . . .

TAKE IT FOR A SPIN

Ask your friend if (s)he feels like doing the following things using *hai voglia di . . .*

1. *guardare la tv* _____

2. *giocare a pallavolo* _____

3. *leggere il giornale* _____

4. *andare al cinema* _____

5. *navigare in Internet* _____

TAKE IT FOR A SPIN

What would you say in the following situations?

1. Your *amica* has just told you that her grandmother married a lawyer twenty years younger than she is. _____

2. *Avete dieci anni* and your mother tells you you're having broccoli for dinner.

   _____

3. A coworker tells you that the Giants signed up a female quarterback. _____

   _____

Adesso let's turn to one of your favorite subjects: *i verbi!*

THE NITTY-GRITTY

KNOW THYSELF: THE DIFFERENCE BETWEEN *SAPERE* (TO KNOW) AND *CONOSCERE* (TO BE ACQUAINTED WITH)

In Italian "to know" can be translated with one of two verbs. *Conoscere* means "to be acquainted with; to be familiar with," and it's most often used when you're talking about people you know or places with which you're familiar. That's why Alba uses *conoscere* when she's talking about a jazz band:

Quattro gatti e un topo. Li conosci?

Four Cats and a Mouse. Do you know them?

Both Livia and Alba use *conoscere* when they're talking about Enzo:

Chi è? Non lo conosco.

Who is he? I don't know him.

Ma, si! Lo conosci!

Yes! You know him!

Sapere, on the other hand, means "to know" in the general sense, i.e., having knowledge of a fact, as when Livia says:

Sai che di solito esco solo il fine-settimana.

You know I usually go out only on weekends.

or knowing how to do something, as when Alba says:

Sai giocare a biliardo?

Do you know how to play pool?

Word on the Street

Note, too, that **sai** (or **sapete**), "you know," is often used as filler in conversations, much like its English counterpart:

Sai, viene anche Enzo.

You know, Enzo's coming, too.

Take a Tip from Me!

Notice that *il fine-settimana* translates as "on weekends." It's the same rule that you learned with the days of the week: the definite article used with a unit of time means "every." You'll see the same usage in prices charged *all'ora* (per hour), i.e., "every hour."

Take a Tip from Me!

Conoscere is perfectly regular: *conosco, conosci, conosce, conosciamo, conoscete, conoscono.* (Yahoo!) *Sapere*, however, has an irregular conjugation, but it should look vaguely familiar, since you already know *dare* and *andare*:

SAPERE (TO KNOW) IN THE PRESENT TENSE			
IO	so	NOI	sappiamo
TU	sai	VOI	sapete
LUI / LEI	sa	LORO	sanno

ACTIVITY 5: **TAKE IT FOR A SPIN**

Fill in the blanks with the appropriate form of *conoscere* or *sapere*.

1. _(voi)_____ mia cugina, Luisa?
2. _(tu)_____ navigare sull'Internet?
3. A che ora comincia il film a RaiUno? —Non lo _(io)_____.
4. È la vostra prima volta a Bologna? —No. La _____ bene.
5. Scusi, _____ quando apre la Fondazione Keats-Shelley?

Let's do one more verb before we leave the workshop:

GET OUTTA HERE!: THE IRREGULAR VERB USCIRE (TO GO OUT)

The verb *uscire* (to go out; to come out) which I hope you'll be using (and thus putting into practice) a lot, is also irregular:

USCIRE (TO GO OUT) IN THE PRESENT TENSE			
IO	esco	NOI	usciamo
TU	esci	VOI	uscite
LUI / LEI	esce	LORO	escono

ACTIVITY 6: **TAKE IT FOR A SPIN**

Answer the questions using full sentences and the clues in parentheses.

1. Quando esci con Enzo? (domani)_____
2. Livia e Alba escono spesso insieme? (Sì)_____

3. *Di solito uscite solo il fine-settimana? (Sì)* _____

4. *Quando esce il giornale? (ogni giorno)* _____

5. *Perché non esci mai? (motorino dal meccanico)* _____

Now back to our show . . .

ACTIVITY 7:   LOOKING AHEAD

Let's play the opposites game again. Insert a "=" if you think the following phrases are similar in meaning and a "≠" if they're not.

1. *in orario* _____ *in ritardo*

2. *Che ore sono?* _____ *Mi può dire l'ora?*

3. *tornare a casa* _____ *uscire*

4. *vi dispiace . . .* _____ *vi piace . . .*

5. *Fantastico!* _____ *Accidenti!*

HEAR . . . SAY 2

We find Livia, Alba, and Enzo waiting at *la fermata* (the bus stop). Livia is getting antsy . . .

Livia: Accidenti! Dov'è l'autobus?

Alba: Cosa dice l'orario? Anche se l'autobus arriva in orario ogni morte di papa . . .

Livia: Uno alle ventuno e dodici, un altro alle ventuno e venticinque, poi alle ventuno e trentotto.

Alba: E che ore sono?

Livia: Non so. Chiediamo . . .

Enzo: Vado io . . . *(approaches man at bus stop)* Scusi, mi può dire l'ora? *(comes back reporting what he's learned)* Sono le dieci meno un quarto.

Livia: Quanto tempo ci vuole per arrivare?

Alba: Non ci vuole molto, ma dobbiamo cambiare linea alla quinta fermata.

Livia: Vi dispiace se torno a casa? Ho tanto da fare domani mattina . . .

Alba: Ma no! Devi venire con noi!

Livia: Veramente non posso.

Alba: Mah!

Livia: Sai che di solito non esco così tardi.

Alba: Ecco l'autobus! Adesso non hai più scuse.

Vero o falso?

		VERO	FALSO
1.	L'autobus è in ritardo.	_____	_____
2.	Secondo Alba, l'autobus di solito arriva in orario.	_____	_____
3.	L'enoteca è abbastanza vicino.	_____	_____
4.	Livia vuole tornare a casa a guardare la tv.	_____	_____
5.	Alla fine, l'autobus arriva.	_____	_____

Allora, avete voglia di lavorare un po'?

WORKSHOP 2

WORDS TO LIVE BY

AS TIME GOES BY: ADVERBS OF TIME, LIKE *OFTEN*, *SELDOM*, ETC.

How often do you usually go out? *Mai? Sempre?* I suspect that it's probably somewhere in between:

una volta	one time; once
ogni tanto	once in a while; every so often
a volte	at times
di solito	usually
spesso	often
sempre	always

I WON'T TAKE NO FOR AN ANSWER: HOW TO CONVINCE AND RESIST BEING CONVINCED

What if you don't feel like going out, but someone is being very insistent, saying things like:

Ma dai!	Come on! (also: Come off it!)
Devi . . .	You have to . . .
Non hai scuse.	You have no excuse.

You have to learn how to say no—politely.

Veramente non posso.	Really, I can't
Lo facciamo un'altra volta.	Let's do it another time.
Preferisco . . .	I'd prefer . . .

One verb that will come in very handy in situations that require being polite and diplomatic is *dispiacere.* Use it when you want to say: "do you mind if . . ."

Ti dispiace se . . .	Do you mind if . . . (sing. infml.)
Le dispiace se . . .	Do you mind if . . . (sing. fml.)
Vi dispiace se . . .	Do you mind if . . . (pl.)

You can say things like *vi dispiace se torno a casa* (do you mind if I go home) like Livia did, but you can also use it to politely ask permission to do something, as in:

Le dispiace se fumo?	Do you mind if I smoke?
Vi dispiace se apro la finestra?	Do you mind if I open the window?

Note that *dispiacere* is used just like *piacere:* with indirect objects (e.g., "to me," "to you," etc.).

Before we move on to grammar, let's review a few transportation-related terms that you need to know.

l'orario	schedule; time-table (masc.)
la fermata	(bus) stop
cambiare linea	to transfer (Lit. to change lines)

Here's something you can say if you just missed the bus:

Accidenti!	Damn!

Vi dispiace se facciamo un esercizio?

ACTIVITY 9:   TAKE IT FOR A SPIN

1.   Tell your friend Marta that she has to come out with you (pl.). _____

     _____

2.   Ask the people waiting with you at the *fermata* if they mind if you smoke. _____

     _____

3. You've just come back from a long night at the office and your friend calls you and suggests checking out the new bar in the neighborhood. You're tired and grumpy and say: "I really can't." _____

    _____

4. Three nights a week you go out with your friends. According to you, this is (every so often) _____. According to your partner, it's (too often)

    _____.

5. You read in your textbook that it's time to do grammar. You think to yourself: _____

    _____

WHAT TIME IS IT?: TELLING TIME

To ask for the time in Italian, say:

Che ore sono?	*What's the time?*
Mi può / puoi dire l'ora?	*Can you tell me the time? (pol. / fam.)*
Sa / Sai l'ora?	*Do you know the time? (pol. / fam.)*

Heads Up!

Volta and *ora* can both be translated as "time," but *volta* refers to an instance of something, as in "one time, two times . . ." or in *c'era una volta* (once upon a time). *L'ora* refers to "clock" time.

When giving the time, the important thing to remember is that in Italian, the time is usually plural because it refers to the number of hours. So, you'd use *sono le* + a plural number, as in:

Sono le due.

It's two o'clock. (*Lit.* They are two [hours].)

Sono le dieci.

It's ten o'clock. (*Lit.* They are ten [hours].)

But *l'una* (one o'clock) is singular because you're only talking about one hour.

È l'una.

It's one o'clock. (*Lit.* It's one [hour].)

mezzogiorno (noon) and *mezzanotte* (midnight) are also singular:

È mezzogiorno.

It's noon.

È mezzanotte.

It's midnight.

To specify minutes past the hour, simply use *e* + the number of *minuti*.

Sono le due e dieci.

It's ten after two.

Sono le dieci e venticinque.

It's 10:25

Or you can say how many minutes remain to the coming hour using *meno*.

Sono le quattro meno cinque. = Sono le trè e cinquantacinque.

It's five to four. (*Lit.* They're four less five.) = It's 3:55.

Sono le undici meno dieci. = Sone le dieci e cinquanta.

It's ten to eleven. (*Lit.* They're eleven less ten.) = It's 10:50.

Instead of specifying the exact number of minutes, you can approximate the time using *un quarto* (a quarter) or *mezzo* (half).

Sono le dieci meno un quarto.

It's a quarter to ten.

Quattro gatti e un topo al Cabiria alle dieci e mezzo.

Four Cats and a Mouse at the Cabiria at 10:30.

When you're talking about the time at which something is supposed to take place, use the preposition *a*.

Facciamo alle nove, nove e un quarto.

Let's make it at nine, a quarter past nine.

C'è il nuovo film di Tornatore all'Odeon alle nove e un quarto.

There's Tornatore's new film at the Odeon at a quarter past nine.

Did You Know?

LIGHTS, CAMERA, ACTION!: THE MOVIE CINEMA PARADISO

Giuseppe Tornatore is one of Italy's most popular contemporary directors. His best-known movie in the United States is *Cinema Paradiso,* a nostalgic look at a young boy's coming of age in a small Sicilian village just after WWII. This Oscar-winner for best foreign language film uses the movies as a backdrop and features one of the most beautiful film montages honoring the kiss. Don't forget the tissues!

Did You Know?

TWENTY-FOUR HUNDRED HOURS: USE OF THE 24-HOUR CLOCK

Note that Italians use the twenty-four-hour clock for all official schedules and appointments. For example, the *orario* at the *fermata* lists scheduled bus arrivals using the twenty-four-hour clock:

Uno alle ventuno e dodici, un altro alle ventuno e venticinque, poi alle ventuno e trentotto.

One at 21:12 (9:12 P.M.), another one at 21:25 (9:25 P.M.), then at 21:38 (9:38 P.M.)

In casual conversation, however, you'd use the twelve-hour clock and simply specify *di mattina* (in the morning; A.M.) or *di sera* (in the evening, P.M.). Note, too, that in Italian the hour and the minutes are separated by a comma instead of a colon. So, 8:45 would be written as 8,45. In general, when dealing with numbers, Italians use a comma where we use a period, and vice versa, e.g.: 1.5 = 1,5; 1,000 = 1.000.

Finally, if you're making plans and you can't make it at a certain time, say

Alle . . . , non posso. Facciamo alle . . .	At . . . , I can't make it. Let's make it at . . .
Diciamo alle . . .	Let's say at . . .

TAKE IT FOR A SPIN

Che ore sono? Answer in Italian.

1.   7:30 A.M. _____

2.   noon _____

3.   8:10 P.M. _____

4.   one o'clock _____

5.   2:45 P.M. _____

6.   11:53 A.M. _____

7.   5:30 P.M. _____

8.   midnight _____

9.   6:03 P.M. _____

LET'S PUT IT IN WRITING

Here's a week in the life of Beppe:

LUNEDÌ
10.15 – Giovanni al caffè greco

MARTEDÌ
9.00 – presentazione a Globetech

MERCOLEDÌ
20.30 – biliardo con Paolo

GIOVEDÌ
13.45 – Dentista!!!

VENERDÌ

SABATO
8.10 – l'autobus per Siena 22.30 – festa per Laura

DOMENICA
15.30 – calcio!!

Cosa fa Beppe . . .

1. *lunedì?*_____

2. *martedì?*_____

3. *mercoledì?*_____

4. *giovedì?*_____

5. *venerdì?*_____

6. *sabato?*_____

7. *domenica?*_____

E adesso devo andare a guardare la mia telenovela. Ci vediamo alla lezione 10!

CRIB NOTES

HEAR...SAY 1

Alba:	What are you doing tonight?
Livia:	I don't know. There's a movie on TV at 9:20. And you?
Alba:	I feel like going out . . .
Livia:	I usually go out only on weekends.
Alba:	Come on! Why don't we go out together? Let's see what there is. Here's the paper.
Livia:	Oh. The horoscope! Do you know what it suggests?
Alba:	What?
Livia:	"Better to stay at home and put everything in order."
Alba:	Are you joking? (*Lit.* Are you taking me for a ride?)
Livia:	I'm serious.
Alba:	Well, let's see . . . There's the new Tornatore film at the Odeon at quarter past nine.
Livia:	I can't stand the actress . . . what's her name?
Alba:	I don't know, but it's not important. Well then, what do you say to some jazz?
Livia:	Who's playing? (*Lit.* Who's there?)
Alba:	*Four Cats and a Mouse* at the Cabiria at

	10:30. Do you know them?
Livia:	No. And you?
Alba:	No. Okay . . . Do you know how to play billiards?
Livia:	No.
Alba:	Then, there's a new wine bar that's very popular.
Livia:	Okay. Let's go there. But how? My scooter's at the mechanic's.
Alba:	We can take the bus. See you at the bus stop at eight.
Livia:	At eight, I can't. Let's make it nine, nine-fifteen.
Alba:	Why?
Livia:	I want to watch my soap opera.
Alba:	Incredible! Okay . . . You know, Enzo's coming, too.
Livia:	Who's he? I don't know him.
Alba:	But, yes. You know him—we have the marketing class with him . . .
Livia:	Oh, yes—Enzo! He's very nice. But how do you know him?
Alba:	We study together once in a while . . .

Livia: Damn! Where's the bus?
Alba: What does the schedule say? Even if the bus arrives on schedule once in a blue moon (*Lit.* every death of a pope) . . .
Livia: One at 21:12, another at 21:25, then at 21:38.
Alba: And what time is it?
Livia: I don't know. Let's ask . . .
Enzo: I'll go. . . . Excuse me, could you tell me the time? . . . It's a quarter to ten.

Livia: How much time do we need to get there?
Alba: We don't need a lot, but we have to transfer at the fifth stop.
Livia: Do you mind if I go home? I have so much to do tomorrow morning.
Alba: No! You have to come with us!
Livia: Really, I can't.
Alba: But!
Livia: You know I don't usually go out this late.
Alba: Here's the bus. You have no more excuses!

ANSWER KEY

ACTIVITY 1

1. ≠; 2. =; 3. ≠; 4. ≠; 5. =

ACTIVITY 2

1. *Livia vuole guardare un film alla tv.*
2. *Alba ha voglia di uscire.*
3. *Livia non vuole guardare il nuovo film di Tornatore perché non sopporta l'attrice.*
4. *"Quattro gatti e un topo" sono i musicisti di jazz.*
5. *Alle otto Livia guarda la sua telenovela.*
6. *Enzo è uno studente nella loro classe di marketing.*

ACTIVITY 3

1. *Hai voglia di guardare la tv?*
2. *Hai voglia di giocare a pallavolo?*
3. *Hai voglia di leggere il giornale?*
4. *Hai voglia di andare al cinema?*
5. *Hai voglia di navigare in Internet?*

ACTIVITY 4

1. *Mi prendi in giro?* or *Dici sul serio?*
2. Since you don't know how to say "yuck" in Italian, it'll have to be: *Non sopporto i broccoli!* or if you have a mouth on you already: *Accidenti!*
3. *Fantastico!* or *Accidenti!* depending on your point of view, I suppose. But *Mi prendi in giro?* or *Dici sul serio?* would work just as well.

ACTIVITY 5

1. *Conoscete;* 2. *Sai;* 3. *so;* 4. *conosco;* 5. *sa*

ACTIVITY 6

1. *Esco con Enzo domani.*
2. *Sì, Livia e Alba escono spesso insieme.*
3. *Sì, di solito usciamo solo il fine-settimana.*
4. *Il giornale esce ogni giorno.*
5. *Non esco mai perché il mio motorino è dal meccanico.*

ACTIVITY 7

1. ≠; 2. =; 3. ≠; 4. ≠; 5. ≠

ACTIVITY 8

1. *vero;* 2. *falso;* 3. *vero;* 4. *falso;* 5. *vero*

ACTIVITY 9

1. *Marta, devi uscire con noi!*
2. *Vi dispiace se fumo?*
3. *Veramente non posso.*
4. *ogni tanto / (troppo) spesso*
5. *Accidenti!*

ACTIVITY 10

1. *Sono le sette e mezzo / sette e trenta (di mattina)*
2. *È mezzogiorno.*
3. *Sono le otto e dieci di sera. / Sono le venti e dieci.*
4. *È l'una.*
5. *Sono le tre meno un quarto. / Sono le tre meno quindici. / Sono le due e quarantacinque. / Sono le quindici meno un quarto / quindici. / Sono le quattordici e quarantacinque.*

6. *Sono le undici e cinquantratre (di mattina). / Sono le dodici meno sette.*
7. *Sono le cinque e mezzo / e trenta (di sera). / Sono le diciassette e mezzo / e trenta.*
8. *È mezzanotte.*
9. *Sono le sei e tre (di sera). / Sono le diciotto e tre.*

ACTIVITY 11

1. *Lunedì alle dieci e un quarto Beppe prende un caffè con Giovanni al Caffè Greco.*
2. *Martedì alle nove Beppe ha una presentazione a Globetech.*
3. *Mercoledì alle otto e mezzo di sera (alle venti e mezzo) Beppe va a giocare a biliardo con Paolo.*
4. *Giovedì alle quattordici meno un quarto (alle tredici e quarantacinque) Beppe va dal dentista.*
5. *Venerdì Beppe non fa niente.*
6. *Sabato alle otto e dieci Beppe parte per Siena e alle ventidue e trenta (dieci e mezzo) va a una festa per Laura.*
7. *Domenica alle tre e mezzo (quindici e trenta)— come tutta l'Italia—Beppe guarda la partita di calcio alla tv.*

10.

YOU MISUNDERSTAND COMPLETELY!

Prendi lucciole per lanterne!

(*Lit.* You're taking fireflies for lanterns!)

You have the wrong number.

COMING UP...

- *Hello?*: Talking on the phone in Italian
- *Do we need milk?*: Shopping at the supermarket
- *Give it to him!*: When a sentence has two pronouns
- *Strut your stuff!*: A review

LOOKING AHEAD

Che ore sono? . . . Cosa?!? . . . È così tardi? Mi dispiace. Sapete, l'autobus non arriva mai in orario . . . Di solito vengo sempre in orario alle lezioni, ma oggi . . . Anyway, *siete fortunati: non conoscete il mio amico Michele* (mee-KEH-leh)*. Questo tipo è sempre in ritardo.* Whenever we agree to meet, *lui arriva con più di quarantacinque minuti di ritardo. Se, per esempio, abbiamo un appuntamento* (an appointment) *alle otto, lui arriva alle nove meno un quarto. A volte alle nove e mezzo. Incredibile!* Things are even worse today. Imagine this: *piove, tira vento, fa freddo,* and I'll be standing *all'angolo* (on the corner) waiting for Michele, when in his stead *signor Trillo Selvaggio* will turn up. *Non conoscete Trillo?* That's what Italians call the sound *un telefonino* (a cell phone) makes. Literally it means "savage ring"—very vivid, *vero?* In any case, after my apprehensive *Sì?,* I hear Michele's voice on the line: *"Senti, sono un po' in ritardo, ma arrivo subito."* Yeah right! I know I'm in for at least another *mezz'ora* in the rain and wind. What we do for friendship . . . *Adesso, basta con le chiacchiere! Facciamo un po' di lavoro.*

ACTIVITY 1: **LET'S WARM UP!**

Match the Italian phrase with its English counterpart.

1.	*Pronto?*	a.	Hello?
2.	*Ha sbagliato numero!*	b.	Leave me alone!
3.	*Con chi parlo?*	c.	to leave a message
4.	*lasciare un messagio*	d.	to try again
5.	*provare di nuovo*	e.	Who's this?
6.	*Mi lasci in pace!*	f.	You have the wrong number!

HEAR . . . SAY 1

Luca is a man of action—*esce quasi tutti i giorni* (he goes out almost every day). Tonight he's off to a party *da Lidia* and he calls his friend Gianni to see if he wants to meet him and go to the party together. He's in such a rush to get there that he doesn't notice one important detail . . .

Alfredo: (*sophisticated voice*) Pronto?
Luca: (*crazed voice*) Gianni, ciao! Sono io, Luca. Senti, vuoi venire con me da Lidia? La festa comincia alle dieci.
Alfredo: Sono già le undici meno un quarto.

Luca:	Nessuno arriva in orario, sai.
Alfredo:	Scusi, ma ha sbagliato numero.
Luca:	Ma, dai! Dobbiamo partire fra poco . . .
Alfredo:	Mi piacciono le feste, ma io non sono Gianni.
Luca:	E allora, con chi parlo?
Alfredo:	Sono Alfredo.
Luca:	Ma dov'è Gianni? Devo parlare con lui.
Alfredo:	Veramente, non lo so. Quale numero vuole?
Luca:	055–26–82–218 (zero cinquantacinque ventisei *ottantadue* duecento diciotto) Ma io non ho tempo per questo.
Alfredo:	(*confused and polite*) Signore, ha sbagliato numero. Può provare di nuovo.
Luca:	Okay, okay. Posso lasciargli un messaggio?
Alfredo:	(*losing patience*) Signore, Le ripeto: non c'è nessun Gianni qui!
Luca:	Sa quando torna?
Alfredo:	(*desperate*) Per favore, mi lasci in pace!
Luca:	(*offended*) Alfredo, non mi piace affatto il Suo tono. Non c'è ragione di arrabbiarsi.
Alfredo:	(*Click.*)
Luca:	Gianni? Alfredo? . . . Ma dove sono? Non c'è nessuno . . . Sono tutti pazzi qui, ve lo dico io!

ACTIVITY 2:   **HOW'S THAT AGAIN?**

Vero o falso? (True or false?) You be the judge . . .

		VERO	FALSO
1.	*All'inizio, Luca pensa di parlare con Gianni.*	_____	_____
2.	*C'è una festa da Lidia stasera alle nove.*	_____	_____
3.	*Luca vuole andare alla festa con Gianni.*	_____	_____
4.	*Alfredo conosce Gianni.*	_____	_____
5.	*Alfredo conosce Luca.*	_____	_____
6.	*Luca conosce Gianni.*	_____	_____

It doesn't look like Luca's very quick on the uptake. Oh, well. Let's hope we fare better.

HELLO?: TALKING ON THE PHONE IN ITALIAN

Well, let's hope the conversations you have in Italy when you *fate una chiamata* (make a phone call) won't be as confusing as Luca and Alfredo's. They shouldn't be if you remember a few simple phrases.

When you answer the phone, say:

Pronto?	Hello?
Sì?	Yes?

Word on the Street

It's an odd phenomenon, but people tend to answer their regular phone with **Pronto?** but their cell phone with **Sì?** Perhaps it's that a call on the cell phone interrupts us at odd moments, so it's more like someone tapping us on the shoulder and we say "yes?" instead of "hello?" *Chi lo sa?* (Who knows?)

If, on the other hand, *chiamate voi* (you're the ones doing the calling) you can ask to speak to someone, by saying:

Posso parlare con . . . , per piacere?	*Can I speak with . . . , please?*
Vorrei parlare con . . .	*I'd like to speak with . . .*

Or, if you're friendly with the person who answers, a simpler phrase will do:

c'è . . . ?	*Is . . . there?*

To be polite, you should always introduce yourself right away. A simple *sono* + your name will do. Or, if you've reached that special moment in a relationship, you can move to a simple *sono io* (it's me), and hope the person on the other end knows who *"io"* is. It's a risk, and you could instead hear:

Chi parla?	*Who's speaking?*

Hey, *chi non risica non rosica* (he who takes no risks, doesn't prosper). If you ask to speak to someone, and the person is there, expect to hear:

Un attimo.	*One moment.*
Te lo / la passo subito. / Glielo / la passo subito.	*Here (s)he is. (infml. / fml.)*
Aspetta / Aspetti in linea, per favore.	*Please hold the line. (infml. / fml.)*

If, on the other hand, the person you're looking for is not available, you'll hear:

In questo momento, non c'è.	*(S)he's not here at the moment.*
Vuoi / Vuole lasciare un messagio?	*Would you like to leave a message? (infml. / fml.)*
Puoi / Può provare di nuovo più tardi.	*You can try again later. (fam. / fml.)*

You can respond with:

Richiamo più tardi.	*I'll call back later.*
Posso lasciare un messaggio?	*Can I leave a message?*

Should you need to spell your name for someone, you can use the Italian alphabet. Sometimes, for clarity, Italians will instead use the name of an Italian city beginning with the letter you want, the way we say " 'v' as in Victor."

ITALIAN ALPHABET

LETTER	PRONOUNCED	CITY NAME	LETTER	PRONOUNCED	CITY NAME
a	ah	Ancona	*n*	EH-nneh	Napoli
b	bee	Bologna	*o*	oh	Otranto
c	chee	Cagliari	*p*	pee	Parma
d	dee	Domodossola	*q*	koo	—
e	eh	Empoli	*r*	EH-rreh	Roma
f	EH-ffeh	Firenze	*s*	EH-sseh	Salerno
g	jee	Genova	*t*	tee	Torino
h	AH-kkah	—	*u*	oo	Udine
i	ee	Isernia	*v*	voo	Venezia
l	EH-lleh	Lucca	*z*	TSEH-tah	Zara
m	EH-mmeh	Milano			

Italians also recognize five letters taken from foreign languages. For these letters, their name alone is usually clear enough.

LETTER	NAME	PRONOUNCED	LETTER	NAME	PRONOUNCED
j	*i lunga*	ee LOOH-gah	*x*	*ics*	eeks
k	*kappa*	KAH-ppah	*y*	*ipsilon /*	EE-psee-lohn /
w	*doppia vu*	DOH-ppyah VOO		*i greca*	ee GREH-kah

Purtroppo in today's modern age, instead of an actual person, you're most likely to reach *una segreteria telefonica* (an answering machine) or someone's *posta vocale* (voice mail). At least you probably won't find that *la linea è occupata* (the line is busy).

If you have the wrong number you'll hear:

Ha sbagliato numero.   *You have the wrong number.*
Che numero ha fatto?   *What number did you dial?*

Or if they're in a particularly bad mood:

Lasciami in pace!   *Leave me alone (Lit. Leave me in peace)!*

Did You Know?

ON THE PHONE: ABOUT TELEPHONE NUMBERS IN ITALY

Traditionally, Italians generally group digits in pairs when giving a phone number. If the phone number consists of seven digits (not all of them in Italy do—some smaller towns have five- or six-digit numbers), they'll usually be grouped: xx–xx–xxx. However, this may be another instance where American culture has left its mark on Europe—you can now see numbers grouped as xxx–xx–xx almost as often as the traditional way. Also, you usually have to dial the city code for the number you are dialing even for intra-city calls. The city code is always given as one unit consisting of three digits, beginning with zero.

Did You Know?

ACTIVITY 3:   **TAKE IT FOR A SPIN!**

Unscramble the following dialogues.

1.   —*Un attimo. Glielo passo subito.*

    —*Buon giorno. Vorrei parlare con il Signor Tozzi.*

    —*Chi parla?*

    —*Pronto?*

    —*Sono Alessandra.*

2.   —*Grazie. Richiamo più tardi.*

    —*In questo moment non c'è.*

    —*Sono Lorenzo. C'è Laura?*

    —*Sì, certo.*

    —*Sì?*

3.   —*Ha sbagliato numero.*

    —*Ciao, Roberto! Sono io.*

    —*Mi dispiace. Provo di nuovo.*

Now let's review some of the major grammar points we've covered since Lesson 5 . . .

STRUT YOUR STUFF!

- The present tense

Well, you now know endings for all regular verbs in the present tense:

	−ARE	−ERE	−IRE
IO	−o	−o	−o
TU	−i	−i	−i
LUI / LEI	−a	−e	−e
NOI	−iamo	−iamo	−iamo
VOI	−ate	−ete	−ite
LORO	−ano	−ono	−ono

Don't forget that certain −ire verbs take an −isc− before all but the noi and voi endings! Let's practice what you've learned.

| ACTIVITY 4: | **TAKE IT FOR A SPIN!** |

Use the correct form of the verbs in parentheses (together with any additional information) to write a fitting response to the questions below.

1. *Cosa prendi come secondo?*

   (prendere il coniglio) _____

2. *Andiamo a un altro ristorante.*

   (se, insistere, tu) _____

3. *Sai cos'è la bistecca fiorentina?*

   (non sapere; chiedere, noi) _____

4. *Quando partono per l'Italia?*

   (partire, sabato, dieci agosto) _____

   _____

5. *Allora, Signore, Le piace la camera al quinto piano?*

   (piacere, non affatto) _____

6. *Non voglio andare lì. Un caffè sicuramente costa un occhio della testa!*

   (offrire, io) _____

7. *I tuoi parenti preferiscono fare un giro turistico o fare un po' di shopping?*
(preferire, fare un po' di shopping) _____

8. *Credete alla leggenda della Fontana di Trevi?*
(non credere) _____

9. *Hai voglia di uscire stasera?*
(Ecco il giornale. vedere cosa c'è, noi) _____

_____

10. *A che ora finisce il film all'Odeon?*
(finire, 10:30 PM) _____

Not only do you know all these regular verbs in the present tense, you've also learned a bunch of irregular verbs: *bere* (to drink), *dire* (to tell; to say), *venire* (to come), *uscire* (to go out), *volere* (to want), *potere* (can; to be able to), *dovere* (must; to have to), and *sapere* (to know). Let's see how well you can throw those around!

TAKE IT FOR A SPIN!

Answer the questions using the information in parentheses.

1. *Di solito, cosa bevi quando ceni?* (vino rosso) _____

_____

2. *Mi prendi in giro?* (dire sul serio) _____

_____

3. *Perché non venite da noi?* (sì, domani pomeriggio) _____

_____

4. *Sai a che ora esce tuo figlio?* (no) _____

_____

5. *Cosa vuole il cliente?* (cambiare camera) _____

_____

6. *Ci vediamo alle nove?* (io, non potere; noi, fare alle dieci) _____

_____

7. *Prendiamo l'autobus, vero?* (sì, dovere comprare i biglietti) _____

_____

8. *Pronto? (potere parlare con Marina)*_____

_____

9. *Mi dica? (noi, volere vedere il menù)*_____

_____

10. *Chi viene alla festa? (la mia fidanzata; anche alcuni suoi amici)*_____

_____

Are you all verbed out? *Non volete vedere mai più i verbi? Non volete nemmeno vedere la "v"* (*Venezia!*) in "verb?" *Non vi interessano né i verbi regolari né i verbi irregolari?* You don't like them *affatto? Vi capisco bene, amici miei,* but it's tough speaking without verbs. *Però, per il momento, non parliamo più dei verbi. Facciamo una pausa* (let's take a break) and let's talk about how to say "no."

• Double negatives

Do you remember how to say "nothing, no one, never . . . ," *niente, nessuno, mai . . .* in Italian? Remember that *non* (not) always goes before the verb, and the other negative goes after it? Good! Now that you have that down, let's take a closer look at *nessuno* (nobody; no one). *Nessuno* is special because it is used without the *non* when it begins the sentence:

Nessuno arriva in orario. = **Non arriva nessuno in orario.**

No one arrives on time.

If you were ambitious in the last lesson and checked out The Fine Print, you may remember that, in addition to being a pronoun meaning "no one," *nessuno* can be an adjective used in front of a singular noun to mean "no, any." When it's used this way, *nessuno,* matches the gender of the noun and follows the same pattern as the indefinite article: *ness-un, ness-un', ness-uno, ness-una.*

Non c'e nessun Gianni qui.

There's no Gianni here.

However, if you're talking about an object that cannot be counted, such as *vino,* you'd use *niente* (nothing) in front of the noun instead.

Qualcosa da bere? Del vino . . . ? —Niente vino, grazie.

Something to drink? Some wine? —No wine, thanks.

Think you can handle that? *Vediamo . . .*

Answer the questions in the negative form.

1.   *Chi viene con noi all'enoteca?* _____

2.   *Cosa c'è da mangiare?* _____

3.   *Prendi la bistecca o il coniglio? (vegetariano)* _____

      _____

4.   *Ti piace giocare a biliardo? (affatto)* _____

      _____

5.   *Prendi sempre l'autobus per andare a scuola?* _____

      _____

6.   *C'è qualche film alla tv stasera?* _____

7.   *Pietro esce ancora con Marina?* _____

8.   *C'è un taxi davanti alla stazione?* _____

9.   *Preferisci guardare la tv o leggere un libro? (non mi piace)* _____

      _____

Basta con la grammatica. Let's get back to to chatting . . .

One of the great things about cell phones is that you can catch someone before they come home and ask them to pick up a few things you need from *il supermercato*. Try to guess some of the things you could find there.

un etto di salame   una bottiglia d'olio   una scatola di pasta   un vasetto di pesto

1.   something you throw in boiling water and cook *al dente* _____

2.   something you put on a piece of *pane* to make *un panino* _____

3.   something you can put on your *insalata* or in your *macchina* _____

4.   something you put on what you cooked in number one _____

So, score one for the *telefonino*, but it has its down side, too. Don't you hate it when you're riding *l'autobus*, and the person next to you gets a call on their *telefonino*, thereby forcing you to just sit there and listen as they a) show off and act important, b) engage in completely meaningless conversation just to pass the time or c) talk to their "honey bun." Well, believe it or not, Italy—cell phone capital of the world (sixty-five percent of the population owns a cell phone)—is no better that way. I guess it just sounds a little better because . . . well . . . it's in Italian.

HEAR . . . SAY 2

Close your eyes and picture yourself on a lovely bus ride through scenic Genova, when—**Trrrrrrrrrillo**—*Selvaggio* strikes again! *Ascoltate* as Nunzio tries to juggle his wife and his *agente di cambio* (stockbroker).

Nunzio:	Sì?
A sua moglie:	Ciao, amore. Cosa c'è? . . . Al supermercato? Vabbe' . . . un etto di salame, una bottiglia d'olio e una scatola di pasta. Sì, te li porto subito . . . Come? Si sente malissimo! . . . I capelli? Non ti piace il taglio? Troppo corti? Ma no, amore, sei bellissima . . . Senti, ho un'altra chiamata. Aspetta un attimo.
A suo agente di cambio:	Sì? Sergio, ciao. Cosa c'è? . . . Caduto? Come? . . . Vendiamo tutto! Sì, sì . . . tutto. Subito! Ciao, ciao.
A se stesso:	(*to himself*) Uffa!
A sua moglie:	(*Trillo Selvaggio again*) Amore, ciao. Ma no. Come ti posso dimenticare? No, no. Mi dispiace . . . È colpa mia. Ma no, i tuoi capelli sono meravigliosi. Sì, un vasetto di pesto. Sì. Ci vediamo fra poco. No, non vado al bar. Te lo giuro . . . Sì, cara. No, cara . . .

Amazing how much you can learn from someone by compulsory eavesdropping! Tell me what you know about our yes-man, Nunzio.

ACTIVITY 8: HOW'S THAT AGAIN?

1. *Chi chiama Nunzio la prima volta?* _____

2. *Cosa deve comprare Nunzio al supermercato?* _____

_____

3. *Chi chiama Nunzio la seconda volta?* _____

4. *Secondo te, cosa succede?* _____

5. *Chi richiama Nunzio?* _____

6. *Qual è il problema della moglie?* _____

Now let's get back to work.

WORKSHOP 2

WORDS TO LIVE BY

Before we leave the world of telephones behind, let's take a look at just a few more useful expressions. If you have a bad connection or find yourself passing through a tunnel while on your *telefonino*, you can say:

Non sento bene.	*I can't hear well.*
Si sente malissimo.	*The connection is really bad.* (**Lit.** *You can hear very badly.*)
Aspetta / Aspetti che richiamo.	*Wait and I'll call back.* (*infml. / fml.*)

Did You Know?

DON'T LEAVE HOME WITHOUT IT: THE UBIQUITOUS CELL PHONES

Nowadays it's hard to find an Italian who would be caught dead without a cell phone. If you're planning on bringing yours over to blend in with the crowd, make sure it's a tri-band because Europe and the United States use different systems. You can also rent a phone and a phone number or buy a pre-paid card for your cell phone. The most popular providers are TIM and Omnitel. You will see their stores all over the place in all major cities. Just walk in and say, *Vorrei comprare una carta prepagata per il mio telefonino* (I'd like to buy a pre-paid phone card for my mobile phone). When you run out of credit, you can buy *una ricarica* (a re-fill) at most Bar-Tabacchi and newsstands. You usually also get fax, voice mail, and e-mail service included in the price of a *carta prepagata*.

You should also be aware that there is no charge for incoming calls on a *telefonino*. This is great if you're the one with the cell phone, but it's not so great if you want to reach a cell phone number from a land line—you'll get charged long-distance rates.

Did you know that Italy has virtually all of the telephone services you're used to in the United States? You can have call waiting service (*una chiamata in attesa*) on your cell phone. If you get another call, simply say:

Aspetta / Aspetti un attimo.	*Wait a second.*
Ho un'altra chiamata.	*I have another call.*
	(*infml. / fml.*)

Did You Know?

But enough of all this high-tech stuff, and let's move to more mundane subjects, like *il supermercato* (the supermarket). Here are some words for various containers, as well as some common items you'll find in the grocery aisle.

DO WE NEED MILK?: SHOPPING AT THE SUPERMARKET

una scatola	box
• *di pasta*	• of pasta
• *di cereali*	• of cereal
• *di biscotti*	• of cookies
un vasetto	jar
• *di sugo al pomodoro*	• of tomato sauce
• *di marmellata*	• of jam
una lattina	can
• *di Coca Cola*	• of Coke
• *di birra*	• of beer

If you're buying *il salame* (salami), *il prosciutto*, *il formaggio*, or another type of cold cut or snack food, you can ask for:

un etto	100 *grams*

If you really want to live *all'italiana* (in the Italian style), you'll keep in mind that Italians are very fashionable, and they make an effort to look stylish even when they're just running out to the *supermercato*. A good *taglio* (haircut) is essential to looking the part.

Vorrei tagliarmi i capelli.	I'd like a haircut.
Vorrei solo una spuntatina.	I'd like just a trim.
Non troppo corti davanti / di dietro.	Not too short in front / in the back.

Finally, here's something you can use with loved ones—phrases you've probably uttered a million times. Why not try it in Italian next time?

È colpa mia.	It's my fault.
Te lo giuro.	I promise.

1.   Call the hairdresser in your hotel, and say you'd like a haircut. _____
_____

2.   Valentino, who thinks of himself as more of an *artista* than *un parrucchiere,* is getting ready to start chopping away at your hair, when you dash his hopes and explain you want just a trim. _____
_____

3.   Your *telefonino* just signaled a call waiting. Tell your friend to hold on a second while you take the other call. _____

4.   A five-year-old's shopping list *da morire*: a jar of Nutella, a box of cookies, six cans of Coke: _____
_____

Heads Up!

If you're talking about a specific measure of something, whether it be its weight or the container it comes in, use *di* without the article. Compare:

Devo comprare <u>del salame</u>.

I have to buy some salami.

Devo comprare <u>un etto di salame</u>.

I have to buy 100 grams of salami.

*Vuoi comprare **dei** biscotti?*

Do you want to buy some cookies?

*Vuoi comprare **una scatola di** biscotti?*

Do you want to buy a box of cookies?

Heads Up!

Back to our grammar review . . .

STRUT YOUR STUFF!

- Saying "some"

Do you remember *come si dice* "some" *in italiano?* The easiest way is just to use the preposition *di*. You can also say *un po' di* (a little bit of) when you're talking about quantities that can't be counted, and *qualche* (some) or *alcuni / alcune* (some) with quantities that can.

But, if you're the type who thinks that "some" is not enough, then you can be more specific with *poco* (a little), *molto* (a lot), *tanto* (much; many), *troppo* (too much; too many). Let's see if you remember *poco* or *molto* . . .

ACTIVITY 10:   TAKE IT FOR A SPIN!

Translate . . .

1.   I'd like some bread. _____

2.   I'd like to see some cell phones. _____

3.   There are so many people! _____

4.   Italy is very beautiful. _____

5.   He says little, but he's very smart. _____

6.   Are there any free rooms? _____

7.   Do you (sing. infml.) want a can of Coke? _____

8.   There are too many tourists in front of the fountain! _____

9.   Some buses arrive late. _____

10.   I know few people in this city. _____

Lo sapevo! (I knew it!) I knew you could do it. Now let's look at object pronouns.

• Direct and indirect object pronouns

The direct and indirect object pronouns in Italian are:

OBJECT PRONOUNS		
	DIRECT	INDIRECT
IO	mi	mi
TU	ti	ti
LEI (FML.)	La	Le
LEI	la	le
LUI	lo	gli
NOI	ci	ci
VOI	vi	vi
LORO	li (m.) le (f.)	gli

Since the object pronouns for the *io, tu, noi,* and *voi* forms are the same, the only ones you really have to try to keep straight are the ones for *lei, lui,* and *loro.* What you do have to remember, however, is that object pronouns go before the verb (e.g. *non **la** sento*) or they can be attached to the end of an infinitive (e.g. *non **la** posso sentire* or *non posso sentir**la***).

ACTIVITY 11:   **TAKE IT FOR A SPIN!**

Rewrite the sentences replacing the underlined object with a pronoun (and be sure to put it in the right place!).

1. *Scrivo una cartolina <u>a Giovanni e Gabriella</u>.* _____

_____

2. *Posso dare <u>il tuo indirizzo</u> a Luca?* _____

_____

3. *Vedete <u>la Colonna di Marco Aurelio</u>?* _____

_____

4. *Di solito prendo <u>un taxi</u> per andare alla stazione.* _____

_____

5. *Io faccio <u>una foto</u>.* _____

_____

6. *Aspetto <u>una chiamata</u> dalle nove e mezzo!* _____

_____

Now answer the questions using the clue in parentheses and an object pronoun.

7. *Mi chiami dopo la cena? (Si)* _____

8. *Ci rispondi domani? (No, la settimana prossima)* _____

9. *Ti posso mandare la foto via e-mail? (Si)* _____

10. *Scusi, che ore sono? (Non sapere)* _____

_____

So what happens when you want to put two object pronouns in a sentence? Good question! Time to learn something new . . .

THE NITTY-GRITTY

GIVE IT TO HIM!: WHEN A SENTENCE HAS TWO PRONOUNS

It's perfectly acceptable to replace both objects in a sentence with pronouns. For example, in English we can say "I'm sending it to him" instead of "I'm sending a postcard to Marco." In Italian you do the same thing. When a direct and an indirect object pronoun appear together in a sentence, the indirect object pronoun comes first, followed by the direct object pronoun. You heard Nunzio using double object pronouns when he said:

Te li porto io.

I'll bring them to you.

Te lo giuro.

I promise you (it).

And Luca, too, when he said:

Sono tutti pazzi qui. Ve lo dico io.

They're all crazy here. I'm telling (it to) you.

Not so bad, right? However, did you notice that the indirect object pronoun changes a little to make things easier to pronounce? You'll mostly be using these combined forms with the direct objects *lo*, *la*, *li*, and *le*. Here they are:

DOUBLE OBJECT PRONOUNS				
	+LO	**+LA**	**+LI**	**+LE**
M I	me lo	me la	me li	me le
T I	te lo	te la	te li	te le
L E	glielo	gliela	glieli	gliele
G L I	glielo	gliela	glieli	gliele
C I	ce lo	ce la	ce li	ce le
V I	ve lo	ve la	ve li	ve le
G L I	glielo	gliela	glieli	gliele

Take a Tip from Me!

Notice that the change in the indirect object pronoun is merely a change from *–i* to *–e*. The biggest difference is that *le* and *gli* both take the form *glie* before a direct object pronoun. Don't forget that *La* is capitalized when it means "you (fml.)."

Take a Tip from Me!

Like single object pronouns, double object pronouns can either come before the verb or be attached to an infinitive. Let's see how it works. The sentence:

> **Do il mio numero a Marco.**

> I'm giving my number to Marco.

Becomes:

> **Glielo do.**

> I'm giving it (*lo*) to him (*glie*).

Likewise:

> **Potete mandare una e-mail a Ada?**

> Can you send an e-mail to Ada?

Becomes:

> **Gliela potete mandare?** or **Potete mandargliela?**

> Can you send it to her?

Take a Tip from Me!

Notice that in English, we often omit one of the pronouns, usually the direct object pronoun. So, *ve lo dico io* literally means "I'm telling you it" but we say simply "I'm telling you." *Te lo giuro* means "I promise you it," but we just say "I promise (you)," and leave out the "it." Ready to try your hand at this?

Take a Tip from Me!

ACTIVITY 12: TAKE IT FOR A SPIN

Rewrite the sentences using double object pronouns.

1. *Scrivo una cartolina a Giovanni e Gabriella.* _____

2. *Posso dare il tuo indirizzo a Luca?* _____

3. *Faccio una foto per voi.* _____

4. *Ti mando la foto via e-mail.* _____

5. *Mi può dire l'ora?* _____

6. *Ci può mostrare la camera?* _____

7. *Le porto subito una forchetta.* _____

8. *Posso lasciare un messagio per lei?* _____

Adesso basta con la grammatica! Ve lo giuro!

LET'S PUT IT IN WRITING

Look at this page from a phone book listing of emergency numbers.

NUMERI DI EMERGENZA E DI UTILITÀ

Pronto Intervento

	CORSO PUBBLICO DI EMERGENZA	113
	CARABINIERI	112
	VIGILI DEL FUOCO	115
	EMERGENZA SANITARIA	118

Numeri d'Utilità

	SOCCORSO STRADALE (AUTOMOBILE CLUB D'ITALIA)	116
	TELEFONO AZZURRO (LINEA GRATUITA PER BAMBINI)	1.96.96
	ORA ESATTA	161
	SVEGLIA AUTOMATICA	114
	INFORMAZIONI ELENCO ABBONATI	12

ACTIVITY 13: TAKE IT FOR A SPIN

Which number would you dial in the following situations?

1. *Fuoco!* (Fire!) _____

2. Your concierge is Gianfranco from the Palazzo Bellini and you need a wake-up call in the morning. _____

3. You want to dial 911. _____

4. Your new rental car just broke down. _____

5. You've had something stolen and want to file a police report. _____

6. You think your high school sweetheart moved to Florence, and you want to look him / her up when you get there. _____

7. You're having a nice romantic dinner, when the guy at the next table appears to be having a heart attack. _____

8. You look at your watch and realize it's still on American time. *"Che ore sono?"* you wonder. _____

CRIB NOTES

HEAR . . . SAY 1

Alfredo:	Hello?
Luca:	Gianni, hi! It's me, Luca. Listen, do you want to come with me to Lidia's? The party starts at ten.
Alfredo:	It's already a quarter to eleven.
Luca:	No one arrives on time, you know.
Alfredo:	I'm sorry, you have the wrong number.
Luca:	Come on! We have to leave soon . . .
Alfredo:	I like parties, but I'm not Gianni.
Luca:	Well then, who's this (*Lit.* with whom am I speaking)?
Alfredo:	It's Alfredo.
Luca:	But where's Gianni? I have to talk to him.
Alfredo:	I really don't know. What number do you want?

Luca:	055-26-82-218. But I don't have time for this.
Alfredo:	Sir, you have the wrong number. You can try again.
Luca:	Okay, okay. Can I leave a message for him?
Alfredo:	Sir, I repeat: there's no Gianni here!
Luca:	Do you know when he'll be back?
Alfredo:	Please, leave me alone (*Lit.* leave me in peace)!
Luca:	Alfredo, I don't like your tone at all. I see no reason to get angry.
Alfredo:	(Click.)
Luca:	Gianni? Alfredo? . . . But where are they? There's no one there . . . They're all crazy here, I'm telling you (*Lit.* I tell you it)!

HEAR . . . SAY 2

Nunzio:	Yes?
To his wife:	Hi, love. What's up? . . . To the supermarket? Okay . . . a bit (*Lit.* 100 grams) of salami, a bottle of oil and a box of pasta. Yes, I'll bring them to you right away . . . What? We have a bad connection. (*Lit.* You can hear very badly) . . . Your hair? You don't like the cut? Too short? No, love, you're beautiful . . . Listen, I have another call. Hold on a second.

To his stockbroker:	Yes? Sergio, hi. What's wrong? . . . Fell? What? . . . Let's sell everything! Yes, yes . . . everything. Now! Bye, bye.
To himself:	Ufffff.
To his wife:	Love, hi! No! How could I forget you? No, no. I'm sorry . . . It's my fault. No, your hair is marvelous. Yes, a jar of pesto sauce. Yes. See you soon. No, I'm not going to the café. I promise. Yes, dear. No, dear . . .

ANSWER KEY

ACTIVITY 1

1. a; 2. f; 3. e; 4. c; 5. d;
6. b

ACTIVITY 2

1. *vero*; 2. *falso (La festa comincia alle dieci.)*;
3. *vero*; 4. *falso*; 5. *falso*; 6. *vero*

ACTIVITY 3

1. —*Pronto?*
   —*Buon giorno. Vorrei parlare con il Signor Tozzi.*
   —*Chi parla?*
   —*Sono Alessandra.*
   —*Un attimo. Glielo passo subito.*
2. —*Sì?*
   —*Sono Lorenzo. C'è Laura?*
   —*In questo momento non c'è.*
   —*Grazie. Richiamo più tardi.*
   —*Sì, certo.*
3. —*Ciao, Roberto! Sono io.*
   —*Ha sbagliato numero.*
   —*Mi dispiace. Provo di nuovo.*

ACTIVITY 4

1. *Come secondo prendo il coniglio.*
2. *Se insisti.*
3. *Non (lo) so. Chiediamo.*
4. *Partono per l'Italia sabato, dieci agosto.*
5. *No, non mi piace affatto la camera al quinto piano.*
6. *Offro io!*
7. *I miei parenti preferiscono fare un po' di shopping,*
8. *No, non crediamo alla leggenda della Fontana di Trevi.*
9. *Ecco il giornale. Vediamo cosa c'è.*
10. *Il film all'Odeon finisce alle dieci e mezzo / alle ventidue e trenta.*

ACTIVITY 5

1. *Di solito, bevo vino rosso con la cena.*
2. *No, dico sul serio.*
3. *Sì, veniamo da voi domani pomeriggio.*
4. *No, non so a che ora esce mio figlio. Or more naturally: Non lo so.*
5. *Il cliente vuole cambiare camera.*
6. *Alle nove non posso; facciamo alle dieci.*
7. *Sì, prendiamo l'autobus. Dobbiamo comprare i biglietti.*
8. *Posso parlare con Marina?*
9. *Vogliamo vedere il menù.*
10. *La mia fidanzata viene alla festa; vengono anche alcuni suoi amici.*

ACTIVITY 6

1. *Non viene nessuno con noi all'enoteca. / Nessuno viene con noi all'enoteca.*
2. *Non c'è niente da mangiare.*
3. *Non prendo né la bistecca né il coniglio. Sono vegetariano / a.*
4. *Non mi piace affatto giocare a biliardo.*
5. *Non prendo mai l'autobus per andare a scuola.*
6. *Non c'è nessun film alla tv stasera.*
7. *No, Pietro non esce più con Marina.*
8. *Non c'è nessun taxi davanti alla stazione.*

9. *Non mi piace né guardare la tv né leggere un libro.*

Or, if you want to sound more natural, you can make some of your answers short (and sweet):
1. *Non viene nessuno.*
2. *Non c'è niente.*
4. *No, non mi piace affatto.*
5. *No, non lo prendo mai.*

ACTIVITY 7

1. *una scatola di pasta;*   2. *un etto di salame;*
3. *una bottiglia d'olio;*   4. *un vasetto di pesto*

ACTIVITY 8

1. *Sua moglie chiama Nunzio la prima volta.* Nunzio's wife calls the first time.
2. *Nunzio deve comprare una scatola di pasta, un etto di salame, una bottiglia d'olio e un vasetto di pesto al supermercato.* Nunzio has to buy a box of pasta, a bit of salami, a bottle of oil, and a jar of pesto sauce.
3. *Il suo agente di cambio (stockbroker) chiama Nunzio la seconda volta.* Nunzio's stockbroker calls the seond tme.
4. *Il prezzo delle azioni è caduto.* Nunzio's stocks crashed.
5. *Sua moglie richiama Nunzio. Or more naturally: Sua moglie lo richiama.* Nunzio's wife calls again. / His wife calls him again.
6. *Non le piace il suo taglio—i suoi capelli sono troppo corti.* She doesn't like her haircut—her hair is too short.

ACTIVITY 9

1. *Vorrei tagliarmi i capelli.*
2. *Vorrei solo una spuntatina.*
3. *Aspetta un attimo. Ho un'altra chiamata.*
4. *Un vasetto di Nutella, una scatola di biscotti, sei lattine di Coca Cola*

ACTIVITY 10

1. *Vorrei un po' di pane / del pane.*
2. *Vorrei vedere dei telefonini / qualche telefonino / alcuni telefonini.*
3. *C'è tanta gente!*
4. *L'Italia è molto bella / bellissima.*
5. *Dice poco, ma è molto intelligente.*
6. *Ci sono delle camere libere? / alcune camere libere? / C'è qualche camera libera?*
7. *Vuoi una lattina di Coca Cola?*
8. *Ci sono troppi turisti davanti alla fontana!*
9. *Alcuni autobus arrivano in ritardo. / Qualche autobus arriva in ritardo.*
10. *Conosco poche persone in questa città. / Conosco poca gente in questa città.*

ACTIVITY 11

1. *Gli scrivo una cartolina.*
2. *Lo posso dare a Luca?*
3. *La vedete?*
4. *Di solito lo prendo per andare alla stazione.*
5. *Io la faccio.*
6. *L'aspetto dalle nove e mezza!*
7. *Sì, ti chiamo dopo cena.*
8. *No. Vi rispondo la settimana prossima.*
9. *Sì, mi puoi mandare / puoi mandarmi la foto via e-mail.*
10. *No, non lo so.*

ACTIVITY 12

1. *Gliela scrivo.*
2. *Glielo posso dare? / Posso darglielo?*
3. *Ve la faccio.*
4. *Te la mando via e-mail.*
5. *Me la può dire? / Può dirmela?*
6. *Ce la può mostrare? / Può mostrarcela?*
7. *Gliela porto subito.*
8. *Glielo posso lasciare. / Posso lasciarglielo.*

ACTIVITY 13

1. 115; 2. 114; 3. 113; 4. 116;
5. 112; 6. 12; 7. 118. 8. 161

11.

BLAME IT ON THE GOVERNMENT!

Piove, governo ladro!

(*Lit.* It's raining, you thief of a government!)

I don't believe it!

COMING UP...

- *Extra! Extra! Read all about it!*: Discussing current events
- *Frankly, my dear . . .* : Expressing your opinion
- *Brace yourself*: Verbs used with pronouns like *myself, yourself, himself,* etc.
- *Verily I do*: Adverbs ending in *–mente*
- *What's done is done*: Talking about the past with the *passato prossimo*

Pronto? Pronto? . . . Si sente malissimo! . . . Sono Ana. Vorrei parlare con i miei studenti. Ci sono? . . . Come? . . . Ho sbagliato numero? . . . No? Allora, me li passa? . . . Sì, sì, aspetto in linea. Grazie mille . . . Well, I thought I'd never get through to you! I must admit I'm not a big fan of telephones. Anyway, now that we're all here, we can let *Trillo Selvaggio* trill away somewhere else. All that *rumore* (noise) makes me want to do something quiet . . . like *leggere il giornale* (read a newspaper). There are few habits I enjoy more than to *sfogliare il giornale* (leafing through the paper), coffee cup in hand, and discussing *le attualità* (current events) or the results of the latest *sondaggio* (opinion poll). *A proposito* (by the way), did you know that, according to a recent survey, Italian fathers dedicate an average of twenty-two minutes a day to their children? Fascinating stuff! But here I am getting carried away with *le notizie* (news) when there's work to be done!

ACTIVITY 1: LET'S WARM UP

Well, now that you have two-thirds of this book under your belt—*Congratulazioni!*—I've decided to challenge you a little. It's just a matching exercise, but this time the phrases and their meanings are in Italian. *In bocca al lupo!*

1. *Non riesco a crederci!*
2. *il diritto di voto*
3. *rendersi conto*
4. *il sindaco*
5. *una cosa da poco*
6. *cambiare tema*

a. *caratteristica di una democrazia*
b. *qualcosa che non è importante*
c. *parlare di un'altra cosa*
d. *Non lo credo!*
e. *sapere una cosa*
f. *la persona più importante di una città*

HEAR...SAY 1

It's a typical morning at the Ciociolas' home. Husband and wife are enjoying a leisurely Sunday breakfast, relaxing with the paper, and exchanging views on what they read. The wife is surprised by one article in particular.

La moglie: Non riesco a crederci!
Il marito: Cosa?

La moglie:	Hai visto il giornale oggi?
Il marito:	Sì, perchè?
La moglie:	Pensano di dare il diritto di voto ai sedicenni.
Il marito:	E tu ti preoccupi? Non sei d'accordo?
La moglie:	Sicuramente no! A sedici anni non hanno imparato ancora niente!
Il marito:	Il mondo resta ai giovani. Infatti, oggi la vita va più in fretta. Oggigiorno i giovani crescono velocemente. Sanno molto più di noi alla loro età.
La moglie:	Sì, ma sono meno maturi e più materialisti. Non si interessano affatto di politica.
Il marito:	Se mi ricordo bene, il giornalista ha parlato con alcuni giovani e loro si rendono conto che il voto è una grande responsabilità.
La moglie:	Allora, non ti ricordi bene cos'ha scritto. Molti giovani hanno detto che non si sentono pronti.
Il marito:	Ma perché ti arrabbi così facilmente? Si tratta solo delle elezioni locali, giusto?
La moglie:	Allora, questo significa che per te l'elezione del sindaco è una cosa da poco?
Il marito:	Certo che non è una cosa da poco, ma . . . Senti, perché non cambiamo tema?

ACTIVITY 2: HOW'S THAT AGAIN?

Vero o falso?

		VERO	FALSO
1.	*Secondo il giornale, i giovani di sedici anni possono già votare.*	_____	_____
2.	*La moglie è d'accordo con la proposta di dare il diritto di voto ai sedicenni.*	_____	_____
3.	*Secondo il giornale, i giovani sanno che il diritto di voto è una grande responsabilità*	_____	_____
4.	*Molti giovani sono pronti per votare.*	_____	_____
5.	*Il marito è d'accordo che l'elezione del sindaco è importante.*	_____	_____

Did You Know?

WORKSHOP 1

WORDS TO LIVE BY

EXTRA! EXTRA! READ ALL ABOUT IT!: DISCUSSING CURRENT EVENTS

As you may or may not know, the Italian political system is very dynamic, with governments sometimes changing faster than you can say *presto.* And *anche se* (even if) *oggigiorno la vita va più in fretta* (nowadays life moves more quickly), *la politica non è una cosa da poco* (politics is no small thing). In Italy, it's a popular subject of discussion, and not something reserved solely for *un / una giornalista* (a journalist). So, it can't hurt for you to know some basic words having to do with *la politica*:

il **diritto di voto**	*the right to vote*
le **elezioni**	*elections (fem. pl.)*
il **candidato**	*candidate*
il **sindaco**	*mayor*
il **capo dello stato**	*the head of state*

Naturalmente (naturally), life and politics are intertwined, and there are many factors that affect how someone feels about a certain *tema* "subject (m.; *temi,* m.pl.)," or *candidato.* Many of the words you use to talk about a *candidato* are similar to ones we use in English:

maturo	mature	**immaturo**	immature
materialista	materialist	**idealista**	idealist
competente	competent	**incompetente**	incompetent

Here are some ways to express how you feel about a particular *tema*:

sentirsi	to feel
preoccuparsi di	to worry about
arrabbiarsi	to get mad
interessarsi di	to be interested in
ricordarsi	to remember
rendersi conto	to realize
trattarsi di	to be about

Or you can simply fall back on:

Sono d'accordo.	I agree.
Non sono d'accordo.	I don't agree.

If you truly don't know what to say, you can always go with:

Non riesco a crederci!	I can't believe it! (Lit. I don't succeed in believing it!)

Another perennially interesting topic of debate is the relationship between *i giovani* (the young) and *i vecchi* (the old). How many times have you heard a sentence begin with *alla loro età . . .* (at their age . . .)? We all know about our *nonni* who walked ten miles to school, barefoot in knee-deep snow! But, as they say all over the world:

Il mondo resta ai giovani.	The world belongs to the young. (Lit. The world is left to the young.)

Before we go and *cambiare tema* (change the subject), *facciamo un esercizio.*

ACTIVITY 3:   TAKE IT FOR A SPIN

What would you say?

1. Your cubicle-mate just won $1,000 dollars on a scratch-off lottery ticket. Hey, that's no small thing: _____

2. Your friend complains that she has too many obligations, that she's constantly running around like a chicken with its head chopped off. Life moves faster nowadays: _____

3. One of the most important moments in the feminist struggle was when women won the right to be heard and participate in elections. What did they earn? _____

_____

4. The new kid on the block gets **your** promotion. You can't believe it! _____

_____

5. Your roommate wants to move some stuff out of his cramped room into the living room. Do you agree or not? _____

Now, like I promised, *cambiamo tema.*

THE NITTY-GRITTY

BRACE YOURSELF: VERBS USED WITH PRONOUNS LIKE MYSELF, YOURSELF, HIMSELF, ETC.

There are certain verbs in Italian that are called reflexive because the action "reflects" back on the subject. Sometimes this makes sense, as in *vestirsi* (to get dressed), which implies putting clothes on oneself. But more often than not, this is merely a grammatical convention, and the verbs we use in English have no "reflexive" meaning. Most of the reflexive verbs you've heard in this lesson fall into the latter category: *interessarsi* (to be interested), *ricordarsi* (to remember), *arrabbiarsi* (to get angry), etc. In fact, you've already been using some of them in expressions like *mi chiamo* and *mi sento.*

Reflexive verbs always end in *–si* in the infinitive. They form their present tense just like regular verbs, but they are preceded by a reflexive pronoun that matches the subject. Here are the reflexive pronouns:

REFLEXIVE PRONOUNS			
myself	*mi*	ourselves	*ci*
yourself	*ti*	yourselves	*vi*
himself / herself / itself; yourself, fml.	*si*	themselves	*si*

Let's see how it works with *divertirsi* (to have fun [*Lit.* to amuse oneself]). *Divertiamoci con divertirsi!*

DIVERTIRSI (TO HAVE FUN) IN THE PRESENT TENSE			
IO	*mi diverto*	NOI	*ci divertiamo*
TU	*ti diverti*	VOI	*vi divertite*
LUI / LEI	*si diverte*	LORO	*si divertono*

Vi ricordate qualche verbo riflessivo nel dialogo? If not, *non vi preoccupate*, here are a few:

E tu ti preoccupi?

And you're worried?

Non si interessano affatto di politica.

They're not at all interested in politics.

Se mi ricordo bene . . .

If I remember well . . .

Ma perché ti arrabbi così facilmente?

But why do you get angry so easily?

Loro si rendono conto che il voto è una grande responsabilità.

They realize that voting is a big responsibility.

Take a Tip from Me!

As you can see, the only trick to use with reflexive verbs is to remember to use the reflexive pronouns, which, I might add, are virtually identical to the direct and indirect object pronouns—the only one that's different is *si*.

Take a Tip from Me!

Other useful reflexive verbs are: *lamentarsi* (to complain), *dimenticarsi* (to forget), *addormentarsi* (to fall asleep), *svegliarsi* (to wake up), *alzarsi* (to get up), and *lavarsi* (to wash).

Allora, non ti ricordi bene cos'ha scritto.

Then you don't remember well what he wrote.

Ti lamenti sempre quando perde il tuo candidato.

You always complain when your candidate loses.

Non dimenticatevi mai di dire "buona notte" prima di andare a letto.

Never forget to say "good night" before going to bed.

ACTIVITY 4: TAKE IT FOR A SPIN

Answer in complete sentences using the clues in parentheses. *Non dimenticatevi i pronomi riflessivi!* (Don't forget your reflexive pronouns!)

1. *T'interessi di politica? (non molto)* _____

    _____

2. *Vi ricordate Pietro, il macellaio? (sì)* _____

_____

3. *Si dimentica sempre di chiamare quando è in ritardo? (sì)* _____

_____

4. *Perché si lamentano? (perché non gli piace la camera)* _____

_____

5. *Vi divertite in Internet? (sì)* _____

_____

6. *Come ti senti oggi? (non bene)* _____

_____

7. *Di solito a che ora si sveglia? (alle sette)* _____

_____

8. *Come si chiama quel tipo nella classe di marketing? (Enzo)* _____

_____

9. *Ti arrabbi quando senti Trillo Selvaggio? (sì, sempre)* _____

_____

10. *È vero che vi addormentate quando fate la grammatica? (no)* _____

_____

If your truthful answer to that last question would have started with *sì*, then **svegliatevi**! We've still got some work to do, but this part's easy. *Ve lo giuro.*

VERILY I DO: ADVERBS ENDING IN –MENTE

As you might imagine, adverbs can describe how an action is performed. In English, we form them by adding –ly to the end of an adjective, as in quick → quickly, slow → slowly, true → truly, easy → easily. In Italian, instead of –ly, you add –mente. *Un gioco da ragazzi, vero?* The only thing you have to remember is to use the **feminine** form of the adjective. Take, for example, the adjective *sicuro* (sure). Its feminine form is *sicura*. Just add –mente, and you get *sicuramente* (surely). If an adjective ends in –e, it's even easier—just add –mente: *veloce* + mente = *velocemente* (quickly).

Oggigiorno, i giovani crescono velocemente.

Nowadays, the young grow up quickly.

Sicuramente, no!

Certainly not! (*Lit.* Surely no!)

Heads Up!

Ready to try your hand at it?

TAKE IT FOR A SPIN

Make adverbs out of these adjectives.

1. *intelligente* _____
2. *gentile* _____
3. *libero* _____
4. *vero* _____
5. *completo* _____
6. *silenzioso* _____
7. *sicuro* _____
8. *felice* _____
9. *serio* _____
10. *facile* _____

Now let's see if things have calmed down in the Ciociola household . . .

LET'S WARM UP

Did you notice some verbs that looked familiar in the first dialogue, but you weren't quite sure if they were the same ones you saw in previous lessons? If so, you're on the ball. Yes, they **are** the same verbs, but they're in the past tense, which is why they look different. You'll find more of them in the dialogue coming up. Try to match the past participle with its infintive . . .

1.	*sentito*	a.	*dire*
2.	*letto*	b.	*fare*
3.	*lasciato*	c.	*imparare*
4.	*detto*	d.	*lasciare*
5.	*fatto*	e.	*leggere*

6.	*portato*	f.	*portare*
7.	*visto*	g.	*ripetere*
8.	*imparato*	h.	*sentire*
9.	*ripetuto*	i.	*vedere*

HEAR ... SAY 2

The morning progresses without casualties, Mrs. Ciociola continues reading the paper, and Mr. Ciociola turns on the TV, when a commercial he sees reminds him . . .

Il marito: A proposito, cos'hai fatto con il mio nuovo vestito? Non so dov'è. Come mi vesto per il lavoro domani?

La moglie: L'ho portato in tintoria . . . Oddio!

Il marito: Cosa c'è? Hai perso il tagliando?

La moglie: "Alluvioni in Lombardia. Una dozzina di persone ha lasciato le loro case . . ."

Il marito: Che disastro!

La moglie: Adesso paghiamo perché abbiamo consumato troppo.

Il marito: Francamente, non mi va di discutere sul clima. C'è qualcosa di meno pesante nel giornale?

La moglie: Sì! Hanno fatto un sondaggio sulla domenica senza traffico.

Il marito: E?

La moglie: Piace a quasi tutti.

Il marito: La gente ha detto che il traffico è il nemico numero uno, più della criminalità . . .

La moglie: Figurati! Dove l'hai sentito dire?

Il marito: L'ho letto nel giornale il mese scorso.

La moglie: Hmm. Non l'ho notato. Ah, ecco una cosa leggera—abbiamo vinto al calcio.

Il marito: Leggera? Ma cosa dici? Il calcio è una cosa molto seria!

ACTIVITY 7: HOW'S THAT AGAIN?

Vero o falso?

		VERO	FALSO
1.	*Il marito vuole discutere temi pesanti.*	_____	_____
2.	*La moglie si preoccupa delle alluvioni in Lombardia.*	_____	_____

3. *Secondo il giornale, la criminalità è più importante per gli Italiani del traffico.* _____ _____

4. *La domenica senza traffico è il nemico numero uno.* _____ _____

5. *Il marito non s'interessa molto di calcio.* _____ _____

Did You Know?

HONK! HONK!: TRAFFIC PROBLEMS AND SOLUTIONS

Traffic truly is a tremendous problem in Italy, largely due to the fact that, while the population has grown and technology has advanced, its city centers have changed very little over the centuries. The result is a lot of people with a lot of cars and *tanti motorini* on narrow streets constructed when cars couldn't even be imagined. The danger is not only road rage, but polluted air which damages both people's health and historic monuments. Various remedies are employed to combat the problem. In Florence and Parma, for example, cars are banned from the historic center. Another solution with popular support all over the country is *la domenica senza traffico* (Sunday without traffic), whereby traffic is banned on the first Sunday of every month.

WORKSHOP 2

WORDS TO LIVE BY

EXTRA! EXTRA! READ ALL ABOUT IT!: DISCUSSING CURRENT EVENTS

Sfortunatamente (unfortunately), when you open a newspaper, you're likely to come across at least *una dozzina di* (a dozen) *articoli* (articles) on topics that are, to say the least, *pesanti* (heavy):

il **disastro**	*disaster*
l'**alluvione**	*flood (fem.)*
il **fuoco**	*fire*
il **terremoto**	*earthquake*
la **criminalità**	*crime*
la **guerra**	*war*
il **nemico**	*enemy*

Word on the Street

Che disastro! is one of those phrases you can get a lot of mileage out of. It can have a rather literal meaning, as was the case in this dialogue, or you can use it whenever you'd use "What a disaster!" in English. *Disastro* can also be used to refer to a person who is a mess, the way we would say "she's a walking disaster."

On the other hand, you can also read about something *meno serio* (less serious), *leggero* (light), even:

il traffico	traffic
il sondaggio	opinion poll
la cronaca mondana	gossip column
le previsioni del tempo	weather forecast (fem. pl.)
il clima	climate (masc.)
i fumetti	comics (masc. pl.)

FRANKLY, MY DEAR . . . : EXPRESSING YOUR OPINION

Either way, *il giornale* is sure to give you plenty of material to *discutere*. Should you get into a heated discussion, here are some phrases to help you connect your arguments:

a proposito	by the way
anche se	even if
francamente	frankly
sinceramente	honestly; sincerely
sicuramente	certainly; definitely

Heads Up!

Notice that in Italian "to discuss something" is to *discutere su* qualcosa.
Notice, too, that *su* combines with definite articles as follows:

su + il = sul	*su + i = sui*
su + la = sulla	*su + le = sulle*
su + l' = sull'	*su + gli = sugli*

Note that *discutere di* is also common.

Heads Up!

If you're not in the mood for political debates, you can always focus on more mundane subjects, like the dry cleaning.

la tintoria	*dry cleaner*
il tagliando	*receipt*
il vestito	*suit or dress*

Word on the Street!

Figurati! comes from the reflexive verb (*che coincidenza!*) *figurarsi,* meaning "to imagine." It can be used to show surprise, as in "Imagine that!" You can also use it as a response when someone asks for permission to do something, as in "of course, don't even think about it!"

ACTIVITY 8:   **TAKE IT FOR A SPIN!**

Fill in the blanks using the choices provided.

> *Figurati!*　　*A proposito*　　*in tintoria*　　*pesanti*　　*discutere*

1. *Queste valigie sono troppo _____. Non le posso portare.*
2. *_____, cosa pensi della domenica senza traffico?*
3. *Devo portare questo vestito _____.*
4. *Ti dispiace se apro la finestra? _____*
5. *Mi piace _____ sulle attualità.*

THE NITTY-GRITTY

WHAT'S DONE IS DONE: **TALKING ABOUT THE PAST WITH THE PASSATO PROSSIMO**

You already know that many of the verbs you heard in the dialogue were in the past tense, specifically in the *passato prossimo.* Since you did an exercise on this already, you know that you need the past participle of a verb (e.g., "taken, walked, gone," etc.) to put it in the past tense. The only other thing you need is the verb *avere* (to have), which you should be able to recite in your sleep at this point. So, the *passato prossimo* = *avere* + past participle.

How do you form a past participle in Italian, you must be wondering? It's not that hard: just take the infinitive of a verb, drop the *–are, –ere,* or *–ire* ending, and add the following endings:

–ato (for –are verbs)	**parl– + ato = parlato**
–uto (for –ere verbs)	**ripet– + uto = ripetuto**
–ito (for –ire verbs)	**sent– + ito = sentito**

Now you try it.

TAKE IT FOR A SPIN

Give the past participle of the following verbs:

1. *capire*_____

2. *studiare*_____

3. *sapere*_____

4. *parlare*_____

5. *lavorare*_____

6. *finire*_____

7. *portare*_____

8. *credere*_____

9. *suggerire*_____

10. *avere*_____

The Fine Print

The great thing about learning how to make a past participle is that you can use them all as adjectives. For example: *un lavoro finito* (a finished job), and *un giro organizzato* (an organized tour).

When you put the present tense of *avere* together with these past participles, you can talk about the past. Remember when *la moglie* says:

Adesso paghiamo perché abbiamo consumato troppo.

We're paying now because we've consumed too much.

Dove l'hai sentito dire?

Where did you hear that (spoken)?

THE PAST TENSE (*PASSATO PROSSIMO*) WITH *AVERE*

	PARLARE (TO SPEAK)	RIPETERE (TO REPEAT)	SENTIRE (TO HEAR)
IO	ho parlato	ho ripetuto	ho sentito
TU	hai parlato	hai ripetuto	hai sentito
LUI / LEI	ha parlato	ha ripetuto	ha sentito
NOI	abbiamo parlato	abbiamo ripetuto	abbiamo sentito
VOI	avete parlato	avete ripetuto	avete sentito
LORO	hanno parlato	hanno ripetuto	hanno sentito

Note, too, that *avere* itself also forms the *passato prossimo* with *avere*: *ho avuto, hai avuto*, etc.

Heads Up!

When you use an object pronoun with the *passato prossimo*, it goes before *avere*.

Ho portato _il vestito_ in tintoria. → _L'ho portato_ in tintoria.

I took the suit to the dry cleaner. → I took it to the dry cleaner.

By the way, if you're really ambitious, you should know that when a direct object pronoun is used with the *passato prossimo*, the past participle acts as an adjective and agrees in gender and number with the object. In the above example, *il vestito→lo*, happens to be masculine, so there's no change, but if we were talking about *la gonna* (the skirt), the sentence would read: *ho portato <u>la gonna</u> in tintoria → <u>l'ho portata</u> in tintoria.*

Okay, let's go for it.

ACTIVITY 10: **TAKE IT FOR A SPIN**

Answer the questions using the *passato prossimo* and "*Sì, . . . ieri.*" For more practice (and challenge!), try using object pronouns in your answer, instead of repeating each element, much as you would in English.

1.   *Hai mandato una cartolina a Massimo?* _____

2.   *Avete parlato con Giovanna?* _____

3.   *Hanno finito il lavoro?* _____

4.   *Ha lasciato un messaggio per me?* _____

5.   *Ti ho portato le foto?* _____

6.   *Hai sentito questa canzone?* _____

7. Hanno ripetuto il giro? _____

8. Avete mangiato la bistecca? _____

9. Ha cambiato camera? _____

10. Hai chiamato il taxi? _____

That wasn't so bad, right? Brace yourselves! There is such a thing as an **irregular** past participle, and those you'll just have to memorize. The good news (or the bad news, depending on how you look at it) is that many common verbs have irregular past participles, so you'll have plenty of occasions to practice them.

IRREGULAR PAST PARTICIPLES

VERB	PAST PARTICIPLE	VERB	PAST PARTICIPLE
fare (to do)	fatto	dire (to say)	detto
scrivere (to write)	scritto	leggere (to read)	letto
vedere (to see)	visto	decidere (to decide)	deciso
chiedere (to ask)	chiesto	prendere (to take)	preso
aprire (to open)	aperto	chiudere (to close)	chiuso
vincere (to win)	vinto	perdere (to lose)	perso
conoscere (to know)	conosciuto	bere (to drink)	bevuto

Take a Tip from Me!

There are many ways to make remembering new words easier: Try to use them as much as you can, use your flash cards, and look for patterns that can help you remember the words in groups. For example, notice that many verbs that end in –dere (*decidere, prendere, chiudere, perdere*) have past participle ending in –so (*deciso, preso, chiuso, perso*). Then there's the group of verbs whose participle ends in –tto, so try to remember these together: *fatto—detto—scritto—letto*. Note also that *conosciuto* isn't truly irregular—there's just an "i" inserted before the ending to retain the soft *sh* sound.

Abbiamo fatto un buon lavoro! Adesso, facciamo un esercizio!

ACTIVITY 11:   TAKE IT FOR A SPIN

Fill in the blanks with the *passato prossimo* of the verbs in parentheses.

1. _____ l'articolo sul terremoto in India? (tu, leggere)

2. _____ quel film? Cosa ne pensate? (voi, vedere)

3. _____ Marina. È molto simpatica. (noi, conoscere)

4. _____ cos'è il coniglio e mi _____
   che è un piatto vegetariano. (io, chiedere; loro, dire) —Figurati!

5. _____ una passeggiata prima di andare a letto. (noi, fare)

6. Mi dispiace, _____ il museo. (loro, chiudere)

7. Chi _____? (vincere)

8. Non mi _____. _____ tutto il
   gruppo. (loro, seguire; io, perdere)

9. Non riesco a crederci! Mario _____ due bottiglie di vino.
   (bere)

10. _____ solo un caffè. Te lo giuro! (prendere)

LET'S PUT IT IN WRITING

A census report and survey conducted by the Italian National Institute of Statistics (ISTAT) in the year 2000 paint an interesting picture of Italians:

L'Italia in Cifre

Spendono 17 500 000 000 euro alla cura del corpo

24,5% fuma

29,8 è l'età quando hanno il primo figlio

60% dei ragazzi in quinta classe usa un profumo

48,3% delle famiglie italiane ha un telefonino

23% delle famiglie italiane ha un computer

8 su 10 italiani mangiano il pranzo a casa

Gli Italiani Hanno Paura di...

Rimanere senza lavoro	49,6%
Criminalità organizzata	42,5%
Immigrazione	31,2%
Droga	27,9%
Traffico urbano	17,8%

Heads Up!

When you're giving statistics in percentages, the verb should be singular, not plural, e.g., *24,5% fuma* (24.5% smoke).

Heads Up!

ACTIVITY 12: TAKE IT FOR A SPIN

Vero o falso?

		VERO	FALSO
1.	*Uno su quattro italiani fumano.*	_____	_____
2.	*Gli italiani diventano genitori molto giovani.*	_____	_____
3.	*Uno su due famiglie italiane ha un computer.*	_____	_____
4.	*Gli italiani hanno paura dell'immigrazione più che della criminalità organizzata.*	_____	_____
5.	*Il fast food è molto popolare in Italia.*	_____	_____
6.	*Il traffico è il problema più grande in Italia.*	_____	_____

Guess what! *Abbiamo finito la lezione! Alla prossima!* Until next time! *Ciao, ciao!*

HEAR ... SAY 1

Wife:	I don't believe it! (*Lit.* I don't succeed in believing it!)
Husband:	What?
Wife:	Did you see the newspaper today?
Husband:	Yes, why?
Wife:	They're thinking of giving the right to vote to sixteen-year-olds.
Husband:	And you're worried? You don't agree?
Wife:	Certainly not! At sixteen, they haven't learned anything yet.
Husband:	The world is left to the young. Also, today life moves more quickly. Nowadays, the young grow up fast. They know a lot more that we did at their age.
Wife:	Yes, but they're less mature and more materialistic. They're not at all interested in politics.
Husband:	If I remember well, the journalist spoke to some young people and they realize that the vote is a big responsibility.
Wife:	Then you don't remember well what he wrote. Many young people said they don't feel ready yet.
Husband:	But why do you get mad so easily? It's only about local elections, right?
Wife:	So, this means that the election of the mayor is of little significance?
Husband:	It's certainly not a matter of no importance, but . . . Listen, why don't we change the subject?

HEAR ... SAY 2

Husband:	By the way, what did you do with my new suit? I don't know where it is. How am I going to get dressed for work tomorrow?
Wife:	I took it to the dry cleaner . . . Oh, God!
Husband:	What's wrong? You lost the receipt (*Lit.* coupon)?
Wife:	"Floods in Lombardy. A dozen people have left their homes."
Husband:	What a disaster!
Wife:	Now we're paying because we consumed too much.
Husband:	Frankly, I don't feel like discussing the

	climate. Is there something less heavy in the paper?
Wife:	Yes. They had an opinion poll about Sundays without traffic.
Husband:	And?
Wife:	Almost everyone likes it.
Husband:	People said that traffic is the number one enemy, more than crime.
Wife:	Imagine that! Where did you hear that?
Husband:	I read it in the paper last month.
Wife:	Hmm. I didn't notice that. Here's something light—we won at soccer.
Husband:	Light? What are you saying? Soccer is a very serious thing!

ANSWER KEY

ACTIVITY 1

1. d; 2. a; 3. e; 4. f; 5. b; 6. c

ACTIVITY 2

1. *falso;* 2. *falso;* 3. *vero;* 4. *falso;*
5. *vero*

ACTIVITY 3

1. *Non è una cosa da poco!*
2. *Oggigiorno, la vita va più in fretta.*
3. *il diritto di voto*
4. *Non riesco a crederci!*
5. *(Non) sono d'accordo.*

ACTIVITY 4

1. *Non m'interesso molto di politica.*
2. *Sì, ci ricordiamo di Pietro.*
3. *Sì, si dimentica sempre di chiamare quando è in ritardo. / Sì, mi dimentico sempre di chiamare quando sono in ritardo.*
4. *Si lamentano perché non gli piace la camera.*
5. *Sì, ci divertiamo in Internet.*
6. *Non mi sento bene oggi.*
7. *Di solito mi sveglio / si sveglia alle sette.*
8. *Quel tipo nella classe di marketing si chiama Enzo.*
9. *Sì, mi arrabbio sempre quando sento Trillo Selvaggio.*
10. *No, non è vero che ci addormentiamo quando facciamo la grammatica.*

1. *intelligentemente*
2. *gentilmente*
3. *liberamente*
4. *veramente*
5. *completamente*
6. *silenziosamente*
7. *sicuramente*
8. *felicemente*
9. *seriamente*
10. *facilmente*

ACTIVITY 6

1. h; 2. e; 3. d; 4. a; 5. b; 6. f;
7. i; 8. c; 9. g

ACTIVITY 7

1. *falso*; 2. *vero*; 3. *falso*; 4. *falso*;
5. *falso*

ACTIVITY 8

1. *pesanti*; 2. *A proposito*; 3. *in tintoria*;
4. *Figurati!*; 5. *discutere*

ACTIVITY 9

1. *capito*; 2. *studiato*; 3. *saputo*;
4. *parlato*; 5. *lavorato*; 6. *finito*;
7. *portato*; 8. *creduto*; 9. *suggerito*;
10. *avuto*

ACTIVITY 10

1. *Sì, ieri ho mandato una cartolina a Massimo.*
   Or: *Sì, gliel'ho mandata ieri.*
2. *Sì, ieri abbiamo parlato con Giovanna.* Or: *Sì, le abbiamo parlato ieri.*
3. *Sì, ieri hanno finito il lavoro.* Or: *Sì, l'hanno finito ieri.*
4. *Sì, ieri ho / ha lasciato un messaggio per te.* Or: *Sì, tel'ho / ha lasciato ieri.*
5. *Sì, ieri mi hai portato le foto.* Or: *Sì, te le ho portate ieri.*
6. *Sì, ieri ho sentito questa canzone.* Or: *Sì, l'ho sentita ieri.*
7. *Sì, ieri hanno ripetuto il giro.* Or: *Sì, l'hanno ripetuto ieri.*
8. *Sì, ieri abbiamo mangiato la bistecca.* Or: *Sì, l'abbiamo mangiata ieri.*
9. *Sì, ieri ho / ha cambiato camera.* Or *Sì, l'ho / ha cambiata ieri.*
10. *Sì, ieri ho chiamato il taxi.* Or: *Sì, l'ho chiamato ieri.*

ACTIVITY 11

1. *Hai letto*; 2. *Avete visto*; 3. *Abbiamo conosciuto*; 4. *Ho chiesto; hanno detto*;
5. *Abbiamo fatto*; 6. *hanno chiuso*;
7. *ha vinto*; 8. *hanno seguito; Ho perso*;
9. *ha bevuto*; 10. *Ho preso*

ACTIVITY 12

1. *vero* 2. *falso* 3. *vero* 4. *falso* 5. *falso*
6. *falso*

12. TO SEE THE WORLD THROUGH ROSE-COLORED GLASSES

Vedere tutto rosa
(*Lit.* To see everything in pink)

Did anyone fall asleep?

So, did the last lesson inspire a bit of *discussione* on the latest *attualità? Avete letto il giornale oggi?* If we could all meet in person, we could do a small *sondaggio* of our own. What would be your favorite subject—*vi interessate di politica, clima, economia, sport?* Or are you the type who prefers *la cronaca mondana, i fumetti,* and *l'oroscopo?* I'm a bit of a news junkie myself, and I like to *sfogliare il giornale,* front to back. Doing it at a small café in Italy is a particularly wonderful pleasure. But then, so many things in Italy are! Can you imagine growing up in Rome or Florence or any town in Italy (*la maggior parte* [the majority] have hidden treasures that would blow your mind!) and taking a school trip to see the Sistine Chapel or to trace Dante's footsteps? *Figuratevi!* Well, Manuela's class in Siena is just that fortunate.

ACTIVITY 1: LET'S WARM UP

The following dialogue has lots of words that sound similar in Italian and English. See if you can match them.

1.	*la cattedrale*	a.	building; edifice
2.	*lo scultore*	b.	cathedral
3.	*l'edificio*	c.	constructed
4.	*lo stile*	d.	design
5.	*gotico*	e.	different; diverse
6.	*l'espressione*	f.	expression
7.	*il disegno*	g.	finished
8.	*le fondamenta*	h.	foundation
9.	*la popolazione*	i.	Gothic
10.	*simile*	j.	marble
11.	*diverso*	k.	population
12.	*costruito*	l.	sculptor
13.	*marmo*	m.	decline
14.	*finito*	n.	similar
15.	*declino*	o.	style

Now we're ready to listen.

HEAR . . . SAY 1

Manuela is *un'insegnante* (a teacher [masc. / fem.]) in Siena. She's taking her *allievi* (students) on a trip to see Siena's own *Duomo.* They've just arrived and they're standing in front of *la cattedrale* (the cathedral).

Manuela:	Due mesi fa, abbiamo visitato il Duomo di Firenze. Questo è il Duomo di Siena. Dall'esterno, sembrano simili, vero? Vi ricordate il nome di questo stile?
Un'allieva:	Gotico!
Manuela:	Bravi!
Un'allieva:	Ma anche la cattedrale di Notre Dame a Parigi è gotica, giusto?
Manuela:	Sì—un bell'esempio. E come vi sembrano la cattedrale di Notre Dame e il Duomo di Siena? Sono simili?
Un'allieva:	Sono tutt'e due cattedrali molto belle . . . ma anche molto diverse.
Manuela:	Perché?
Un'allieva:	La cattedrale di Notre Dame è tutta grigia. Sembra più seria . . . mi fa un po' paura.
Manuela:	Come vedete, lo stile gotico ha avuto un'espressione diversa in Italia. Questo disegno di marmo bianco, rosa e verde è più leggero, meno scuro.
Un'allieva:	Quando l'hanno costruita?
Manuela:	Hanno finito la cattedrale, come la vedete oggi, nel Trecento.
Un'allieva:	Sette secoli fa! Quant'è vecchia!
Manuela:	Poi hanno cominciato a costruire un edificio molto più grande—le fondamenta si vedono ancora—però improvvisamente è arrivata la peste.
Un'allieva:	E cos'è successo?
Manuela:	Nel 1348 (milletrecentoquarantotto), la maggior parte della popolazione di Siena è morta. Questo ha segnato l'inizio del declino di Siena e non hanno mai finito la cattedrale. Adesso, entriamo . . .

ACTIVITY 2: HOW'S THAT AGAIN?

Vero o falso . . . with a twist! Choose the group in which **all** of the statements are true.

A.
1. *Manuela e i suoi allievi hanno già visitato il Duomo di Firenze.*
2. *Il Duomo di Siena non è gotico.*
3. *Nel 1348 (milletrecentoquarantotto) hanno finito il Duomo di Siena.*

B.
1. *Manuela e i suoi allievi fanno una visita al Duomo di Siena.*
2. *Dall'esterno, il Duomo di Siena è simile al Duomo di Firenze.*
3. *La cattedrale di Notre Dame e il Duomo di Siena sono in stile gotico.*

C. 1. *Manuela e i suoi allievi fanno una visita al Duomo di Firenze.*
    2. *Lo stile gotico ha un'espressione più leggera in Italia che in Francia.*
    3. *Non hanno mai finito il Duomo di Siena.*

Now you get to see how much all those words that were *simili* helped you understand Manuela.

WORKSHOP 1

WORDS TO LIVE BY

HOW BEAUTIFUL!: APPRECIATING THE SIGHTS

You already know how to talk about *le cose da vedere*, but here are a few more words that will help you discuss art and architecture, topics that are sure to come up in Italy!

If you're talking about *uno scultore* or *una scultrice* (a sculptor), or any *artista* (artist [masc. / fem.]) for that matter, an important consideration is how *influente* (influential) he or she is. Is he or she *vivo* (living) or *morto* (dead)?

What materials did they use?

il marmo	marble
il legno	wood
il bronzo	bronze

What type of *edificio* (building) did he or she work on? Is it *simile* (similar to) or *diverso* (different) from any other works you know? Which *stile* (style [m.]) does it represent?

gotico	Gothic
romanico	Romanesque
classico	classical
moderno	modern

How does it look *dall'esterno* (from the outside) and *dentro* (inside)? You can examine it from *il tetto* (the roof) to *il pavimento* (the floor).

Word on the Street

You already know that you can make all sorts of exclamations with the formula *che* + a noun, as in: *Che idiota!* Now you can expand your repertoire with adjectives, by using **come** + an adjective (*Com'è bello!*) or **quanto** + adjective (*Quant'è vecchio!*). They both translate into English as "How beautiful / old!" You can use them interchangeably.

You can also talk about *l'espressione* (the expression [fem.]) of the style. Was it *leggero* or *serio?* What colors were used? *Chiari* (clear; light) or *scuri* (dark)?

nero	black
bianco	white
grigio	gray
rosso	red
rosa	pink
blu	blue
verde	green
giallo	yellow
marrone	brown
viola	purple

Take a Tip from Me!

Colors are adjectives, and as such, they follow the noun they're describing and agree with it in gender and number. *Blu, rosa,* **and** *viola,* **however, are invariable—they stay the same no matter what the gender or number of the noun.**

Take a Tip from Me!

Or maybe you avoid talking about art like la peste (the plague)? I certainly hope not! Now let's see how good an artist you would make.

ACTIVITY 3:	**TAKE IT FOR A SPIN**

What colors result from mixing other colors?

1. *bianco + nero* = _____

2. *bianco + rosso* = _____

3. *blu + giallo* = _____

4. *rosso + nero* = _____

5. *blu + rosso* = _____

Now let's play the game of opposites!

Give the opposite of each term.

1. *scuro* _____

2. *leggero* _____

3. *bianco* _____

4. *classico* _____

5. *diverso* _____

THE NITTY-GRITTY

CHE BELLO!: USING THE ADJECTIVE *BELLO* (BEAUTIFUL)

The adjective *bello*, meaning "beautiful," is one I'm sure you'll be using quite a bit in Italy. Remember that, unlike most adjectives, it usually comes before the noun. Its forms are similar to *quello* (that).

THE FORMS OF *BELLO* (BEAUTIFUL) BEFORE A NOUN		
	SINGULAR	PLURAL
MASCULINE		
before a consonant	*bel*	*bei*
before a vowel	*bell'*	*begli*
FEMININE		
before a consonant	*bella*	*belle*
before a vowel	*bell'*	*belle*

In fact, you've already heard it used in the expression:

Che bella giornata!

What a beautiful day!

And Manuela used it to praise her *allievi*:

Un bell'esempio!

A good example!

You probably also recognize it in the expression *Che bello!* (How beautiful!) where it's used alone, without a noun. *Bello* can also come **after** a noun, when it is used for emphasis, or together with *molto* or another adverb.

Sono tutt'e due cattedrali molto belle.

They're both very beautiful cathedrals.

When *bello* is used alone or after a noun, it acts just like any other adjective:

THE FORMS OF *BELLO* WHEN USED ALONE OR AFTER A NOUN		
	SINGULAR	PLURAL
MASCULINE	bello	belli
FEMININE	bella	belle

Heads Up!

Before nouns beginning with *s* + a consonant or with *z*, use *bello* if they're singular and *begli* if they're plural.

Heads Up!

ACTIVITY 5: TAKE IT FOR A SPIN

Fill in the blanks with the appropriate form of *bello.*

1. *Abbiamo visitato il Duomo e la Pinacoteca Nazionale.*
   —Che _____ giro!

2. *Quest'edificio è un _____ esempio di architettura gotica.*

3. *Cosa ti prende? —Ho visto una ragazza molto _____.*
   Non la posso dimenticare.

4. *Enzo ha comprato una macchina gialla. —Un _____ colore*
   per un taxi!

5. *Che _____ giornata! Perché non andiamo a fare una*
   passeggiata? C'è il sole, fa fresco . . . —Sì, fa _____
   tempo. Va bene. Andiamo.

A little tired of appreciating the beauty of all things? Well, let's get down to brass tacks . . .

THE COUNTDOWN: THE NUMBERS 101–1,000,000,000

Whether you're talking about *la storia* (history) or how you made your millions (or hundreds, whichever the case may be), you'll need to know some numbers higher than *cento*. It can't be easier: it works just like in English.

NUMBERS FROM 100 TO 1,000,000,000			
cento	100	*mille*	1,000
centouno	101	*milledue*	1,002
centodue	102	*milletrentaquattro*	1,034
centotrè	103	*millecento*	1,100
centodieci	110	*milleduecentoquarantacinque*	1,245
centoventi	120	*duemila*	2,000
centotrentatrè	133	*tremila*	3,000
centoquarantacinque	145	*diecimila*	10,000
duecento	200	*sessantamila*	60,000
trecento	300	*centomila*	100,000
quattrocento	400	*seicentomila*	600,000
cinquecento	500	*ottocentocinquantamila*	850,000
seicento	600	*novecentonovantanovemilanovecento-novantanove*	999,999
settecento	700	*un milione*	1,000,000
ottocento	800	*due milioni*	2,000,000
novecento	900	*un miliardo*	1,000,000,000

Heads Up!

The word *mille* (thousand) has an irregular plural form: *mila* (thousands). Note the single "*l.*"

Heads Up!

So, now you can talk about the year in which an event occurred. You say *in*, just like in English, but you also need the definite article (don't forget those combined forms!).

Nel 1348 (milletrecentoquarantotto), la maggior parte della popolazione di Siena è morta.

In 1348, the majority of Siena's population died.

Leonardo da Vinci è nato nel 1452 (millequattrocentocinquantadue).

Leonardo da Vinci was born in 1452.

You can also talk about centuries using the numbers *duecento*, *trecento*, *quattrocento*, etc. In this case, they're capitalized and introduced by a definite article. So, *il Cinquecento* refers to the 1500s or the sixteenth century. Note also: The twenty-first century (the 2000s) is called *il Duemila*. The eleventh century (or the 1000s) is called *l' undicesimo secolo*.

> **Hanno finito la cattedrale, come la vedete oggi, nel Trecento.**

> They finished the cathedral, as you see it today, in the fourteenth century (the 1300s).

La storia is great, but . . . Show me the money! Right?

> **Ho trovato duecento euro per la strada.**

> I found 200 euros on the street.

> **Quel tipo ha vinto un milione al Totocalcio!**

> That guy won a million on Totocalcio!

ACTIVITY 6: **TAKE IT FOR A SPIN**

Say the following years out loud and write which century they're in. As a bonus, see if you can guess why they're significant.

1. 1984 _____
2. 1492 _____
3. 1776 _____
4. 2001 _____
5. 1088 _____
6. 1265 _____
7. 1499 _____
8. 1508 _____
9. 1633 _____
10. 1996 _____

Good work! Now let's get back to our show . . .

ACTIVITY 7: **LET'S WARM UP**

Simile o diverso? (Similar or different?) You be the judge!

1. *sbadigliare—addormentarsi*   _____   _____

2. *noioso—interessante*   _____   _____

3. *addormentarsi—andare a letto*   _____   _____

4. *normale—strano*   _____   _____

5. *presto—tardi*   _____   _____

6. *dentro—all'esterno*   _____   _____

7. *andare a letto—alzarsi*   _____   _____

8. *una bell' interpretazione—un disastro*   _____   _____

9. *rimanere senza fiato—non interessarsi di*   _____   _____

10. *ho dimenticato—non mi ricordo*   _____   _____

Let's find out how the rest of Manuela's day went.

HEAR . . . SAY 2

Felice, Manuela's friend and coworker, *si preoccupa* because he didn't see her at school today. He gives her a *chiamata* after work to check on her . . .

Una voce: Pronto?

Felice: Buona sera. Sono Felice. C'è Manuela?

Una voce: Sì. Un attimo che la chiamo . . . Manueeeeeeela! Telefonooooooo! . . . Felice.

Manuela: *(out of breath)* Ciao, Felice!

Felice: Manuela, sei rimasta senza fiato! Lo so che sono un tipo "superbono" ma devi controllarti.

Manuela: Ma, dai! Sai che non sei i mio genere. Scherzi a parte, sono appena tornata. Salire al quarto piano a piedi non è una cosa da poco.

Felice: Da dove sei tornata?

Manuela: Sono andata a vedere il Duomo con la mia classe.

Felice: Ho dimenticato! Allora, ecco perché non ti ho vista a scuola oggi. Gli è piacuta la gita?

Manuela: *(sarcastically)* Sì, tanto!

Felice: Che cosa gli è piaciuto di più?

Manuela: I "fumetti."

Felice:	Quali "fumetti"?
Manuela:	I disegni di marmo sul pavimento dentro il Duomo.
Felice:	Come sono creativi! Una bella interpretazione—davvero moderna!
Manuela:	Infatti, mi è piaciuto questo parallelo. È importante trovare un nesso tra l'arte dei tempi passati e la vita dei nostri giorni.
Felice:	Vedi tutto rosa, Manuela! Altre reazioni interessanti?
Manuela:	Gli ho detto che più di quaranta artisti hanno lavorato alle cinquantasei scene per quasi duecento anni—sono svenuti!
Felice:	L'idea di un lavoro che dura più di una vita non si può più capire.
Manuela:	Non so. Nel passato, quella non era un'idea così strana.
Felice:	È vero. Ma oggigiorno—quando le lettere si scambiano via Internet in due secondi e la cena si prepara in due minuti—un lavoro che dura più di un'ora è diventato una cosa strana!
Manuela:	Almeno, la gita è andata meglio dell'anno scorso.
Felice:	Perché?
Manuela:	L'anno scorso, un'allieva si è addormentata. Tipico! "Che noia!"—lo sbadiglio contagioso! (*no response from Felice*) . . . Felice? Ci sei?
Felice:	Sì, sì, scusa. Ho sbadigliato anch'io.

ACTIVITY 8: HOW'S THAT AGAIN?

Vero o falso?

		VERO	FALSO
1.	Manuela è andata a scuola oggi.	_____	_____
2.	La gita è piaciuta agli allievi.	_____	_____
3.	Un'allieva si è addormentata oggi.	_____	_____
4.	Più di quaranta artisti hanno lavorato al pavimento del Duomo.	_____	_____
5.	Gli artisti hanno lavorato per due anni.	_____	_____
6.	Ci sono cinquantasei scene in marmo sul pavimento del Duomo.	_____	_____

If you think learning Italian is hard, just think about those artists who worked on their marble mosaics for almost 200 years! Kind of puts things in perspective, doesn't it? *Al lavoro!* (Get to work!)

The art treasures of Italy will make most people *rimanere senza fiato* (breathless [*Lit.* to remain without breath]). Of course, so does *salire* (climbing) up four flights of stairs (as in Manuela's case), but what's your point?

The great thing about art is that it's all really a question of *interpretazione* (interpretation [fem.]). Your *reazione* (reaction [fem.]) and mine can be completely different. The important thing is that you **have** a reaction, and good art will elicit just that. Regardless of how long ago the artwork was created, you'll be able to find *un nesso* (a connection) or *un parallelo* (a parallel) between *il passato* (the past) *e il presente* (the present). Hopefully, it'll make you *svenire* (faint) rather than *sbadigliare* (yawn). Either way, here are some adjectives you can use to *scambiare* (exchange) ideas about your *interpretazione*.

strano	strange
tipico	typical
creativo	creative
noioso	boring
interessante	interesting

Word on the Street

Che noia! (How boring! How annoying!) is a useful expression, I'm sure you'll agree. But lest you become boring yourselves, here are a few colorful alternatives: *Che coma!* (*Lit.* What a coma!), *Che depressione!* (*Lit.* What a depression!). And if something's "heavy" (and thus for most teenagers *noioso*), you can say: *Che pizza!* (*Lit.* What a pizza!) or *Che mattone!* (*Lit.* What a brick!).

ACTIVITY 9: TAKE IT FOR A SPIN

What would you say?

1. It's June, and you're looking for something to watch on TV, but all you find are reruns. You say: _____

2. You walk outside your house and see a monkey on your porch. You think: _____

_____

3. You just found out that it took more than forty artists almost 200 years to create the biblical scenes in marble that decorate the floor of Siena's *Duomo*. _____

   _____

4. Many theories have been proposed to explain this phenomenon. One says that when this occurs, a person sucks in a lot of air, leaving those around him with less than they need, causing them to do the same thing in an effort to inhale more oxygen. The phenomenon is known as: _____

5. Voltaire's hero Candide experiences some of the worst horrors and treacheries imaginable, but he insists that this is the best of all possible worlds. You could say about him: _____

Now it's time to face *il nemico numero uno* again: *la grammatica*.

THE NITTY-GRITTY

LET BYGONES BE BYGONES: MORE ON THE *PASSATO PROSSIMO*

In these dialogues, you probably recognized a lot of past participles, but many of them were used a little differently than in the previous lesson. Can you identify the difference? Let's look at some examples:

Cos'è successo?

What happened?

Però improvvisamente è arrivata la peste.

But suddenly the plague arrived.

Sono appena tornata.

I've just come back.

Sono andata a vedere il Duomo.

I went to see the Duomo.

Un allieva si è addormentata.

A student fell asleep.

So, did you notice that these past participles are preceded by a form of *essere* (to be) and not *avere* (to have)? If you were particularly astute, you may also have noticed that not all of the past participles ended in –o. Instead, they appear to act as adjectives and agree with the subject. Well, there's the whole mystery solved!

There is a group of verbs that forms the *passato prossimo* with *essere*. These verbs are all intransitive (meaning they don't take a direct object), and they often involve movement. The past participle then agrees with the subject. The most common verbs in this group include: *essere* (whose past participle is *stato*), *andare, arrivare, venire, uscire, partire, stare, rimanere, tornare, diventare, piacere,* and all the reflexive verbs. Two other important verbs conjugated with *essere* are *nascere* (to be born), whose past participle is *nato,* and *morire* (to die), whose past participle is *morto.*

Nel 1348, la maggior parte della popolazione di Siena è morta.

In 1348, the majority of Siena's population died.

Dove siete andanti? —Siamo usciti al ristorante con i miei.

Where did you go? —We went out to a restaurant with my family.

Now, let's practice.

ACTIVITY 10:   **TAKE IT FOR A SPIN**

Change the following sentences to the *passato prossimo.*

1. *Torniamo da Roma.* _____

2. *Elena e Tommaso partono per l'Italia.* _____

    _____

3. *Vado a vedere i monumenti.* _____

4. *Elisabetta non si alza mai prima delle nove.* _____

    _____

5. *Felice si preoccupa per Manuela.* _____

    _____

6. *Oggi Marina si veste di nero.* _____

7. *Ti piace la cattedrale di Notre Dame?* _____

    _____

8. *Esco con Enzo stasera.* _____

9. *Gli allievi si divertono a scuola.* _____

    _____

10. *Vieni sola?* _____

The adjective *solo* means "alone," but when it's introduced by *da*, as in *da solo*, the expression means "by myself / yourself / himself, etc."

As I mentioned, the *passato prossimo* is used when talking about something that began and was finished in the past. It refers to a point in time, however extended. You'll often hear it used together with expressions of time that help place an event in a moment of time:

- To specify how long ago something happened, indicate the amount of time that has passed and add *fa*.

un'ora fa	*an hour ago*
cinque giorni fa	*five days ago*
due settimane fa	*two weeks ago*
dieci anni fa	*ten years ago*

Due settimane fa, abbiamo visitato il Duomo di Firenze.

Two weeks ago, we visited the Duomo in Florence.

Sono partiti dieci giorni fa.

They left ten days ago.

Manuela è arrivata cinque minuti fa.

Manuela arrived five minutes ago.

- To specify a moment in the past, say:

l'anno scorso / passato	*last year*
il mese scorso / passato	*last month*
la settimana scorsa / passata	*last week*
lunedì scorso / passato	*last Monday*

Almeno, la gita è andata meglio dell'anno scorso.

At least the excursion went better than last year.

Sabato scorso, abbiamo fatto un giro della città.

Last Saturday, we took a tour of the city.

La settimana passata non siamo andati a scuola.

Last week we didn't go to school.

TAKE IT FOR A SPIN

Answer the following questions using the hint in parentheses. Try to answer as naturally as possible—you don't have to repeat all of the information in the question, and you can use object pronouns to shorten your answer.

1. *Quando ti ha scritto Stefano? (il mese scorso)* _____

    _____

2. *Quando sono arrivati a Siena? (due settimane fa)* _____

    _____

3. *Quando è partito il treno per Roma? (un'ora fa)* _____

    _____

4. *Quando avete parlato a Lotte? (la settimana scorsa)* _____

    _____

5. *Quando ti ho dato i soldi? (due anni fa)* _____

    _____

6. *Quando sei andato in Italia? (nel 1999)* _____

    _____

7. *Quando avete visto l'ultimo film di Tornatore? (il mese scorso)* _____

    _____

8. *Quando è nata sua figlia? (tre mesi fa)* _____

    _____

9. *Quando hanno finito la cattedrale? (nel Trecento)* _____

    _____

10. *Quando ha chiamato Felice? (cinque minuti fa)* _____

    _____

Adesso, cambiamo tema . . .

THIS IS HOW IT'S DONE: USING THE IMPERSONAL *SI*

When you want to make a general statement without specifying a subject, or if you want to talk about a custom or habit, you can use the pronoun *si* + the *Lei / lui / lei* form of a verb in the present tense. In English, statements like this are usually made using the passive form or non-specific subjects like "you," "they," or "one."

Si vendono qui biglietti per l'autobus?

Are bus tickets sold here?

Le lettere si scambiano via Internet in due secondi.

Letters are exchanged via the Internet in two seconds.

La cena si prepara in due minuti.

Dinner is made in two minutes.

Le fondamenta si vedono ancora.

One can still see the foundation. / The foundation can still be seen.

L'idea di un lavoro che dura più di una vita non si può più capire.

The idea of a job that lasts more than a lifetime can no longer be understood.

ACTIVITY 12: TAKE IT FOR A SPIN

Translate the following sentences using the impersonal *si*.

1. One can see the whole city from here! _____
   _____

2. One never eats pasta with risotto. _____
   _____

3. Can one see the room? _____
   _____

4. English is spoken here. _____
   _____

5. Are telephone cards sold here? _____
   _____

6. This idea can't be understood. _____
   _____

7. You have to pay before going in. (One has to pay before going in.) _____
   _____

8. They speak Italian in Switzerland, too. _____

_____

All done! See you next time!

CRIB NOTES

HEAR...SAY 1

Manuela:	Two months ago, we visited the Duomo in Florence. This is Siena's Duomo. From the outside, they seem similar, don't they? Do you remember the name of this style?
A Student:	Gothic!
Manuela:	Excellent!
A Student:	But the Notre Dame cathedral in Paris is also Gothic, isn't it?
Manuela:	Yes, a beautiful example. And how do the cathedral of Notre Dame and Siena's Duomo seem to you? Are they similar?
A Student:	They're both very beautiful cathedrals . . . but they are also very different.
Manuela:	Why?
A Student:	The Notre Dame cathedral is all gray. It seems more serious . . . it scares me a little.
Manuela:	As you can see, the Gothic style was expressed very differently in Italy. This design with white, pink, and green marble is lighter, less dark.
A Student:	When did they build the cathedral?
Manuela:	They finished it, as you see it today, in the fourteenth century.
A Student:	Seven centuries ago! It's so old! (*Lit.* How old it is!)
Manuela:	Then they started working on a structure that was much bigger—the foundation can still be seen—but suddenly the plague arrived.
A Student:	And what happened?
Manuela:	In 1348, the majority of Siena's population died. This marked the beginning of Siena's decline and they never finished the cathedral. Now, let's go in . . .

HEAR...SAY 2

A Voice:	Hello?
Felice:	Good evening. This is Felice. Is Manuela there?
A Voice:	Yes. One moment and I'll call her . . . Manueeeeeeela! Telephooooone! . . . Felice.
Manuela:	Hi, Felice!
Felice:	Manuela, you're out of breath! I know I'm a hunk of a guy, but you have to control yourself.
Manuela:	Come off it! You know you're not my type. Seriously, though, I've just come back. Climbing up to the fourth floor on foot is no small thing.
Felice:	Where did you come back from?
Manuela:	I went to see the Duomo with my class.
Felice:	I forgot. So, that's why I didn't see you in school today. Did they like the excursion?
Manuela:	Yes, so much!
Felice:	What did they like the best?
Manuela:	The "comics."
Felice:	Which "comics"?
Manuela:	The marble designs on the floor of the Duomo.
Felice:	How creative they are! A beautiful interpretation—truly modern!
Manuela:	Actually, I liked this parallel. It's important to find a connection between the art of the past and our lives today.
Felice:	You see the world through rose-colored glasses (*Lit.* you see everything in pink), Manuela! Any other interesting reactions?
Manuela:	I told them that more than forty artists worked on the fifty-six scenes for close to 200 years—they fainted!
Felice:	The idea of a job that lasts more than a lifetime can't be understood anymore.

Manuela:	I don't know. In the past, that wasn't such a strange idea.	Manuela:	At least the trip went better than last year.
Felice:	It's true. But today—when you can exchange letters via the Internet in two seconds and dinner can be made in two minutes—a job that lasts more than an hour has become a strange thing.	Felice:	Why?
		Manuela:	Last year, a student fell asleep. Typical! "How boring!"—the contagious yawn! no response from Felice . . . Felice? Are you there?
		Felice:	Yes, yes, sorry. I yawned, too.

ANSWER KEY

ACTIVITY 1

1. b; 2. l; 3. a; 4. o; 5. i; 6. f;
7. d; 8. h; 9. k; 10. n; 11. e; 12. c;
13. j; 14. g; 15. m

ACTIVITY 2

The statements in group B are all true. In A, only the first statement is true. In C, only the second is true.

ACTIVITY 3

1. *grigio;* 2. *rosa;* 3. *verde;* 4. *marrone;*
5. *viola*

ACTIVITY 4

1. *chiaro;* 2. *serio* or *pesante;* 3. *nero;*
4. *moderno;* 5. *simile*

ACTIVITY 5

1. *bel;* 2. *bell';* 3. *bella;* 4. *bel;*
5. *bella; bel*

ACTIVITY 6

1. 1984—*millenovecentottantaquattro; il Novecento;* Name of George Orwell's famous work
2. 1492—*millequattrocentonovantadue; il Quattrocento;* Columbus sailed the ocean blue
3. 1776—*millesettecentosettantasei; il Settecento;* U.S. Declaration of Independence signed
4. 2001—*duemilauno; il duemila;* Beginning of the new millennium, name of Arthur C. Clarke's famous work and Stanley Kubrick's *film influente.*
5. 1088—*milleottantotto; l'undicesimo secolo;* Europe's first university founded in Bologna
6. 1265—*milleduecentosessantacinque; il Duecento;* Dante Alighieri is born
7. 1499—*millequattrocentonovantanove; il Quattrocento;* Leonardo Da Vinci finishes the *Last Supper* in Milan

8. 1508—*millecinquecentotto; il Cinquecento;* Michelangelo begins work on the Sistine Chapel
9. 1633—*milleseicentotrentatrè; il Seicento;* Galileo Galilei faces the Inquisition
10. 1996—*millenovecentonovantasei; il Novecento;* Marcello Mastroianni, one of Italy's legendary actors and Federico Fellini's alter ego in 8½, dies

ACTIVITY 7

1. *simile;* 2. *diverso;* 3. *simile;* 4. *diverso;*
5. *diverso;* 6. *diverso;* 7. *diverso;*
8. *diverso;* 9. *diverso;* 10. *simile*

ACTIVITY 8

1. *falso;* 2. *vero* (o *falso*—depends on how sarcastic she was when saying it); 3. *falso;*
4. *vero;* 5. *falso;* 6. *vero*

ACTIVITY 9

1. *Che noia! / Che depressione!;* 2. *Strano!;*
3. *Interessante!* or *Mi prendi in giro?*
4. *lo sbadiglio contagioso;* 5. *Vede tutto rosa!*

ACTIVITY 10

1. *Siamo tornati / e da Roma.*
2. *Elena e Tommaso sono partiti per l'Italia.*
3. *Sono andato / a a vedere i monumenti.*
4. *Elisabetta non si è alzata mai prima delle nove.*
5. *Felice si è preoccupato per Manuela.*
6. *Oggi Marina si è vestita di nero.*
7. *Ti è piaciuta la cattedrale di Notre Dame?*
8. *Sono uscito / a con Enzo stasera.*
9. *Gli allievi si sono divertiti a scuola.*
10. *Sei venuta sola?*

ACTIVITY 11

1. *Stefano mi ha scritto il mese scorso.* → *Mi ha scritto il mese scorso.*
2. *Sono arrivati a Siena due settimane fa.* → *Sono arrivati due settimane fa.*

3. *Il treno per Roma è partito un'ora fa.* → *È partito un'ora fa.*
4. *Abbiamo parlato a Lotte la settimana scorsa.* → *Le abbiamo parlato la settimana scorsa.*
5. *Mi hai dati soldi due anni fa.* → *Me li hai dati due anni fa.*
6. *Sono andato / a in Italia nel 1999.*
7. *Abbiamo visto l'ultimo film di Tornatore il mese scorso.* → *L'abbiamo visto il mese scorso.*
8. *Sua figlia è nata tre mesi fa.* → *È nata tre mesi fa.*
9. *Hanno finito la cattedrale nel Trecento.* → *L'hanno finita nel Trecento.*
10. *Felice ha chiamato cinque minuti fa.* → *Ha chiamato cinque minuti fa.*

ACTIVITY 12

1. *Da qui si vede tutta la città.*
2. *La pasta non si mangia mai con il risotto.*
3. *Si può vedere la camera?*
4. *Si parla inglese qui. / Qui si parla inglese.*
5. *Qui si vendono le carte / schede telefoniche. / Si vendono le carte / schede telefoniche qui.*
6. *Non si può capire questa idea. / Questa idea non si può capire.*
7. *Si deve pagare prima di entrare.*
8. *L'italiano si parla anche in Svizzera.*

13. THE SWAN SONG

Il canto del cigno

Would you like a tissue?

While we're in the business of getting cultured, let's look at another famous Italian art form: *l'opera* (the opera). While it's true that the first thing to *venire in mente* (come to mind) when you think of Italy's impressive cultural heritage are its famous *pittori* and *scultori* (especially those associated with *l'arte del rinascimento*), music and the opera probably come in a close second. In fact, *l'opera è nata in Italia* in the 1700s, and it really developed as an art form in the 1800s. Famous *compositori* (composers) like Verdi, Puccini, and Bellini drew their *ispirazione* (inspiration [fem.]) from *canti popolari* (folk songs). *Il pubblico* (the audience) would in turn take their favorite *aria* back to the *piazza*, where it would eventually become a popular *canzone* (song [fem.]). But enough talking about opera—let's go for the real thing. In this lesson we get to *assistere a uno spettacolo* (see a show) in the *Arena di Verona* . . .

ACTIVITY 1: LET'S WARM UP

Choose the best answer . . .

1. *Uno spettacolo* is . . .
    a. a spaceship
    b. a spectrogram
    c. a show

2. *Un direttore d'orchestra* is . . .
    a. an usher
    b. a conductor
    c. an orchestra stand

3. *Indimenticabile* means
    a. indecent
    b. unforgettable
    c. demented

4. If you're *sotto le stelle*, you're spending an evening
    a. outside
    b. inside
    c. south of the border

5. *Sta zitto!* means
    a. Check out that zit!
    b. Zipper up!
    c. Hush up!

Now, clean your ears, and listen up!

Paolo and Francesco were supposed to go to the opera together at *l'Arena di Verona*. Unfortunately Paolo ends up sick and gives his ticket to his friend, Simona, who's visiting from out of town. Francesco and Simona have never met, so they talk on the phone beforehand to decide where to meet and how they will recognize each other. Francesco says he'll be wearing a *borsalino*, the hat made famous by Humphrey Bogart, but designed by an Italian. Simona is waiting at *il luogo dell'appuntamento*, when someone approaches . . .

Francesco: Ciao. Sei Simona, giusto?

Simona: Ciao, Borsalino! Sei Francesco?

Francesco: Entriamo? Lo spettacolo comincia tra poco.

Simona: (*on their way in*) Mi dispiace per Paolo, ma sono felicissima di potere venire al suo posto. Al mio paese c'era un teatro piccolissimo dove andavo all'opera quasi ogni sabato con i miei. Preferivo sempre *La Bohème* . . . è l'opera più bella di Puccini.

Francesco: Sono d'accordo, anche se, secondo me, la sua opera più interessante è *La Tosca*. Puccini è davvero il compositore più profondo del mondo.

Simona: Può darsi.

Francesco: Com'erano gli spettacoli in un teatro così piccolo?

Simona: Beh! Il nostro tenore non era un Pavarotti, però avevo dieci anni e tutto mi sembrava proprio magico.

Francesco: Anch'io non perdevo maì l'occasione di assistere a un'opera. I miei amici mi tormentavano—mi chiamavano "Puccini".

Simona: Povero te! A proposito, hai visto il programma? Abbiamo la fortuna di vedere Katia Ricciarelli, la grande cantante, e Riccardo Muti, il grande direttore d'orchestra, la stessa sera!

Francesco: E grazie a Paolo, abbiamo posti davanti.

Simona: L'anno scorso ho visto *La Traviata* di Verdi con la Ricciarelli. È stata veramente indimenticabile, qualcosa di meraviglioso . . . (*no response from Francesco, who appears to be deep in thought*) Franceso?

Francesco: Penso a Katia Ricciarelli. L'ho vista cinque anni fa nella *Carmen* . . . Non so . . . Non era così brava. Sembrava un po' . . . stanca.

Simona: È chiaro che abbiamo delle opinioni diverse. A mio parere, è il miglior soprano dei nostri giorni.

Francesco: Un'esagerazione, forse, ma certamente ha avuto tanto successo.

Simona: (*trying to get things back on a good note*) Ma che piacere vedere tutt'e due sotto le stelle di Verona!

Francesco:	È l'occasione di una vita!
Simona:	Paolo mi parlava spesso dell'Arena di Verona. Secondo lui, è il teatro più bello del mondo.
Francesco:	A dire la verità, preferisco un teatro intimo a questa grande arena.
Simona:	Allora, un giorno devi visitare il mio paese. Il nostro deve essere il teatro più intimo d'Italia!
Francesco:	Sst. Sta zitta! Comincia!

HOW'S THAT AGAIN?

1. *A quale opera assistono Simona e Francesco?* _____

   _____

2. *Chi è il compositore?* _____

3. *Secondo Francesco, chi è il compositore più profondo del mondo?* _____

   _____

4. *Cosa pensa Simona di Katia Ricciarelli? Francesco è d'accordo?* _____

   _____

5. *Riccardo Muti canta con Katia Ricciarelli?* _____

6. *L'Arena di Verona è un teatro grande o intimo?* _____

   _____

Did You Know?

LA DONNA È MOBILE: OPERA IN ITALY

Milan's La Scala is Italy's best-known and most-respected opera house, but virtually every city holds its performers to high standards. You may remember an incident in the 1990s when an angry audience booed the famous *tenore* Pavarotti, who later said he deserved it due to his poor performance. L'Arena di Verona is one of the largest and best-preserved ancient Roman amphitheaters in the world. In the summer, it welcomes up to 22,000 people a night to its opera festival, which is known for its splashy sets and spectacular productions. If you go, be sure to take or rent a cushion. Two thousand-year-old seats can be pretty uncomfortable.

Ah, the opera! Let's see if you can *cantare* (sing) your way through the workshop.

WORKSHOP 1

WORDS TO LIVE BY

APPRECIATING THE ARTS: A NIGHT OUT AT THE OPERA

Assistere a un'opera (to attend an opera) in Italy is truly *l'occasione di una vita* (the chance of a lifetime)—especially if the setting is as romantic as the Arena di Verona, where you can enjoy the music *sotto le stelle* (under the stars). *Il programma* (notice that it's masculine, even though it ends in *−a*) will give you a good indication of whether *lo spettacolo* (the performance; the show) is likely to be good. Just look at who's involved.

il compositore / la compositrice	composer (masc. / fem.)
il / la regista	director (masc. / fem.)
il direttore / la direttrice d'orchestra	conductor; orchestra director (masc. / fem.)
il / la cantante	singer
il soprano	soprano (Notice that the word is masculine even though it refers to a female singer.)
il contralto	alto (Notice the masculine gender just like for **soprano**.)
il tenore	tenor
il basso	bass

If you're at a loss for words when trying to describe the performance, here are a few poignant adjectives:

magico	magical
indimenticabile	unforgettable
meraviglioso	fantastic; marvelous
profondo	profound
intimo	intimate
grande	great

Heads Up!

Tutti e due (or *tutt'e due*) means "both." If you want to say "all three" or "all four" just change the number: *tutti e tre, tutti e quattro . . .*

Heads Up!

Word on the Street

Another way you can describe someone is by comparing him or her to a famous person, like when Simona says: *il nostro tenore non era un Pavarotti,* meaning "our tenor was no Pavarotti." All you do is stick an indefinite article (*un / una*) in front of the name, as in: *mio figlio è un artista—certamente non è un Michelangelo, ma ha talento,* "my son is an artist—certainly he's no Michelangelo, but he's got talent."

IF YOU ASK ME . . . : **EXPRESSING YOUR OPINION**

Be careful when you're throwing around superlative adjectives. Some people might interpret your genuine statement as *un'esagerazione* (an exaggeration [fem.]). If your interlocutor doesn't see things your way, here are a few ways to get your opinion across.

secondo me . . .	I think . . . ; if you ask me . . . (Lit. according to me)
a mio parere	in my opinion
a dire la verità . . .	to tell you the truth . . .
preferisco . . . **X** . . . **a** . . . **Y** . . .	I prefer . . . X . . . to . . . Y . . .
spero di sì / no	I hope so / not

And if you're not in the mood to argue, it might be easier to say simply:

Può darsi.	Maybe. It could be.

If someone says they like something, *mi piace . . .* , or don't like something, *non mi piace . . .* , you can express a contrary opinion with:

A me, invece, no.	I, on the other hand, don't.
A me, invece, sì.	I, on the other hand, do.

Finally, if *un vicino / una vicina* (neighbor [masc. / fem.] is rustling with candy or continually discussing what's happening on stage, you might want to turn around and politely but firmly say:

Silenzio, per favore!	Silence, please!

Or not so politely:

Sssssst!	Psssst!
Sta zitto / a!	Be quiet!

I'm sure you can think of plenty of other occasions where some of these phrases could come in handy. Here's your chance to try them out . . .

TAKE IT FOR A SPIN

Two friends are whispering during a show. Translate:

Chiara:	Do you like the show?
Del Vecchio:	To tell you the truth, I don't like it much.
Chiara:	I, on the other hand, do. In my opinion, it's a great interpretation! Unforgettable!
Del Vecchio:	An exaggeration, if you ask me. But it could be. The tenor is fantastic . . .
Chiara:	What's his name?
Del Vecchio:	Let's see . . . here's the program.
Una vicina:	Silence, please!

Now for the subject that's *il più interessante del mondo: la grammatica.*

THE NITTY-GRITTY

THE BEST OF THE BEST: THE RELATIVE SUPERLATIVE

You already know how to compare two things using *meno* and *più*. That's called the comparative. But what if you're comparing more than two things? Like when Simona says:

Il nostro deve essere il teatro più intimo d'Italia.

Ours has to be the most intimate theater in Italy.

La Bohème è l'opera più bella di Puccini.

La Bohème is Puccini's most beautiful opera. (*Lit.* the most beautiful opera of Puccini)

In cases like these, you need the superlative. And guess what: *È la cosa più facile del mondo!* It's the easiest thing in the world! *Dico sul serio.* (Seriously.) All you do is use the definite article before the comparative form. While in English we use prepositions like "in" ("in the world") or "of" ("of the lot") to show what the point of reference is, in Italian they keep it simple and always use *di*. The basic formula is:

il / la + noun + più / meno + adjective + di

Secondo lui, è il teatro più bello del mondo.

According to him, it's the most beautiful theater in the world.

As in English, you don't always have to specify exactly what you're comparing something to. Sometimes it's implied, as when Francesco says:

La sua opera più interessante è La Tosca.

His most interesting opera is *Tosca.*

Heads Up!

Remember that the adjectives *migliore* (better) and *peggiore* (worse) are already comparative, so you just add *il / la;* no need for *più / meno* before them. Remember, too, that they come before the noun.

A mio parere, è il miglior soprano dei nostri giorni.

In my opinion, she's the best soprano of our time.

Heads Up!

Now, let's get superlative!

ACTIVITY 4:   TAKE IT FOR A SPIN

Make superlative statements, according to the example:

> La Bohème / opera / + / bella / Puccini
>
> La Bohème è l'opera più bella di Puccini.

1.   *Riccardo Muti / direttore d'orchestra / + / buono / mondo* _____

     _____

2.   *Calcio / sport / + / popolare / tutti* _____

     _____

3.   *Verdi / compositore / + / conosciuto* _____

     _____

4.   *Navigare in rete / passatempo / + / popolare / mondo* _____

     _____

5.   *il terremoto / disastro / + / orribile* _____

     _____

6.   *questo / ristorante / – / caro / zona* _____

     _____

7.   *Elisabetta / guida / simpatica / + / tutte* _____

     _____

8.   *Gianfranco / portiere / pazzo / + / mondo* _____

     _____

9. _Chianti / vino / + / delizioso / mondo_ _____

_____

10. _Italiano / lingua / + / bella / mondo_ _____

_____

THE WAY WE WERE: TALKING ABOUT THE PAST USING THE IMPERFETTO

Did you notice that when Simona was talking about her weekly visits to the opera when she was a child, she wasn't using the _passato prossimo_?

> **. . . andavo all'opera quasi ogni sabato con i miei. La Bohème mi piaceva sempre di più.**
>
> . . . I used to go to the opera almost every Saturday with my folks. I always liked _La Bohème_ the most.
>
> **. . . tutto mi sembrava magico!**
>
> . . . everything seemed magical to me!

When you're talking about things you would do regularly in the past or how things used to be, you should use the _imperfetto_ and not the _passato prossimo_. But here's the good news: The imperfect is pretty easy to form—it has only one set of endings for all three verb groups. Just drop the _–re_ from the infinitive, and replace it with the appropriate ending: _–vo, –vi, –va, –vamo, –vate, –vano_.

THE IMPERFECT TENSE OF REGULAR VERBS		
	PARLARE (TO SPEAK)	_LEGGERE_ (TO READ)	_FINIRE_ (TO FINISH)
IO	_parla–vo_	_legge–vo_	_fini–vo_
TU	_parla–vi_	_legge–vi_	_fini–vi_
LEI / LUI	_parla–va_	_legge–va_	_fini–va_
NOI	_parla–vamo_	_legge–vamo_	_fini–vamo_
VOI	_parla–vate_	_legge–vate_	_fini–vate_
LORO	_parla–vano_	_legge–vano_	_fini–vano_

So, now that you know that the imperfect is easy to form, let's spend a little more time discussing when to use it. As we said, it's mainly used to talk about habitual actions in the past. It's often the tense you use when you're talking about memories of the past, how things used to be, as when Francesco says:

Anch'io non perdevo l'occasione di assistere a un'opera.

I, too, wouldn't miss a chance to see an opera.

I miei amici mi tormentavano—mi chiamavano "Puccini."

My friends used to torture me—they used to call me "Puccini."

Phrases like:

- **ogni sera / giorno / anno**
- **spesso**
- **sempre**
- **tutte le mattine**
- **tutto il giorno / tutti i giorni**
- **da bambino / bambina**
- **da piccolo / piccola**

should be an automatic "trigger" for the imperfect, when you're talking about the past. Just as *dieci anni fa* or *l'anno scorso* would be automatic "triggers" for the *passato prossimo*.

Paolo mi parlava spesso dell'Arena di Verona.

Paolo often talked to me about the Arena di Verona.

Finally, the imperfect is a descriptive tense, and it should be used when you're talking about the state of things in the past, how you felt, or how old you were.

Avevo dieci anni . . .

I was ten years old . . .

It follows, then, that the verb *essere* is mainly used in the imperfect when you're talking about the past. It's irregular:

ESSERE (TO BE) IN THE IMPERFECT			
I O	*ero*	N O I	*eravamo*
T U	*eri*	V O I	*eravate*
LEI / LUI	*era*	L O R O	*erano*

C'era un teatro piccolissimo.

There was a very small theater.

Com'erano gli spettacoli a un teatro cosi piccolo?

How were the shows at such a small theater?

Nel passato, quella non era un'idea così strana.

In the past, that wasn't such a strange idea.

Take a Tip from Me!

The difference between the *imperfetto* and the *passato prossimo* is one of the more challenging issues in Italian grammar. Think of the *passato prossimo* when you're talking about something as an event or an occurrence, rather than a process. For example, speaking of Katia Ricciarelli, Francesco says *l'ho vista cinque anni fa nella* Carmen using the *passato prossimo* because what's important is the fact that he saw her—he's describing something that happened at a specific moment in time. But he says, "*non era così brava; sembrava un po' . . . stanca*" using the imperfect because he's <u>describing</u> her. Likewise, Simona says, "*Paolo mi parlava spesso dell'Arena di Verona*" because she wants to stress that Paolo told her about the theater many times. If he had simply mentioned it once or twice, she would have said, "*Paolo mi ha parlato dell'Arena di Verona.*" The truth is, it usually takes a lot of exposure to get a feel for which tense to use when. The reality is you'll probably be making mistakes for quite a while. But making mistakes is one of the best ways to learn something. So, don't obsess too much about being right or wrong. Do your best, and whatever you do, <u>speak</u> and <u>listen</u> as much as you can—it's the only way to really learn. So, let's get to it!

Take a Tip from Me!

ACTIVITY 5: TAKE IT FOR A SPIN

Change the sentences into the imperfect tense.

1. *Il soprano è veramente meraviglioso!* _____

_____

2. *Vado all'opera ogni sabato.* _____

_____

3. *Gli allievi hanno sempre delle interpretazioni originali.* _____

_____

4. *Sbadiglio sempre durante la classe di matematica.* _____

_____

5. *Ogni anno mi scrivono una cartolina.* _____

_____

6. *Gli piace leggere il giornale e discutere sulle attualità.* _____

_____

7. *Parla spesso della criminalità.* _____

_____

8. *Hai otto anni.* _____

_____

9. *Si sentono per telefono tutte le mattine.* _____

_____

10. *Tutta la mia famiglia dorme sempre fino a tardi.* _____

_____

Now let's get back to the Arena di Verona and see if Simona and Francesco have managed to find some common ground or if their night out is going *di male in peggio* (from bad to worse) . . .

ACTIVITY 6: LET'S WARM UP

See if you can identify the following theater terms.

1.	*la scenografia*		a.	costumes
2.	*i costumi*		b.	intermission
3.	*la rappresentazione*		c.	the end
4.	*l'intervallo*		d.	set design
5.	*la fine*		e.	performance

HEAR . . . SAY 2

Despite sitting in front of a woman who sneezed throughout most of *il primo atto* (the first act) and made *un sacco di rumore* (a ton of noise) trying to get out *un fazzoletto* (a tissue), Simona and Francesco seem to be enjoying the evening. *All'intervallo* (at intermission), they exchange some impressions . . .

Simona: Sicuramente una grande interpretazione! Mi piace tantissimo.

Francesco: A me, invece, no.

Simona: Davvero? A me sì. La scenografia, i costumi, la rappresentazione . . . tutto mi sembra ottimo.

Francesco:	Secondo me, è tutto un po' esagerato.
Simona:	Non è vero. Devi perderti nella musica . . .
Francesco:	Non mi perdo così facilmente.
Simona:	Ma questa voce! Mio padre diceva sempre del soprano al nostro teatro: "canta come un angelo!" Si può dire senza dubbio della Ricciarelli.
Francesco:	Sì, sì, ma c'è ancora qualcosa che non mi convince . . .

As the curtains drops signaling *la fine* (the end), Simona looks over at Francesco and is surprised to find him wiping away *qualche lacrima* (some tears).

Simona:	Ma cosa c'è, Francesco?
Francesco:	*(sniff)* È l'opera più triste di tutte! . . . *sniff, sniff* . . . Ogni volta che vedo uno spettacolo commovente è più forte di me, piango.
Simona:	*(trying not to laugh)* Ti serve un fazzoletto?
Francesco:	No, no grazie. Sto meglio. Passa subito. *(takes it anyway)*
Simona:	Ma adesso, l'opera ti ha convinto?
Francesco:	Sì, purtroppo, sì . . .

ACTIVITY 7:   HOW'S THAT AGAIN?

Vero o falso?

	VERO	FALSO
1. L'opera è piaciuta a Simona.	_____	_____
2. Secondo Francesco, la scenografia è un po' esagerata.	_____	_____
3. Per Simona, il soprano canta come un angelo.	_____	_____
4. All'intervallo, Francesco dice che l'opera è commovente.	_____	_____
5. Alla fine, Francesco piange perché l'opera non gli è piaciuta.	_____	_____

Well, it's nice to know Francesco's heart isn't made of stone after all. How can anyone resist crying at *La Bohème, una storia così commovente, così triste . . .* ? But I suppose we should find out what all those words mean first.

WORKSHOP 2

APPRECIATING THE ARTS: MORE ABOUT A NIGHT OUT AT THE OPERA

If you want to sound like you know what you're talking about, you might want to comment on some of the supporting elements in an opera, besides *la rappresentazione* (the performance) itself.

il palcoscenico	*stage*
la scenografia	*set design*

Here are a few more adjectives you can use to discuss whether *lo spettacolo* was able to *convincere* (convince [past participle: *convinto*]) *il pubblico* (the audience).

esagerato	*overdone; exaggerated*
commovente	*moving*
triste	*sad*
ottimo	*excellent*

Take a Tip from Me!

Notice that *esagerazione* and *esagerare* derive from the same stem. Keeping an eye out for these relationships is a great way to increase your vocabulary. Once you know the verb, you can often guess what the noun form or the adjective is. For example, how would you say "exaggerated; overdone" in Italian? If you guessed *esagerato*, you're right! Just think of all the other places you could apply this kind of rule: *preparare—preparazione—preparato; immaginare—immaginazione—immaginato,* and so on, and so on . . .

Take a Tip from Me!

Now let's look at the sequence of events:

il primo atto	*the first act*
l'intervallo	*intermission*
la fine	*the end (fem.)*

Before you break out the *fazzoletti* (tissues), you'll need to take that very important first step: buying *i biglietti* (tickets). Where do you prefer to sit?

Vorrei . . .	I'd like . . .
• **un posto in platea.**	• *an orchestra seat.*
• **un posto in prima / seconda galleria**	• *a mezzanine / balcony seat*
• **dei posti davanti / di dietro**	• *seats up front / in the rear*

ACTIVITY 8: TAKE IT FOR A SPIN

Translate the following sentences into Italian.

1. At intermission, let's get a glass of wine. _____

    _____

2. That was the most moving performance of all! _____

    _____

3. Did the opera convince you? _____

    _____

4. Are tickets for the opera sold here? _____

    _____

5. I'd like a balcony seat. _____

THE NITTY-GRITTY

Now, let's take a look at disjunctive pronouns—and I don't mean Simona and Francesco!

FROM ME TO YOU: PRONOUNS USED AFTER A PREPOSITION

"Disjunctive pronouns" is just a fancy name for pronouns you use after a preposition. They're also often used for emphasis, and you've seen them in phrases like *secondo me*, and *a me, invece, no.* Here they are, in all their glory:

PRONOUNS USED AFTER A PREPOSITION			
IO	*me*	NOI	*noi*
TU	*te*	VOI	*voi*
LEI	*lei / Lei*	LEI	*lei*
LUI	*lui*	LORO	*loro*

These pronouns must be used with the prepositions *per, con, su, di,* and *tra / fra.* With the preposition *a,* they are used only for added emphasis. The great news about these pronouns is that, except for *me* and *te,* they're identical to the subject pronouns, and you've pretty much been using them all along. In Lesson 2, Delphine orders a snack:

Una pasta con crema per me.

A pastry with cream for me.

In Lesson 4, Antonella talks about her father's reaction to her grandmother's new boyfriend:

Mio padre non parla con lei.

My father's not talking to her.

In Lesson 5, Teresa comments about Brad Pitt:

È un po' vecchio per me, ma non importa . . . è super bono!

He's a bit old for me, but it doesn't matter . . . he's really hot!

And so on . . . in effect, you get a freebie on this one. You already know this stuff!

Word on the Street

Here's a bonus: Disjunctive pronouns can also be used following an adjective in exclamations, such as *Povero te!* (Poor you!) or *Beato lui!* (Lucky him!)

ACTIVITY 9: TAKE IT FOR A SPIN

Fill in the blanks using disjunctive pronouns.

1. *Devo parlare con (Angela) _____ .*

2. *Sono andata a vedere un'opera con (Francesco e Simona) _____ .*

3. *Secondo (io) _____ , la scenografia è un po' strana.*

4. *Per (il marito) _____ , il calcio è la cosa più importante del mondo.*

5. *A (Marina e Gabriella) _____ piace lo spettacolo. A (io) _____ , invece, no.*

6. *Non ci sono più biglietti per stasera. —Poveri (noi) _____ !*

Adesso cambiamo tema . . .

THE WAY WE WERE: MORE ON THE *IMPERFETTO*

Before we go, let's look at some verbs that are irregular in the imperfect. Again, the good news is that there are very few of them, and their endings are perfectly regular: They just have irregular stems. The stems should look familiar.

IRREGULAR VERBS IN THE IMPERFECT TENSE	
fare	*fac–*
dire	*dic–*
bere	*bev–*

Mio padre diceva sempre del soprano al nostro teatro, "Canta come un angelo!".

My father always used to say about the soprano in our theater, "She sings like an angel!"

All'intervallo spesso bevevo vino bianco.

At intermission, I would often drink white wine.

Gli allievi facevano un giro della città ogni anno.

The students used to take a tour of the city every year.

ACTIVITY 10: TAKE IT FOR A SPIN

Fill in the blanks using the imperfect tense.

1. *Mi ricordo che mia nonna sempre (fare)_____ pettegolezzi con le sue amiche.*

2. *Da bambino, (bere, io)_____ un bicchiere di latte prima di andare a letto.*

3. *(Dire, io)_____ sempre che La Bohème è l'opera più triste di tutte!*

4. *Quando (essere, voi)_____ piccoli, vi (portare, noi)_____ al teatro ogni fine-settimana.*

5. *Paolo mi (dire)_____ spesso di andare all'Arena di Verona!*

Curtain falls. *La fine.*

CRIB NOTES

HEAR ... SAY 1

Francesco:	Hi. You're Simona, right?
Simona:	Hi, Borsalino! You're Francesco?
Francesco:	Should we go in? The show is starting in a little bit.
Simona:	I'm sorry for Paolo, but I'm so happy to be able to come in his place. In my hometown, there was a very small theater where I would go to the opera almost every Saturday with my folks. I always liked *La Bohème* the most . . . it's Puccini's most beautiful opera.
Francesco:	I agree, even if, according to me, his most interesting opera is *Tosca*. Puccini is truly the most profound composer in the world.
Simona:	Maybe.
Francesco:	How were the shows at such a small theater?
Simona:	Well! Our tenor was no Pavarotti, but I was ten years old and everything seemed magical to me.
Francesco:	I would also never miss a chance to see an opera. My friends used to make fun of me (*Lit.* torment me)—they would call me "Puccini."
Simona:	Poor you! By the way, have you seen the program? We have the good fortune to see Katia Ricciarelli, the great singer, and Riccardo Muti, the great orchestra director, on the same night!
Francesco:	And, thanks to Paolo, we have seats up front.
Simona:	Last year, I saw Verdi's *La Traviata* with Ricciarelli. She was truly unforgettable, something marvelous . . . Francesco?
Francesco:	I'm thinking about Katia Ricciarelli. I saw her five years ago in *Carmen*. . . . I don't know . . . She wasn't that great. She seemed a bit . . . tired.
Simona:	It's clear we have different opinions. In my opinion, she's the best soprano of our time.
Francesco:	An exaggeration, perhaps, but she certainly has had much success.
Simona:	But what a pleasure to see both of them under the stars of Verona!
Francesco:	It's the occasion of a lifetime!
Simona:	Paolo often talked to me about the Arena di Verona. According to him, it's the most beautiful theater in the world.
Francesco:	To tell you the truth, I prefer an intimate theater to this big arena.
Simona:	Well then, one day you have to visit my hometown. Ours has to be the most intimate theater in Italy!
Francesco:	Psst. Be quiet! It's starting.

HEAR ... SAY 2

Simona:	Certainly a great interpretation. I like it so much.
Francesco:	I, on the other hand, don't.
Simona:	Really? I do. The set design, the costumes, the performance . . . everything seems excellent.
Francesco:	If you ask me, it's all a bit overdone.
Simona:	That's not true. You have to lose yourself in the music.
Francesco:	I don't lose myself that easily.
Simona:	But that voice! My father used to say about the soprano at our little theater: "She sings like an angel!" That can be said about Ricciarelli without a doubt.
Francesco:	Yes, yes, but there's still something that doesn't convince me . . .
Simona:	But what's wrong, Francesco?
Francesco:	sniff . . . It's the saddest opera of all! . . . sniff, sniff . . . Every time I see a performance this moving, it's stronger than me, I cry.
Simona:	Do you need a tissue?
Francesco:	No, no, thank you. I'm better. It'll pass quickly.
Simona:	So, now, has the opera convinced you?
Francesco:	Yes, unfortunately, yes.

ACTIVITY 1

1. c;   2. b;   3. b;   4. a;   5. c

ACTIVITY 2

1. *Simona e Francesco assistono a* La Bohème.
2. *Il compositore è Puccini.*
3. *Secondo Francesco, Puccini è il compositore più profondo del mondo.*
4. *Per Simona, Katia Ricciarelli è il miglior soprano dei nostri giorni. Francesco non è d'accordo. Non gli sembra così brava.*
5. *No, Riccardo Muti non canta con Katia Riccarelli. Lui è il direttore d'orchestra.*
6. *L'Arena di Verona è un teatro grande.*

ACTIVITY 3

Chiara:	*Ti piace lo spettacolo?*
Del Vecchio:	*A dire la verità, non mi piace molto.*
Chiara:	*A me, invece, sì. A mio parere, è una grande interprezione! Indimenticabile!*
Del Vecchio:	*Un'esagerazione, secondo me. Però può darsi. Il tenore è meraviglioso . . .*
Chiara:	*Come si chiama?*
Del Vecchio:	*Vediamo . . . ecco il programma.*
A neighbor:	*Silenzio, per favore!*

ACTIVITY 4

1. *Riccardo Muti è il migliore direttore d'orchestra del mondo.*
2. *Il calcio è lo sport più popolare di tutti.*
3. *Verdi è il compositore più conosciuto.*
4. *Navigare in rete è il passatempo più popolare del mondo.*
5. *Il terremoto è il disastro più orribile.*
6. *Questo è il ristorante meno caro della zona.*
7. *Elisabetta è la guida più simpatica di tutte.*
8. *Gianfranco è il portiere più pazzo del mondo.*
9. *Il Chianti è il vino più delizioso del mondo.*
10. *L'italiano è la lingua più bella del mondo.*

ACTIVITY 5

1. *Il soprano era veramente meraviglioso!*
2. *Andavo all'opera ogni sabato.*
3. *Gli allievi avevano sempre delle interpretazioni originali.*
4. *Sbadigliavo sempre durante la classe di matematica.*
5. *Ogni anno mi scrivevano una cartolina.*
6. *Gli piaceva leggere il giornale e discutere sulle attualità.*
7. *Parlava spesso della criminalità.*
8. *Avevi otto anni.*
9. *Si sentivano per telefono tutte le mattine.*
10. *Tutta la mia famiglia dormiva sempre fino a tardi.*

ACTIVITY 6

1. d;   2. a;   3. e;   4. b;   5. c

ACTIVITY 7

1. *vero;*   2. *vero;*   3. *vero;*   4. *falso;*
5. *falso*

ACTIVITY 8

1. *All'intervallo, prendiamo un bicchiere di vino.*
2. *Questo è stato lo spettacolo più commovente di tutti! / Questa è stata la rapprezentazione più commovente di tutte!*
3. *Ti ha convinto l'opera?*
4. *Si vendono qui i biglietti per l'opera?*
5. *Vorrei un posto in seconda galleria.*

ACTIVITY 9

1. *lei;*   2. *loro;*   3. *me;*   4. *lui;*   5. *loro; me;*
6. *noi*

ACTIVITY 10

1. *faceva;*   2. *bevevo;*   3. *Dicevo;*
4. *eravate; portavamo;*   5. *diceva*

L E S S O N

14. BIRDS OF A FEATHER FLOCK TOGETHER

Chi s'assomiglia si piglia.
(*Lit.* Those who are alike take each other.)

This is for you!

Spero che vi siete divertiti all'opera! But I also imagine you might be a little "cultured out," having spent two lessons talking about *l'arte*, whether it's Italy's *pittori e scultori famosi* or its *grandi direttori d'orchestra e soprani.* Still, you can't beat *un posto davanti* at a place like *l'Arena di Verona!* But let's leave all that behind *per il momento*, and turn to something all of us in today's consumer society enjoy: *fare lo shopping!* There's no shopping like the shopping you do around *Natale* (Christmas). Fortunately, Italy just might be *il miglior paese del mondo* to find the perfect *regalo* (gift)—at least if you're a *turista.* For most Italians, who are used to everything that Italy has to offer, finding a gift that's *originale* (original) is no small feat. Like most Americans, Italians usually walk away with something as exciting as a new *cravatta* (tie) or *camicia* (shirt). The trick is to get creative, as you're about to see . . .

ACTIVITY 1: LET'S WARM UP

Matchmaker, matchmaker . . .

1.	*Lo prendo!*	a.	Can you wrap it for me?
2.	*Me lo può incartare?*	b.	How original you are!
3.	*Ci voglio pensare.*	c.	The chance of a lifetime!
4.	*Ripasserò.*	d.	I'll take it!
5.	*Quanto sei originale!*	e.	I'll pass by again.
6.	*Un'occasione della vita!*	f.	I want to think about it.

ACTIVITY 2: LET'S WARM UP

. . . matchmake some more.

If you read about what's coming up, you know that you'll encounter verbs in the future tense in this lesson. See if you can match the verb in the future tense with its infinitive.

1.	*ripasserò*	a.	*aprire*
2.	*sarà*	b.	*essere*
3.	*farai*	c.	*portare*
4.	*piacerà*	d.	*ripassare*
5.	*mi riposerò*	e.	*fare*
6.	*apriremo*	f.	*piacere*
7.	*porterai*	g.	*riposarsi*

Adesso, andiamo a fare un po' di shopping!

Gabriella, whom you met way back in Lesson 1, and her sister, Sandra, are doing their Christmas shopping together. Gabriella is buying something for Giovanni, but her quirky *sorella minore* finds her choices rather uninspired. Gabriella has something up her sleeve, though . . .

Gabriella:	Lo prendo. Me lo può incartare, per piacere?
La commessa:	Certo. E quell'altro?
Gabriella:	No, grazie. Ci voglio pensare . . . ripasserò.
Sandra:	Cos'hai comprato per Giovanni, a parte questa cravattona, troppo grande secondo me?
Gabriella:	Una camicia, come al solito.
Sandra:	Quanto sei originale!
Gabriella:	Ed anche il nuovo libro di Eco e il nuovo CD di Carmen Consoli.
Sandra:	Un po' meglio ma . . .
Gabriella:	Vedrai . . . il grande regalo sarà una settimana libera.
Sandra:	Come libera?
Gabriella:	Non so—ma avrà l'occasione di fare quello che vorrà. Non avrà nessuna responsabilità a casa.
Sandra:	Un'occasione della vita! E tu, cosa farai?
Gabriella:	Io? Finalmente mi riposerò! Lui è stato molto stressato in questi ultimi mesi.
Sandra:	Allora, è un regalo per te o per lui?
Gabriella:	Per tutt'e due.
Sandra:	Come sei generosa!
Gabriella:	Che ore sono?
Sandra:	Saranno le sei.
Gabriella:	Me ne vado. Ci vediamo domani sera.
Sandra:	Apriremo tutti i regali insieme?
Gabriella:	Sì, certo. I bambini saranno felicissimi! Ti ricordi quando eravamo piccole? Non vedevamo l'ora di aprire i regali!
Sandra:	Si, a parte quelli della nonna. Ogni Natale ci regalava dei calzini!
Gabriella:	È vero! Ma i vecchi ci compravano tanti giocattoli . . . a proposito, porterai il nuovo ragazzo?
Sandra:	Il contorno, lo porterò certamente . . . il nuovo ragazzo, non sono sicura . . . Lo saprai quando arriveremo.

Vero o falso?

		VERO	FALSO
1.	Gabriella ha comprato una cravatta per suo marito.	_____	_____
2.	A Sandra piace la cravatta.	_____	_____
3.	Gabriella ha comprato un regalo per sé stessa.	_____	_____
4.	La nonna di Gabriella e Sandra comprava dei giocattoli per le sue nipoti ogni Natale.	_____	_____
5.	Sandra porterà il contorno alla cena di Natale.	_____	_____

On your way *da negozio a negozio* (from store to store), why don't you stop by the workshop?

WORKSHOP 1

WORDS TO LIVE BY

While *fare lo shopping* is fun for most people, around *Natale* it can also be *da impazzire* (maddening)! Whether you prefer shopping in *un grande magazzino* (a department store), *un centro commerciale*, or a small *negozio* (store; boutique), *scegliere un regalo non è una cosa da poco* (choosing a gift)! It's not a bad idea to go *a vedere le vetrine* (window shopping), before you decide what you'd like to *regalare* (give as a gift). In the end, however, most people just round up the usual suspects:

un libro	book
un CD	CD
un lettore di CD	CD player
un aggeggio	gadget

DRESSED TO THE NINES: CLOTHING ITEMS

Items of *l'abbigliamento* (clothing) are also popular choices:

la camicia	shirt
la camicetta	blouse
il pullover	sweater

i pantaloni	pants
i jeans	jeans
il vestito	dress; suit
la giacca	jacket
il cappotto	coat
le scarpe	shoes
i calzini	socks

Just be sure you know the person's size: *la taglia* for clothing and *il numero* for shoes. Or if you want to avoid all that, *gli accessori* (accessories) will often do the trick, too:

la cravatta	tie
la cintura	belt
i guanti	gloves
la sciarpa	scarf
l'ombrello	umbrella
l'orologio	watch
la collana	necklace
il braccialetto	bracelet
l'anello	ring

To see something, ask:

Mi può mostrare . . . ?	*Can you show me . . . ?*
Vorrei vedere . . .	*I'd like to see*
Vorrei provare . . .	*I'd like to try on . . .*

Or *il commesso / la commessa* (salesperson [masc. / fem.]) might offer:

Le posso mostrare qualcosa?	*Can I show you something?*
Posso darLe un suggerimento?	*Can I offer a suggestion?*
Posso consigliarLa?	*Can I recommend something?*

If you like what you see, just say:

Lo / La prendo!	*I'll take it! (masc. / fem.)*
Me lo / la può incartare?	*Can you wrap it (masc. / fem.) for me?*
Mi fa un pacco?	*Can you wrap it up (Lit. . . . make a package)?*
Mi dà un sacchetto?	*Can I have a bag?*

If, on the other hand, you haven't quite made up your mind, you can politely say:

Do solo un'occhiata.	*I'm just looking.*
Ci voglio pensare.	*I want to think about it.*
Ripasserò.	*I'll stop by again.*

Whatever you decide, don't get *stressato* (stressed)! People usually *non vedono l'ora* (can't wait) to open their gifts. And after all, *è il pensiero che conta* (it's the thought that counts)!

TAKE IT FOR A SPIN

Unscramble the following dialogues.

1. —*Sì, lo prendo. Me lo può incartare?*
   —*Sì, certo. Eccolo.*
   —*Buon giorno. Posso mostrarle qualcosa?*
   —*Certo, e Le do un sacchetto.*
   —*Sì. Mi può mostrare l'orologio in vetrina?*
   —*Grazie.*
   —*Le piace?*

2. —*Ci voglio pensare. Ripasserò.*
   —*Vorrei vedere quella camicia bianca.*
   —*. . . Allora, la prende?*
   —*Vuole provarla?*
   —*Sì, grazie.*

3. —*No, grazie. Do solo un'occhiata.*
   —*Cerca un regalo?*
   —*Posso consigliarLa?*
   —*Sì.*

Did You Know?

I'LL TAKE IT!: A GUIDE TO SHOPPING AND GIFT-GIVING

Italy is truly a shopper's delight! Italians are extremely fashion conscious and insist on the finest quality in everything. Contrary to popular belief, bargaining is <u>not</u> the norm in Italy, except at outdoor markets, where it's expected. In fact, many stores will display a *prezzi fissi* sign (meaning "fixed prices"). One of my favorite things about shops in Italy, however, is that virtually all of them display prices in the *vetrina*, so you can instantly tell which *negozio* falls within your price range. In general, the best buys in Italy are leather goods, ceramics, jewelry, handicrafts, and of course their famous *scarpe* and *abbigliamento*.

But each *regione* of Italy has its specialty. Shop for leather and fine paper products in Firenze; for glassware and lace in Venezia; for ceramics in Siena, Vietri, and many towns in Sicilia; for coral in Napoli; for wooden handcrafts in Calabria, Sicilia, and the Dolomiti. Finally, don't be confused by the *ingresso libero* (free entry) sign that decorates many shop windows. All it means is that you're free to go in without an appointment, which is what you're probably used to anyway. So, whip out your *contanti* (cash) and *carte di credito* (credit cards) and let the fun begin!

| ACTIVITY 5: | **TAKE IT FOR A SPIN** |

Label all the items of clothing *nella vetrina*.

Before you get carried away in a shopping frenzy, let's buckle down and spend some time on *la grammatica*.

WHAT WILL BE WILL BE: THE FUTURE TENSE AND ITS USES

The great news about the future tense is that, just like the *imperfetto*, it has one set of endings for all three verb groups. Just drop the final –*e* from the infinitive, and tag on one of the endings:

–ò	–emo
–ai	–ete
–à	–anno

There's not much of a "catch" to this rule either: the only thing to remember is that the –*a*– in –*are* verbs changes to –*e*–. Here's how it works:

THE FUTURE TENSE OF REGULAR VERBS			
	COMPRARE	PRENDERE	APRIRE
IO	comprer–ò	prender–ò	aprir–ò
TU	comprer–ai	prender–ai	aprir–ai
LEI / LUI	comprer–à	prender–à	aprir–à
NOI	comprer–emo	prender–emo	aprir–emo
VOI	comprer–ete	prender–ete	aprir–ete
LORO	comprer–anno	prender–anno	aprir–anno

The future tense is generally used in Italian exactly as it is in English:

Apriremo tutti i regali insieme?

Will we open all the gifts together?

Porterai il nuovo fidanzato?

Will you bring your new boyfriend?

Il contorno, lo porterò certamente. Il fidanzato, non sono sicura.

The side dish, I'll certainly bring. The boyfriend, I'm not sure.

Reflexive verbs work just as they did in the present tense; the pronoun goes before the verb:

Finalmente mi riposerò.

I'll finally rest.

Heads Up!

Because the –a–in the –are ending changes to –e–when forming the future tense, verbs ending in –care and –gare take an h to keep the "hard" sound of their stem (e.g. pagare → pagherò; cercare → cercherò). Likewise, verbs ending in –ciare and –giare drop the i from their stem because the –e– already makes the c and g "soft" (e.g. cominciare → comincerò; mangiare → mangerò).

So, let's give it a go!

TAKE IT FOR A SPIN

Change the sentences from the present to the future tense, adding *domani*.

1. *Partiamo per le vacanze di Natale.* _____

   _____

2. *Festeggiano insieme.* _____

   _____

3. *Aprite i regali?* _____

   _____

4. *Compro un lettore di CD.* _____

   _____

5. *Ti riposi dopo la festa?* _____

   _____

6. *Sandra porta il contorno e Ridzi porta i dolci.* _____

   _____

7. *Prendo il treno per Napoli.* _____

   _____

8. *Invitiamo tutti i nostri amici.* _____

   _____

9. *Fabrizio non ha vinto un premio.* _____

   _____

10. *Esce il nuovo libro di Eco.* _____

    _____

LET'S DO THE CI CI CI: MORE ON THE MULTIFACETED PRONOUN *CI*

Let's see . . . so far you've learned that *ci* can mean:

"us"	as in: *Ci porterà alla festa.* (He'll take us to the party).
"to / for us"	as in: *Ci compreranno un regalo.* (They'll buy a gift for us).
"there"	as in: *Non ci vado più.* (I don't go there anymore).
"ourselves"	as in: *Ci svegliamo presto la mattina.* (We wake up early in the morning).

You'd think that four different usages would be enough for a two-letter word, but no—there's another one left. The pronoun *ci* can also replace a phrase that begins with the preposition *a* or *in*. For example:

Voglio pensare <u>a questo regalo</u>. → <u>Ci</u> voglio pensare.

I want to think about this gift. → I want to think about it.

Ci penso io.

I'll take care of it.

The pronoun *ci* here means "about / of it" because we say *pensare <u>a</u> qualcosa*. You've already seen this usage in the expressions:

Non ci credo.

I don't believe (in) it.

Non riesco a crederci!

I can't believe it!

Ci is used because we say *credere <u>a</u> qualcosa*. Got it? Good—let's take it for a spin.

ACTIVITY 7:   TAKE IT FOR A SPIN

Answer the questions using *ci* and any information in parentheses.

1. *Credi alla leggenda alla Fontana di Trevi? (no)* _____

   _____

2. *Pensate alle vostre vacanze in Italia? (sì, spesso)* _____

   _____

3. *Chi preparerà la cena stasera? (pensare, io)* _____

4. *Siete già stati a Roma? (mai)* _____

   _____

5. *I bambini credono a Babbo Natale (Santa Claus)? (purtroppo, no)* _____

   _____

Now that we're all shopped and grammared out, we get to eavesdrop on a nice Natale family dinner . . .

LET'S WARM UP

Let's play odd one out. Cross out the word or phrase that doesn't belong.

1.	*il tavolo*	*il piatto*	*il televisore*	*la sala da pranzo*
2.	*cucinare*	*guardare la tv*	*pulire*	*lavare*
3.	*fantastico*	*malaccio*	*simpatico*	*meraviglioso*
4.	*la cravatta*	*il cuscino*	*la camicia*	*il vestito*
5.	*il balcone*	*il corridoio*	*il bagno*	*la sala da pranzo*

HEAR . . . SAY 2

Din dan! Was that the doorbell? Look, it's Sandra and her side dish . . . oops! I meant boyfriend. *Poverino* (the poor thing), he's been traveling for hours and all he can think about is making it to the bathroom in time. In the process, he also makes a bit of an odd first impression . . .

Sandra:	Buona sera. Buon Natale!
Gabriella:	Buon Natale! Entrate . . .
Sandra:	Questo è Ridzi.
Sandra:	Ciao, Ridzi. Si accomodi.
Ridzi:	Grazie. Scusate, ma dov'è il bagno?
Gabriella:	Ce n'è uno alla fine del corridoio, accanto alla cucina, e un altro al primo piano dopo la cameretta dei bambini. Noi saremo nella sala da pranzo.
Giovanni:	Te lo mostrerò io e così potrai vedere la casa.
Sandra:	Cosa ne pensi?
Gabriella:	Non è malaccio, è simpatico. Ma ha appena detto due parole. Vedremo . . .

With the introductions out of the way, the dinner goes swimmingly, and *la conversazione* takes the typical turns . . .

Ridzi: . . . Mmmm. Le lasagne sono fantastiche, Gabriella.
Gabriella: . . . Avete visto la mostra all'Istituto Olandese . . .
Sandra: . . . Non sopporto questi politici ipocriti che . . .

Everyone seems to be having a great time, and they're so engrossed in conversa-tion that they almost forget it's *Natale*. Giovanni glances at his *orologio* and announces . . .

Giovanni: (*clinking his glass*) Din, din, din! È mezzanotte! Vediamo cosa ci ha portato Babbo Natale . . .
Sandra: Ma dove sono i bambini?
Gabriella: Saranno sotto il tavolo. Si addormentano lì ogni Natale.
Giovanni: Una camicia . . . di nuovo. Grazie, tesoro. Oh! Carmen Consoli—mi conosci bene. Ma perché non apri tu il mio regalo?
Gabriella: Una scatolina? Cosa c'è dentro?
Giovanni: Non so. Vedrai . . .
Gabriella: Un foglio di carta?
Giovanni: Cosa dice?
Gabriella: "La titolare di questo tagliando avrà sette giorni interi per sé stessa. Non cucinerà, non pulirà, non addormenterà i bambini, potrà scegliere il canale alla tv (cosa che mi dà tanta pena) e comincerà ogni giorno con la colazione a letto." Che buon'idea! Adesso vediamo il tuo.
Giovanni: "Il titolare di questo tagliando . . ."
Sandra: Chi s'assomiglia si piglia.

ACTIVITY 9: HOW'S THAT AGAIN?

1. *Sandra ha portato il suo ragazzo a cena?* _____

2. *Come si chiama il fidanzato?* _____

3. *Ridzi piace a Gabriella?* _____

4. *Cos'ha cucinata Gabriella?* _____

5. *Dove sono i bambini a mezzanotte?* _____

6. *Che regalo di Natale ha comprato Giovanni per Gabriella?* _____

_____

Did You Know?

WORKSHOP 2

WORDS TO LIVE BY

'TIS THE SEASON: CELEBRATIONS AND DINNER CONVERSATION

We've talked all about shopping and presents, but we haven't talked about the most basic part of holidays: greetings. Here are some general greetings you can use on all occasions:

Auguri!	Best wishes!
Tante cose!	All the best! (Lit. So many things!)
Congratulazioni!	Congratulations!

If you want to be more specific, here are some of the major causes for celebration and the appropriate words for well-wishing:

il Capodanno	New Year's Day	**Buon Anno!**	Happy New Year!
la Pasqua	Easter; Passover	**Buona Pasqua!**	Happy Easter!; Happy Passover!
il Natale	Christmas	**Buon Natale!**	Merry Christmas!
il compleanno	birthday	**Buon compleanno!**	Happy birthday!
l'onomastico	name day	**Buon onomastico!**	Happy name day!
l'anniversario	anniversary	**Buon anniversario!**	Happy anniversary!

Of course, no celebration would be complete without:

Salute!	Cheers!
Cin Cin!	

That *Natale* is probably the most important family holiday in Italy can be summed up in the saying: *Natale con i tuoi, Pasqua con chi vuoi*, which means "Christmas with the family and Easter with whomever you want."

HOME SWEET HOME: ALL THE ROOMS THAT MAKE A HOME

As you may remember from Lesson 4, *casa mia*, whether it's referring to *un palazzo* (a palace), *una casa* (a house), or *un appartamento* (an apartment) is a place of tremendous importance for most Italians. Let's get to know *la casa* a little better, at least in its physical form:

il soggiorno	*living room*
la sala da pranzo	*dining room*
la camera (da letto)	*bedroom*
la cucina	*kitchen*
il bagno	*bathroom*
il balcone	*balcony*
il corridoio	*hallway; corridor*
la porta	*door*
la finestra	*window*

Did You Know?

WHERE ARE WE?: COUNTING FLOORS IN ITALIAN

In Italian, they count the floors of a house differently. What we call the first (or ground) floor is *il pianterreno,* our second floor is their *primo piano* (*Lit.* first floor), our third their *secondo piano,* etc.

Naturally, making a house a home takes a lot of work. Before you can open the door with a smile and say:

Si accomodi.	*Make yourself at home. (formal)*

there's plenty of work to be done!

cucinare	*to cook*
pulire	*to clean*
lavare	*to wash*

At the sight of these words, most of us will think *mi dà tanta pena* (it pains me). That's why small gestures, like Gabriella and Giovanni's gifts to each other, where *il titolare* (the bearer) of *il tagliando* (the coupon), gets a week off from his or her *faccende domestiche* (household chores [fem.pl.]) can go a long way to making a happy home.

Dove sono?

1. *Qui si mangia:* _____

2. *Qui si dorme:* _____

3. *Qui si entra in casa:* _____

4. *Qui si prepara la cena:* _____

5. *Qui si guarda la tv:* _____

6. *Qui si passa da una stanza all'altra:* _____

7. *Qui ci si può sedere fuori:* _____

8. *Da qui c'è una bella vista:* _____

Auguri! Now there's more work to be done.

THE NITTY-GRITTY

WHAT WILL BE WILL BE: THE FUTURE TENSE OF *ESSERE* (TO BE) AND *AVERE* (TO HAVE)

Before you get bent out of shape, let me tell you that even irregular verbs are pretty easy in the future tense. There aren't that many of them, and the endings are the same. You just have to memorize the irregular stem. First let's look at *essere* and *avere*:

THE FUTURE TENSE OF *ESSERE* (TO BE)			
I O	sarò	N O I	saremo
T U	sarai	V O I	sarete
LEI / LUI	sarà	L O R O	saranno

THE FUTURE TENSE OF *AVERE* (TO HAVE)			
I O	avrò	N O I	avremo
T U	avrai	V O I	avrete
LEI / LUI	avrà	L O R O	avranno

Here are a few more common verbs with irregular future stems. As with the *imperfetto*, they all take the standard future tense endings.

IRREGULAR FUTURE TENSE VERB STEMS	
fare (to do)	*far–*
dare (to give)	*dar–*
andare (to go)	*andr–*
vedere (to see)	*vedr–*
sapere (to know)	*sapr–*
potere (can)	*potr–*
dovere (must)	*dovr–*
volere (to want)	*vorr–*
venire (to come)	*verr–*

Take a Tip from Me!

Notice that with *fare* and *dare,* all that happens is that the –*a*– doesn't change to an –*e*–. For most of the remaining verbs, you just drop the –*e*– from the infinitive ending, which will probably happen naturally, even if you forget the "irregular stem," simply because it's easier to pronounce that way.

Take a Tip from Me!

The Fine Print

In addition to the usages we discussed in Workshop 1, the future tense can also be used to express probability in the present, as when Gabriella asks Sandra what time it is in the first dialogue, and Sandra responds:

Saranno le sei.

It must be six.

Or when Sandra asks where the *bambini* are in the second dialogue, and Gabriella answers:

Saranno sotto il tavolo.

They must be under the table.

ACTIVITY 11:   TAKE IT FOR A SPIN

Fill in the blanks with the future tense of the appropriate verb.

1. *La cena di Natale (essere)* _____ *fenomenale!*

2. *Cosa (dare, tu)* _____ *a tua moglie per Natale?*

3. *Domani sera (andare, voi)* _____ *a vedere un'opera all'Arena di Verona?*

4. *Se non (piacere)* _____ *a tua sorella, (potere, Lei)* _____ *cambiarlo.*

5. *Domani (vedere, io)* _____ *la loro nuova casa.*

6. *Cosa (fare, tu)* _____ *domani dopo la lezione?*

7. *Dov'è Gabriella? (essere)* _____ *al negozio.*

8. *Al nuovo lavoro, (avere, io)* _____ *tante responsabilità.*

9. *Venite alla festa! (fare)* _____ *tante conoscenze!*

10. *Quando (vedere, loro)* _____ *Pietro? —Fra due settimane.*

Now a little something to wrap things up . . .

—INO, –ETTO, –UCCIO, –ONE: SUFFIXES AND THEIR MANY USES

Italian culture being as vibrant as it is, how could their language not be? Sometimes a word on its own just doesn't say it all; it requires additional color, nuance, tone. In English, we do this by describing it with other words; in Italian, they just tag on one of their suffixes, like *–issimo*, which you already know. At this point, don't worry about memorizing all of them, just try to recognize them when you hear them.

COMMON SUFFIXES	
SUFFIX	**MEANING**
–ello / –ella –etto / etta –ino / –ina	small
–uccio / –uccia	small or expresses endearment
–one / –ona –accio / –accia –astro / –astra	large
–azzo / –azza	ugliness or poor quality

ACTIVITY 12: TAKE IT FOR A SPIN

Can you find instances of the use of suffixes in the dialogues? Try to guess what each means:

1. *una cravattona* _____

2. *la cameretta dei bambini* _____

3. *malaccio* _____

4. *Tesorino!* _____

5. *scatolina* _____

Auguri! Avete finito la lezione! Alla prossima!

CRIB NOTES

Gabriella: I'll take it. Can you wrap it for me, please?

Saleswoman: Sure. And that other one?

Gabriella: No, thanks. I want to think about it. . . . I'll come back.

Sandra: What did you buy for Giovanni, apart from this big tie, too big, if you ask me?

Gabriella: A shirt, as usual.

Sandra: How original you are!

Gabriella: And also Eco's new book and Carmen Consoli's new CD.

Sandra: A little better, but . . .

Gabriella: You'll see . . . The big present will be a week free.

Sandra: Free how?

Gabriella: I don't know—but he'll have the chance to do what pleases him. He won't have any responsibilities at home.

Sandra: The chance of a lifetime! And you, what will you do?

Gabriella: Me? Finally, I'll rest! He's been very stressed these last few months.

Sandra: So, is it a gift for you or for him?

Gabriella: For both of us.

Sandra: How generous you are!

Gabriella: What time is it?

Sandra: It must be six.

Gabriella: I'm leaving. See you tomorrow night.

Sandra: Will we open all the presents together?

Gabriella: Yes, of course. The kids will be so happy! Do you remember when we were little? We couldn't wait to open our presents!

Sandra: Yes, except for the ones from Grandmother. She gave us socks as a gift every Christmas.

Gabriella: That's true. But our folks would always buy us lots of toys . . . by the way, will you bring your new boyfriend?

Sandra: The side dish I'll bring for sure . . . the new boyfriend, I'm not sure . . . you'll find out when we get there.

Sandra: Hello. Merry Christmas!

Gabriella: Merry Christmas! Come in . . .

Sandra: This is Ridzi.

Sandra: Hi, Ridzi. Make yourself at home.

Ridzi: Thanks. Excuse me, but where's the bathroom?

Gabriella: There's one at the end of the corridor, next to the kitchen, and another one on the second (*Lit.* first) floor after the kids' small bedroom. We'll be in the dining room.

Giovanni: I'll show you and that way you'll be able to see the apartment.

Sandra: What do you think of him?

Gabriella: He's not so bad, he's nice. But he's barely said two words. We'll see . . .

With the introductions out of the way, the dinner goes swimmingly, and *la conversazione* takes the typical turns . . .

Ridzi: . . . Hmmm. The lasagna is fantastic, Gabriella.

Gabriella:	. . . Have you seen the exhibit at the Dutch Institute?
Sandra:	. . . I can't stand these hypocritical politicians who . . .

Everyone seems to be having a great time, and they're so engrossed in conversation that they almost forget it's *Natale*. Giovanni glances at his *orologio* and announces . . .

Giovanni:	Clink, clink, clink! It's midnight! Let's see what Santa Claus brought us . . .
Sandra:	But where are the kids?
Gabriella:	They must be under the table. They fall asleep there every Christmas.
Giovanni:	A shirt . . . again. Thank you, sweetheart (*Lit.* little treasure). Oh! Carmen Consoli—you know me

well. Now why don't you open my present?

Gabriella:	A little box. What's inside?
Giovanni:	I don't know. You'll see . . .
Gabriella:	A piece of paper?
Giovanni:	What does it say?
Gabriella:	"The bearer of this coupon will have seven whole days for herself. She will not cook, will not clean, will not put the kids to bed, she'll be able to choose the channel on TV (which causes me great pain) and she'll begin each day with breakfast in bed." What a good idea! Now let's see yours . . .
Giovanni:	"The bearer of this coupon . . ."
Sandra:	Birds of a feather flock together!

ANSWER KEY

ACTIVITY 1

1. d; 2. a; 3. f; 4. e; 5. b; 6. c

ACTIVITY 2

1. d; 2. b; 3. e; 4. f; 5. g; 6. a;
7. c

ACTIVITY 3

1. *vero*; 2. *falso*; 3. *falso*; 4. *falso*;
5. *vero*

ACTIVITY 4

1. —*Buon giorno. Posso mostrarLe qualcosa?*
   —*Sì. Mi può mostrare l'orologio in vetrina?*
   —*Sì, certo. Eccolo.*
   —*Grazie.*
   —*Le piace?*
   —*Sì, lo prendo. Me lo può incartare?*
   —*Certo, e Le do un sacchetto.*
2. —*Vorrei vedere quella camicia bianca.*
   —*Vuole provarla?*
   —*Sì, grazie.*
   —*. . . Allora, la prende?*
   —*Ci voglio pensare. Ripasserò.*
3. —*Cerca un regalo?*
   —*Sì.*
   —*Posso darLe un suggerimento?*
   —*No, grazie. Do solo un'occhiata.*

ACTIVITY 5

1. *il capello*, €80; 2. *il pullover*, €120;
3. *la giacca*, €360; 4. *i pantaloni*, €160;
5. *la cintura*, €90; 6. *le scarpe*, €280

ACTIVITY 6

1. *Domani partiremo per le vacanze di Natale.*
2. *Domani festeggeranno insieme.*
3. *Aprirete i regali domani?*
4. *Domani comprerò un lettore di CD.*
5. *Ti riposerai dopo la festa domani?*
6. *Domani Sandra porterà il contorno e Ridzi porterà i dolci.*
7. *Domani prenderò il treno per Napoli.*
8. *Domani inviteremo tutti i nostri amici.*
9. *Fabrizio non vincerà un premio domani.*
10. *Domani uscirà il nuovo libro di Eco.*

ACTIVITY 7

1. *No, non ci credo.*
2. *Sì, ci pensiamo spesso.*
3. *Ci penso io.*
4. *Non ci siamo mai stati.*
5. *Purtroppo, no. I bambini non ci credono.*

ACTIVITY 8

1. *il televisore* (hopefully!); 2. *guardare la tv;*
3. *malaccio;* 4. *il cuscino;* 5. *il balcone*

ACTIVITY 9

1. *Sì, Sandra ha portato il suo fidanzato a cena.*
2. *Il fidanzato si chiama Ridzi.*
3. *Sì e no—non è sicura.*
4. *Gabriella ha cucinato le lasagne.*
5. *A mezzanotte i bambini dormivano sotto il tavolo.*
6. *Giovanni ha "comprato" una settimana libera per Gabriella.*

ACTIVITY 10

1. *la sala da pranzo;* 2. *la camera da letto;* 3. *la porta;* 4. *la cucina;* 5. *il soggiorno;* 6. *il corridoio;* 7. *il balcone;* 8. *la finestra*

ACTIVITY 11

1. *sarà;* 2. *darai;* 3. *andrete;* 4. *piacerà; potrà;* 5. *vedrò;* 6. *farai;* 7. *Sarà;* 8. *avrò;* 9. *Farete;* 10. *vedranno*

ACTIVITY 12

1. a big tie; 2. the kids' small bedroom; 3. very / so bad; 4. little treasure; 5. small box

15. WHEN PIGS FLY . . .

Quando voleranno gli asini . . .
(*Lit.* When donkeys fly . . .)

Gimme the remote control!

COMING UP...

- *Come on down!*: The joys of pop culture
- *You fool!*: Insults and comebacks
- *Watch it!*: How to give commands and order people around
- *Ne, ne, ne*: The pronoun *ne* and its many uses
- *Strut your stuff!*: A review

So, we've talked about *le attualità* and *l'alta cultura* (high culture)—*l'opera, l'arte, l'architettura*—but that doesn't paint the full picture of what Italy is all about. It's not as serious as all that. Believe it or not, Italians have as much of a taste for *la cultura di massa* (mass / popular culture) as most Americans do. The popularity of *le telenovele, i varietà* (variety shows), and *i giochi a premi* (game shows) will attest to that. Come to think of it, being a *concorrente* (contestant) on *un gioco a premi* is not a bad way to come into some extra spending money for *Natale* and really make a statement with an expensive *regalo*. But most of us are content to play along at home and *sognare* of the millions we're going to win some day. So, *accendiamo la tv* (let's turn on the TV), and let's have some fun—*divertiamoci*! And speak of the devil, *Il Quiz* happens to be on with its over-the-top *presentatore* (host) and a brand new *concorrente*, Fabrizio.

ACTIVITY 1: **LET'S WARM UP**

It's the matching game again . . . *in italiano*!

1.	*le stupidaggini*	a.	*tema*
2.	*Me ne frego!*	b.	*Mai!*
3.	*scherzare*	c.	*idiota*
4.	*Quando voleranno gli asini!*	d.	*Sta zitto!*
5.	*argomento*	e.	*Non m'importa!*
6.	*cretino*	f.	*prendere in giro*
7.	*Chiudi il becco!*	g.	*le cose stupide*

Adesso siete pronti per giocare.

HEAR . . . SAY 1

Ada *e suo fratello* Adriano never seem to agree on anything, least of all on which TV show to watch. Ada's in the *soggiorno* with *il telecomando* (remote control) in hand, watching *Il Quiz*, when Adriano walks in and begins to do what all brothers do: make fun of her, argue with her, and grab for *il telecomando*.

Il presentatore:	Buona sera, meraviglioso pubblico! Pronti, prontissimi per giocare per un milione di euro! . . .
Adriano:	*(grabbing the remote and changing channels)* Cosa c'è alla tv?
Ada:	Dammi il telecomando! Guardavo il Quiz quando l'hai preso.

Adriano:	Non ho nessuna voglia di guardare quelle stupidaggini!
Ada:	Non sono stupidaggini. *(regaining control of the remote)* È un programma da cui si può imparare molto. Se non ti piace, leggi un libro.
Adriano:	Leggilo tu!
Ada:	Allora, fa' il cruciverba, ascolta la musica, pulisci la camera . . . me ne frego!
Adriano:	Ma c'è la partita tra il Milan e la Juventus. Volevo guardarla!
Ada:	Non m'interessa il calcio.
Il presentatore:	. . . La domanda che vale mille euro è: Quale grande compositore italiano ha scritto *La Bohème*? 1. Verdi? 2. Puccini? 3. Rossini? o 4. Bellini?
Ada:	Puccini!
Adriano:	Testa di rapa!
Il concorrente:	L'ha scritta Puccini.
Ada:	Hai visto? Scherza quanto vuoi, ma un giorno, sarò una concorrente e vincerò tanti soldi!
Adriano:	Sì—quando voleranno gli asini!
Ada:	Non ti darò un euro!
Il presentatore:	. . . Mi dia la Sua risposta definitiva, Fabrizio.
Il concorrente:	Puccini—risposta definitiva.
Il presentatore:	Vediamo cosa dice il computer . . . sì! Ha vinto mille euro. Continuiamo? . . . il prossimo argomento è lo sport e la domanda vale due mila . . .
Adriano:	Finalmente qualcosa d'interessante!
Ada:	Chiudi il becco!
Il presentatore:	Quale squadra di calcio ha vinto il maggior numero di Coppe dei campioni? 1. La Roma? 2. La Fiorentina? 3. La Juventus? o 4. Il Milan?
Il concorrente:	Hmmm. Non sono sicuro . . . posso eliminare la Roma e il Milan— no, volevo dire la Fiorentina . . .
Il presentatore:	Allora, ha già eliminato due possibilità e ne sono rimaste solo due . . .
Adriano:	Che idiota!
Il presentatore:	. . . Non si affretti . . . ci pensi un po' . . .
Adriano:	*(screaming at the TV)* È il Milan, cretino!
Ada:	Non urlare! Sii gentile!
Il concorrente:	. . . La Juventus, risposta definitiva.

Il presentatore:	La Juventus. Vediamo . . . secondo il computer, il Milan ha vinto . . .
Adriano:	Te l'ho detto! Vincerò io i milioni!
Il presentatore:	. . . più titoli europei, però la Juventus è la squadra campione italiana. Bravo, Fabrizio! Ha dato la risposta giusta!
Ada:	Cosa dicevi? Chi, esattamente, è il cretino? Parliamo un po' di queste "stupidaggini" . . .
Adriano:	Non ne voglio parlare!

ACTIVITY 2: HOW'S THAT AGAIN?

Vero o falso?

		VERO	FALSO
1.	*Ada guardava* Il Quiz *alla tv quando Adriano è entrato.*	_____	_____
2.	*Anche Adriano vuole guardare il gioco a premi.*	_____	_____
3.	*Puccini ha scritto* La Bohème.	_____	_____
4.	*Il Milan è la squadra campione italiana.*	_____	_____
5.	*Adriano ha dato la risposta giusta.*	_____	_____
6.	*A questo punto, il concorrente ha vinto due mila euro.*	_____	_____
7.	*Ada sogna di vincere un milione di euro.*	_____	_____

Heads Up!

When talking about quantities or amounts (of cash, for example!), and you're using millions and billions (*milione* or *miliardo*), the noun that follows has to be introduced by *di*. With hundreds and thousands no such introductions are necessary!

While the bickering continues, *mettiamoci al lavoro!* (Let's get to work!).

WORKSHOP 1

COME ON DOWN!: THE JOYS OF POP CULTURE

Whether you're watching *a casa* or you're part of *il pubblico* (the audience) in *lo studio* (the studio), the appeal of *un gioco a premi* (a game show) is that regular folks, like you and me, get to go on as *un / una concorrente* (a contestant [m. / f.]) and walk away with sometimes hefty *vincite* (winnings [f. pl.]) . . . and fifteen minutes of fame.

    Prepararsi bene (to prepare well) is important, but really it all comes down to *la fortuna*. After all, you have no control over which *argomento* (subject) your *domanda* (question) is about. And all anyone cares about is whether your *risposta* (answer) is *corretta / giusta* (right) or *sbagliata* (wrong). A good strategy is this: *eliminare* (to eliminate) *le risposte* (the answers) that you know are *sbagliate*. Then you just have to *scegliere* (choose) among the remaining *possibilità*. So, pick your favorite *canale* (channel [masc.]) and let the games begin!

    If *un gioco a premi* is not your speed, there are plenty of other *programmi alla tv*:

lo spettacolo di varietà	*variety show*
i cartoni animati	*cartoons*
il documentario	*documentary*
il telegiornale	*the news*
la telenovela	*soap opera*
la commedia	*comedy*
una partita di calcio	*a soccer game*

Heads Up!

Notice that in Italian they say *alla tv* (or *alla radio*), while we say "<u>on</u> TV" (or "<u>on</u> the radio"). This is another example of the "flexibility" of prepositions. They're the hardest words to translate!

Did You Know?

Did You Know?

GOAL!: SOCCER FEVER IN ITALY

Italians are *pazzi* over *il calcio,* which is hands-down the national sport. Sunday afternoons people are glued to their television sets, watching the truly bizarre cult show *Quelli che di calcio.* It's a sports show crossed with a variety show crossed with David Letterman's Stupid Human Tricks. There's a studio audience and guests who include anyone from soccer players' moms and psychics to top models and actresses. As they follow the results of all the matches being played in Italy, they air strange segments featuring men dressed like babies lying in bathtubs, others dressed like chickens interviewing fans, etc. I've seen it quite a few times. I have to admit that I still don't quite get it. I'm convinced it holds the key to being a true Italian!

YOU FOOL!: INSULTS AND COMEBACKS

So sit back, relax, *prendete il telecomando* (take the remote control), and *accendete la tv* (turn on the TV). You can *cambiare canale* (change channels) to your heart's content. Just don't forget to *spegnere la tv* (turn off the TV) before going *a letto.* Of course, if you're part of the typical family, it won't go as smoothly as all that. You can expect to argue quite a bit over what to watch, and harsh words might be exchanged, but please use them sparingly!

Cretino!	Cretin! / Idiot!
Testa di rapa!	Nerd! (Lit. Beet head!)
Chiudi il becco!	Shut your trap! (Lit. Shut your beak!)
Me ne frego!	I don't give a damn! / I couldn't care less!
Quando voleranno gli asini!	When pigs fly! (Lit. When donkeys fly!)

ACTIVITY 3:   TAKE IT FOR A SPIN

Choose the word that best completes each sentence.

eliminare	spegnere	il telecomando
cambiare canale	accendere	prepararsi

1. Dov'è _____? Non sopporto questo programma!

2. Ragazzi, _____ la tv. La partita tra Roma e Lazio comincia tra poco.

3. Mario è un uomo tipico—_____ ogni due secondi.

4. Bambini, _____ la tv e _____ per andare a letto.

5. Nella vita, devi _____ i problemi uno per uno.

TAKE IT FOR A SPIN

What would you say?

1. You're at a party and a George Clooney look-alike walks over to you, only to start talking about little-known facts about the mating habits of ants. You nod obligingly while thinking, "What a nerd!" _____

2. You learn that your ex is getting married. You insist you don't care. _____
    _____

3. The same person's been asking you out for eons and wants to know when you'll finally agree to a date. Tired of being nice, you indicate that the chances are less than slim. _____

4. As you light up a cigarette and launch into a piece of *tiramisù,* your friend reminds you of your New Year's resolutions: to quit smoking and go on a diet. You tell him / her, not so politely, to shut up. _____

5. Some jerk speeds through the crosswalk, almost knocking you down. You wave your fist in the air and yell, _____

Adesso, diamo un'occhiata alla grammatica.

THE NITTY-GRITTY

WATCH IT!: **HOW TO GIVE COMMANDS AND ORDER PEOPLE AROUND**

The imperative is used to give commands or direct suggestions, as in:

Leggi un libro.

Read a book.

You've been using the imperative in the *noi* and *voi* forms ever since Lesson 3, because the imperative forms are identical to the present tense. The same is true for the *tu* form of *–ere* and *–ire* verbs; *infatti*, all you have to remember is that the imperative of the *Lei* form ends in *–a*, and you know the imperative for these two verb groups. With *–are* verbs the present tense *tu* and *Lei* forms "switch places:" in the imperative the *tu* form ends in *–a* and the *Lei* form ends in *–i*. To sum up:

THE IMPERATIVE OF REGULAR VERBS

	–ARE	–ERE	–IRE
TU	–a	–i	
LEI (FML.)	–i	–a	
NOI		–iamo	
VOI	–ate	–ete	–ite

Can you remember a few examples of the imperative from the dialogue? *Il presentatore* instructs Fabrizio (using the *Lei* form):

Ci pensi un po'.

Think about it a little bit.

Non si affretti.

Don't rush.

And Ada tells her brother (naturally, using the *tu* form):

. . . ascolta la musica, pulisci la camera.

. . . listen to music, clean your room.

Scherza quanto vuoi . . .

Joke as much as you want . . .

Chiudi il becco!

Shut your trap!

Non urlare!

Don't scream!

Heads Up!

When you're giving a negative command in the *tu* form, use the infinitive form of the verb, as in: *non parlare, non scrivere,* and *non dormire.*

Before you get to test your command of the command form, let's look at how you use pronouns with the imperative. In general, the object pronouns are attached to the end of the verb:

Leggilo tu!

You read it!

Divertitevi!

Have fun!

Non leggerlo.

Don't read it.

Guardatelo!

Watch it!

Divertiamoci un po'!

Let's have a little fun!

However, with the *Lei* command form, pronouns **always** come before the verb.

Mi dica.

What would you like? (*Lit.* Tell me.)

Me ne parli un po'.

Talk to me about it a little.

Okay, let's try it out!

ACTIVITY 5:   TAKE IT FOR A SPIN

Translate!

1.   Don't watch TV! (*tu*) _____

2.   Change the channel. (*Lei*) _____

3.   Open your gifts! (*tu*) _____

4.   Kids, (go to) sleep! _____

5.   Don't close the window. (*Lei*) _____

6.   Believe me! (*tu*) _____

7.   Write to Manuela! (*voi*) _____

8.   Buy me a coffee! (*tu*) _____

9.   Let's read the newspaper! _____

10.   Talk to your mother! (*tu*) _____

Before we get back to the show, let's take a quick look at the pronoun *ne*.

You've already encountered the pronoun *ne* in the expression *quanti ne vuole?*, "how many (of them) would you like?" And you've probably noticed it butting in here and there throughout the dialogues. That's because it's a very versatile little word. It has two main functions.

- *Ne*, meaning "some of it / them"

In the example above, *ne* is used as a partitive, and it means "some / any (of it / them, etc.)." If you remember the context, Barbara wants to buy bus tickets:

> **Ha <u>biglietti per l'autobus</u>? —Sì, certo. Quanti <u>ne</u> vuole?**
>
> Do you have bus tickets? —Yes, of course. How many (of them) would you like?

In the latest dialogue, you heard *il presentatore* say:

> **Ha eliminato due <u>possibilità</u>. <u>Ne</u> sono rimaste due.**
>
> You've eliminated two possibilities. There are two (of them) left.

The Fine Print

When *ne* is used to mean "of it / them" it functions as a direct object. This means that in the *passato prossimo*, the past participle agrees with the gender and number of the noun that *ne* is replacing. So, we say *ne sono rimast<u>e</u> due* because *ne* stands for *possibilità*. For example:

> **Quante cartoline hai comprato? —Ne ho comprate dieci.**
>
> How many postcards did you buy? —I bought ten (of them).

Notice, too, that in English we often omit the phrase "of them," but in Italian you have to remember to use *ne*.

- *Ne*, meaning "about it / them"

In addition to meaning "of it / them," *ne* can also replace any phrase that is introduced by the preposition *di*, in much the same way that *ci* replaces a phrase introduced by the preposition *a*. It then means "about it / them." For example, Ada says:

> **Parliamo un po' <u>di queste "stupidaggini"</u>** . . .
>
> Let's talk a bit about these "stupidities" . . .

And Adriano responds:

> **Non _ne_ voglio parlare.**
>
> I don't want to talk about it.

Here *ne* refers back to the phrase *di queste "stupidaggini."* Let's look at some other examples.

> **Abbiamo parlato _della partita_.** → **_Ne_ abbiamo parlato.**
>
> We talked about the game. → We talked about it.
>
> **Abbiamo bisogno _di un nuovo televisore_.** → **_Ne_ abbiamo bisogno.**
>
> We need a new TV set. → We need it.

In this context, *ne* is often used with phrases like *parlare di, avere voglia di, avere paura di,* or *avere bisogno di.*

> **Hai voglia _di andare a una partita di calcio_?** → **_Ne_ hai voglia?**
>
> Do you feel like going to a soccer game? → Do you feel like it?

Notice that when *ne* replaces a phrase that begins with *di*, there is no agreement of the past participle.

Heads Up!

You may have noticed that we say, *"Cosa ne pensi?"* (What do you think about it?) but *"Ci voglio pensare"* (I want to think about it). Well, that's because *pensare* has two different meanings, which both translate the same way into English. *Pensare di* means "to think about" in the sense of having an opinion about something or someone: *"Cosa pensi di Sandra? —È molto simpatica."* *Pensare a,* on the other hand, means "to think about" in the sense of "to consider, to reflect upon" or "to have something or someone on one's mind." *"Pensi all'Italia? —Ci penso spesso."*

Let's see *quanto sapete del pronome ne. Ne sapete tanto? Vediamo . . .*

ACTIVITY 6: TAKE IT FOR A SPIN

Rewrite the sentences replacing the underlined phrase with *ne*, as in the example. Don't forget the past participle agreement where it's needed!

Fabrizio ha avuto due <u>domande</u>. → *Fabrizio ne ha avute due.*

1. *Ha eliminato due <u>possibilità</u>.*
2. *Simona e Francesco hanno parlato <u>dell'opera</u>.*
3. *Abbiamo bisogno <u>di pane</u>.*
4. *Ho letto tanti <u>articoli sulla domenica senza traffico</u>.*
5. *Avete invitato cinque <u>amici alla cena di Natale</u>.*

Now answer the following questions using *ne* and any information in parentheses, as in the example.

Quante opere con Katia Ricciarelli hai visto? (due) —Ne ho viste due.

6. *Quante cartoline avete scritto? (twenty)* _____

7. *Hai voglia di uscire? (no)* _____

8. *Hanno comprato dei regali? (sì, tanti)* _____

9. *Ha già fatto qualche domanda? (sì, tre)* _____

10. *Quante camere da letto ha la casa di Giovanni e Gabriella? (due)* _____

Now back to our show! *Bentornati!* (Welcome back!)

ACTIVITY 7: LET'S WARM UP

Matchmaker, matchmaker, make me a match . . .

1.	*Vieni qua!*	a.	Do me a favor!
2.	*Dammi una mano!*	b.	I have my doubts.
3.	*Abbia pazienza!*	c.	Come here!
4.	*Ho cambiato idea.*	d.	Such is life.
5.	*Vengo subito!*	e.	Give me a hand!
6.	*Fammi un favore!*	f.	I changed my mind.
7.	*Ho i miei dubbi.*	g.	I'm coming right away!
8.	*Così è la vita.*	h.	Be patient!

HEAR . . . SAY 2

In an effort to stop the bickering, Ada and Adriano's mother calls to them from another room . . .

La mamma:	Ada! Vieni qua! Dammi una mano!
Ada:	Vengo subito. Ecco il telecomando, cretino. Ma quando tornerò, me lo ridarai.
Adriano:	Finalmente, posso guardare la partita in pace . . . ma sentiamo la prossima domanda . . .
Il presentatore:	Giochiamo per quattro mila . . . L'argomento è la geografia e la domanda è: Qual è la regione più grande d'Italia? 1. il Piemonte? 2. la Toscana? 3. la Sicilia? o 4. la Sardegna?
Fabrizio:	(*getting nervous*) L'abbiamo imparato in quinta elementare, ma tanto tempo fa . . .
Il presentatore:	Mi faccia un favore: abbia pazienza! Non si preoccupi. Cosa sta pensando? Me lo dica . . .
Fabrizio:	È una delle isole, credo. La Sicilia sembra più grande . . . però, ho i miei dubbi . . . Non ho ancora deciso.
Adriano:	(*now completely engrossed*) Secondo me è la Sicilia.
Ada:	(*returns, thrilled to have caught her brother still watching* Il Quiz) Ah! Ma come mai guardi queste "stupidaggini"?
Adriano:	Ma cosa ne pensi tu? La Sardegna o la Sicilia?
Ada:	(*baiting him*) Sono sicura che . . .
Adriano:	Cosa? Dimmelo!
Ada:	. . . che sei tu la testa di rapa!
Adriano:	Mah! (*about to retort, but stops to hear Fabrizio's answer*)
Fabrizio:	Ho cambiato idea. Dirò la Sardegna, risposta definitiva.
Il presentatore:	Per quanto riguarda il tipo di regione, ha ragione—è una delle isole. Purtroppo, pero, è la Sicilia. Mi dispiace, Fabrizio. Ha giocato bene . . .
Fabrizio:	Così è la vita . . .
Adriano e Ada:	(*both yell at the TV*) Cretino!

ACTIVITY 8: HOW'S THAT AGAIN?

Vero o falso?

		VERO	FALSO
1.	*Ada va a aiutare sua madre.*	_____	_____
2.	*Adriano cambia canale e adesso guarda la partita di calcio.*	_____	_____

3. *La domanda che tratta della geografia*
   vale dieci mila euro. _____ _____

4. *La Sicilia è la regione più grande d'Italia.* _____ _____

5. *Fabrizio sa la risposta giusta.* _____ _____

6. *Adriano sa la risposta giusta.* _____ _____

Well, it seems that even bickering rivals will band together when they find someone else to make fun of. *Adesso, continuiamo la lezione?*

WORKSHOP 2

WORDS TO LIVE BY

In general, the dialogues in this lesson provide lots of expressions whose use far exceeds a game show appearance. Use them at will:

Venga qua. / Vieni qua.	Come here! (fml. / infml.)
Vengo subito.	I'll be right there!
Mi faccia / Fammi un favore.	Do me a favor. (fml. / infml.)
Mi dia / Dammi una mano.	Give me a hand. (fml. / infml.)
Ho i miei dubbi.	I have my doubts.
Ho cambiato idea.	I've changed my mind.
Così è la vita!	Such is life!
Abbia / Abbi pazienza!	Be patient! (fml. / infml.)
Non si preoccupi. / Non preoccuparti.	Don't worry. (fml. / infml.)
Infatti . . .	In fact . . .
per quanto riguarda . . . (+ noun)	as far as . . . (+ noun) . . . is concerned

Let's also take a quick look at *la geografia* (jeh-oh-grah-FEE-ah), "geography," in this case, political geography:

il paese	country; town
lo stato	nation, state
la regione	region
la città	city
il comune	municipality
il villaggio	village

Did You Know?

THE MAP OF ITALY: ITALY AND ITS REGIONS

Italy has a population of circa 60 million people. It is comprised of twenty *regioni,* each with its own history, cultural heritage, and character. In fact, many of the regions used to be countries in their own right. Here are Italy's *regioni* together with their *capitali* (capital cities) from north to south: La Valle d'Aosta—Aosta, Il Piemonte—Torino, La Liguria—Genova, La Lombardia—Milano, Il Veneto—Venezia, Il Trentino Alto Adige—Trento, Il Friuli Venezia Giulia—Trieste, L'Emilia Romagna—Bologna, La Toscana—Firenze, Le Marche—Ancona, L'Umbria—Perugia, Il Lazio—Roma, L'Abruzzo—L'Aquila, Il Molise—Campobasso, La Campania—Napoli, La Puglia—Bari, La Basilicata—Potenza, La Calabria—Reggio Calabria, La Sicilia—Palermo, La Sardegna—Cagliari. (A map with all these various regions is in the back of the book.)

Did You Know?

ACTIVITY 9:   **TAKE IT FOR A SPIN**

What would you say?

1. Your friend is just sitting there watching as you're trying to move an antique (and heavy!) dresser across your living room. Finally, you look at him in disbelief and ask for help: _____

2. You want to ask your brother to pick up your kids from school. You call him and say: "Do me a favor!" _____

3. Your friend calls you up with a surefire scheme to make *i milioni!* It sounds like a pyramid scheme to you. You don't want to be rude, but say you have your doubts:

   _____

4. Your intercom sounds and it's your boss yelling, *"Venga qua!"* You jump and say:

   _____

5. Your best friend complains that he'll never learn how to snowboard. You encourage him to be patient: _____

6. You're about to buy a pretzel from a street vendor, when you see him rubbing the pretzels with dirty hot dog water and putting salt on them. He looks up at you and says, *"Mi dica?"* You tell him you've changed your mind and you're no longer hungry: _____

7. You just found out that your partner left you, your house was repossessed, you lost your job, and your best friend moved to Madagascar. Trying to keep things in perspective, you simply say: _____

Basta con le chiacchiere! Preparatevi per un po' di lavoro!

THE NITTY-GRITTY

WATCH IT!: MORE COMMANDS

What would a new verb form be without irregular verbs? Well, fortunately, if you paid attention in the dialogues and in the vocabulary workshop, you should be in pretty good shape. Here are some common verbs that have irregular imperatives:

IRREGULAR IMPERATIVES				
	TU	**LEI**	**NOI**	**VOI**
AVERE	abbi	abbia	abbiamo	abbiate
ESSERE	sii	sia	siamo	siate
ANDARE	va'	vada	andiamo	andate
DARE	da'	dia	diamo	date
DIRE	di'	dica	diciamo	dite
FARE	fa'	faccia	facciamo	fate
STARE	sta'	stia	stiamo	state
USCIRE	esci	esca	usciamo	uscite
VENIRE	vieni	venga	veniamo	venite

Again, the *noi* and *voi* forms are exactly the same as in the present tense (except for the *voi* form of *avere: abbiate*), so you don't have to worry about those. Just concentrate on the *tu* and *Lei* forms. An important thing to remember is that when a pronoun is attached to the end of *va', da', di', fa',* or *sta',* the first letter of the pronoun is doubled:

Dammi il telecomando!

Give me the remote control!

Dammi una mano.

Give me a hand.

Fammi un favore.

Do me a favor.

Notice, too, that double object pronouns behave just like a single pronoun:

Dimmelo!

Tell me!

Me lo dica.

Tell me.

How many more irregular imperatives can you find in the dialogues? List all of them.

Now get ready to order someone around on your own!

Say that you don't want to do the proposed activities and instruct your interlocutor(s) to do it themselves, as in the example:

Guardare Il Quiz? Nemmeno morto! (tu) Guardalo tu!

1. *Scrivere la e-mail? Non posso. (noi insieme)* _____

    _____

2. *Dare il biglietto a Simona? Ma cosa ti prende?! (tu)* _____

    _____

3. *Andare a un museo? Sono stanchissimo! (Lei)* _____

    _____

4. *Uscire con quegli idioti? Hai perso la testa? (tu)* _____

    _____

5. *Trovare un nuovo lavoro? Perché? (Lei)* _____

6. *Prendere l'autobus? Ma dai! (tu)* _____

7. *Divertirsi a scuola? Impossibile! (noi, alla festa)* _____

    _____

8. *Non preoccuparsi? Ma come? (tu)* _____

9. *Ripetere le regole? Io le conosco. (tu)* _____

10. *Fare gli esercizi? Nemmeno morto! (Lei)* _____

STRUT YOUR STUFF!

Before we go, lest you've already forgotten all about the *passato prossimo* and the *imperfetto* and plan to communicate entirely by giving commands or talking about the future, let's do a quick review of the past tenses.

- A review of the past

If by now you don't know that the *passato prossimo* is formed with *avere* or *essere* and the past participle of the main verb, and that the *imperfetto* is formed by replacing the final –*re* with –*vo* / –*vi* / –*va* / –*vamo* / –*vate* / –*vano*, then you're in trouble! Go directly to Lesson 11, do not pass go, do not collect $200. If, on the other hand, you have that much down, then you're in good shape. Let's spend some time on the tricky stuff.

ACTIVITY 12: TAKE IT FOR A SPIN

Try to jot down as many verbs as you can think of that are conjugated in the *passato prossimo* with *essere*. While you're at it, write down their past participle, too.

_____ _____ _____
_____ _____ _____
_____ _____ _____
_____ _____ _____
_____ _____ _____

Now let's see how many irregular past participles you remember.

ACTIVITY 13: TAKE IF FOR A SPIN

Give the past participle.

1. *fare* _____
2. *essere* _____
3. *dire* _____
4. *leggere* _____
5. *aprire* _____
6. *prendere* _____

9. *chiudere* _____
10. *perdere* _____
11. *rimanere* _____
12. *bere* _____
13. *piacere* _____
14. *chiedere* _____

7. *vedere* _____   15. *decidere* _____

8. *vincere* _____

Let's take a look at one of the stickier rules: Adverbs of time, like *già*, *ancora*, *sempre*, and *mai* go between *avere* or *essere* and the past participle, as when *il presentatore* says:

Hai già eliminato due possibilità.

You've already eliminated two possibilities.

or when Fabrizio responds:

Non ho ancora deciso.

I haven't decided yet.

Okay, now let's put it all together and do some talking in the past.

ACTIVITY 14:   **TAKE IT FOR A SPIN**

Answer the questions below using the information in parentheses. Replace any underlined phrases with pronouns.

1.   *Avete visto il programma Quelli che di calcio? (mai)* _____

_____

2.   *Fabrizio è già stato un candidato di un gioco a premi? (due anni fa)* _____

3.   *Chi ha scritto l'opera Aida? (Verdi)* _____

4.   *Vi siete divertiti? (tanto)* _____

5.   *Hanno mandato la e-mail a sua madre o a suo padre? (non . . . né . . . né)* _____

_____

6.   *Dove hai sentito questo? (leggere nel giornale, l'anno scorso)* _____

_____

7.   *Quando hanno costruito la cattedrale? (nel Trecento)* _____

_____

8.   *A che ora ti sei alzata e quando sei arrivata al lavoro? (alle otto e mezzo, alle*

nove e dieci) _____

9.   *Cos'ha comprato per Giovanni? (una cravatta)* _____

_____

10. *Avete finito l'esercizio?* (non ancora) _____

_____

But one of the trickiest things when talking about the past is knowing when to use the *passato prossimo* and when to use the *imperfetto*. Remember that the *imperfetto* is a descriptive tense and as such, it's often used to describe a "background" action that was going on when something else happened, as when Ada says:

Guardavo Il Quiz quando tu sei entrato.

I was watching *The Quiz* when you came in.

Other examples could be:

Leggevo il giornale quando mi hanno telefonato.

I was reading the paper when they called me.

Word on the Street

You can also use the imperfect of *volere* to mitigate a statement, as when Fabrizio says, "*Volevo dire la Fiorentina*" (I wanted to say Fiorentina). It's the same way we would say "I wanted to ask you a question" instead of "I want to ask you a question" or "*Volevo vedere la camicia in vetrina*" (I wanted to see the shirt in the window).

Why don't you try it out?

ACTIVITY 15: TAKE IT FOR A SPIN

Fill in the blanks using the verbs in parentheses in the appropriate past tense.

1. *Ada (guardare)* _____ *la tv quando (arrivare)* _____ *suo fratello.*

2. *Fabrizio (pensare)* _____ *alla Fiorentina quando (dire)* _____ *il Milan.*

3. *La domenica, tutti (dormire)* _____ *fino a tardi.*

4. *Quest'anno mi (comprare, loro)* _____ *un nuovo vestito per Natale.*

5. *Ieri sera, Simona e Francesco (andare)* _____ *a vedere un'opera all'Arena di Verona.*

6. *Ogni anno Manuela (portare)* _____ *i suoi allievi a vedere il Duomo di Siena.*

7. (leggere, voi) _____ le ultime notizie sul terremoto in India?

8. Luca (volere) _____ parlare con Gianni quando (chiamare) _____ Alfredo.

9. Livia di solito (uscire) _____ solo il fine-settimana, ma una volta (uscire) _____ con Alba e Enzo dopo la classe.

10. Quando Chiara e il signor Del Vecchio (arrivare) _____ a Piazza di Spagna, c'(essere) _____ il sole e (tirare) _____ vento.

11. Giancarlo (dare) _____ la stessa camera a tutt'e due i signori Johnson. (fare, lui) _____ sempre errori simili.

12. Lotte (avere) _____ una fame da lupo quando (vedere) _____ una trattoria.

13. A Laura (piacere) _____ fare la chat in italiano ogni sera.

14. (sentire, voi) _____? La nonna di Antonella (sposarsi) _____ con un uomo molto più giovane di lei.

15. A Bracciano Paola (prendere) _____ un taxi per andare alla festa.

16. Barbara e Delphine (prendere) _____ le vacanze insieme ogni anno.

17. Quando (essere) _____ piccolo, Pietro (sognare) _____ di diventare un macellaio.

Well, this is it for your Italian lessons. Or is it? I hope this is just the beginning of a long and lasting relationship with the Italian language and Italian-speaking cultures. Remember that regular and abundant exposure to the language is the best way to learn it. So keep using what's around you—TV, radio, newspapers, and the Internet. Travel to Italy if you can, make friends with your Italian neighbors, join chat rooms, write e-mails . . . and don't be afraid to make mistakes. It's the effort that counts and most people will appreciate it! As for me, I certainly hope to meet with you again. *Buona fortuna, cari amici!*

HEAR...SAY 1

Host:	Good evening, marvelous audience! We're ready, really ready to play for one million euros!
Adriano:	What's on TV?
Ada:	Give me the remote control! I was watching *The Quiz* when you took it.
Adriano:	I have no desire to watch such stupidities.
Ada:	They're not stupidities. It's a show you can learn a lot from. If you don't like it, read a book.
Adriano:	You read it!
Ada:	Well, then, do a crossword puzzle, listen to music, clean your room . . . I couldn't care less!
Adriano:	But the game between Milan and Juventus is on. I wanted to watch it!
Ada:	I'm not interested in soccer.
Host:	. . . The question that's worth 1,000 euros is: Which great Italian composer wrote *La Bohème*? 1. Verdi? 2. Puccini? 3. Rossini? or 4. Bellini?
Ada:	Puccini!
Adriano:	Nerd! (*Lit.* Beet head!)
Contestant:	Puccini wrote it.
Ada:	Did you see? Joke as much as you want, but one day, I'll be a contestant, and I'll win a lot of money!
Adriano:	Yeah—when pigs (*Lit.* donkeys) fly!
Ada:	I won't even give you one euro!
Host:	. . . Give me your final answer, Fabrizio.
Contestant:	Puccini—final answer.

Host:	Let's see what the computer says . . . Yes! You've won 1,000 euros. Shall we go on? . . . The next subject is sports and the question is worth 2,000 . . .
Adriano:	Finally something interesting!
Ada:	Shut up! (*Lit.* Shut your beak!)
Host:	Which soccer team won the greatest number of Champions' Cups? 1. Roma? 2. Fiorentina? 3. Juventus? or 4. Milan?
Contestant:	Hmmm. I'm not sure . . . I can eliminate Roma and Milan—no, I wanted to say Fiorentina . . .
Host:	So, you've already eliminated two possibilities and you have only two left . . .
Adriano:	What an idiot!
Host:	. . . Don't rush . . . Think about it a little . . .
Adriano:	It's Milan, cretin!
Ada:	Don't scream! Be nice!
Contestant:	. . . Juventus, final answer.
Host:	Juventus. Let's see . . . According to the computer, Milan won . . .
Adriano:	I told you! I'll win the million!
Host:	. . . the most European titles, but Juventus is the Italian champion. Excellent, Fabrizio! You found the right answer!
Ada:	What were you saying? Who, exactly, is the cretin? Let's talk a little about these "stupidities" . . .
Adriano:	I don't want to talk about it!

HEAR...SAY 2

Mother:	Ada! Come here! Give me a hand.
Ada:	I'll be right there. Here's the remote, cretin. But when I come back, you'll give it to me.
Adriano:	Finally, I can watch the game in peace . . . but let's hear the next question . . .
Host:	We're playing for 4,000 . . . The subject is geography, and the question is: Which region is the largest in Italy? 1. Piemonte? 2. Tuscany? 3. Sicily? or 4. Sardinia?
Fabrizio:	We learned this in fifth grade, but that was a long time ago . . .

Host:	Do me a favor: be patient! Don't worry. What are you thinking? Tell me . . .
Fabrizio:	It's one of the islands, I think. Sicily seems bigger . . . but I have my doubts . . . I haven't decided yet.
Adriano:	In my opinion, it's Sicily.
Ada:	Ah! How come you're watching these "stupidities?"
Adriano:	But what do you think (about it)? Sardinia or Sicily?
Ada:	I'm sure that . . .
Adriano:	What? Tell me!
Ada:	. . . that **you're** the nerd!
Adriano:	But!

| Fabrizio: | I changed my mind. I'll say Sardinia, final answer. | | sorry, Fabrizio. You played well . . . |
| Host: | In fact, you're right as far as the type of region is concerned—it is one of the islands. Unfortunately, it's Sicily. I'm | Fabrizio:
Adriano
and Ada: | Such is life . . .
Cretin! |

ANSWER KEY

ACTIVITY 1

1. g;   2. e;   3. f;   4. b;   5. a;   6. c;
7. d

ACTIVITY 2

1. *vero*;   2. *falso*;   3. *vero*;   4. *falso*;
5. *falso*;   6. *vero*;   7. *vero*

ACTIVITY 3

1. *il telecomando*;   2. *accendete*;   3. *cambia canale*;   4. *spegnete; preparatevi*;   5. *eliminare*

ACTIVITY 4

1. *(Che) Testa di rapa!*   2. *Me ne frego!*
3. *Quando voleranno gli asini!*   4. *Chiudi il becco!*   5. *Cretino!*

ACTIVITY 5

1. *Non guardare la tv!*
2. *Cambia (il) canale.*
3. *Apri i tuoi regali!*
4. *Bambini, dormite!*
5. *Non chiuda la finestra.*
6. *Credimi!*
7. *Scrivete a Manuela!*
8. *Comprami un caffè.*
9. *Leggiamo il giornale!*
10. *Parla a tua madre!*

ACTIVITY 6

1. *Ne ha eliminate due.*
2. *Simona e Francesco ne hanno parlato.*
3. *Ne abbiamo bisogno.*
4. *Ne ho letti tanti.*
5. *Ne avete invitati cinque.*
6. *Ne abbiamo scritte venti.*
7. *No, non ne ho voglia.*
8. *Sì, ne hanno comprati tanti.*
9. *Sì, ne ha già fatte tre.*
10. *Ne ha due.*

ACTIVITY 7

1. c;   2. e;   3. h;   4. f;   5. g;   6. a;
7. b;   8. d

ACTIVITY 8

1. *vero*;   2. *falso*;   3. *falso*;   4. *vero*;
5. *falso*;   6. *vero*

ACTIVITY 9

1. *Dammi una mano!*   2. *Fammi un favore!*
3. *Ho i miei dubbi.*   4. *Vengo subito!*
5. *Abbi pazienza!*   6. *Ho cambiato idea. Non ho più fame.*   7. *Così è la vita.*

ACTIVITY 10

Sii gentile.
Mi dia la Sua risposta definitiva.
Vieni qua!
Mi faccia un favore: abbia pazienza.

ACTIVITY 11

1. *Scriviamola insieme.*   2. *Daglielo tu!*
3. *Vada Lei a un museo.*   4. *Esci tu con loro.*
5. *Lo trovi Lei.*   6. *Prendilo tu!*   7. *Divertiamoci alla festa. / Ci vada Lei!*   8. *Non ti preoccupare. / Non preoccuparti.*   9. *Ripetile tu.*   10. *Li faccia Lei.*

ACTIVITY 12

andare / andato	arrivare / arrivato	diventare / diventato
entrare / entrato	essere / stato	morire / morto
nascere / nato	partire / partito	piacere / piaciuto
rimanere / rimasto	ritornare / ritornato	stare / stato
tornare / tornato	uscire / uscito	venire / venuto

Plus all reflexive verbs, like:

addormentarsi / addormentato	alzarsi / alzato	arrabbiarsi / arrabbiato
divertirsi / divertito	interessarsi / interessato	lamentarsi / lamentato
preoccuparsi / preoccupato	prepararsi / preparato	ricordarsi / ricordato
sentirsi / sentito	svegliarsi / svegliato	vestirsi / vestito

ACTIVITY 13

1. *fatto;*   2. *stato;*   3. *detto;*   4. *letto;*
5. *aperto;*   6. *preso;*   7. *visto;*   8. *vinto;*
9. *chiuso;*   10. *perso;*   11. *rimasto;*
12. *bevuto;*   13. *piaciuto;*   14. *chiesto;*
15. *deciso*

ACTIVITY 14

1. *No, non l'abbiamo mai visto.*
2. *Sì, Fabrizio è già stato un candidato di un gioco a premi due anni fa.*
3. *L'ha scritta Verdi.*
4. *Ci siamo divertiti tanto.*
5. *Non l'hanno mandata né a sua madre né a suo padre.*

6. *L'ho letto nel giornale, l'anno scorso.*
7. *L'hanno costruita nel Trecento.*
8. *Mi sono alzata alle otto e mezzo e sono arrivata al lavoro alle nove e dieci.*
9. *Gli ha (ho) comprato una cravatta.*
10. *Non l'abbiamo ancora finito.*

ACTIVITY 15

1. *guardava; è arrivato;*   2. *pensava; ha detto;*
3. *dormivano;*   4. *hanno comprato;*
5. *sono andati;*   6. *portava;*   7. *Avete letto;*
8. *voleva; ha chiamato;*   9. *usciva; è uscita;*
10. *sono arrivati; era; tirava;*   11. *ha dato; Faceva;*   12. *aveva; ha visto;*   13. *piaceva;*
14. *Avete sentito; si è sposata;*   15. *ha preso;*
16. *prendevano;*   17. *era; sognava*

APPENDIX A

A SHORTCUT TO ITALIAN GRAMMAR

A. Words, words, words . . .

1. TYPICAL NOUN AND ADJECTIVE ENDINGS

	SINGULAR	PLURAL
FEMININE	-a	-e
MASCULINE	-o	-i
FEM. OR MASC.	-e	-i

2. PRONOUNS

SUBJECT	DIRECT OBJECT	INDIRECT OBJECT	REFLEXIVE	AFTER A PREPOSITION
(I, you, we . . .)	(me, him, us . . .)	(to me, to you, to them . . .)	(myself, herself . . .)	(with / for / etc. me, you . . .)
io	mi	mi	mi	me
tu	ti	ti	ti	te
Lei	La	Le	Si	voi
lui	lo	gli	si	lui
lei	la	le	si	lei
noi	ci	ci	ci	noi
voi	vi	vi	vi	voi
loro (m.)	li	gli	si	loro
loro (f.)	le	gli	si	loro

3. DOUBLE OBJECT PRONOUNS—COMBINED FORMS

When a direct and indirect object pronoun appear together in a sentence, they are combined, as follows:

	+LO (him; it, m.)	+LA (her; it, f.)	+LI (them, m.)	+LE (them, f.)
MI (to me)	me lo	me la	me li	me le
TI (to you, infml.)	te lo	te la	te li	te le
LE (to her; to you, fml.)	glielo	gliela	glieli	gliele
GLI (to him)	glielo	gliela	glieli	gliele
CI (to us)	ce lo	ce la	ce li	ce le
VI (to you, pl.)	ve lo	ve la	ve li	ve le
GLI (to them)	glielo	gliela	glieli	gliele

4. ARTICLES

| | | INDEFINITE (a, an) | DEFINITE (the) | |
		SINGULAR	SINGULAR	PLURAL
MASCULINE	before a consonant	un	il	i
	before a vowel	un	l'	gli
	before s + consonant or z	uno	lo	gli
FEMININE	before a consonant	una	la	le
	before a vowel	un'	l'	le

5. PREPOSITIONS + DEFINITE ARTICLE COMBINED FORMS

When a definite article follows the prepositions *a*, *da*, *di*, *in*, or *su*, they are combined into one word, as follows:

	+*IL*	+*LO*	+*I*	+*GLI*	+*LA*	+*LE*	+*L'*
A (to; in)	al	allo	ai	agli	alla	alle	all'
DA (from)	dal	dallo	dai	dagli	dalla	dalle	dall'
DI (of; from)	del	dello	dei	degli	della	delle	dell'
IN (in)	nel	nello	nei	negli	nella	nelle	nell'
SU (on)	sul	sullo	sui	sugli	sulla	sulle	sull'

6. DEMONSTRATIVE ADJECTIVES

| | | QUESTO | | QUELLO | |
		SINGULAR (this)	PLURAL (these)	SINGULAR (that)	PLURAL (those)
MASCULINE	before a consonant	questo	questi	quel	quei
	before a vowel	quest'	questi	quell'	quegli
	before s + consonant or z	questo	questi	quello	quegli
FEMININE	before a consonant	questa	queste	quella	quelle
	before a vowel	quest'	queste	quell'	quelle

7. DEMONSTRATIVE PRONOUNS

	QUESTO		QUELLO	
	SINGULAR (this one)	PLURAL (these)	SINGULAR (that one)	PLURAL (those)
MASCULINE	questo	questi	quello	quelli
FEMININE	questa	queste	quella	quelle

8. POSSESSIVE ADJECTIVES AND PRONOUNS

	MASCULINE		FEMININE	
	SINGULAR	PLURAL	SINGULAR	PLURAL
my / mine	il mio	i miei	la mia	le mie
your / yours (infml.)	il tuo	i tuoi	la tua	le tue
your / yours (fml.)	il Suo	i Suoi	la Sua	le Sue
his, her / his, hers	il suo	i suoi	la sua	le sue
our / ours	il nostro	i nostri	la nostra	le nostre
your / yours (pl.)	il vostro	i vostri	la vostra	le vostre
their / theirs	il loro	i loro	la loro	le loro

9. QUESTION WORDS

Chi?	Who?
Cosa / che cosa / che?	What?
Quando?	When?
Dove?	Where?
Perché?	Why?
Come?	How?
Quale?	Which?

[Note: **quale**→**qual'** before a vowel, except before è; **quale**→**quali** in plural.]

10. ADVERBS OF QUANTITY

poco	*un po'*	*abbastanza*	*molto*	*tanto*	*troppo*
little	a little	enough	a lot; much	much	too much

mai	ogni tanto	a volte	spesso	sempre
never	every so often	at times	often	always

12. REGULAR VERBS

A. THE PRESENT TENSE

To form the present tense, drop the *–are / –ere / –ire* ending, and replace it with the appropriate personal ending:

	-ARE	-ERE	-IRE
IO	-o	-o	-o
TU	-i	-i	-i
LUI / LEI	-a	-e	-e
NOI	-iamo	-iamo	-iamo
VOI	-ate	-ete	-ite
LORO	-ano	-ono	-ono

Don't forget that some *–ire* verbs, like *finire, preferire, capire, pulire,* and *costruire* take an *–isc–* before the ending.

B. THE *PASSATO PROSSIMO*

The *passato prossimo* = the present tense of *avere / essere* + past participle. Past participles are formed by replacing the *–are / –ere / –ire* endings with:

-are → -ato
-ere → -uto
-ire → -ito

Most verbs form the *passato prossimo* with *avere*, but all reflexive verbs, as well as intransitive verbs expressing movement, are conjugated with *essere*. The most common verbs conjugated with *essere* include:

	VERBS THAT FORM THE *PASSATO PROSSIMO* WITH *ESSERE*
andare	to go
arrivare	to arrive
diventare	to become
entrare	to enter
essere	to be
morire	to die
nascere	to be born
partire	to leave; to depart
piacere	to like; to be pleasing to
restare	to stay
ritornare	to return
stare	to stay; to be
tornare	to return
uscire	to go out
venire	to come

C. THE IMPERFECT

To form the imperfect (*l'imperfetto*), drop the *-re* from the infinitive, and replace it with the appropriate personal ending:

	-ARE / -ERE / -IRE
IO	*-vo*
TU	*-vi*
LUI / LEI	*-va*
NOI	*-vamo*
VOI	*-vate*
LORO	*-vano*

D. THE FUTURE TENSE

To form the future tense, drop the final *-e* from the infintive, and add the appropriate personal ending. For *-are* verbs the *-a* in the *-are* ending changes to an *-e:*

	-ARE / -ERE / -IRE
IO	*-ò*
TU	*-ai*
LUI / LEI	*-à*
NOI	*-emo*
VOI	*-ete*
LORO	*-anno*

E. THE IMPERATIVE

The imperative is formed as follows:

	-ARE	-ERE	-IRE
TU	-a	same as present tense	
LEI (FML.)	-i	-a	
NOI	same as present tense		
VOI	same as present tense		

Remember that verbs that take an *–isc–* before the ending in the present tense, do so in the imperative, as well.

B. Putting words together into sentences

1. MAKING STATEMENTS

The basic word order in Italian is the same as in English:

subject—verb—object

Marco è italiano

Marco is Italian.

However, because the verb in Italian tells you who the subject is, you can shuffle things around pretty freely in order to emphasize one piece of information over another. So, for example, you could just as easily say:

È italiano Marco.

if you want to stress the fact that Marco is Italian and not some other nationality.

2. ASKING QUESTIONS

When you're asking a simple yes / no question, you have two choices:

1. Simply raise your voice at the end of the sentence:

    Marco è italiano?

2. Move the verb to the front of the sentence, immediately followed by the element you want to emphasize:

    È italiano Marco? (stresses his nationality)

    È Marco italiano? (stresses that you're asking about Marco)

3. ADJECTIVES

Remember that in Italian most adjectives follow the noun:

Marco è un uomo italiano.

Marco is an Italian man.

However, certain common adjectives come before the noun:

- possessives (_il mio amico, la tua amica, le nostre amiche_ . . .)
- _buono (un buon partito)_
- _bello (una bella ragazza)_
- _questo (quest'estate)_
- _quello (quel libro)_

APPENDIX B

EXCEPTIONS THAT CONFIRM THE RULE
A. Irregular verbs

1. Following are the full conjugations of some of the most common irregular verbs. They are all given in the following order: *io, tu, Lei/lui/lei, noi, voi,* and loro

	PRESENT TENSE	*PASSATO PROSSIMO*	*IMPERFETTO*	FUTURE	IMPERATIVE
ANDARE (TO GO)	vado	sono andato / a	andavo	andrò	
	vai	sei andato / a	andavi	andrai	vai / va'
	va	è andato / a	andava	andrà	vada
	andiamo	siamo andati / e	andavamo	andremo	andiamo
	andate	siete andati / e	andavate	andrete	andate
	vanno	sono andati / e	andavano	andranno	
AVERE (TO HAVE)	ho	ho avuto	avevo	avrò	
	hai	hai avuto	avevi	avrai	abbi
	ha	ha avuto	aveva	avrà	abbia
	abbiamo	abbiamo avuto	avevamo	avremo	abbiamo
	avete	avete avuto	avevate	avrete	abbiate
	hanno	hanno avuto	avevano	avranno	
BERE (TO DRINK)	bevo	ho bevuto	bevevo	berrò	
	bevi	hai bevuto	bevevi	berrai	bevi
	beve	ha bevuto	beveva	berrà	beva
	beviamo	abbiamo bevuto	bevevamo	berremo	beviamo
	bevete	avete bevuto	bevevate	berrete	bevete
	bevono	hanno bevuto	bevevano	berranno	
DARE (TO GIVE)	do	ho dato	davo	darò	
	dai	hai dato	davi	darai	dai / da'
	dà	ha dato	dava	darà	dia
	diamo	abbiamo dato	davamo	daremo	diamo
	date	avete dato	davate	darete	date
	danno	hanno dato	davano	daranno	
DIRE (TO SAY)	dico	ho detto	dicevo	dirò	
	dici	hai detto	dicevi	dirai	dici / di'
	dice	ha detto	diceva	dirà	dica
	diciamo	abbiamo detto	dicevamo	diremo	diciamo
	dite	avete detto	dicevate	direte	dite
	dicono	hanno detto	dicevano	diranno	

	PRESENT TENSE	PASSATO PROSSIMO	IMPERFETTO	FUTURE	IMPERATIVE
DOVERE[1] (MUST; TO HAVE TO)	devo devi deve dobbiamo dovete devono	ho dovuto hai dovuto ha dovuto abbiamo dovuto avete dovuto hanno dovuto	dovevo dovevi doveva dovevamo dovevate dovevano	dovrò dovrai dovrà dovremo dovrete dovranno	
ESSERE (TO BE)	sono sei è siamo siete sono	sono stato / a sei stato / a è stato / a siamo stati / e siete stati / e sono stati / e	ero eri era eravamo eravate erano	sarò sarai sarà saremo sarete saranno	sii sia siamo siate
FARE (TO DO; TO MAKE)	faccio fai fa facciamo fate fanno	ho fatto hai fatto ha fatto abbiamo fatto avete fatto hanno fatto	facevo facevi faceva facevamo facevate facevano	farò farai farà faremo farete faranno	fai / fa' faccia facciamo fate
POTERE (CAN; TO BE ABLE TO)	posso puoi può possiamo potete possono	ho potuto hai potuto ha potuto abbiamo potuto avete potuto hanno potuto	potevo potevi poteva potevamo potevate potevano	potrò potrai potrà potremo potrete potranno	
SAPERE (TO KNOW)	so sai sa sappiamo sapete sanno	ho saputo hai saputo ha saputo abbiamo saputo avete saputo hanno saputo	sapevo sapevi sapeva sapevamo sapevate sapevano	saprò saprai saprà sapremo saprete sapranno	sai sappia sappiamo sapete
STARE (TO STAY)	sto stai sta stiamo state stanno	sono stato / a sei stato / a è stato / a siamo stati / e siete stati / e sono stati / e	stavo stavi stava stavamo stavate stavano	starò starai starà staremo starete staranno	stai stia stiamo state
USCIRE (TO GO OUT)	esco esci esce usciamo uscite escono	sono uscito / a sei uscito / a è uscito / a siamo usciti / e siete usciti / e sono usciti / e	uscivo uscivi usciva uscivamo uscivate uscivano	uscirò uscirai uscirà usciremo uscirete usciranno	esci esca usciamo uscite

---

[1] *Dovere* (must), *potere* (can), and *volere* (to want) can be used with either *avere* or *essere* in the *passato prossimo* depending on what verb follows, e.g., *ho dovuto parlare* (I had to speak) or *sono dovuto / a andare* (I had to go).

	PRESENT TENSE	*PASSATO PROSSIMO*	*IMPERFETTO*	FUTURE	IMPERATIVE
VENIRE (TO COME)	vengo	sono venuto / a	venivo	verrò	
	vieni	sei venuto / a	venivi	verrai	vieni
	viene	è venuto / a	veniva	verrà	venga
	veniamo	siamo venuti / e	venivamo	verremo	veniamo
	venite	siete venuti / e	venivate	verrete	venite
	vengono	sono venuti / e	venivano	verranno	
VOLERE (TO WANT)	voglio	ho voluto	volevo	vorrò	
	vuoi	hai voluto	volevi	vorrai	vuoi
	vuole	ha voluto	voleva	vorrà	voglia
	vogliamo	abbiamo voluto	volevamo	vorremo	vogliamo
	volete	avete voluto	volevate	vorrete	volete
	vogliono	hanno voluto	volevano	vorranno	

2. COMMON IRREGULAR PAST PARTICIPLES

VERB	PAST PARTICIPLE	VERB	PAST PARTICIPLE
aprire	aperto	offrire	offerto
chiedere	chiesto	perdere	perso
decidere	deciso	prendere	preso
dire	detto	rimanere	rimasto
essere	stato	scegliere	scelto
fare	fatto	scrivere	scritto
leggere	letto	spegnere	spento
mettere	messo	vedere	visto
morire	morto	vincere	vinto
nascere	nato	vivere	vissuto

3. COMMON IRREGULAR FUTURE STEMS

VERB	FUTURE STEM
andare	andr-
bere	berr-
dare	dar-
dire	dir-
dovere	dovr-
fare	far-
potere	potr-
sapere	sapr-
venire	verr-
volere	vorr-

B. Irregular adjectives

1. *BELLO* (BEAUTIFUL)

THE FORMS OF *BELLO* BEFORE A NOUN

		SINGULAR	PLURAL
MASCULINE	before a consonant	*bel*	*bei*
	before a vowel	*bell'*	*begli*
	before s + consonant, *gn*, *ps*, or *z*	*bello*	*begli*
FEMININE	before a consonant	*bella*	*belle*
	before a vowel	*bell'*	*belle*

THE FORMS OF *BELLO* WHEN USED ALONE OR AFTER A NOUN

	SINGULAR	PLURAL
MASCULINE	*bello*	*belli*
FEMININE	*bella*	*belle*

C. Issues with gender

Some nouns ending in −*a* are masculine, while others ending in −*o* are feminine. Here are some of the most common examples:

1. FEMININE NOUNS ENDING IN −*O*

la foto (le foto, pl.)	*photograph*
la radio (le radio, pl.)	*radio*
la mano (le mani, pl.)	*hand*
l'auto (le auto, pl.)	*car*
la pallavolo	*volleyball*

il **cinema**	*movie theater*
il **clima**	*climate*
il **programma**	*program*
il **cruciverba**	*crossword puzzle*

In fact, all nouns ending in –*ema* (of Greek origin) are masculine:

il **tema (i temi, pl.)**	*topic, subject*
il **sistema (i sistemi, pl.)**	*system*
il **teorema (i teoremi, pl.)**	*theory*

D. Issues with number

1. SINGULAR → PLURAL SPELLING CHANGES

A. NOUNS AND ADJECTIVES ENDING IN –*ISTA*

Nouns and adjectives ending in –*ista* in the singular can be either masculine or feminine. When they change to the plural, they end in –*e* if you're talking about a group of women and in –*i* if you're talking about a group of men. For example:

il **turista** → i **turisti**	*male tourist → male tourists*
la **turista** → le **turiste**	*female tourist → female tourists*
il **taxista** → i **taxisti**	*male taxi driver → male taxi drivers*
la **taxista** → le **taxiste**	*female taxi driver → female taxi drivers*

B. NOUNS AND ADJECTIVES ENDING IN –*CA* / –*GA* AND –*CO* / –*GO*

Nouns and adjectives that end in –*ca* or –*ga* take an –*h*– before the plural ending –*e*.

l'**amica** → le **amiche**	*friend → friends*
simpatica → **simpatiche**	*nice*

Nouns and adjectives ending in –*co* / –*go* take an –*h*– before the plural ending –*i*, when the stress is on the next to last syllable:

l'**albergo** → gli **alberghi**	*hotel → hotels*
lungo → **lunghi**	*long*
BUT: l'**amico** → gli **amici**	*friend → friends*

Otherwise, there is no –h– inserted:

il **meccanico** → i **meccanici**   *mechanic → mechanics*
simpatico → **simpatici**   *nice*

C. NOUNS ENDING IN –CIA / –GIA

If the –i– is stressed, then the change is regular: the –a simply changes to –e

la **farmacia** → le **farmacie**   *pharmacy → pharmacies*
la **bugia** → le **bugie**   *lie → lies*

If, however, the –i– is not stressed, then –ia changes to –e:

la **doccia** → le **docce**   *shower → showers*
la **pioggia** → le **piogge**   *rain → rains*

D. NOUNS ENDING IN –IO

If the –i– is stressed then the change is regular: the –o changes to –i, giving you a double –ii:

lo **zio** → gli **zii**   *uncle → uncles*

If, on the other hand, the –i– is not stressed, then one of the double –ii is dropped:

il **figlio** → i **figli**   *son → sons, children*
il **premio** → i **premi**   *prize → prizes*

2. NOUNS THAT DON'T CHANGE

Some nouns have the same form whether they're singular or plural:

A. NOUNS ENDING IN AN ACCENTED VOWEL:

la **città** → le **città**   *city → cities*
l'**università** → le **università**   *university → universities*

B. NOUNS ENDING IN A CONSONANT (GENERALLY OF FOREIGN ORIGIN):

il **bar** → i **bar**   *café → cafés*
il **computer** → i **computer**   *computer → computers*
il **film** → i **film**   *movie → movies*
la **e-mail** → le **e-mail**   *e-mail → e-mails*

C. NOUNS THAT ARE ABBREVIATED FORMS OF LONGER WORDS

la foto → le foto   *photograph → photographs (from **fotografia**)*
l'auto → le auto   *car → cars (from **automobile**)*

D. COMPOUND NOUNS FORMED FROM TWO WORDS:

il cruciverba → i cruciverba   *crossword puzzle → crossword puzzles*
l'asciugacappelli → gli asciugacappelli   *hair dryer → hair dryers*

3. NOUNS THAT CHANGE GENDER WHEN THEY CHANGE NUMBER

Some nouns change their gender when they become plural:

l'urlo → le urla   *scream → screams*
l'uovo → le uova   *egg → eggs*

4. NOUNS THAT ARE GENERALLY USED ONLY IN THEIR PLURAL FORM

le elezioni   *elections*
le fondamenta   *foundations (of a building)*

APPENDIX C

WHEN YOU'RE STUCK FOR WORDS . . .

DECIDING ON A LANGUAGE . . .

Do you speak English?	*Parla inglese?*
I don't speak Italian.	*Non parlo (l')italiano.*
I don't understand.	*Non capisco.*
Can you repeat that, please?	*Puo ripetere, per favore?*
What does . . . mean?	*Cosa significa . . . ?*

TRAVELING . . .

Here's my passport.	*Ecco il mio passaporto.*
I'm American.	*Sono americano / americana.*
I'm Canadian.	*Sono canadese.*
My name is . . .	*Mi chiamo . . .*
Where can I exchange dollars?	*Dove posso cambiare dei dollari?*
What's the exchange rate?	*Qual è il tasso di cambio?*
These are my suitcases.	*Queste sono le mie valigie.*
I've lost my luggage.	*Ho perso le mie valigie.*
Where is . . .	*Dov'è . . .*
• the taxi?	• *il taxi?*
• the train station?	• *la stazione ferroviaria?*
• the bus stop?	• *la fermata dell'autobus?*
• the underground?	• *la metropolitana?*
• the car rental?	• *l'autonoleggio?*
• the phone?	• *il telefono?*
I'd like a ticket to . . .	*Vorrei un biglietto per . . .*
• one-way	• *solo andata*
• round-trip	• *andata e ritorno*
When is the next train to . . . ?	*Quand'è il prossimo treno per . . . ?*
This seat is taken.	*Questo posto è occupato.*
At what time do we arrive?	*A che ora si arriva?*
My car won't start.	*La macchina non parte.*
I'm out of gas.	*Sono rimasto senza benzina.*
Fill it up.	*Faccia il pieno.*
How do I get to . . . ?	*Come si va a . . . ?*
Is this the road to . . . ?	*È questa la strada per . . . ?*
Do I go . . .	*Devo andare . . .*
• straight?	• *diritto?*
• to the right?	• *a destra?*
• to the left?	• *a sinistra?*
• to the light?	• *al semaforo?*
Where can I park?	*Dove posso parcheggiare?*

IN A RESTAURANT . . .

Can you recommend a good restaurant?	*Può consigliarmi un buon ristorante?*
Is it expensive / affordable?	*È costoso / economico?*
Do I need a reservation?	*Si deve prenotare?*
I'd like to reserve . . .	*Vorrei prenotare . . .*
• a table for two / four.	• *un tavolo per due / quattro.*
• for tonight.	• *per questa sera.*
• for tomorrow.	• *per domani.*
• a table outside.	• *un tavolo fuori / all'aperto.*
The menu, please.	*Il menù, per piacere.*
I'm vegetarian.	*Sono vegetariano / vegetariana.*
What's . . . ?	*Cos'è . . . ?*
To begin . . .	*Per cominciare . . .*
Next . . .	*Poi . . .*
I'll have this. (point to item on menu)	*Prendo questo.*
Where's the restroom?	*Dov'è la toletta?*
The check, please.	*Il conto, per favore.*
Please keep the change.	*Tenga pure il resto.*

AT THE HOTEL . . .

Are there any free rooms?	*Ci sono delle camere libere?*
I'd like a . . . room.	*Vorrei una camera . . .*
• single	• *singola.*
• double (one bed)	• *matrimoniale.*
• double (two beds)	• *doppia.*
I have a reservation.	*Ho una prenotazione.*
Do you have a city map?	*Ha una pianta della città?*
I'd like to order room service.	*Vorrei ordinare qualcosa in camera.*
Can you give me a wake-up call?	*Mi può dare la sveglia?*
Where's . . .	*Dov'è . . .*
• the museum?	• *il museo?*
• the center?	• *il centro?*
• the bank?	• *la banca?*
• the post office?	• *la posta?*
Is there an organized tour?	*C'è un giro organizzato?*

ON A SHOPPING SPREE . . .

I'd like to see . . .	*Vorrei vedere . . .*
Can you show me . . .	*Mi può mostrare . . .*
• this?	• *questo?*
• that?	• *quello?*
• the one in the window?	• *quello in vetrina?*
I'm looking for . . .	*Cerco . . .*
• a gift.	• *un regalo.*
• a souvenir.	• *un ricordo.*
Can I try this on?	*Posso provare questo?*
My (clothing) size is . . .	*La mia taglia è . . .*
I wear (shoe) size . . .	*Porto il numero . . .*
How much is it?	*Quant'è?*
Can you gift-wrap it for me?	*Me lo / la può incartare?*
I'm just looking.	*Do solo un'occhiata.*

THE WORST CASE SCENARIO . . .

Help!	*Aiuto!*
Look out!	*Attenzione!*
Fire!	*Fuoco!*
Thief!	*Al ladro!*
Stop!	*Alt!*
Call . . .	*Chiami . . .*
• an ambulance!	• *il pronto soccorso!*
• the police!	• *la polizia!*
I need . . .	*Ho bisogno di . . .*
• a doctor.	• *un medico.*
• a dentist.	• *un dentista.*
I don't feel well.	*Non mi sento bene.*
I have . . .	*Ho . . .*
• a headache.	• *mal di testa.*
• a stomachache.	• *mal di stomaco.*
• a pain in my throat.	• *mal di gola.*
• a fever.	• *la febbre.*
• a cold.	• *il raffreddore.*
• the flu.	• *l'influenza.*
• a rash.	• *un'irritazione.*
• an allergy to . . .	• *un'allergia a . . .*
Is it serious?	*È grave?*
Is it contagious?	*È contagioso?*
Do I need a prescription?	*Ho bisogno di una ricetta?*
Can I have a bill for my insurance?	*Mi può fare una ricevuta per l'assicurazione?*

APPENDIX D

HOW TO SOUND LIKE AN ITALIAN

A. SPICE UP YOUR CONVERSATION!

Beh!	Well . . . , Um . . . , So . . .
Mah!	But! Oh! Ugh!
Vabbe'!	Okay!
Accidenti!	Damn!
Cavolo!	Shoot! Wow!
Ma dai!	Come on! Come off it! Gimme a break!
Non esiste!	No way!
Meno male!	Thank God!
Magari!	I wish!
Figurati!	Just imagine! or Of course (you can)!
Uffa!	Hmph! Argh! Ugh!
Che disastro!	What a disaster!
Mi prendi in giro?	Are you kidding me?
Dico sul serio!	I'm serious!
. . . da morire!	. . . to die for!
Roba da pazzi!	Crazy stuff!

B. A WORD FOR THE WISE

In bocca al lupo! —Crepi!	Good luck! (*Lit.* In the mouth of the wolf!) — Here, here! (*Lit.* May he die!)
Chi dorme non pecca, ma non piglia pesci.	The early bird gets the worm. (*Lit.* He who sleeps doesn't sin, but neither does he catch any fish.)
Finché la va, la va.	As long is it lasts, it lasts.
Chi la dura, la vince.	Slow and steady wins the race. (*Lit.* He who lasts, wins.)
È arrivato come il cacio sui maccheroni.	Just what was needed! (*Lit.* It arrived like cheese on macaroni!)
Volere è potere.	Where there's a will, there's a way. (*Lit.* To want is to be able.)
Non si può avere la botte piena e la moglie ubriaca.	You can't have your cake and eat it, too. (*Lit.* You can't have your bottle full and your wife drunk.)
Meglio soli che male accompagnati.	It's better to be alone than in bad company.
Mal comune mezzo gaudio.	Misery loves company. (*Lit.* Shared misery is half joy.)

Poca brigata, vita beata.	Two's company, three's a crowd. (*Lit.* Small brigade, blissful life.)
Piove, governo ladro!	Blame it on the government. (*Lit.* It's raining, you thief of a government!)
Chi s'assomiglia si piglia.	Birds of a feather flock together. (*Lit.* Those who are alike, take each other)
Vale più la pratica che la grammatica.	Practice makes perfect! (*Lit.* Practice is worth more than grammar!)
Chi non risica, non rosica.	He who takes no risks doesn't prosper.
Quando volerano gli asini.	When pigs fly! (*Lit.* When donkeys fly!)

APPENDIX E

SURFING THE INTERNET IN ITALIAN

The Web is a great place to learn more about Italian language and culture. A good place to start is about.com, which provides loads of great information on Italy, all in English. When you're feeling a little more confident, try one of your favorite major Web sites with the extension **.it**. You'll be surprised at what you'll find. Here's just a small selection:

- **www.yahoo.it**
- **www.msn.it**
- **cnnitalia.it**
- **www.iol.it** (the Italian counterpart to AOL)

Here are some other sites you can check out, depending on your mood and interests:

- *Viaggiare*

www.wandering.com offers personal accounts of traveling in Italy. Read all about it or add your own experience.

- *Studiare*

www.it-schools.com has information on Italian-language schools in Italy. This is a great place to start when you're ready to experience the real thing!

- *Leggere*

www.voicebuster.it has the lowdown on urban legends in Italian, and it's a great place to practice your language skills: Read about an urban legend in Italian, and then check your comprehension by reading the story in English.

www.aforisma.it features anything and everything you can imagine that might fill up your *tempo libero:* from *barzellette* (jokes) to *aforismi* (sayings) to *ricette* (recipes).

www.fabula.it is the perfect place for anyone who likes to read and write—*in italiano*, of course. You'll probably get more and more out of this site as your proficiency in Italian increases.

- *Ascoltare*

www.musicaitaliana.it has everything you always wanted to know about Italian music, but were afraid to ask (or admit!).

www.rockol.it/classifiche.asp features the Italian Top 10 list.
www.liverock.it has the lowdown on all the bands touring in Italy.

- *Un po' di tutto*

www.italian-american.com is the official Italian-American Web site of New York, with great links and information about Italian history and culture and its place in the United States.

APPENDIX F

WHAT DO ALL THOSE GRAMMAR TERMS REALLY MEAN?

ADJECTIVE	a word that describes a noun; e.g. *buono* (good), *rosso* (red), *simpatico* (nice). Don't forget that in Italian, adjectives usually come **after** the noun and they always agree with it in gender and number, e.g., *un ragazzo simpatico,* but *una ragazza simpatica.*
ADVERB	a word that describes an action (a verb), a quality (an adjective), or another adverb, e.g., *velocemente* (quickly), *molto* (very), and *spesso* (often). Adverbs never change for agreement.
AGREEMENT	changing a word to match the grammatical features of another word. In Italian, adjectives and articles agree with the gender and number of the nouns they describe, e.g., **il** *ragazzo simpatico,* **la** *ragazza simpatica,* **i** *ragazzi simpatici,* **le** *ragazze simpatiche.*
ARTICLE	*a / an* or *the.* Definite articles mean "the" and indefinite articles mean "a / an." In Italian, articles match the gender and number of the noun, e.g., **un / il** *panino* but **una / la** *pizza.*
COMPARATIVE	"more" or "less." An expression comparing two people or things or two qualities. In Italian, the comparative is expressed with *più di* (more than) and *meno di* (less than), e.g., *Marina è più giovane di Marco* (Marina is younger than Marco).
CONJUGATION	changing a verb to show who the subject is and when the action takes place (i.e. tense—past, present, future). For example, *io parlo,* but *tu parli, lei parla.*
CONJUNCTION	a word that connects other words or phrases. The most common conjunctions are: *e* (and), *ma* (but), and *o* (or).
DEMONSTRATIVE	"this" and "that." In Italian, demonstratives match the gender and number of the nouns they describe or replace, e.g., *questo / quel panino* but *questa / quella pizza.*
DIRECT OBJECT	in the sentence *Scrivo una cartolina a Marco* (I'm writing a postcard to Marco), the direct object is *una cartolina* (a postcard). Direct objects receive the action of the verb, usually without the "help" of a preposition, like *a* (to) or *per* (for).
GENDER	strictly a grammatical category. In Italian, nouns, adjectives, and articles have gender; they can be masculine or feminine.
IMPERFECT	the past tense used to describe ongoing or habitual actions or states of being; useful for description and memories of the past.

IMPERSONAL VERB	a verb that is used to make a general statement, where the subject is a general *you, one,* or *they,* as in *qui si parla inglese,* (they speak English here).
INDIRECT OBJECT	in the sentence *Scrivo una cartolina a Marco* (I'm writing a postcard to Marco), the indirect object is *a Marco* (to Marco). Indirect objects receive the action of the verb, usually with the "help" of a preposition, like *a* (to) or *per* (for).
INFINITIVE	the basic form of a verb (the one you'll find in a dictionary), before it's been changed (or conjugated) to show who the subject is or when the action takes place
INTRANSITIVE VERB	a verb that cannot take a direct object, e.g., *venire* (to come).
NOUN	a person, place, thing, or idea
NUMBER	There are two numbers: "one" or "more than one," also called "singular" and "plural"
PARTITIVE	words expressing a partial quantity of an item that cannot be counted, like *water, rice,* or *pie,* i.e., "some / a little / any **of.**" In Italian, the partitive is expressed with the preposition *di* (which combines with definite articles) or the expressions *un po' di* (a little bit of), *alcuni / alcune* (some), or *qualche* (some).
PASSIVE	when the subject and the object "switch places"; used to emphasize the object, as in "The cathedral was built in 1873." Often used to translate impersonal statements from Italian, e.g., *qui si parla inglese* (English is spoken here).
PAST PARTICIPLE	the form of a verb (usually ending in *–ato, –uto,* or *–ito*) used to form the *passato prossimo* or used as an adjective, e.g., *ho parlato* (I spoke) or *sono andata* (I went).
POSSESSIVE	*my / mine, your / yours,* etc. A word that shows ownership. In Italian, possessives agree in gender and number with the object or person **possessed,** not the owner.
PREPOSITION	*to, from, on, in,* etc. A connective word that shows spatial, temporal, or other relationships between other words.
PRONOUN	*I, him, mine, this one,* etc. A word that takes the place of a noun.
REFLEXIVE VERB	a verb conjugated with a reflexive pronoun: *mi* (myself), *ti* [yourself (sing. fam.)], *si* [him / herself; yourself (sing. pol.); yourselves], *ci* (ourselves), *vi* (youselves). Sometimes, the action actually "reflects" back on the subject, as in *mi vesto* [I'm getting dressed (i.e. dressing myself)]; sometimes, there is nothing inherently "reflexive" about the action, as in *divertirsi* (to have fun), *ricordarsi* (to remember), etc.
SUFFIX	an ending that is attached to a word to change its meaning, e.g., *–issimo,* meaning "very," *–ino,* meaning "small," or *–mente,* the equivalent of our "-ly," which changes an adjective to an adverb.

SUPERLATIVE	*most, least,* etc. An expression indicating the highest degree and used when comparing three or more things, people, or qualities, e.g., *è la ragazza più bella del mondo* (she's the most beautiful girl in the world).
TENSE	the time of an action or state of being, i.e., past, present, future, etc.
VERB	a word showing an action or a state of being, e.g., *parlare* (to speak), *essere* (to be).

GLOSSARY

List of Abbreviations

adj.	adjective	m.	masculine
adv.	adverb	n.	noun
coll.	colloquial	pl.	plural
f.	feminine	prep.	preposition
fml.	formal	sing.	singular
infml.	informal	v.	verb
interj.	interjection		
isc.	add –isc– before all endings but *noi* and *voi*		

ITALIAN–ENGLISH*

*A note on the pronunciations: Stressed syllables are marked in uppercase. Words such as prepositions, pronouns, articles, and conjunctions, which usually contain a single syllable, are in lowercase as they are not normally stressed.

A

a [AH] *to; in; at; until*
A domani. [ah doh-MAH-nee] *See you tomorrow.*
a piedi [ah PYEH-dee] *on foot*
A più tardi. [ah PYOO TAHR-dee] *See you later.*
A presto. [ah PREH-stoh] *See you soon.*
a proposito [ah proh-POH-zee-toh] *by the way*
abitare [ah-bee-TAH-reh] *to live*
accendere [ah-CHEHN-deh-reh] *to light (an appliance, the light, a cigarette)*
accessori [ah-cheh-SSOH-ree] *accessories (m.pl.)*
Accidenti! [ah-chee-DEHN-tee] *Wow!; Damn!*
accomodarsi [ah-koh-moh-DAHR-see] *to make oneself comfortable*
Si accomodi. [see ah-KOH-moh-dee] *Make yourself at home.*
accordo [ah-KKOHR-doh] *agreement*
D'accordo. [dah-KKOHR-doh] *Okay.; Agreed.*

acqua [AH-kwah] *water*
acqua minerale [AH-kwah mee-neh-RAH-leh] *mineral water*
addormentarsi [ah-ddohr-mehn-TAHR-see] *to fall asleep*
aereo [ah-EH-reh-oh] *airplane*
affrettarsi [ah-ffreh-TTAHR-see] *to hurry; to rush*
agente [ah-JEHN-teh] *agent (m./f.)*
aggeggio [ah-JJEH-jjoh] *gadget*
agosto [ah-GOH-stoh] *August*
aiutare [ah-yoo-TAH-reh] *to help*
aiuto [ah-YOO-toh] *help*
Aiuto! [ah-YOO-toh] *Help!*
albergo [ahl-BEHR-goh] *hotel*
alcuni/–e [ahl-KOO-nee/eh] *some (m. pl./f. pl.)*
allergia [ah-llehr-JEE-ah] *allergy*
allora [ah-LLOH-rah] *so; then; well*
alluvione [ah-lloo-VYOH-neh] *flood (f.)*
alto [AHL-toh] *high; tall*
altro [AHL-troh] *other (adj.); another (n.)*
alzarsi [ahl-TSAHR-see] *to get up*
amare [ah-MAH-reh] *to love*
amico/–a [ah-MEE-koh/-ah] *friend (m./f.)*

anche [AHN-keh] *also, too*
Anch'io. [ahnk-EE-oh] *Me, too.*
anche se [AHN-keh seh] *even if*
andare [ahn-DAH-reh] *to go*
Come va? [KOH-meh VAH] *How's it going?*
Ti va di… [tee VAH dee] *Do you feel like . . . (doing something)*
anello [ah-NEH-lloh] *ring*
angolo [AHN-goh-loh] *corner*
animale [ah-nee-MAH-leh] *animal (m.)*
anniversario [ah-nee-vehr-SAH-ree-oh] *anniversary*
anno [AH-nnoh] *year*
antipasto [ahn-tee-PAH-stoh] *appetizer*
aperitivo [ah-peh-ree-TEE-voh] *apertif, before-dinner drink*
appartamento [ah-ppahr-tah-MEHN-toh] *apartment*
aprile [ah-PREE-leh] *April*
argomento [ahr-goh-MEHN-toh] *subject; topic*
aria [AH-ree-ah] *air; aria*
aria condizionata [AH-ree-ah kohn-dee-tsee-oh-NAH-tah] *air-conditioning*

arrabbiarsi [ah-rrah-BBYAHR-see] *to get angry*

arrivare [ah-ree-VAH-reh] *to arrive*

Arrivederci! [ah-ree-veh-DEHR-chee] *Good-bye!*

ArrivederLa! [ah-ree-veh-DEHR-lah] *Good-bye! (fml.)*

arrosto [ah-RROH-stoh] *roast; roasted*

arte [AHR-teh] *art (f.)*

articolo [ahr-TEE-koh-loh] *article*

asciugacapelli [ah-shoo-gah-kah-PEH-llee] *hair dryer (m.)*

asciugamano [ah-shoo-gah-MAH-noh] *towel*

ascoltare [ah-skohl-TAH-reh] *to listen*

aspettare [ah-speh-TTAH-reh] *to wait*

assistere [ah-SSEE-steh-reh] *to attend; to help*

   assistere a uno spettacolo [ah-SSEE-steh-reh ah OO-noh speh-TTAH-koh-loh] *to see a show*

Attenzione! [ah-ttehn-TSYOH-neh] *Watch out!; Careful!*

attimo [AH-ttee-moh] *moment*

atto [AH-ttoh] *act*

   primo atto [PREE-moh AH-ttoh] *first act*

attore [ah-TTOH-reh] *actor (m.)*

attrice [ah-TTREE-cheh] *actress (f.)*

attualità [ah-ttoo-ah-lee-TAH] *current events (f.pl.)*

Auguri! [ah-oo-GOO-ree] *Best wishes! Congratulations!*

autobus [OW-toh-boos] *bus (m.)*

autunno [ow-TOO-nnoh] *autumn*

avere [ah-VEH-reh] *to have*

   avere . . . anni [ah-VEH-reh AH-nnee] *to be . . . years old (Lit. to have . . . years)*

   avere fame [ah-VEH-reh FAH-meh] *to be hungry*

   avere fortuna [ah-VEH-reh fohr-TOO-nah] *to be lucky*

   avere fretta [ah-VEH-reh FREH-ttah] *to be in a hurry*

   avere ragione [ah-VEH-reh rah-JOH-neh] *to be right*

   avere sete [ah-VEH-reh SEH-teh] *to be thirsty*

   avere voglia di [ah-VEH-reh VOH-lyah dee] *to feel like (doing something)*

avvocatessa [ah-vvoh-kah-TEH-ssah] *lawyer (f.)*

avvocato [ah-vvoh-KAH-toh] *lawyer (m.)*

B

bagno [BAH-nyoh] *bath*

balcone [bahl-KOH-neh] *balcony (m.)*

ballare [bah-LLAH-reh] *to dance*

bambino/–a [bahm-BEE-noh/-ah] *child; baby (m./f.)*

bandiera [bahn-DYEH-rah] *flag*

bar [BAHR] *café (m.)*

barista [bah-REE-stah] *bartender (m./f.)*

basso [BAH-ssoh] *low; short; bass (voice)*

battaglia [bah-TAH-lyah] *battle*

bello [BEH-lloh] *beautiful; handsome*

bene [BEH-neh] *well*

bere [BEH-reh] *to drink*

bianco [BYAHN-koh] *white*

bicchiere [bee-KYEH-reh] *glass (m.)*

biglietto [bee-LYEH-ttoh] *ticket*

biliardo [bee-lee-YAHR-doh] *billiards*

birra [BEE-rrah] *beer*

biscotto [bee-SKOH-ttoh] *cookie*

bistecca [bee-STEH-kkah] *steak*

blu [BLOO] *blue*

braccialetto [brah-chah-LEH-ttoh] *bracelet*

bronzo [BROHN-dzoh] *bronze*

brutto [BROO-ttoh] *ugly*

buono [BWOH-noh] *good*

   Buon anno! [BWOHN AH-nnoh] *Happy New Year!*

   Buon divertimento! [BWOHN dee-vehr-tee-MEHN-toh] *Have fun!*

   Buon giorno. [BWOHN JOHR-noh] *Hello.*

   un buon partito [oon BWOHN pahr-TEE-toh] *a good catch*

   Buona sera. [BWOH-nah SEH-rah] *Good evening.*

C

caffè [kah-FFEH] *coffee; café*

calcio [KAHL-choh] *soccer*

caldo [KAHL-doh] *hot*

   Ho caldo. [OH KAHL-doh] *I'm hot.*

   Fa caldo. [FAH KAHL-doh] *It's hot.*

calzino [kahl-TSEE-noh] *sock*

cambiare [kahm-BYAH-reh] *to change*

   cambiare idea [kahm-BYAH-reh ee-DEH-ah] *to change one's mind*

   cambiare linea [kahm-BYAH-reh LEE-neh-ah] *to transfer, to change lines (transportation)*

---

camera [KAH-meh-rah] *room*

   camera (da letto) [KAH-meh-rah dah LEH-ttoh] *bedroom*

   camera doppia [KAH-meh-rah DOH-ppyah] *double room (two beds)*

   camera matrimoniale [KAH-meh-rah mah-tree-moh-nee-AH-leh] *double room (one bed)*

   camera singola [KAH-meh-rah SEEN-goh-lah] *single room*

cameriere/–a [kah-mehr-YEH-reh/ah] *waiter/waitress*

camicetta [kah-mee-CHEH-ttah] *blouse*

camicia [kah-MEE-chah] *shirt*

canale [kah-NAH-leh] *channel (m.)*

candidato/–a [kahn-dee-DAH-toh/ah] *candidate (m./f.)*

cane [KAH-neh] *dog (m.)*

capelli [kah-PEH-llee] *hair*

capire [kah-PEE-reh] *to understand (isc.)*

capo [KAH-poh] *head; boss*

Capodanno [kah-poh-DAH-nnoh] *New Year's Day*

cappotto [kah-PPOH-ttoh] *coat*

cappuccino [kah-ppoo-CHEE-noh] *coffee with steamed milk*

carezza [kah-REH-tsah] *caress*

carino [kah-REE-noh] *cute*

carne [KAHR-neh] *meat (f.)*

carta [KAHR-tah] *card; paper*

   carta di credito [KAHR-tah dee KREH-dee-toh] *credit card*

   carta stradale [KAHR-tah strah-DAH-leh] *road map*

   carta telefonica [KAHR-tah teh-leh-FOH-nee-kah] *phone card*

cartolina [kahr-toh-LEE-nah] *postcard*

cartone animato [kahr-TOH-neh ah-nee-MAH-toh] *cartoon (m.)*

casa [KAH-zah] *house; home*

caso [KAH-zoh] *case*

cassaforte [kah-ssah-FOHR-teh] *safe-deposit box (f.)*

castello [kah-STEH-lloh] *castle*

cattedrale [kah-tteh-DRAH-leh] *cathedral (f.)*

cavolo [KAH-voh-loh] *cabbage*

   Cavolo! [KAH-voh-loh] *Wow!; Darn!*

celibe [CHEH-lee-beh] *(m.) single, unmarried*

cena [CHEH-nah] *dinner*

cento [CHEHN-toh] *hundred*
  per cento [pehr CHEHN-toh]
    percent
cercare [chehr-KAH-reh] *to look for*
  cercare di [chehr-KAH-reh dee] *to try*
cereali [cheh-reh-AH-lee] *cereal*
  (m. pl.)
certamente [chehr-tah-MEHN-teh]
  certainly
certo [CHEHR-toh] *certain (adj.);*
  certainly (adv.)
che [KEH] *that; what*
  Che peccato! [keh peh-KAH-toh]
    What a pity!
chi [KEE] *who*
  Chi lo sa? [KEE loh SAH] *Who*
    knows?
chiamare [kyah-MAH-reh] *to call*
chiamarsi [kyah-MAHR-see] *to be*
  called; to be named
chiamata [kyah-MAH-tah] *call*
  fare una chiamata [FAH-reh OO-
    nah kyah-MAH-tah] *to make a*
    phone call
  una chiamata in attesa [OO-nah
    kyah-MAH-tah een ah-TTEH-zah]
    call-waiting
chiaro [KYAH-roh] *clear; light-*
  colored
chiave [KYAH-veh] *key (f.)*
chiedere [KYEH-deh-reh] *to ask*
chiesa [KYEH-zah] *church*
ci [chee] *us; to us; there*
  c'è [CHEH] *there is*
  ci sono [chee SOH-noh] *there are*
  Ci vediamo! [chee veh-DYAH-moh]
    See you!
Ciao! [chow] *Hello!; Bye!*
cinema [CHEE-neh-mah] *cinema (m.)*
cinquanta [cheen-KWAHN-tah] *fifty*
cinque [CHEEN-kweh] *five*
cintura [cheen-TOO-rah] *belt*
città [chee-TAH] *city*
classico [KLAH-see-koh] *classic*
cliccare [klee-KKAH-reh] *to click*
cliente [klee-EHN-teh] *client (m./f.)*
clima [KLEE-mah] *climate (m.)*
coda [KOH-dah] *line; tail*
coincidenza [koh-een-chee-DEHN-
  tsah] *coincidence; connection*
  (transportation)
colazione [koh-lah-TSYOH-neh]
  breakfast (f.)
collana [koh-LLAH-nah] *necklace*
colonna [koh-LOH-nnah] *column*
coltello [kohl-TEH-lloh] *knife*

come [KOH-meh] *how*
  Come sta? [KOH-meh STAH] *How*
    are you? (fml.)
  Come stai? [KOH-meh STAH-ee]
    How are you? (infml.)
  Come va? [KOH-meh VAH] *How's*
    it going?
commovente [koh-mmoh-VEHN-teh]
  emotionally moving;
  compelling
competente [kohm-peh-TEHN-teh]
  competent
compleanno [kohm-pleh-AH-nnoh]
  birthday
  Buon compleanno! [BWOHN
    kohm-pleh-AH-nnoh] *Happy*
    birthday!
completo [kohm-PLEH-toh] *complete*
  al completo [ahl kohm-PLEH-toh]
    filled up; booked
compositore [kohm-poh-zee-TOH-
  reh] *composer (m.)*
compositrice [kohm-poh-zee-TREE-
  cheh] *composer (f.)*
computer [kohm-PYOO-tehr]
  computer (m.)
comune [koh-MOO-neh]
  municipality (m.)
con [KOHN] *with*
  Con piacere. [kohn pyah-CHEH-reh]
    Gladly.
concorrente [kohn-koh-RREHN-teh]
  contestant (m./f.)
condividere [kohn-dee-VEE-deh-reh]
  to share
Congratulazioni! [kohn-grah-too-
  lah-TSYOH-nee]
  Congratulations!
coniglio [koh-NEE-lyoh] *rabbit*
conoscenza [koh-noh-SHEHN-tsah]
  acquaintance
conoscere [koh-NOH-sheh-reh] *to*
  know; to be acquainted with;
  to have surface knowledge of
consigliare [kohn-see-LYAH-reh] *to*
  suggest; to recommend; to
  counsel
contanti [kohn-THAN-tee] *cash*
  (m. pl)
contento [kohn-TEHN-toh] *happy,*
  content
conto [KOHN-toh] *bill*
contorno [kohn-TOHR-noh] *side dish*
contralto [kon-TRAHL-toh] *alto*
convincere [kohn-VEEN-cheh-reh] *to*
  convince

coperta [koh-PEHR-tah] *blanket*
cornetto [kohr-NEH-ttoh] *croissant*
corretto [koh-RREH-ttoh] *correct;*
  laced with alcohol
corridoio [koh-rree-DOH-yoh]
  hallway, corridor
corso [KOHR-soh] *course*
corto [KOHR-toh] *short*
cosa [KOH-zah] *thing; what*
  una cosa da poco [OO-nah KOH-
    zah dah POH-koh] *a trifle;*
    something of little importance
  Cosa ne dici di . . . ? [KOH-zah neh
    DEE-chee di] *What do you say*
    to . . . ?
così [koh-ZEE] *like this, so*
  così così [koh-ZEE koh-ZEE] *so-so*
costare [koh-STAH-reh] *to cost*
costruito [koh-stroo-EE-toh] *built*
costume [koh-STOO-meh] *suit;*
  costume; bathing suit (m.)
cravatta [krah-VAH-ttah] *tie*
creativo [kreh-ah-TEE-voh] *creative*
credere [KREH-deh-reh] *to believe*
  Non ci credo! [nohn chee KREH-
    doh] *I don't believe it!*
crema [KREH-mah] *cream; custard*
criminalità [kree-mee-nah-lee-TAH]
  crime
cronaca mondana [KROH-nah-kah
  mohn-DAH-nah] *gossip column*
cucchiaio [koo-KYAH-yoh] *spoon*
cucina [koo-CHEE-nah] *kitchen*
cucinare [koo-chee-NAH-reh] *to cook*
cugino/–a [koo-JEE-noh/-a] *cousin*
  (m./f.)
cuscino [koo-SHEE-noh] *pillow*

D

da [DAH] *at; to; for; from*
dare [DAH-reh] *to give*
  dare contro a [DAH-reh KOHN-troh
    ah] *to contradict someone*
  dare un film [DAH-reh OON
    FEELM] *to show a movie*
  dare una festa [DAH-reh OO-nah
    FEH-stah] *to throw a party*
  Ma, dai! [MAH DAH-ee] *Oh, come*
    on!; Come off it!; Gimme a
    break!
davanti [dah-VAHN-tee] *in front*
davvero [dah-VVEH-roh] *really*
decidere [deh-CHEE-deh-reh] *to*
  decide
decimo (DEH-chee-moh) *tenth*

decisione [deh-chee-ZYOH-neh] decision (f.)

declino [deh-KLEE-noh] decline

delizioso [deh-lee-TSYOH-zoh] delicious

denaro [deh-NAH-roh] money

dentro [DEHN-troh] inside

desiderare [deh-zee-deh-RAH-reh] to desire

Desidera? [deh-ZEE-deh-rah] Can I take your order?

destra [DEH-strah] right side

dettaglio [deh-TTAH-lyoh] detail

di [dee] of; from; 's (possession)

di dietro [dee DYEH-troh] in the back

di nuovo [dee NWOH-voh] again; all over

di solito [dee SOH-lee-toh] usually

dicembre [dee-CHEHM-breh] December

dieci [DYEH-chee] ten

dietro [DYEH-troh] behind

digestivo [dee-jeh-STEE-voh] after-dinner drink

dimenticare [dee-mehn-tee-KAH-reh] to forget

dimenticarsi [dee-mehn-tee-KAHR-see] to forget

dio [DEE-oh] God

dire [DEE-reh] to say; to tell

A dire la verità . . . [ah DEE-reh lah veh-ree-TAH] To tell you the truth . . .

direttore [dee-reh-TTOH-reh] director; boss

direttore d'orchestra [dee-reh-TTOH-reh dohr-KEH-strah] orchestra director

direttrice [dee-reh-TREE-cheh] director; boss (f.)

diritto [dee-REE-ttoh] right (privilege); straight

disastro [dee-ZAH-stroh] disaster

disegno [dee-ZEH-nyoh] design; drawing

dispiacere [dee-spyah-CHEH-reh] to displease

Mi dispiace. [mee dee-SPYAH-che] I'm sorry.

Vi dispiace se . . . [vee dee-SPYAH-che seh] Do you mind if . . .

diverso [dee-VEHR-soh] different; diverse; several; various

divertimento [dee-vehr-tee-MEHN-toh] fun; amusement

divertirsi [dee-vehr-TEER-see] to have fun

Divertitevi! [dee-vehr-TEE-teh-vee] Have fun! (pl.)

dividere [dee-VEE-deh-reh] to divide

doccia [DOH-chah] shower

documentario [doh-koo-mehn-TAH-ree-oh] documentary

dolce [DOHL-cheh] sweet (adj.); dessert (n.) (m.)

domanda [doh-MAHN-dah] question

domani [doh-MAH-nee] tomorrow

domenica [doh-MEH-nee-kah] Sunday

dottore [doh-TTOH-reh] doctor (m.)

dottoressa [doh-ttoh-REH-ssah] doctor (f.)

dove [DOH-veh] where

dovere [doh-VEH-reh] must; to have to; to owe

Quanto Le devo? [KWAHN-toh LEH DEH-voh] How much do I owe you?

due [DOO-eh] two

duro [DOO-roh] hard

E

e [eh] and

è [EH] he/she is; you are (fml.)

ecco [EH-kkoh] here you go; here it is

edificio [eh-dee-FEE-choh] building; edifice

elegante [eh-leh-GAHN-teh] elegant

elezioni [eh-leh-TSYOH-nee] elections (f. pl.)

eliminare [eh-lee-mee-NAH-reh] to eliminate

e–mail [ee-MAYL] e-mail (f.)

enoteca [eh-noh-TEH-kah] wine bar

entrare [ehn-TRAH-reh] to enter

esagerato [eh-zah-jeh-RAH-toh] exaggerated; overdone

esagerazione [eh-zah-jeh-rah-TSYOH-neh] exaggeration (f.)

esattamente [eh-zah-ttah-MEHN-teh] exactly

esatto [eh-ZAH-ttoh] exactly (adv.); exact (adj.)

esistere [eh-ZEE-steh-reh] to exist

espressione [eh-spreh-SYOH-neh] expression (f.)

essere [EH-sseh-reh] to be

estate [eh-STAH-teh] summer (f.)

esterno [eh-STEHR-noh] outside

età [eh-TAH] age

alla loro età [AH-llah LOH-roh eh-TAH] at their age

etto [EH-ttoh] 100 grams

F

faccende domestiche [fah-CHEHN-deh doh-MEH-stee-keh] household chores (f. pl.)

fagioli [fah-JOH-lee] beans (m. pl.)

falso [FAHL-soh] false

fame [FAH-meh] hunger

Ho fame. [OH FAH-meh] I'm hungry.

famoso [fah-MOH-zoh] famous

fantastico [fahn-TAH-stee-koh] fantastic

fare [FAH-reh] to do; to make

fare due chiacchiere [FAH-reh DOO-eh KYAH-kyeh-reh] to chat

fare finta [FAH-reh FEEN-tah] to pretend

fare giardinaggio [FAH-reh jahr-dee-NAH-jjoh] to do the gardening

fare la chat [FAH-reh lah CHEHT] to chat on-line

fare la coda [FAH-reh lah KOH-dah] to wait in line

fare le spese [FAH-reh leh SPEH-zeh] to go shopping

fare pettegolezzi [FAH-reh peh-tteh-goh-LEH-tsee] to gossip

fare una passeggiata [FAH-reh OO-nah pah-sseh-JAH-ttah] to take a walk

Non fare così! [nohn FAH-reh koh-ZEE] Don't be like that!

farmacia [fahr-mah-CHEE-ah] pharmacy

fastidioso [fah-stee-dee-OH-zoh] annoying

favoloso [fah-voh-LOH-zoh] fabulous

fazzoletto [fah-tsoh-LEH-ttoh] tissue

febbraio [feh-BBRAH-yoh] February

felice [feh-LEE-cheh] happy

fenomenale [feh-noh-meh-NAH-leh] phenomenal

fermarsi [fehr-MAHR-see] to stop (oneself)

fermata [fehr-MAH-tah] stop (transportation)

ferro [FEH-rroh] iron

festa [FEH-stah] party

festeggiare [feh-steh-JJAH-reh] to celebrate

fiato [fee-AH-toh] *breath*
  senza fiato [SEHN-tsah fee-AH-toh]
  breathless
fidanzato/–a [fee-dahn-TSAH-
  toh/ah] *fiancé(e);
  boyfriend/girlfriend*
figlio/–a/–i [FEE-lyoh/-ah/-ee] *son;
  daughter; children*
film [FEELM] *movie (m.)*
fine [FEE-neh] *end (f.)*
  fine–settimana [FEE-neh-seh-ttee-
  MAH-nah] *weekend (m.)*
finestra [fee-NEH-strah] *window*
finire [fee-NEE-reh] *to finish (isc.)*
finito [fee-NEE-toh] *finished*
fon [FOHN] *hair dryer (m.)*
fondamenta [fohn-dah-MEHN-teh]
  foundation of a building (f. pl.)
fontana [fohn-TAH-nah] *fountain*
forchetta [fohr-KEH-ttah] *fork*
formaggio [fohr-MAH-jjoh] *cheese*
forse [FOHR-seh] *maybe*
fortuna [fohr-TOO-nah] *luck*
  Buona fortuna! [BWOH-nah fohr-
  TOO-nah] *Good luck!*
foto [FOH-toh] *photograph (f.)*
fra [FRAH] *between; among; in
  (time)*
francamente [frahn-kah-MEHN-teh]
  frankly
francobollo [frahn-koh-BOH-lloh]
  stamp
fratello [frah-TEH-lloh] *brother*
freddo [FREH-ddoh] *cold*
  Ho freddo. [OH FREH-ddoh] *I'm
  cold.*
  Fa freddo. [FAH FREH-ddoh] *It's cold.*
fresco [FREH-skoh] *fresh; cool
  (temperature)*
fretta [FREH-ttah] *rush*
frigo–bar [FREE-goh-BAHR] *minibar
  (m.)*
frizzante [free-TSAHN-teh] *fizzy;
  carbonated*
frutta [FROO-ttah] *fruit*
fuoco [FWOH-koh] *fire*
fuori [FWOH-ree] *outside*
  fuori di sè [FWOH-ree dee SEH]
  beside oneself

G

galleria [gah-LEH-ree-ah] *gallery;
  mezzanine, balcony*
gamba [GAHM-bah] *leg*
garage [gah-RAHZH] *garage (m.)*

gatto [GAH-ttoh] *cat*
gemelli/–e [jeh-MEH-llee/eh] *twins
  [m./f. pl.]*
genitori [jeh-nee-TOH-ree] *parents
  (m. pl.)*
gennaio [jeh-NNAH-yoh] *January*
gente [JEHN-teh] *people (f. sing.)*
gentile [jehn-TEE-leh] *nice, kind*
geografia [jeh-oh-grah-FEE-ah]
  geography
giacca [JAH-kkah] *jacket*
giallo [JAH-lloh] *yellow*
gioco [JOH-koh] *game*
  gioco a premi [JOH-koh ah PREH-
  mee] *game show*
giornale [johr-NAH-leh] *newspaper
  (m.)*
giornalista [johr-nah-LEE-stah]
  journalist (m./f.)
giornata [johr-NAH-tah] *day*
giorno [JOHR-noh] *day*
giovane [JOH-vah-neh] *young*
giovedì [joh-veh-DEE] *Thursday*
giro [JEE-roh] *tour; ride; walk; drive*
giugno [JOO-nyoh] *June*
giusto [JOO-stoh] *right; correct;
  just*
gli [lyee] *to him; to it (m.); to them
  (m.); the (m. pl.)*
gomma [GOH-mmah] *gum; rubber*
gotico [GOH-tee-koh] *Gothic*
grande [GRAHN-deh] *large, big;
  great*
  grande magazzino [GRAHN-deh
  mah-gah-DZEE-noh] *department
  store*
Grazie. [GRAH-tsyeh] *Thanks.*
grigio [GREE-joh] *gray*
guanti [GWAHN-tee] *gloves (m. pl.)*
guardare [gwahr-DAH-reh] *to watch*
  Ma guarda un po'! [mah GWAHR-
  dah oon POH] *Fancy that!*
guerra [GWEH-rrah] *war*
guidare [gwee-DAH-reh] *to drive*

H

hobby [OH-bee] *hobby (m.)*
hotel [oh-TEHL] *hotel (m.)*

I

i [ee] *the (m. pl.)*
idea [ee-DEH-ah] *idea*
  Che buon'idea! [keh BWOHN ee-
  DEH-ah] *Good idea!*

idealista [ee-deh-ah-LEE-stah] *idealist
  (m./f.)*
idiota [ee-dee-OH-tah] *idiot (m./f.)*
il [eel] *the (m. sing.)*
illustrazione [ee-loo-strah-TSYOH-
  neh] *illustration (f.)*
immaturo [ee-mah-TOO-roh]
  immature
in [een] *in; at; to; by*
  in fondo [een FOHN-doh] *at the
  bottom*
  in gamba [een GAHM-bah] *smart;
  capable (coll.)*
  in orario [een oh-RAH-ree-oh] *on
  time*
  in ordine [een OHR-dee-neh] *in
  order*
  in ritardo [een ree-TAHR-doh] *late*
  in treno [een TREH-noh] *by train*
incantevole [een-kahn-TEH-voh-leh]
  enchanting
incartare [een-kahr-TAH-reh] *to
  wrap; to gift wrap*
incluso [een-KLOO-zoh] *included*
incompetente [een-kohm-peh-TEHN-
  teh] *incompetent*
incredible [een-kreh-DEE-bee-leh]
  incredible; unbelievable
indimenticabile [een-dee-mehn-tee-
  KAH-bee-leh] *unforgettable*
indirizzo [een-dee-REE-tsoh]
  address
influente [een-floo-EHN-teh]
  influential
insalata [een-sah-LAH-tah] *salad*
insegnante [een-seh-NYAN-teh]
  teacher (m./f.)
insieme [een-SYEH-meh] *together*
insistere [een-SEES-teh-reh] *to
  insist*
intelligente [een-teh-lee-JEHN-teh]
  intelligent
interessante [een-teh-reh-SSAHN-
  teh] *interesting*
interessarsi [een-teh-reh-SSAHR-see]
  to be interested
interesse [een-teh-REH-sseh] *interest
  (m.)*
interpretazione [een-tehr-preh-tah-
  TSYOH-neh] *interpretation (f.)*
intervallo [een-tehr-VAH-lloh]
  intermission; interval
intimo [EEN-tee-moh] *intimate*
invece di [een-VEH-cheh dee]
  instead of
inverno [een-VEHR-noh] *winter*

invitare [een-vee-TAH-reh] *to invite*
io [EE-oh] *I*
ipocondriaco/–a [ee-poh-kohn-DREE-ah-koh/ah] *hypochondriac (m./f.)*

jeans [JEENS] *jeans (m. pl.)*

la [lah] *her; it (f.); the (f. sing.)*
La [lah] *you (fml.)*
là [LAH] *there*
lamentarsi [lah-mehn-TAHR-see] *to complain*
lasciare [lah-SHAH-reh] *to leave*
  Mi lasci in pace! [mee LAH-shee een PAH-cheh] *Leave me alone (Lit. in peace)! (fml.)*
lattina [lah-TTEE-nah] *can*
lavare [lah-VAH-reh] *to wash*
lavarsi [lah-VAHR-see] *to wash oneself*
le [leh] *to her; to it (f.); them (f.); the (f. pl.)*
Le [leh] *to you (fml.)*
legge [LEH-jjeh] *law (f.)*
leggenda [leh-JJEHN-dah] *legend*
leggere [LEH-jjeh-reh] *to read*
leggero [leh-JJEH-roh] *light*
legno [LEH-nyoh] *wood*
lei [LAY] *she; her (after prep.)*
Lei [LAY] *you (fml.)*
lettore di CD [leh-TTOH-reh dee CHEE-DEE] *CD player (m.)*
lezione [leh-TSYOH-neh] *lesson (f.)*
lì [LEE] *there*
libero [LEE-beh-roh] *free; unoccupied*
libro [LEE-broh] *book; pound*
lieto [lee-EH-toh] *pleased*
  Molto lieto. [MOHL-toh lee-EH-toh] *Pleased to meet you.*
linea [LEE-neh-ah] *line*
lingua [LEEN-gwah] *language; tongue*
litro [LEE-troh] *liter*
lo [loh] *him; it (m.); the (m. sing.)*
lontano [lohn-TAH-noh] *far, distant*
loro [LOH-roh] *they; them; their; theirs*
luglio [LOO-lyoh] *July*
lui [LOO-ee] *he; him (after prep.)*
lunedì [loo-neh-DEE] *Monday*

luogo [LWOH-goh] *place*
lupo [LOO-poh] *wolf*
  avere una fame da lupo [ah-VEH-reh OO-nah FAH-meh dah LOO-poh] *to be hungry like the wolf*
  In bocca al lupo! [een BOH-kkah ahl LOO-poh] *Good luck! (Lit. In the mouth of the wolf!)*

ma [mah] *but*
Ma, dai! [mah DAH-ee] *Come on!; Come off it!*
macchina [MAH-kee-nah] *car*
macellaio/–a [mah-cheh-LAH-yoh/-ah] *butcher (m./f.)*
madre [MAH-dreh] *mother (f.)*
Magari! [mah-GAH-ree] *Don't I wish!*
maggio [MAH-jjoh] *May*
maggiore [mah-JJOH-reh] *bigger; older*
  la maggior parte [lah MAH-jjohr PAHR-teh] *most, the majority*
mandare [mahn-DAH-reh] *to send*
mangiare [mahn-JAH-reh] *to eat*
marito [mah-REE-toh] *husband*
marmellata [mahr-meh-LLAH-tah] *jam, marmalade*
marmo [MAHR-moh] *marble*
marrone [mah-RROH-neh] *brown*
martedì [mahr-teh-DEE] *Tuesday*
marzo [MAHR-zoh] *March*
materialista [mah-teh-ree-ah-LEE-stah] *materialist (m./f.)*
maturità [mah-too-ree-TAH] *high-school graduation*
maturo [mah-TOO-roh] *mature*
meccanico/–a [meh-KAH-nee-koh/-ah] *mechanic (m./f.)*
medievale [meh-dee-eh-VAH-leh] *medieval*
meglio [MEH-lyoh] *better*
meno [MEH-noh] *less*
mentre [MEHN-treh] *while*
menù [meh-NOO] *menu (m.)*
meraviglioso [meh-rah-vee-LYOH-zoh] *fantastic; marvelous*
mercoledì [mehr-koh-leh-DEE] *Wednesday*
mese [MEH-zeh] *month (m.)*
messaggio [meh-SSAH-jjoh] *message*
mezzo [MEH-dzoh] *half*

mi [mee] *me; to me; myself*
  Mi dica? [mee DEE-kah] *Can I help you?/Tell me!*
  Mi dispiace. [mee dee-SPYAH-cheh] *I'm sorry.*
migliore [mee-LYOH-reh] *better (adj.)*
mila [MEE-lah] *thousands (m. pl.)*
miliardo [mee-lee-AHR-doh] *billion*
milione [mee-lee-OH-neh] *million (m.)*
mille [MEE-lleh] *thousand (m.)*
minestra [mee-NEH-strah] *soup*
minore [mee-NOH-reh] *smaller; younger*
minuto [mee-NOO-toh] *minute (n.)*
mio [MEE-oh] *my; mine*
moderno [moh-DEHR-noh] *modern*
moglie [MOH-lyeh] *wife (f.)*
molto [MOHL-toh] *a lot (adv.); many (adj.)*
mondo [MOHN-doh] *world*
monumento [moh-noo-MEHN-toh] *monument*
morto [MOHR-toh] *dead*
motorino [moh-toh-REE-noh] *motorbike*
museo [MOO-seh-oh] *museum*
musica [MOO-zee-kah] *music*

Natale [nah-TAH-leh] *Christmas (m.)*
naturale [nah-too-RAH-leh] *natural*
naturalmente [nah-too-rahl-MEHN-teh] *naturally*
navigare [nah-vee-GAH-reh] *to navigate*
né . . . né [NEH NEH] *neither . . . nor . . .*
neanche [neh-AHN-keh] *not even*
negozio [neh-GOH-tsyoh] *store; boutique*
nemico [NEH-mee-koh] *enemy*
nemmeno [neh-MMEH-noh] *not even*
nero [NEH-roh] *black*
nesso [NEH-ssoh] *connection*
nessuno [neh-SSOO-noh] *no one; nobody*
nevicare [neh-vee-KAH-reh] *to snow*
niente [NYEHN-teh] *nothing*
nipote [nee-POH-teh] *grandchild; nephew/niece (m./f.)*
no [NOH] *no*
noi [NOY] *we; us (after prep.)*
noioso [noh-YOH-zoh] *boring*

nome [NOH-meh] *name (m.)*
non [nohn] *not*
  non . . . affatto [nohn ah-FFAH-ttoh] *not at all*
  non . . . ancora [nohn ahn-KOH-rah] *not yet*
  non . . . mai [nohn MAHY] *never*
  non . . . più [nohn PYOO] *no more; no longer*
nonno/–a/–i [NOH-nnoh/-ah/-ee] *grandfather; grandmother; grandparents*
nono [NOH-noh] *ninth*
normale [nohr-MAH-leh] *normal; regular*
nostro [NOH-stroh] *our; ours*
notizie [noh-TEE-tsee-eh] *news (f. pl.)*
notte [NOH-tteh] *night (f.)*
novanta [noh-VAHN-tah] *ninety*
nove [NOH-veh] *nine*
novembre [noh-VEHM-breh] *November*
nubile [NOO-bee-leh] *single, unmarried (f.)*
numero [NOO-meh-roh] *number*
nuovo [NWOH-voh] *new*

O

o [oh] *or*
occasione [oh-kah-ZYOH-neh] *occasion (f.)*
  occasione di una vita [oh-kah-ZYOH-neh dee OO-nah VEE-tah] *chance of a lifetime*
occupazione [oh-kkoo-pah-TSYOH-neh] *occupation (f.)*
offrire [oh-FFREE-reh] *to offer*
  Offro io. [OH-ffroh EE-oh] *It's on me.*
oggi [OH-jjee] *today*
oggigiorno [oh-jee-JOHR-noh] *nowadays*
ombrello [ohm-BREH-lloh] *umbrella*
onomastico [oh-noh-MAH-stee-koh] *name day*
oppure [oh-PPOO-reh] *otherwise, else, or*
ora [OH-rah] *time; hour*
  Che ore sono? [keh OH-reh SOH-noh] *What time is it?*
  Sa/Sai l'ora? [SAH/SAH-ee LOH-rah] *Do you have the time? (fml./infml.)*
orario [oh-RAH-ree-oh] *timetable, schedule*

originale [oh-ree-jee-NAH-leh] *original*
orologio [oh-roh-LOH-joh] *watch*
oroscopo [oh-ROH-skoh-poh] *horoscope*
ottanta [oh-TTAHN-tah] *eighty*
ottavo [oh-TTAH-voh] *eighth*
ottimista [oh-ttee-MEE-stah] *optimist (m./f.); optimistic (m./f.)*
ottimo [OH-ttee-moh] *excellent*
otto [OH-ttoh] *eight*
ottobre [oh-TTOH-breh] *October*

P

padre [PAH-dreh] *father (m.)*
paese [pah-EH-zeh] *country; town (m.)*
pagare [pah-GAH-reh] *to pay*
pagina [PAH-jee-nah] *page*
palazzo [pah-LAH-tsoh] *palace*
palcoscenico [pahl-koh-SHEH-nee-koh] *stage*
palestra [pah-LEH-strah] *gym*
pallavolo [PAH-llah-VOH-loh] *volleyball (f.)*
panino [pah-NEE-noh] *sandwich*
pantaloni [pahn-tah-LOH-nee] *pants (m. pl.)*
parallelo [pah-rah-LLEH-loh] *parallel*
parenti [pah-REHN-tee] *relatives (m. pl.)*
parere [pah-REH-reh] *viewpoint; opinion*
  A mio parere . . . [ah MEE-oh pah-REH-reh] *In my opinion . . .*
parlare [pahr-LAH-reh] *to speak*
parrucchiere/–a [pah-rroo-KYEH-reh/ah] *hairdresser (m./f.)*
Pasqua [PAH-skwah] *Easter; Passover*
passare [pah-SSAH-reh] *to pass*
passatempo [pah-ssah-TEHM-poh] *pastime*
pasta [PAH-stah] *pasta; pastry*
pasticceria [pah-stee-cheh-REE-ah] *pastry shop*
patate [pah-TAH-teh] *potatoes (f. pl.)*
pavimento [pah-vee-MEHN-toh] *floor*
pazzo [PAH-tsoh] *crazy*
peccato [peh-KAH-toh] *sin*
  Che peccato! [keh peh-KKAH-toh] *What a shame!*
peggio [PEH-jjoh] *worse (adv.)*
peggiore [peh-JJOH-reh] *worse (adj.)*

pensare [pehn-SAH-reh] *to think*
pensiero [pehn-SYEH-roh] *thought*
pensione [pehn-SYOH-neh] *small hotel (f.)*
pepe [PEH-peh] *pepper (m.)*
per [PEHR] *for*
  per favore [pehr fah-VOH-reh] *please*
  per piacere [pehr pyah-CHEH-reh] *please*
perché [pehr-KEH] *why*
  Perché non . . . [pehr-KEH NOHN] *Why don't . . . (we do something)*
perdere [PEHR-deh-reh] *to lose*
permettere [pehr-MEH-tteh-reh] *to permit, to allow*
pesce [PEH-sheh] *fish (m.)*
pessimista [peh-see-MEE-stah] *pessimist (m./f.); pessimistic (m./f.)*
peste [PEH-steh] *plague (f.)*
piacere [pyah-CHEH-reh] *pleasure (m.); to like, to be pleasing to (v.)*
  Piacere. [pyah-CHEH-reh] *Nice to meet you.*
  Mi piace/piacciono . . . [mee PYA-cheh pyah-CHO-noh] *I like . . .*
piangere [PYAHN-jeh-reh] *to cry*
piano [PYAH-noh] *floor (n.); slowly (adv.)*
pianta [PYAHN-tah] *map*
piazza [PYAH-tsah] *city square*
piccolo [PEE-kkoh-loh] *small*
piovere [PYOH-veh-reh] *to rain*
pittura [pee-TTOO-rah] *painting (including the art form)*
più [PYOO] *more*
pizzetta [pee-TSEH-ttah] *small pizza*
poco [POH-koh] *little*
polline [POH-llee-neh] *pollen (m.)*
popolare [poh-poh-LAH-reh] *popular; folk*
popolazione [poh-poh-lah-TSYOH-neh] *population (f.)*
porta [POHR-tah] *door*
portare [pohr-TAH-reh] *to bring; to take*
portiere [pohr-TYEH-reh] *concierge; doorman (m./f.)*
possibile [poh-SSEE-bee-leh] *possible*
possibilità [poh-ssee-bee-lee-TAH] *possibility*

posta [POH-stah] *mail*
  C'è posta per te. [CHEH POH-stah pehr TEH] *You've got mail.*
  posta vocale [POH-stah voh-KAH-leh] *voice mail*
posto [POH-stoh] *place; seat*
potere [poh-TEH-reh] *to be able to*
povero [POH-veh-roh] *poor*
pranzo [PRAHN-tsoh] *lunch; dinner*
preferire [preh-feh-REE-reh] *to prefer (isc.)*
Prego. [PREH-goh] *You're welcome.; Here you are.*
prendere [PREHN-deh-reh] *to take*
  Cosa ti prende? [KOH-zah tee PREHN-deh] *What's gotten into you?*
  prendere in giro [PREHN-deh-reh een JEE-roh] *to pull someone's leg (Lit. to take for a ride)*
prenotazione [preh-noh-tah-TSYOH-neh] *reservation (f.)*
preoccuparsi [preh-oh-kkoo-PAHR-see] *to worry*
prepagato [preh-pah-GAH-toh] *pre-paid*
preparare [preh-pah-RAH-reh] *to prepare*
prepararsi [preh-pah-RAHR-see] *to prepare (oneself)*
presentare [preh-zehn-TAH-reh] *to introduce; to present*
presentatore [preh-zehn-tah-TOH-reh] *host of a show (m.); presenter*
presentatrice [preh-zehn-tah-TREE-cheh] *host of a show; presenter (f.)*
presidente [preh-zee-DEHN-teh] *president (m./f.)*
presto [PREH-stoh] *early*
previsione [preh-vee-ZYOH-neh] *forecast (f.)*
  previsioni del tempo [preh-vee-ZYOH-nee dehl TEHM-poh] *weather forecast (f. pl.)*
primavera [pree-mah-VEH-rah] *spring*
primo [PREE-moh] *first; first course (at a meal)*
principe [PREEN-chee-peh] *prince (m.)*
principessa [preen-chee-PEH-ssah] *princess*
professore [proh-feh-SSOH-reh] *professor (m.)*
professoressa [proh-feh-ssoh-REH-ssah] *professor (f.)*

profondo [proh-FOHN-doh] *profound*
programma [proh-GRAH-mmah] *program (m.)*
pronto [PROHN-toh] *ready; right away; hello (phone)*
  Pronto? [PROHN-toh] *Hello? (phone)*
proprio [PROH-pree-oh] *really; just; own*
prosciutto [proh-SHOO-ttoh] *ham; prosciutto*
provare [proh-VAH-reh] *to try; to try on*
pubblicità [poo-bblee-chee-TAH] *commercial*
pubblico [POO-bblee-koh] *audience; public*
pulire [poo-LEE-reh] *to clean*
pullover [POOL-oh-vehr] *sweater (m.)*
purtroppo [poor-TROH-ppoh] *unfortunately*

Q

qua [KWAH] *here*
qualche [KWAHL-keh] *some*
qualcosa [kwahl-KOH-zah] *something*
qualcuno [kwahl-KOO-noh] *someone*
quando [KWAHN-doh] *when*
quanto/-a; quanti/-e [KWAHN-toh/ah/ee/eh] *how much; how many*
  Quanti ne abbiamo oggi? *What's today's date?*
quaranta [kwah-RAHN-tah] *forty*
quartino [kwahr-TEE-noh] *a quarter of a liter*
quarto [KWAHR-toh] *fourth; quarter*
quattro [KWAH-ttroh] *four*
quello [KWEH-lloh] *that; that one*
questo [KWEH-stoh] *this; this one*
qui [KWEE] *here*
quinto [KWEEN-toh] *fifth*

R

radio [RAH-dee-oh] *radio (f.)*
ragazza [rah-GAH-tsah] *girl; girlfriend*
ragazzo [rah-GAH-tsoh] *boy; boyfriend*
rappresentazione [rah-ppreh-zehn-tah-TSYOH-neh] *performance (f.)*

reazione [reh-ah-TSYOH-neh] *reaction (f.)*
regalare [reh-gah-LAH-reh] *to give a gift*
regalo [reh-GAH-loh] *present; gift*
regione [reh-JOH-neh] *region (f.)*
regista [reh-JEE-stah] *film/theater director (m./f.)*
regola [REH-goh-lah] *rule*
rendersi conto [REHN-dehr-see KOHN-toh] *to realize; to become aware of*
restare [reh-STAH-reh] *to stay*
rete [REH-teh] *Web, Internet (f.)*
ricarica [ree-KAH-ree-kah] *refill (telephone card)*
richiamare [ree-kyah-MAH-reh] *to call again*
ricordarsi [ree-kohr-DAHR-see] *to remember*
ricordo [ree-KOHR-doh] *memory*
ridere [REE-deh-reh] *to laugh*
rilassarsi [ree-lah-SSAHR-see] *to relax*
rinascimento [ree-nah-shee-MEHN-toh] *Renaissance*
ripasso [ree-PAH-ssoh] *review*
ripetere [ree-PEH-teh-reh] *to repeat*
rispondere [ree-SPOHN-deh-reh] *to answer*
risposta [ree-SPOH-stah] *answer*
ristorante [ree-stoh-RAHN-teh] *restaurant (m.)*
ritardo [ree-TAHR-doh] *delay*
  in ritardo [een ree-TAHR-doh] *late*
rosa [ROH-zah] *pink*
rosso [ROH-ssoh] *red*
rovine [roh-VEE-neh] *ruins (f.pl.)*

S

sabato [SAH-bah-toh] *Saturday*
salame [sah-LAH-meh] *salami (m.)*
sala [SAH-lah] *room*
  sala da pranzo [SAH-lah dah PRAHN-tsoh] *dining room*
sale [SAH-leh] *salt (m.)*
salire [sah-LEE-reh] *to climb*
salone [sah-LOH-neh] *hair salon (m.)*
Saluti! [sah-LOO-tee] *Greetings; Cheers!*
sapere [sah-PEH-reh] *to know (a fact); to have in depth knowledge of*
sapone [sah-POH-neh] *soap (m.)*
sbadiglio [zbah-DEE-lyoh] *yawn*

sbagliare [zbah-LYAH-reh] *to make a mistake*
   Ha sbagliato numero. [ah zbah-LYAH-toh NOO-meh-roh] *You've got the wrong number.*
sbagliato [zbah-LYAH-toh] *wrong*
scale [SKAH-leh] *stairs (f. pl.)*
scambiare [skahm-BYAH-reh] *to exchange*
scambio [SKAHM-byoh] *exchange*
scarpa [SKAHR-pah] *shoe*
scatola [SKAH-toh-lah] *box*
scegliere [SHEH-lyeh-reh] *to choose*
scenografia [sheh-noh-grah-FEE-ah] *set design*
scheda [SKEH-dah] *card*
   scheda telefonica [SKEH-dah teh-leh-FOH-nee-kah] *phone card*
scrivere [SKREE-veh-reh] *to write*
scultore [skool-TOH-reh] *sculptor (m.)*
scultrice [skool-TREE-cheh] *sculptor (f.)*
scultura [skool-TOO-rah] *sculpture (including the art form)*
scuro [SKOO-roh] *dark*
scusa [SKOO-zah] *excuse*
   Scusa/–i [SKOO-zah/-ee] *Excuse me. (fml./infml.)*
se [seh] *if*
   se no [seh NOH] *else; or else*
secondo [seh-KOHN-doh] *second; second course (at a meal)*
   Secondo me... [seh-KOHN-doh MEH] *In my opinion . . .*
segno [SEH-nyoh] *sign*
segretario/–a [seh-greh-TAH-ree-ah] *secretary*
segreteria telefonica [seh-greh-tah-REE-ah teh-leh-FOH-nee-kah] *answering machine*
sei [SAY] *you are (infml.); six*
sembrare [sehm-BRAH-reh] *to seem*
sempre [SEHM-preh] *always*
sentire [sehn-TEE-reh] *to hear; to sense; to smell*
sentirsi [sehn-TEER-see] *to feel*
   Non mi sento bene. [NOHN mee SEHN-toh BEH-neh] *I don't feel well*
senza [SEHN-tsah] *without*
   senz'altro [SEHN-tsahl-troh] *of course*
sera [SEH-rah] *evening*
   Buona sera. [BWOH-nah SEH-rah] *Good evening.*
serio [SEH-ree-oh] *serious*

servire [sehr-VEE-reh] *to serve; to need*
   Mi serve... [mee SEHR-veh] *I need . . .*
sessanta [seh-SSAHN-tah] *sixty*
sesso [SEH-ssoh] *sex; gender*
sesto [SEH-stoh] *sixth*
settanta [seh-TTAHN-tah] *seventy*
sette [SEH-tteh] *seven*
settembre [seh-TTEHM-breh] *September*
settimana [seh-ttee-MAH-nah] *week*
settimo [SEH-ttee-moh] *seventh*
sfogliare [sfoh-LYAH-reh] *to leaf through*
si [see] *himself; herself; yourself (fml.)*
sì [SEE] *yes*
siamo [SYAH-moh] *we are*
sicuramente [see-koo-rah-MEHN-teh] *surely*
sicuro [see-KOO-roh] *sure, certain*
siete [SYEH-teh] *you are (pl.)*
sigaretta [see-gah-REH-ttah] *cigarette*
silenzioso [see-lehn-TSYOH-zoh] *quiet*
simile [SEE-mee-leh] *similar*
simpatico [seem-PAH-tee-koh] *nice; likeable; cute*
sinagoga [see-nah-GOH-gah] *synagogue*
sinceramente [seen-cheh-rah-MEHN-teh] *sincerely*
sindaco [SEEN-dah-koh] *mayor*
sinistra [see-NEE-strah] *left*
sito [SEE-toh] *site*
soggiorno [soh-JJOHR-noh] *living room*
soldi [SOHL-dee] *money (m. pl.)*
sole [SOH-leh] *sun (m.)*
solo [SOH-loh] *alone; only*
somma [SOH-mmah] *quantity; sum; amount*
sondaggio [sohn-DAH-jjoh] *survey; opinion poll*
sono [SOH-noh] *I am; they are*
sopportare [soh-ppohr-TAH-reh] *to stand; to support*
sopra [SOH-prah] *on top; over*
soprano [soh-PRAH-noh] *soprano*
sorella [soh-REH-lah] *sister*
sorridere [soh-RREE-deh-reh] *to smile*
sotto [SOH-ttoh] *below; beneath; under*
spegnere [SPEH-nyeh-reh] *to turn off (the light, an appliance); to put out*

spettacolo [speh-TTAH-koh-loh] *show*
   spettacolo di varietà [speh-TTAH-koh-loh dee vah-ree-eh-TAH] *variety show*
sposare [spoh-ZAH-reh] *to marry*
sposato [spoh-ZAH-toh] *married*
spremuta [spreh-MOO-tah] *fresh juice*
spuntatina [spoon-tah-TEE-nah] *trim (haircut)*
stadio [STAH-dee-oh] *stadium*
stagione [stah-JOH-neh] *season*
stanza [STAHN-tsah] *room*
   stanza di chat [STAHN-tsah DEE CHEHT] *chat room*
stasera [stah-SEH-rah] *tonight*
stato [STAH-toh] *state*
statua [STAH-too-ah] *statue*
stazione [stah-TSYOH-neh] *station (f.)*
stella [STEH-llah] *star*
stile [STEE-leh] *style (m.)*
strada [STRAH-dah] *avenue; street*
strano [STRAH-noh] *strange*
studente [stoo-DEHN-teh] *student (m.)*
studentessa [stoo-dehn-TEH-ssah] *student (f.)*
studiare [stoo-dee-AH-reh] *to study*
studio [STOO-dee-oh] *studio; a study*
stupendo [stoo-PEHN-doh] *stupendous*
subito [SOO-bee-toh] *right away*
succo [SOO-kkoh] *juice*
suggerire [soo-jjeh-REE-reh] *to suggest (isc.)*
sugo [SOO-goh] *sauce*
su [soo] *on*
   sul serio [sool SEH-ree-oo] *seriously*
suo [SOO-oh] *his, her; his, hers*
Suo [SOO-oh] *your (fml.); yours (fml.)*
super bono [SOO-pehr BOH-noh] *hot (attractive)*
svegliarsi [zveh-LYAHR-see] *to wake up*

T

taglia [TAH-lyah] *size (clothing)*
tagliando [tah-LYAHN-doh] *coupon; stub*
taglio [TAH-lyoh] *cut; haircut*
tanto [TAHN-toh] *so much (adv.); so many (adj.)*
   Tante cose! [TAHN-teh KOH-zeh] *All the best!*
   Tante grazie. [TAHN-teh GRAH-tsyeh] *Thank you very much.*

tardi [TAHR-dee] *late*

tavolo [TAH-voh-loh] *table*

taxi [TAH-ksee] *taxi, cab*

taxista [tahk-SEE-stah] *taxi driver (m./f.)*

telefonare [teh-leh-foh-NAH-reh] *to call*

telefonino [teh-leh-foh-NEE-noh] *cell phone*

telegiornale [teh-leh-johr-NAH-leh] *TV news*

telenovela [teh-leh-noh-VEH-lah] *TV soap opera*

televisione [teh-leh-vee-ZYOH-neh] *television (programming) (f.)*

televisore [teh-leh-vee-ZOH-reh] *television set (m.)*

tema [TEH-mah] *subject (m.)*

tempo [TEHM-poh] *weather; time*
  Che tempo fa? [keh TEHM-poh FAH] *What's the weather like?*
  Fa bel tempo. [FAH BEHL TEHM-poh] *It's nice out.*
  Non ho tempo [NOHN oh TEMP-poh] *to keep; to hold*

tenere [teh-NEH-reh] *to keep; to hold*

tennis [TEH-nnees] *tennis (m.)*

tenore [teh-NOH-reh] *tenor (m.)*

terremoto [teh-rreh-MOH-toh] *earthquake*

terzo [TEHR-tsoh] *third*

tesoro [teh-ZOH-roh] *treasure*

tetto [TEH-ttoh] *roof*

ti [tee] *you (infml.); to you (infml.); yourself*

tintoria [teen-toh-REE-ah] *dry-cleaner*

tipico [TEE-pee-koh] *typical*

tipo [TEE-poh] *type; guy (coll.)*

tirare [tee-RAH-reh] *to pull*

titolare [tee-toh-LAH-reh] *bearer; holder (m./f.)*

toletta [toh-LEH-ttah] *restroom*

tomba [TOHM-bah] *tomb*

topo [TOH-poh] *mouse*

troppo [TROH-ppoh] *too much (adv.); too many (adj.)*

tornare [tohr-NAH-reh] *to return; to come back*

torre [TOH-rreh] *tower*

tovagliolo [toh-vah-LYOH-loh] *napkin*

tra [TRAH] *between; among; in (time)*

traffico [TRAH-ffee-koh] *traffic*

tramezzino [trah-meh-TSEE-noh] *triangle-shaped sandwich*

trasferire [trah-sfeh-REE-reh] *to transfer (isc.)*

trattarsi [trah-TTAHR-see] *to be about; to deal with; to have to do with*
  Si tratta di . . . [see TRAH-ttah dee] *It's about . . . ; It has to do with . . .*

tre [TREH] *three*

treno [TREH-noh] *train*

trenta [TREHN-tah] *thirty*

triste [TREE-steh] *sad*

trovare [troh-VAH-reh] *to find*

trovarsi [troh-VAHR-see] *to be located*

tu [too] *you (infml.)*

tuo [TOO-oh] *your (infml.); yours (infml.)*

turista [too-REE-stah] *tourist (m./f.)*

turistico [too-REE-stee-koh] *touristy*

tv [tee-VOO] *TV (f.)*

U

ultimo [OOL-tee-moh] *last, latest*

un [oon] *a; one (m.)*

una [OO-nah] *a; one (f.)*

università [oo-nee-vehr-see-TAH] *university*

uscire [oo-SHEE-reh] *to go out*

V

valere [vah-LEH-reh] *to be worth*
  (Non) vale la pena. [nohn VAH-leh lah PEH-na] *It's (not) worth it.*

valigie [vah-LEE-jeh] *luggage (f. pl.)*

vandalismo [vahn-dah-LEE-zmoh] *vandalism*

vasetto [vah-ZEH-ttoh] *jar*

vecchio [VEH-kyoh] *old; former*

vedere [veh-DEH-reh] *to see*
  Ci vediamo! [chee veh-DYAH-moh] *See you!*

vegetariano [veh-jeh-tah-ree-AH-noh] *vegetarian*

velocemente [veh-loh-cheh-MEHN-teh] *quickly*

venditore [vehn-dee-TOH-reh] *salesman (m.)*
  venditore di fumo [vehn-dee-TOH-reh dee FOO-moh] *poseur; con-artist (Lit. smoke salesman)*

venditrice [vehn-dee-TREE-cheh] *saleswoman (f.)*

venerdì [veh-nehr-DEE] *Friday*

venire [veh-NEE-reh] *to come*

venti [VEHN-tee] *twenty*

vento [VEHN-toh] *wind*
  Tira vento. [TEE-rah VEHN-toh] *It's windy.*

veramente [veh-rah-MEHN-teh] *really; truly*

verde [VEHR-deh] *green*
  numero verde [NOO-meh-roh VEHR-deh] *toll-free number*

vero [VEH-roh] *true; real*

vertigine [vehr-TEE-jee-neh] *dizziness (f.); vertigo*
  Ho le vertigini. [OH leh vehr-TEE-jee-nee] *I'm dizzy.*

vestito [veh-STEE-toh] *suit; dress*

vetrina [veh-TREE-nah] *store window*

via [VEE-ah] *street; by*

viaggiare [vyah-JJAH-reh] *to travel*

vicino [vee-CHEE-noh] *near; close*

vicino/–a [vee-CHEE-noh/ah] *neighbor (m./f.)*

villaggio [vee-LLAH-jjoh] *village*

vincere [VEEN-cheh-reh] *to win*

vincite [VEEN-chee-teh] *winnings (f.pl.)*

vino [VEE-noh] *wine*

vita [VEE-tah] *life; lifetime*

vivo [VEE-voh] *alive; living; lively*

voi [VOY] *you (pl.)*

voglia [VOH-lyah] *willingness; wish*
  Ho voglia di [OH VOH-lyah dee] *I feel like . . . (doing something)*

volere [voh-LEH-reh] *to want*

volta [VOHL-tah] *time; instance*
  a volte [ah VOHL-teh] *at times*
  C'era una volta . . . [CHEH-rah OO-nah VOHL-tah] *Once upon a time . . .*

vorrei [voh-RAY] *I'd like*

vostro [VOH-stroh] *your (pl.); yours (pl.)*

votare [voh-TAH-reh] *to vote*

voto [VOH-toh] *vote*

Z

zero [TSEH-roh] *zero*

zio/–a [TSEE-oh/–ah] *uncle; aunt*

zona [TSOH-nah] *zone; neighborhood; area*

zuccherino [tsoo-kkeh-REE-noh] *a cinch*

zucchero [TSOO-kkeh-roh] *sugar*

A

a *un* [oon] *(m.); una* [OO-nah] *(f.)*
able (to be) *potere* [poh-TEH-reh]
above *sopra* [SOH-prah]
accessories *accessori* [ah-cheh-SSOH-ree] *(m. pl.)*
acquaintance *conoscenza* [koh-noh-SHEHN-tsah]
act *atto* [AH-ttoh]
　first act *primo atto* [PREE-moh AH-ttoh]
actor *attore* [ah-TTOH-reh] *(m.)*
actress *attrice* [ah-TTREE-cheh] *(f.)*
address *indirizzo* [een-dee-REE-tsoh]
after *dopo* [DOH-poh]
　after–dinner drink *digestivo* [dee-jeh-STEE-voh]
again *di nuovo* [dee NWOH-voh]; *ancora* [ahn-KOH-rah]
age *età* [eh-TAH]
　at their age *alla loro età* [AH-llah LOH-roh eh-TAH]
agent *agente* [ah-JEHN-teh] *(m./f.)*
agreement *accordo* [ah-KKOHR-doh]
　Agreed. *D'accordo.* [dah-KKOHR-doh]
air *aria* [AH-ree-ah]
　air–conditioning *aria condizionata* [AH-ree-ah kohn-dee-tsee-oh-NAH-tah]
airplane *aereo* [ah-EH-reh-oh]
alive *vivo* [VEE-voh]
allergy *allergia* [ah-llehr-JEE-ah]
allow (to) *permettere* [pehr-MEH-tteh-reh]
alone *solo* [SOH-loh]
also *anche* [AHN-keh]
alto *contralto* [kon-TRAHL-toh]
always *sempre* [SEHM-preh]
among *fra* [FRAH]; *tra* [TRAH]
amount *somma* [SOH-mmah]
amusement *divertimento* [dee-vehr-tee-MEHN-toh]
and *e* [EH]
animal *animale* [ah-nee-MAH-leh] *(m.)*
anniversary *anniversario* [ah-nee-vehr-SAH-ree-oh]
annoying *fastidioso* [fah-stee-dee-OH-zoh]

another *un altro/-a* [oon AHL-troh/ah]
answer *risposta* [ree-SPOH-stah]
answer (to) *rispondere* [ree-SPOHN-deh-reh]
answering machine *segreteria telefonica* [seh-greh-teh-REE-yah teh-leh-FOH-nee-kah]
apartment *appartamento* [ah-ppahr-tah-MEHN-toh]
aperitif (before–dinner drink) *aperitivo* [ah-peh-ree-TEE-voh]
appetizer *antipasto* [ahn-tee-PAH-stoh]
April *aprile* [ah-PREE-leh]
area *zona* [DZOH-nah]
aria *aria* [AH-ree-ah]
arrive (to) *arrivare* [ah-ree-VAH-reh]
art *arte* [AHR-teh] *(f.)*
article *articolo* [ahr-TEE-koh-loh]
ask (to; for) *chiedere* [KYEH-deh-reh]
　to ask a question *fare una domanda* [FAH-reh OO-nah doh-MAHN-dah]
at *da* [dah]; *a* [ah]; *in* [een]
　at the bottom *in fondo* [een FOHN-doh]
attend (to) *assistere* [ah-SSEE-steh-reh]
attractive *attraente*, [ah-trah-EHN-teh]; *super bono* [soo-pehr BOH-noh] *(coll.)*
audience *pubblico* [POO-bblee-koh]
August *agosto* [ah-GOH-stoh]
aunt *zia* [TSEE-ah]
autumn *autunno* [ow-TOO-nnoh]
avenue *strada* [STRAH-dah]

B

baby *bambino/-a* [bahm-BEE-noh/-ah] *(m./f.)*
balcony *balcone* [bahl-KOH-neh]; *galleria* [gah-LEH-ree-ah]
bartender *barista* [bah-REE-stah] *(m./f.)*
bass (voice) *basso* [BAH-ssoh]
bath *bagno* [BAH-nyoh]
battle *battaglia* [bah-TAH-lyah]
be able (to) *potere* [poh-TEH-reh]

beans *fagioli* [fah-JOH-lee] *(m. pl.)*
bearer *titolare* [tee-toh-LAH-reh]
beautiful *bello* [BEH-lloh]
beer *birra* [BEE-rrah]
be (to) *essere* [EH-sseh-reh]
　to be…years old (Lit. to have…years) *avere…anni* [ah-VEH-reh AH-nnee]
　to be hungry *avere fame* [ah-VEH-reh FAH-meh]
　to be lucky *avere fortuna* [ah-VEH-reh fohr-TOO-nah]
　to be in a hurry *avere fretta* [ah-VEH-reh FREH-ttah]
　to be right *avere ragione* [ah-VEH-reh rah-JOH-neh]
　to be thirsty *avere sete* [ah-VEH-reh SEH-teh]
behind *dietro* [DYEH-troh]
believe (to) *credere* [KREH-deh-reh]
　I don't believe it! *Non ci credo!* [NOHN chee KREH-doh]
below *sotto* [SOH-ttoh]
belt *cintura* [cheen-TOO-rah]
best *il/la migliore* [eel/lah mee-LYOH-reh] *(adj.); il/la meglio* [eel/lah MEH-lyoh] *(adv.)*
　Best wishes! *Auguri!* [ah-oo-GOO-ree]
better *meglio* [MEH-lyoh] *(adv.); migliore* [mee-LYOH-reh] *(adj.)*
between *fra* [FRAH]; *tra* [TRAH]
big *grande* [GRAHN-deh]
bigger *più grande* [pyoo GRAHN-deh]
bill *conto* [KOHN-toh]
billiards *biliardo* [bee-LYAHR-doh]
billion *miliardo* [mee-LYAHR-doh]
birthday *compleanno* [kohm-pleh-AH-nnoh]
　Happy birthday! *Buon compleanno!* [BWOHN kohm-pleh-AH-nnoh]
black *nero* [NEH-roh]
blanket *coperta* [koh-PEHR-tah]
blouse *camicetta* [kah-mee-CHEH-ttah]
blue *blu* [BLOO]
book *libro* [LEE-broh]
booked *al completo* [ahl kohm-PLEH-toh]

boring *noioso* [noh-YOH-zoh]

boss *capo* [KAH-poh]

boutique *negozio* [neh-GOH-tsyoh]

box *scatola* [SKAH-toh-lah]

boy *ragazzo* [rah-GAH-tsoh]

boyfriend *ragazzo* [rah-GAH-tsoh]

bracelet *braccialetto* [brah-chah-LEH-ttoh]

breakfast *colazione* [koh-lah-TSYOH-neh] *(f.)*

breath *fiato* [fee-AH-toh]
  breathless *senza fiato* [SEHN-tsah fee-AH-toh]

bring (to) *portare* [pohr-TAH-reh]

bronze *bronzo* [BROHN-dzoh]

brother *fratello* [frah-TEH-loh]

brown *marrone* [mah-RROH-neh]

building *edificio* [eh-dee-FEE-choh]

built *costruito* [koh-stroo-EE-toh]

bus *autobus* [OW-toh-boos] *(m.)*

but *ma* [mah]

butcher *macellaio/-a* [mah-cheh-LAH-yoh/-ah] *(m./f.)*

by *via* [VEE-ah]; *in* [een]
  by the way *a proposito* [ah proh-POH-zee-toh]
  by train *in treno* [een TREH-noh]

Bye! *Ciao!* [CHOW]

C

café *bar* [BAHR] *(m.)*; *caffè* [kah-FFEH] *(m.)*

call *chiamata* [kyah-MAH-tah]
  to make a phone call *fare una chiamata* [FAH-reh OO-nah kyah-MAH-tah]

call (to) *chiamare* [kyah-MAH-reh]; *telefonare* [teh-leh-foh-NAH-reh]
  call again (to) *richiamare* [REE-kyah-MAH-reh]

call waiting *chiamata in attesa* [kyah-MAH-tah een ah-TTEH-zah]

called (to be) *chiamarsi* [kyah-MARH-see]

can *lattina* [lah-TTEE-nah]

candidate *candidato/-a* [kahn-dee-DAH-toh/ah] *(m./f.)*

car *macchina* [MAH-kee-nah]

carbonated *frizzante* [free-TSAHN-teh]

card *carta* [KAHR-tah]; *scheda* [SKEH-dah]
  credit card *carta di credito* [KAHR-tah dee KREH-dee-toh]

telephone card *scheda telefonica* [SKEH-dah teh-leh-FOH-nee-kah]

Careful (be)! *Attenzione!* [ah-ttehn-TSYOH-neh]

caress *carezza* [kah-REH-tsah]

cartoon *cartone animato* [kahr-TOH-neh ah-nee-MAH-toh] *(m.)*

case *caso* [KAH-zoh]

cash *contanti* [kohn-THAN-tee] *(m. pl.)*

castle *castello* [kah-STEH-lloh]

cat *gatto* [GAH-ttoh]

cathedral *cattedrale* [kah-tteh-DRAH-leh] *(f.)*

CD player *lettore di CD* [leh-TTOH-reh DEE CHEE-DEE]

celebrate (to) *festeggiare* [feh-steh-JAH-reh]; *celebrare* [cheh-leh-BRAH-reh]

cell phone *telefonino* [teh-leh-foh-NEE-noh]

cereal *cereali* [cheh-reh-AH-lee] *(m. pl.)*

certain *certo* [CHEHR-toh]

certainly *certamente* [chehr-tah-MEHN-teh]; *certo* [CHEHR-toh]

change (to) *cambiare* [kahm-BYAH-reh]
  to change one's mind *cambiare idea* [kahm-BYAH-reh ee-DEH-ah]
  to change lines *cambiare linea* [kahm-BYAH-reh LEE-neh-ah]

channel *canale* [kah-NAH-leh] *(m.)*

chat (to) *fare due chiacchiere* [FAH-reh DOO-eh KYAH-kyeh-reh]
  to chat on-line *fare la chat* [FAH-reh lah CHEHT]

cheese *formaggio* [fohr-MAH-jjoh]

Cheers! *Saluti!* [sah-LOO-tee]

child *bambino/-a* [bahm-BEE-noh/-ah] *(m./f.)*

children *figli* [FEE-lyee]

choose (to) *scegliere* [SHEH-lyeh-reh]

chore (household) *faccenda domestica* [fah-CHEHN-dah doh-MEH-stee-kah]

Christmas *Natale* [nah-TAH-leh] *(m.)*
  Merry Christmas! *Buon Natale!* [BWOHN nah-TAH-leh]

church *chiesa* [KYEH-zah]

cigarette *sigaretta* [see-gah-REH-ttah]

cinch *zuccherino* [tsoo-keh-REE-noh]

cinema *cinema* [CHEE-neh-mah] *(m.)*

city *città* [chee-TAH]

city square *piazza* [PYAH-tsah]

classic *classico* [KLAH-see-koh]

clean (to) *pulire* [poo-LEE-reh]

clear *chiaro* [KYAH-roh]

click (to) *cliccare* [klee-KKAH-reh]

client *cliente* [klee-EHN-teh] *(m./f.)*

climate *clima* [KLEE-mah] *(m.)*

climb (to) *salire* [sah-LEE-reh]

coat *cappotto* [kah-PPOH-ttoh]

coffee *caffè* [kah-FFEH]

coincidence *coincidenza* [koh-een-chee-DEHN-tsah]

cold *freddo* [FREH-ddoh]
  I'm cold. *Ho freddo.* [OH FREH-ddoh]
  It's cold. *Fa freddo.* [FAH FREH-ddoh]

column *colonna* [koh-LOH-nnah]
  gossip column *cronaca mondana* [KROH-nah-kah mohn-DAH-nah]

come (to) *venire* [veh-NEE-reh]
  Come off it! *Ma, dai!* [mah DAH-ee]

commercial *pubblicità* [poo-bblee-chee-TAH]

compelling *commovente* [koh-mmoh-VEHN-teh]

competent *competente* [kohm-peh-TEHN-teh]

complain (to) *lamentarsi* [lah-mehn-TAHR-see]

complete *completo* [kohm-PLEH-toh]

composer *compositore* [kohm-poh-zee-TOH-reh] *(m.)*; *compositrice* [kohm-poh-zee-TREE-cheh] *(f.)*

computer *computer* [kohm-PYOO-tehr] *(m.)*

concierge *portiere* [pohr-TYEH-reh] *(m./f.)*

Congratulations! *Congratulazioni!* [kohn-grah-too-lah-TSYOH-nee]

connection *nesso* [NEH-ssoh]; *coincidenza* [koh-een-chee-DEHN-tsah] *(transportation)*

contestant *concorrente* [kohn-koh-RREHN-teh] *(m./f.)*

contradict (to) *dare contro a* [DAH-reh KOHN-troh ah]

convince (to) *convincere* [kohn-VEEN-cheh-reh]

cook (to) *cucinare* [koo-chee-NAH-reh]

cookie *biscotto* [bee-SKOH-ttoh]
cool *fresco* [FREH-skoh]
corner *angolo* [AHN-goh-loh]
correct *giusto* [JOO-stoh]; *corretto* [koh-RREH-ttoh]
corridor *corridoio* [koh-ree-DOH-yoh]
cost (to) *costare* [koh-STAH-reh]
costume *costume* [koh-STOO-meh] *(m.)*
counsel (to) *consigliare* [kohn-see-LYAH-reh]
country *paese* [pah-EH-zeh] *(m.)*
coupon *tagliando* [tah-LYAHN-doh]
course *corso* [KOHR-soh]
  of course *senz'altro* [SEHN-tsahl-troh]
cousin *cugino/-a* [koo-JEE-noh/-a] *(m./f.)*
crazy *pazzo* [PAH-tsoh]; *matto* [MAH-ttoh]
cream *crema* [KREH-mah]
creative *creativo* [kreh-ah-TEE-voh]
crime *criminalità* [kree-mee-nah-lee-TAH]
croissant *cornetto* [kohr-NEH-ttoh]
cry (to) *piangere* [PYAHN-jeh-reh]
current events *attualità* [ah-ttoo-ah-lee-TAH] *(f. pl.)*
cut *taglio* [TAH-lyoh] *(n.)*
cute *carino* [kah-REE-noh]; *simpatico* [seem-PAH-tee-koh]

D

dance (to) *ballare* [bah-LLAH-reh]
dark *scuro* [SKOO-roh]
daughter *figlia* [FEE-lyah]
day *giorno* [JOHR-noh]; *giornata* [johr-NAH-tah]
dead *morto* [MOHR-toh]
December *dicembre* [dee-CHEHM-breh]
decide (to) *decidere* [deh-CHEE-deh-reh]
decision *decisione* [deh-chee-ZYOH-neh] *(f.)*
decline (n.) *declino* [deh-KLEE-noh]
delay *ritardo* [ree-TAHR-doh]
delicious *delizioso* [deh-lee-TSYOH-zoh]
depart (to) *partire* [pahr-TEE-reh]
department store *grande magazzino* [GRAHN-deh mah-gah-TSEE-noh]
design *disegno* [dee-ZEH-nyoh]

desire (to) *desiderare* [deh-zee-deh-RAH-reh]
dessert *dolce* [DOHL-cheh]
detail *dettaglio* [deh-TTAH-lyoh]
different *diverso* [dee-VEHR-soh]
dinner *cena* [CHEH-nah]
director *direttore* [dee-reh-TTOH-reh] *(m.)*; *direttrice* [dee-reh-TREE-cheh] *(f.)*
  film/theater director *regista* [reh-JEE-sta]
disaster *disastro* [dee-ZAH-stroh]
  What a disaster! *Che disastro!* [KEH dee-ZAH-stroh]
dish *piatto* [PYAH-ttoh]
  side dish *contorno* [kohn-TOHR-noh]
displease (to) *dispiacere* [dee-spyah-CHEH-reh]
distant *lontano* [lohn-TAH-noh]
diverse *diverso* [dee-VEHR-soh]
divide (to) *dividere* [dee-VEE-deh-reh]
dizziness *vertigine* [vehr-TEE-jee-neh] *(f.)*
  I'm dizzy. (from the height) *Ho le vertigini.* [OH leh vehr-TEE-jee-nee]
do (to) *fare* [FAH-reh]
doctor *dottore* [doh-TTOH-reh] *(m.)*; *dottoressa* [doh-ttoh-REH-ssah] *(f.)*; *medico* [MEH-dee-koh]
documentary *documentario* [doh-koo-mehn-TAH-ree-oh]
dog *cane* [KAH-neh] *(m.)*
door *porta* [POHR-tah]
doorman *portiere* [pohr-TYEH-reh] *(m./f.)*
dress *vestito* [veh-STEE-toh]
drink (to) *bere* [BEH-reh]
drive (to) *guidare* [gwee-DAH-reh]
dry cleaner *tintoria* [teen-toh-REE-ah]

E

early *presto* [PREH-stoh]
earthquake *terremoto* [teh-rreh-MOH-toh]
Easter *Pasqua* [PAH-skwah]
eat (to) *mangiare* [mahn-JAH-reh]
eight *otto* [OH-ttoh]
eighth *ottavo* [oh-TAH-voh]
eighty *ottanta* [oh-TTAHN-tah]
elections *elezioni* [eh-leh-TSYOH-nee] *(f. pl.)*
elegant *elegante* [eh-leh-GAHN-teh]
eliminate (to) *eliminare* [eh-lee-mee-NAH-reh]

e–mail *e-mail* [ee-MAYL] *(f.)*
enchanting *incantevole* [een-kahn-TEH-voh-leh]
end *fine* [FEE-neh] *(f.)*
enemy *nemico* [NEH-mee-koh]
enter (to) *entrare* [ehn-TRAH-reh]
even if *anche se* [AHN-keh seh]
evening *sera* [SEH-rah]
  Good evening. *Buona sera.* [BWOH-nah SEH-rah]
exact *esatto* [eh-ZAH-ttoh]
exactly *esattamente* [eh-zah-tah-MEHN-teh]; *esatto* [eh-ZAH-ttoh]
exaggerated *esagerato* [eh-zah-jeh-RAH-toh]
exaggeration *esagerazione* [eh-zah-jeh-rah-TSYOH-neh] *(f.)*
excellent *ottimo* [OH-ttee-moh]; *eccellente* [eh-cheh-LEHN-teh]
exchange (to) *scambiare* [skahm-BYAH-reh]
exchange *scambio* [SKAHM-byoh]
excuse *scusa* [SKOO-zah]
  Excuse me. *Scusa/-i.* [SKOO-zah/-ee] *(infml./fml.)*
exist (to) *esistere* [eh-ZEE-steh-reh]
expect (to) *aspettare* [ah-speh-TTAH-reh]
expression *espressione* [eh-spreh-SYOH-neh] *(f.)*

F

fabulous *favoloso* [fah-voh-LOH-zoh]
fall asleep (to) *addormentarsi* [ah-ddohr-mehn-TAHR-see]
false *falso* [FAHL-soh]
famous *famoso* [fah-MOH-zoh]; *conosciuto* [koh-noh-SHOO-toh]
fantastic *fantastico* [fahn-TAH-stee-koh]; *meraviglioso* [meh-rah-vee-LYOH-zoh]
father *padre* [PAH-dreh] *(m.)*
February *febbraio* [feh-BRAH-yoh]
feel (to) *sentirsi* [sehn-TEER-see]; *sentire* [sehn-TEER-see]
  to feel like (doing something) *avere voglia di* [ah-VEH-reh VOH-lyah dee]
  I don't feel well. *Non mi sento bene.* [NOHN mee SEHN-toh BEH-neh]
fiancé(e) *fidanzato/-a* [fee-dahn-TSAH-toh/ah] *(m./f.)*
fifth *quinto* [KWEEN-toh]

fifty *cinquanta* [cheen-KWAHN-tah]

find (to) *trovare* [troh-VAH-reh]

finish (to) *finire* [fee-NEE-reh] *(isc.)*

finished *finito* [fee-NEE-toh]

fire *fuoco* [FWOH-koh]

Fire! *Al fuoco!* [FWOH-koh]

first *primo* [PREE-moh]

fish *pesce* [PEH-sheh] *(m.)*

five *cinque* [CHEEN-kweh]

flag *bandiera* [bahn-DYEH-rah]

flood *alluvione* [ah-lloo-VYOH-neh] *(f.)*

floor *pavimento* [pah-vee-MEHN-toh]; *piano* [PYAH-noh] *(story of a building)*

for *per* [PEHR]; *da* [DAH]

forecast *previsione* [preh-vee-ZYOH-neh] *(f.)*

weather forecast *previsioni del tempo* [preh-vee-ZYOH-nee dehl TEHM-poh]

forget (to) *dimenticare* [dee-mehn-tee-KAH-reh]; *dimenticarsi* [dee-mehn-tee-KAHR-see]

fork *forchetta* [fohr-KEH-ttah]

former *vecchio* [VEH-kyoh]

forty *quaranta* [kwah-RAHN-tah]

foundation *fondazione* [fohn-dah-TSYOH-neh]; *fondamenta* [fohn-dah-MEHN-tah] *(of a building) (f. pl.)*

fountain *fontana* [fohn-TAH-nah]

four *quattro* [KWAH-ttroh]

fourth *quarto* [KWAHR-toh]

frankly *francamente* [frahn-kah-MEHN-teh]

free *libero* [LEE-beh-roh]; *gratis* [GRAH-tees]

fresh *fresco* [FREH-skoh]

from *da* [dah]; *di* [dee]

Friday *venerdì* [veh-nehr-DEE]

friend *amico/-a* [ah-MEE-koh/-ah] *(m./f.)*

fruit *frutta* [FROO-ttah]

fun *divertimento* [dee-vehr-tee-MEHN-toh]

to have fun *divertirsi* [dee-vehr-TEER-see]

Have fun! (pl.) *Divertitevi!* [dee-vehr-TEE-teh-vee]

G

gadget *aggeggio* [ah-JJEH-jjoh]

gallery *galleria* [gah-LEH-ree-ah]

game *gioco* [JOH-koh]

game show *gioco a premi* [JOH-koh ah PREH-mee]

garage *garage* [gah-RAHZH] *(m.)*

gardening *giardinaggio* [jahr-dee-NAH-jjoh]

gender *sesso* [SEH-ssoh]; *genere* [JEH-neh-reh]

geography *geografia* [jeh-oh-grah-FEE-ah]

get angry (to) *arrabbiarsi* [ah-rrah-BBYAHR-see]

get up (to) *alzarsi* [ahl-TSAHR-see]

gift *regalo* [reh-GAH-loh]

girl *ragazza* [rah-GAH-tsah]

girlfriend *ragazza* [rah-GAH-tsah]; *fidanzata* [fee-dahn-TSAH-tah]

give (to) *dare* [DAH-reh]

to give a gift *regalare* [reh-gah-LAH-reh]

gladly *con piacere* [kohn pyah-CHEH-reh]

glass *bicchiere* [bee-KYEH-reh] *(m.)*

gloves *guanti* [GWAHN-tee] *(m. pl.)*

go (to) *andare* [ahn-DAH-reh]

How's it going? *Come va?* [KOH-meh VAH]

to go out *uscire* [oo-SHEE-reh]

God *dio* [DEE-oh]

good *buono* [BWOH-noh]

a good catch *un buon partito* [oon BWOHN pahr-TEE-toh]

Good afternoon. *Buon pomeriggio.* [BWOHN poh-meh-REE-jjoh]

Good evening. *Buona sera.* [BWOH-nah SEH-rah]

Good–bye! *Arrivederci!* [ah-rree-veh-DEHR-chee]; *ciao; ArrivederLa!* [ah-rree-veh-DEHR-lah] *(fml.)*

gossip (to) *fare pettegolezzi* [FAH-reh peh-tteh-goh-LEH-tsee]

Gothic *gotico* [GOH-tee-koh]

graduation *maturità* [mah-too-ree-TAH] *(high school); laurea* [LAH-oo-reh-ah] *(college)*

grandchild *nipote* [nee-POH-teh] *(m./f.)*

grandfather *nonno* [NOH-nnoh]

grandmother *nonna* [NOH-nnah]

grandparents *nonni* [NOH-nnee]

gray *grigio* [GREE-joh]

great *grande* [GRAHN-deh]

green *verde* [VEHR-deh]

greetings *saluti* [sah-LOO-tee]

gum *gomma* [GOH-mmah]

gym *palestra* [pah-LEH-strah]

H

hair *capelli* [kah-PEH-llee]

hair dryer *fön* [FOHN]; *asciugacappelli* [ah-SYOO-gah-kah-PPEH-lli]

hair salon *salone* [sah-LOH-neh]

haircut *taglio* [TAH-lyoh]

hairdresser *parrucchiere/-a* [pah-roo-KYEH-rreh/rrah] *(m./f.)*

half *mezzo* [MEH-dzoh]

hallway *corridoio* [koh-ree-DOH-yoh]

ham *prosciutto* [proh-SHOO-ttoh]

happy *contento* [kohn-TEHN-toh]; *felice* [feh-LEE-cheh]

Happy New Year! *Buon anno!* [BWOHN AH-nnoh]

hard *duro* [DOO-roh]

have (to) *avere* [ah-VEH-reh]

Have fun! *Buon divertimento!* [BWOHN dee-vehr-tee-MEHN-toh]

he *lui* [LOO-ee]

head *capo* [KAH-poh]

hear (to) *sentire* [sehn-TEE-reh]

Hello! *Buon giorno.* [BWOHN JOHR-noh]; *Ciao!* [CHOW] *(infm.); Salve.* [SAHL-veh]

Hello? *Pronto?* [PROHN-toh] *(telephone)*

help *aiuto* [ah-YOO-toh]

Help! *Aiuto!* [ah-YOO-toh]

help (to) *aiutare* [ah-yoo-TAH-reh]; *assistere* [ah-SSEE-steh-reh]

her *la* [lah]; *le* [leh] *(to her)*

hers *suo* [SOO-oh]

herself *si* [see]

here *qua* [KWAH]; *qui* [KWEE]

Here you go./Here it is. *Ecco.* [EH-koh]

high *alto* [AHL-toh]

him *lo* [loh]; *gli* [lyee] *(to him); lui* [LOO-ee] *(after prep.)*

himself *si* [see]

his *suo* [SOO-oh]

hobby *hobby* [OH-bee] *(m.)*

hold (to) *tenere* [teh-NEH-reh]

holder *titolare* [tee-toh-LAH-reh] *(m./f.)*

horoscope *oroscopo* [oh-ROH-skoh-poh]

host (of a show) *presentatore* [preh-zehn-tah-TOH-reh] *(m.);*

presentatrice [preh-zehn-tah-TREE-cheh] *(f.)*

hot *caldo* [KAHL-doh]

  I'm hot. *Ho caldo.* [OH KAHL-doh]

  It's hot. *Fa caldo.* [FAH KAHL-doh]

hotel *albergo* [ahl-BEHR-goh]; *hotel* [oh-TEHL]

hour *ora* [OH-rah]

house *casa* [KAH-zah]

how *come* [KOH-meh]

  How are you? (infml.) *Come stai?* [KOH-meh STAH-ee]

  How are you? (fml.) *Come sta?* [KOH-meh STAH]

  how much *quanto/-a* [KWAHN-toh]

  how many *quanti/-e* [KWAHN-tee/teh]

  How's it going? *Come va?* [KOH-meh VAH]

hundred *cento* [CHEHN-toh]

hunger *fame* [FAH-meh]

hungry (to be) *avere fame* [ah-VEH-reh FAH-meh]

hurry (to) *affrettarsi* [ah-ffreh-TTAHR-see]

husband *marito* [mah-REE-toh]

hypochondriac *ipocondriaco/-a* [ee-poh-kohn-DREE-ah-koh/kah] *(m./f.)*

I

I *io* [EE-oh]

idea *idea* [ee-DEH-ah]

  Good idea! *Che buon'idea!* [keh BWOHN ee-DEH-ah]

idealist *idealista* [ee-deh-ah-LEE-stah] *(m./f.)*

idiot *idiota* [ee-dee-OH-tah] *(m./f.)*

if *se* [seh]

illustration *illustrazione* [ee-loo-strah-TSYOH-neh] *(f.)*

immature *immaturo* [ee-mah-TOO-roh]

in *in* [een]

  in front *davanti* [dah-VAHN-tee]

  in order *in ordine* [een OHR-dee-neh]

  in the back *di dietro* [dee DYEH-troh]

included *incluso* [een-KLOO-zoh]

incompetent *incompetente* [een-kohm-peh-TEHN-teh]

incredible *incredibile* [een-kreh-DEE-bee-leh]

influential *influente* [een-floo-EHN-teh]

inside *dentro* [DEHN-troh]

insist (to) *insistere* [een-SEES-teh-reh]

instead of *invece di* [een-VEH-cheh dee]

intelligent *intelligente* [een-teh-lee-JEHN-teh]

interest *interesse* [een-teh-REH-sseh] *(m.)*

interested (to be) *interessarsi* [een-teh-reh-SSAHR-see]

interesting *interessante* [een-teh-reh-SSAHN-teh]

intermission *intervallo* [een-tehr-VAH-lloh]

interpretation *interpretazione* [een-tehr-preh-tah-TSYOH-neh] *(f.)*

interval *intervallo* [een-tehr-VAH-lloh]

intimate *intimo* [EEN-tee-moh]

introduce (to) *presentare* [preh-zehn-TAH-reh]

invite (to) *invitare* [een-vee-TAH-reh]

iron *ferro* [FEH-rroh]

it *la* [lah]; *lo* [loh]

J

jacket *giacca* [JAH-kkah]

jam *marmellata* [mahr-meh-LLAH-tah]

January *gennaio* [jeh-NAH-yoh]

jar *vasetto* [vah-ZEH-ttoh]

jeans *jeans* [JEENS] *(m. pl.)*

journalist *giornalista* [johr-nah-LEE-stah] *(m./f.)*

juice *succo* [SOO-koh]

  fresh juice *spremuta* [spreh-MOO-tah]

July *luglio* [LOO-lyoh]

June *giugno* [JOO-nyoh]

just *proprio* [PROH-pree-oh]; *appena* [ah-PPEH-nah]; *giusto* [JOO-stoh]

K

key *chiave* [KYAH-veh] *(f.)*

keep (to) *tenere* [teh-NEH-reh]

kind *gentile* [jehn-TEE-leh] *(adj.)*

kitchen *cucina* [koo-CHEE-nah]

knife *coltello* [kohl-TEH-lloh]

know (to) *conoscere* [koh-NOH-sheh-reh] *(to be acquainted with)*; *sapere* [sah-PEH-reh] *(to know about or how to)*

L

language *lingua* [LEEN-gwah]

large *grande* [GRAHN-deh]

last *ultimo* [OOL-tee-moh]

late *in ritardo* [een ree-TAHR-doh]; *tardi* [TAHR-dee]

latest *ultimo* [ool-tee-moh]

laugh (to) *ridere* [REE-deh-reh]

law *legge* [LEH-jeh] *(f.)*

lawyer *avvocato* [ah-voh-KAH-toh] *(m.)*; *avvocatessa* [ah-voh-kah-TEH-ssah] *(f.)*

leaf through (to) *sfogliare* [sfoh-LYAH-reh]

leave (to) *lasciare* [lah-SHAH-reh]

  Leave me alone (Lit. in peace)! *Mi lasci in pace!* [mee LAH-shee een PAH-cheh]

left *sinistra* [see-NEE-strah]

leg *gamba* [GAHM-bah]

legend *leggenda* [leh-JEHN-dah]

less *meno* [MEH-noh]

lesson *lezione* [leh-TSYOH-neh] *(f.)*

life *vita* [VEE-tah]

light *leggero* [leh-JJEH-roh] *(adj.)*; *luce* [LOO-cheh] *(n. f.)*

light (to) *accendere* [ah-CHEHN-deh-reh]

line *coda* [KOH-dah]; *linea* [LEE-neh-ah]

  to wait in line *fare la coda* [FAH-reh lah KOH-dah]

listen (to) *ascoltare* [ah-skohl-TAH-reh]

liter *litro* [LEE-troh]

little *poco* [POH-koh] *(adv.)*; *piccolo* [PEE-kkoh-loh] *(adj.)*

live (to) *abitare* [ah-bee-TAH-reh]

look (to) *guardare* [gwahr-DAH-reh]

look for (to) *cercare* [chehr-KAH-reh]

lose (to) *perdere* [PEHR-deh-reh]

love (to) *amare* [ah-MAH-reh]

low *basso* [BAH-ssoh]

luck *fortuna* [fohr-TOO-nah]

  Good luck! *Buona fortuna!* [BWOH-nah fohr-TOO-nah]/*In bocca al lupo!* [een BOH-kkah ahl LOO-poh]

luggage *valigie* [vah-LEE-jeh] *(f. pl.)*

lunch *pranzo* [PRAHN-tsoh]

M

mail *posta* [POH-stah]
   You've got mail. *C'è posta per te.* [CHEH POH-stah pehr TEH]
   voice mail *posta vocale* [POH-stah voh-KAH-leh]
make (to) *fare* [FAH-reh]
   to make a mistake *sbagliare* [zbah-LYAH-reh]
   to make oneself comfortable *accomodarsi* [ah-koh-moh-DAHR-see]
   Make yourself comfortable. *Si accomodi.* [see ah-KOH-moh-dee]
many *molto* [MOHL-toh]; *tanto* [TAHN-toh]
map *mappa* [MAH-ppah]; *carta* [KAHR-tah]; *pianta* [PYAN-tah]
   road map *carta stradale* [KAHR-tah strah-DAH-leh]
marble *marmo* [MAHR-moh]
March *marzo* [MAHR-zoh]
married *sposato* [spoh-ZAH-toh]
marry (to) *sposare* [spoh-ZAH-reh]
marvelous *meraviglioso* [meh-rah-vee-LYOH-zoh]
materialist *materialista* [mah-teh-ree-ah-LEE-stah] *(m./f.)*
mature *maturo* [mah-TOO-roh]
May *maggio* [MAH-joh]
maybe *forse* [FOHR-seh]
mayor *sindaco* [SEEN-dah-koh]
me *mi* [mee]
meat *carne* [KAHR-neh] *(f.)*
mechanic *meccanico/-a* [meh-KAH-nee-koh/-ah] *(m./f.)*
medieval *medievale* [meh-dee-eh-VAH-leh]
memory *ricordo* [ree-KOHR-doh]
menu *menù* [meh-NOO] *(m.)*
message *messaggio* [meh-SSAH-jjoh]
million *milione* [mee-LYOH-neh] *(m.)*
mine *mio* [MEE-oh]
minibar *frigo-bar* [FREE-goh-BAHR] *(m.)*
minute (n.) *minuto* [mee-NOO-toh]
modern *moderno* [moh-DEHR-noh]
moment *attimo* [AH-ttee-moh]; *momento* [moh-MEHN-toh]
Monday *lunedì* [loo-neh-DEE]
money *denaro* [deh-NAH-roh]; *soldi* [SOHL-dee] *(m. pl.)*
month *mese* [MEH-zeh] *(m.)*
monument *monumento* [moh-noo-MEHN-toh]

more *più* [PYOO]
most *la maggior parte* [lah MAH-jjohr PAHR-teh]
mother *madre* [MAH-dreh] *(f.)*
motorbike *motorino* [moh-toh-REE-noh]
mouse *topo* [TOH-poh]
movie *film* [FEELM] *(m.)*
   to show a movie *dare un film* [DAH-reh oon FEELM]
moving (emotionally) *commovente* [koh-mmoh-VEHN-teh]
much *molto* [MOHL-toh]; *tanto* [TAHN-toh]
   too much *troppo* [TROH-ppoh]
municipality *comune* [koh-MOO-neh] *(m.)*
museum *museo* [MOO-seh-oh]
music *musica* [MOO-zee-kah]
must *dovere* [doh-VEH-reh]
my *mio* [MEE-oh]
myself *mi* [MEE]

N

name *nome* [NOH-meh] *(m.)*
   My name is… *Mi chiamo . . .* [mee KYAH-moh]
   name day *onomastico* [oh-noh-MAH-stee-koh]
   named (to be) *chiamarsi* [kyah-MAHR-see]
napkin *tovagliolo* [toh-vah-LYOH-loh]
natural *naturale* [nah-too-RAH-leh]
naturally *naturalmente* [nah-too-rahl-MEHN-teh]
navigate (to) *navigare* [nah-vee-GAH-reh]
near *vicino* [vee-CHEE-noh]
necklace *collana* [koh-LLAH-nah]
need (to) *avere bisogno di* [ah-VEH-reh bee-ZOH-nyoh dee]; *servire* [sehr-VEE-reh]
   I need… *Mi serve . . .* [mee SEHR-veh]
neighbor *vicino/-a* [vee-CHEE-noh/ah] *(m./f.)*
neighborhood *zona* [DZOH-nah]
neither…nor… *non . . . né . . . né* [nohn NEH NEH]
nephew *nipote* [nee-POH-teh] *(m.)*
never *non . . . mai* [nohn MAH-ee]
new *nuovo* [NWOH-voh]
New Year's Day *Capodanno* [kah-poh-DAH-nnoh]

news *notizie* [noh-TEE-tsee-eh] *(f. pl.)*; *telegiornale* [teh-leh-johr-NAH-leh] *(m.)*
newspaper *giornale* [johr-NAH-leh] *(m.)*
nice *simpatico* [seem-PAH-tee-koh]; *carino* [kah-REE-noh]; *gentile* [jehn-TEE-leh]
niece *nipote* [nee-POH-teh] *(f.)*
night *notte* [NOH-tteh] *(f.)*
nine *nove* [NOH-veh]
ninety *novanta* [noh-VAHN-tah]
ninth *nono* [NOH-noh]
no *no* [NOH]
   no longer *non . . . più* [nohn PYOO]
   no more *non . . . più* [nohn PYOO]
nobody *nessuno* [neh-SSOO-noh]
normal *normale* [nohr-MAH-leh]
not *non* [nohn]
   not at all . . . *affatto* [ah-FFAH-ttoh]
   not even . . . *neanche* [neh-AHN-keh]; . . . *nemmeno* [neh-MMEH-noh]
   not yet . . . *ancora* [ahn-KOH-rah]
nothing *non . . . niente* [nohn NYEHN-teh]
November *novembre* [noh-VEHM-breh]
nowadays *oggigiorno* [oh-jee-JOHR-noh]
number *numero* [NOO-meh-roh]
   toll–free number *numero verde* [noo-meh-roh VEHR-deh]

O

occasion *occasione* [oh-kah-ZYOH-neh] *(f.)*
occupation *occupazione* [oh-kkoo-pah-TSYOH-neh] *(f.)*
October *ottobre* [oh-TOH-breh]
of *di* [dee]
offer (to) *offrire* [oh-FFREE-reh]
old *vecchio* [VEH-kyoh]
older *maggiore* [mah-JJOH-reh]
on *su* [soo]
   on foot *a piedi* [ah PYEH-dee]
   on time *in orario* [een oh-RAH-ree-oh]
   on top *sopra* [SOH-prah]
one *uno* [OO-noh] *(m.)*; *una* [OO-nah] *(f.)*
only *solo* [SOH-loh]
opinion *parere* [pah-REH-reh] *(m.)*

In my opinion... *A mio parere* . . . [ah MEE-oh pah-REH-reh]/*Secondo me* . . . [seh-KOHN-doh MEH]

opinion poll *sondaggio* [sohn-DAH-jjoh]

optimist *ottimista* [oh-tee-MEE-stah] *(m./f.)*

optimistic *ottimista* [oh-tee-MEE-stah] *(m./f.)*

or *o* [oh]

original *originale* [oh-ree-jee-NAH-leh]

other *altro* [AHL-troh]

otherwise *oppure* [oh-PPOO-reh]

our *nostro* [NOH-stroh]

ours *nostro* [NOH-stroh]

outer *esterno* [eh-STEHR-noh]

outside *fuori* [FWOH-ree]

owe (to) *dovere* [doh-VEH-reh]
How much do I owe you? *Quanto Le devo?* [KWAHN-toh leh DEH-voh]

own *proprio* [PROH-pree-oh]

page *pagina* [PAH-jee-nah]

painting *pittura* [pee-TTOO-rah]

palace *palazzo* [pah-LAH-tsoh]

pants *pantaloni* [pahn-tah-LOH-nee] *(m. pl.)*

paper *carta* [KAHR-tah]

parallel *parallelo* [pah-rah-LLEH-loh]

parents *genitori* [jeh-nee-TOH-ree] *(m. pl.)*

party *festa* [FEH-stah]
to throw a party *dare una festa* [DAH-reh OO-nah FEH-stah]

pass (to) *passare* [pah-SSAH-reh]

Passover *Pasqua ebraica* [PAH-skwah eh-BRAH-ee-kah]

pasta *pasta* [PAH-stah]

pastry *pasta* [PAH-stah]
pastry shop *pasticceria* [pah-stee-cheh-REE-ah]

pastime *passatempo* [pah-ssah-TEHM-poh]

pay (to) *pagare* [pah-GAH-reh]

people *gente* [JEHN-teh] *(f. sing.)*

pepper *pepe* [PEH-peh]

percent *per cento* [pehr CHEHN-toh]

performance *rappresentazione* [rah-ppreh-zehn-tah-TSYOH-neh] *(f.)*

pessimist *pessimista* [peh-see-MEE-stah] *(m./f.)*

pessimistic *pessimista* [peh-see-MEE-stah] *(m./f.)*

pharmacy *farmacia* [fahr-mah-CHEE-ah]

phenomenal *fenomenale* [feh-noh-meh-NAH-leh]

photo(graph) *foto (grafia)* [FOH-toh (grah-FEE-ah)] *(f.)*

pillow *cuscino* [koo-SHEE-noh]

pink *rosa* [ROH-zah]

place *luogo* [LWOH-goh]; *posto* [POH-stoh]

plague *peste* [PEH-steh] *(f.)*

please *per favore* [pehr fah-VOH-reh]; *per piacere* [pehr pyah-CHEH-reh]

please (to) *piacere* [pyah-CHEH-reh]

pleased *lieto* [lee-EH-toh]
Pleased to meet you. *Molto lieto.* [MOHL-toh lee-EH-toh]; *Piacere.* [pyah-CHEH-reh]

pleasure *piacere* [pyah-CHEH-reh] *(m.)*

pollen *polline* [POH-llee-neh] *(m.)*

poor *povero* [POH-veh-roh]

popular *popolare* [poh-poh-LAH-reh]

population *popolazione* [poh-poh-lah-TSYOH-neh] *(f.)*

possibility *possibilità* [poh-ssee-bee-lee-TAH]

possible *possibile* [poh-SEE-bee-leh]

post office *posta* [POH-stah]

postcard *cartolina* [kahr-toh-LEE-nah]

potato *patata* [pah-TAH-tah]

pound *libro* [LEE-broh]

prefer (to) *preferire* [preh-feh-REE-reh] *(isc.)*

pre–paid *prepagato* [preh-pah-GAH-toh]

prepare (to) *preparare* [preh-pah-RAH-reh]; *prepararsi* [preh-pah-RAHR-see] *(oneself)*

present *regalo* [reh-GAH-loh]

president *presidente* [preh-zee-DEHN-teh] *(m./f.)*

pretend (to) *fare finta di* [FAH-reh FEEN-tah dee]

prince *principe* [PREEN-chee-peh] *(m.)*

princess *principessa* [preen-chee-PEH-ssah]

professor *professore* [proh-feh-SSOH-reh] *(m.)*; *professoressa* [proh-feh-ssoh-REH-ssah] *(f.)*

profound *profondo* [proh-FOHN-doh]

program *programma* [proh-GRAH-mmah] *(m.)*

public *pubblico* [POO-bblee-koh]

pull (to) *tirare* [tee-RAH-reh]

quarter *quarto* [KWAHR-toh]

question *domanda* [doh-MAHN-dah]

quickly *velocemente* [veh-loh-cheh-MEHN-teh]

quiet *silenzioso* [see-lehn-TSYOH-zoh]; *quieto* [kwee-EH-toh]

rabbit *coniglio* [koh-NEE-lyoh]

radio *radio* [RAH-dee-oh] *(f.)*

rain (to) *piovere* [PYOH-veh-reh]

reaction *reazione* [reh-ah-TSYOH-neh] *(f.)*

read (to) *leggere* [LEH-jjeh-reh]

ready *pronto* [PROHN-toh]

realize (to) *rendersi conto* [REHN-dehr-see KOHN-toh]

really *davvero* [dah-VVEH-roh]; *proprio* [PROH-pree-oh]; *veramente* [veh-rah-MEHN-teh]

receipt *tagliando* [tah-LYAHN-doh]; *ricevuta* [ree-cheh-VOO-tah]

red *rosso* [ROH-ssoh]

region *regione* [reh-JOH-neh] *(f.)*

regular *normale* [nohr-MAH-leh]

relatives *parenti* [pah-REHN-tee] *(m. pl.)*

relax (to) *rilassarsi* [ree-lah-SSAHR-see]

remember (to) *ricordarsi* [ree-kohr-DAHR-see]

Renaissance *rinascimento* [ree-nah-shee-MEHN-toh]

repeat (to) *ripetere* [ree-PEH-teh-reh]

reservation *prenotazione* [preh-noh-tah-TSOY-neh] *(f.)*

restaurant *ristorante* [ree-stoh-RAHN-teh] *(m.)*

restroom *toletta* [toh-LEH-ttah]; *toilette* [twah-LEHT]

Is there a restroom? *C'è una toletta?* [CHEH OO-nah toh-LEH-ttah]

return (to) *tornare* [tohr-NAH-reh]; *ritornare* [ree-tohr-NAH-reh]

review *ripasso* [ree-PAH-ssoh]

right *destra* [DEH-strah] *(side)*; *diritto* [dee-REE-ttoh] *(privilege)*; *giusto* [JOO-stoh] *(correct)*

right away *subito* [SOO-bee-toh]

ride *giro* [JEE-roh]

ring *anello* [ah-NEH-lloh]

roast *arrosto* [ah-RROH-stoh]

roasted *arrosto* [ah-RROH-stoh]

roof *tetto* [TEH-ttoh]

room *camera* [KAH-meh-rah]; *sala* [SAH-lah]; *stanza* [STAHN-tsah]
bedroom *camera (da letto)* [KAH-meh-rah dah LEH-ttoh]
chat room *stanza di chat* [STAHN-tsah dee CHEHT]
double room (two beds) *camera doppia* [KAH-meh-rah DOH-ppyah]

room *(continued)*
double room (one bed) *camera matrimoniale* [KAH-meh-rah mah-tree-moh-nee-AH-leh]
single room *camera singola* [KAH-meh-rah SEEN-goh-lah]
dining room *sala da pranzo* [SAH-lah dah PRAHN-tsoh]
living room *soggiorno* [soh-JJOHR-noh]

ruins *rovine* [roh-VEE-neh] *(f. pl.)*

rule *regola* [REH-goh-lah]

rush *fretta* [FREH-ttah]

rush (to) *affretarsi* [ah-ffreh-TTAHR-see]

S

sad *triste* [TREE-steh]

safe *sicuro* [see-KOO-roh]
safe–deposit box *cassaforte* [kah-ssah-FOHR-teh] *(f.)*

salad *insalata* [een-sah-LAH-tah]

salami *salame* [sah-LAH-meh] *(m.)*

salesman *venditore* [vehn-dee-TOH-reh]

saleswoman *venditrice* [vehn-dee-TREE-cheh]

salon *salone* [sah-LOH-neh] *(m.)*

salt *sale* [SAH-leh] *(m.)*

sandwich *panino* [pah-NEE-noh]

Saturday *sabato* [SAH-bah-toh]

sauce *sugo* [SOO-goh]

say (to) *dire* [DEE-reh]

schedule *orario* [oh-RAH-ree-oh]

sculptor *scultore* [skool-TOH-reh] *(m.)*; *scultrice* [skool-TREE-cheh] *(f.)*

sculpture *scultura* [skool-TOO-rah]

season *stagione* [stah-JOH-neh] *(f.)*

seat *posto* [POH-stoh]

second *secondo* [seh-KOHN-doh]

secretary *segretaria* [seh-greh-TAH-ree-ah]

see (to) *vedere* [veh-DEH-reh]
to see a show *assistere a uno spettacolo* [ah-SSEE-steh-reh ah OO-noh speh-TTAH-koh-loh]
See you! *Ci vediamo!* [chee veh-DYAH-moh]
See you later. *A più tardi.* [ah PYOO TAHR-dee]
See you soon. *A presto.* [ah PREH-stoh]
See you tomorrow. *A domani.* [ah doh-MAH-nee]

seem (to) *sembrare* [sehm-BRAH-reh]

send (to) *mandare* [mahn-DAH-reh]

sense (to) *sentire* [sehn-TEE-reh]

September *settembre* [seh-TEHM-breh]

serious *serio* [SEH-ree-oh]

seriously *sul serio* [sool SEH-ree-oo]

serve (to) *servire* [sehr-VEE-reh]

set design *scenografia* [sheh-noh-grah-FEE-ah]

seven *sette* [SEH-tteh]

seventh *settimo* [SEH-ttee-moh]

seventy *settanta* [seh-TTAHN-tah]

several *diverso* [dee-VEHR-soh]; *parecchio* [pah-REH-kkyoh]

sex *sesso* [SEH-ssoh]

share (to) *condividere* [kohn-dee-VEE-deh-reh]

she *lei* [LAY]

shirt *camicia* [kah-MEE-chah]

shoe *scarpa* [SKAHR-pah]

shopping *spese* [SPEH-zeh] *(f. pl.)*
to go shopping *fare le spese* [FAH-reh leh-SPEH-zeh]

short *basso* [BAH-ssoh]; *corto* [KOHR-toh]

show *spettacolo* [speh-TTAH-koh-loh]
variety show *spettacolo di varietà* [speh-TTAH-koh-loh dee vah-ree-eh-TAH]

shower *doccia* [DOH-chah]

sign *segno* [SEH-nyoh]

similar *simile* [SEE-mee-leh]

sin *peccato* [peh-KAH-toh]

sincerely *sinceramente* [seen-cheh-rah-MEHN-teh]

single (unmarried) *single* [SEEN-guhl]; *celibe* [CHEH-lee-beh] *(m.)*; *nubile* [NOO-bee-leh] *(f.)*

sister *sorella* [soh-REH-lah]

site *sito* [SEE-toh]

six *sei* [SAY]

sixth *sesto* [SEH-stoh]

sixty *sessanta* [seh-SSAHN-tah]

size *taglia* [TAH-lyah] *(clothing)*; *numero* [NOO-meh-roh] *(shoes)*

slowly *piano* [PYAH-noh]

small *piccolo* [PEE-kkoh-loh]
small hotel *pensione* [pehn-SYOH-neh] *(f.)*

smaller *minore* [mee-NOH-reh]

smell *sentire* [sehn-TEE-reh]

smile (to) *sorridere* [soh-RREE-deh-reh]

snow (to) *nevicare* [neh-vee-KAH-reh]

so *allora* [ah-LLOH-rah]; *così* [koh-ZEE] *(like this)*
so–so *così così* [koh-ZEE koh-ZEE]

soap *sapone* [sah-POH-neh] *(m.)*
soap opera *telenovela* [teh-leh-noh-VEH-lah]

soccer *calcio* [KAHL-choh]

sock *calzino* [kahl-TSEE-noh]

some *qualche* [KWAHL-keh]; *alcuni/-e* [ahl-KOO-nee/eh] *(m./f. pl.)* di + article

someone *qualcuno* [kwahl-KOO-noh]

something *qualcosa* [kwahl-KOH-zah]

son *figlio* [FEE-lyoh]

soprano *soprano* [soh-PRAH-noh]

Sorry. *Mi dispiace.* [mee dee-SPYAH-che]

soup *minestra* [mee-NEH-strah]

speak (to) *parlare* [pahr-LAH-reh]

spoon *cucchiaio* [koo-KYAH-yoh]

spring *primavera* [pree-mah-VEH-rah]

square (city) *piazza* [PYAH-tsah]

stadium *stadio* [STAH-dee-oh]

stage *palcoscenico* [pahl-koh-SHEH-nee-koh]

stairs *scale* [SKAH-leh] *(f. pl.)*

stamp *francobollo* [frahn-koh-BOH-lloh]

stand (to) *sopportare* [soh-ppohr-TAH-reh] *(a person)*

star *stella* [STEH-llah]

state *stato* [STAH-toh]

station *stazione* [stah-TSYOH-neh] *(f.)*

statue *statua* [STAH-too-ah]

stay (to) *stare* [STAH-reh]; *restare* [reh-STAH-reh]

steak *bistecca* [bee-STEH-kkah]

stop (to) *fermarsi* [fehr-MAHR-see]

stop (transportation) *fermata* [fehr-MAH-tah]

store *negozio* [neh-GOH-tsyoh]
  store window *vetrina* [veh-TREE-nah]

strange *strano* [STRAH-noh]

street *via* [VEE-ah]

student *studente* [stoo-DEHN-teh] *(m.)*; *studentessa* [stoo-dehn-TEH-ssah] *(f.)*

studio *studio* [STOO-dee-oh]

study (to) *studiare* [stoo-dee-AH-reh]

stupendous *stupendo* [stoo-PEHN-doh]

style *stile* [STEE-leh] *(m.)*

subject *argomento* [ahr-goh-MEHN-toh]; *tema* [TEH-mah] *(m.)*

suggest (to) *suggerire* [soo-jjeh-REE-reh] *(isc.)*; *consigliare* [kohn-see-LYAH-reh]

suit *vestito* [veh-STEE-toh]; *costume* [koh-STOO-meh]

sum *somma* [SOH-mmah]

summer *estate* [eh-STAH-teh] *(f.)*

sun *sole* [SOH-leh] *(m.)*

Sunday *domenica* [doh-MEH-nee-kah]

sure *sicuro* [see-KOO-roh]

surely *sicuramente* [see-koo-rah-MEHN-teh]

survey *sondaggio* [sohn-DAH-jjoh]

sweater *pullover* [POOL-oh-vehr] *(m.)*

sweet *dolce* [DOHL-cheh]

synagogue *sinagoga* [see-nah-GOH-gah]

T

table *tavolo* [TAH-voh-loh]

take (to) *prendere* [PREHN-deh-reh]

tall *alto* [AHL-toh]

taxi *taxi* [TAH-ksee]
  taxi driver *taxista* [tahk-SEE-stah] *(m./f.)*

teacher *insegnante* [een-seh-NYAN-teh] *(m./f.)*; *maestro/a*

telephone *telefono* [teh-LEH-foh-noh]
telephone card *carta/scheda telefonica* [KAHR-tah/SKEH-dah teh-leh-FOH-nee-kah]

television (programming) *televisione* [teh-leh-vee-ZYOH-neh]

television set *televisore* [teh-leh-vee-ZOH-reh] *(m.)*

tell (to) *dire* [DEE-reh]
  To tell you the truth... *A dire la verità* . . . [ah DEE-reh lah veh-ree-TAH]

ten *dieci* [DYEH-chee]

tennis *tennis* [TEH-nnees] *(m.)*

tenor *tenore* [teh-NOH-reh] *(m.)*

tenth *decimo* [DEH-chee-moh]

Thank you (very much). *(Tante) grazie.* [TAHN-teh GRAH-tsyeh]

Thanks. *Grazie.* [GRAH-tsyeh]

that *che* [keh]; *quello* [KWEH-lloh]

the *il* [eel] *(m. sing.)*; *la* [lah] *(f. sing.)*; *lo* [loh] *(m. sing.)* *i/gli* [ee/lyee] *(m. pl.)*; *le* [leh] *(f. pl.)*

their *loro* [LOH-roh]

theirs *loro* [LOH-roh]

them *loro* [LOH-roh]; *le* [leh]

then *allora* [ah-LLOH-rah]

there *ci* [chee]; *lì* [LEE]; *là* [LAH]
  there are *ci sono* [chee SOH-noh]
  there is *c'è* [CHEH]

they *loro* [LOH-roh]

thing *cosa* [KOH-zah]

think (to) *pensare* [pehn-SAH-reh]

third *terzo* [TEHR-tsoh]

thirty *trenta* [TREHN-tah]

this *questo* [KWEH-stoh]

thought *pensiero* [pehn-SYEH-roh]

thousand *mille* [MEE-lleh] *(m.)*; *mila* [MEE-lah] *(pl.)*

three *tre* [TREH]

Thursday *giovedì* [joh-veh-DEE]

ticket *biglietto* [bee-LYEH-ttoh]

tie *cravatta* [krah-VAH-ttah]

time (clock) *ora* [OH-rah]
  What time is it? *Che ore sono?* [KEH OH-reh SOH-noh]
  Do you have the time? (fml./infml.) *Sa/Sai l'ora?* [SAH/SAH-ee LOH-rah]

time (instance) *volta* [VOHL-tah]; *tempo* [TEHM-poh]
  at times *a volte* [ah VOHL-teh]
  Once upon a time... *C'era una volta* . . . [CHEH-rah OO-nah VOHL-tah]

timetable *orario* [oh-RAH-ree-oh]

tissue *fazzoletto* [fah-tsoh-LEH-ttoh]

to *a* [ah] + city; *in* [een] + country/continent/state/region

today *oggi* [OH-jjee]

together *insieme* [een-SYEH-meh]

tomb *tomba* [TOHM-bah]

tomorrow *domani* [doh-MAH-nee]

tongue *lingua* [LEEN-gwah]

tonight *stasera* [stah-SEH-rah]

too *anche* [AHN-keh]
  Me too. *Anch'io.* [ahnk-EE-oh]
  too many *troppi/-e* [TROH-ppee/ppeh]
  too much *troppo* [TROH-ppoh]

topic *argomento* [ahr-goh-MEHN-toh]; *tema* [TEH-mah] *(m.)*

tour *giro* [JEE-roh]

tourist *turista* [too-REE-stah] *(m./f.)*

touristy *turistico* [too-REE-stee-koh]

towel *asciugamano* [ah-shoo-gah-MAH-noh]

tower *torre* [TOH-rreh] *(m.)*

town *paese* [pah-EH-zeh] *(m.)*

traffic *traffico* [TRAH-ffee-koh]

train *treno* [TREH-noh]

transfer (to) *cambiare linea* [kahm-BYAH-reh LEE-neh-ah] *(transportation)*; *trasferire* [trah-sfeh-REE-reh] *(isc.)*

travel (to) *viaggiare* [vyah-JJAH-reh]

treasure *tesoro* [teh-ZOH-roh]

trifle *cosa da poco* [KOH-zah dah POH-koh]

trim (haircut) *spuntatina* [spoon-tah-TEE-nah]

true *vero* [VEH-roh]

try (to) *cercare di* [chehr-KAH-reh dee]; *provare* [proh-VAH-reh] *(to try on)*

Tuesday *martedì* [mahr-teh-DEE]

turn off (to) *spegnere* [SPEH-nyeh-reh]

TV *tv* [tee-VOO] *(f.)*

twenty *venti* [VEHN-tee]

twins *gemelli/-e* [jeh-MEH-llee/eh] *(m./f. pl.)*

two *due* [DOO-eh]

type *tipo* [TEE-poh]

typical *tipico* [TEE-pee-koh]

U

ugly *brutto* [BROO-ttoh]

umbrella *ombrello* [ohm-BREH-lloh]

unbelievable *incredibile* [een-kreh-DEE-bee-leh]

uncle *zio* [TSEE-oh]

under *sotto* [SOH-ttoh]

understand (to) *capire* [kah-PEE-reh] *(isc.)*

unforgettable *indimenticabile* [een-dee-mehn-tee-KAH-bee-leh]

unfortunately *purtroppo* [poor-TROH-ppoh]

university *università* [oo-nee-vehr-see-TAH]

us *ci* [chee]; *noi* [NOY] *(after prep.)*

usually *di solito* [dee SOH-lee-toh]

V

vandalism *vandalismo* [vahn-dah-LEE-zmoh]

various *diverso* [dee-VEHR-soh]

vegetarian *vegetariano* [veh-jeh-tah-ree-AH-noh]

viewpoint *parere* [pah-REH-reh]

village *villaggio* [vee-LLAH-jjoh]

volleyball *pallavolo* [PAH-llah-VOH-loh] *(f.)*

vote *voto* [VOH-toh]

vote (to) *votare* [voh-TAH-reh]

W

wait (to) *aspettare* [ah-speh-TTAH-reh]

to wait in line *fare la coda* [FAH-reh lah KOH-dah]

waiter *cameriere* [kah-mehr-YEH-reh]

waitress *cameriera* [kah-mehr-YEH-rah]

wake up (to) *svegliarsi* [zveh-LYAHR-see]

walk *passeggiata* [pah-sseh-JAH-ttah]; *giro* [JEE-roh]

to take a walk *fare una passeggiata* [FAH-reh OO-nah pah-sseh-JAH-ttah]

want (to) *volere* [voh-LEH-reh]

war *guerra* [GWEH-rrah]

wash (to) *lavare* [lah-VAH-reh]; *lavarsi* [lah-VAHR-see] *(oneself)*

watch *orologio* [oh-roh-LOH-joh]

Watch out! *Attenzione!* [ah-ttehn-TSYOH-neh]

watch (to) *guardare* [gwahr-DAH-reh]

water *acqua* [AH-kwah]

mineral water *acqua minerale* [AH-kwah mee-neh-RAH-leh]

we *noi* [NOY]

weather *tempo* [TEHM-poh]

What's the weather like? *Che tempo fa?* [KEH TEHM-poh FAH]

The weather's nice. *Fa bel tempo.* [FAH BEHL TEHM-poh]

Web *rete* [REH-teh] *(f.)*

Wednesday *mercoledì* [mehr-koh-leh-DEE]

week *settimana* [seh-ttee-MAH-nah]

weekend *fine-settimana* [FEE-neh-seh-ttee-MAH-nah] *(m.)*

welcome *benvenuto* [behn-veh-NOO-toh]

Welcome! *Benvenuti!* [behn-veh-NOO-tee]

You're welcome. *Prego.* [PREH-goh]

well *bene* [BEH-neh] *(adv.)*; *allora* [ah-LLOH-rah] *(interj.)*

what *cosa* [KOH-zah]; *che* [KEH]

What a pity! *Che peccato!* [KEH peh-KAH-toh]

What do you say to . . . ? *Cosa ne dici di . . . ?* [KOH-zah neh DEE-chee dee]

when *quando* [KWAHN-doh]

where *dove* [DOH-veh]

while *mentre* [MEHN-treh]

white *bianco* [BYAHN-koh]

who *chi* [KEE]; *che* [keh]

Who knows? *Chi lo sa?* [KEE loh SAH]

why *perché* [pehr-KEH]

Why don't . . . (we do something) *Perché non . . .* [pehr-KEH NOHN]

wife *moglie* [MOH-lyeh] *(f.)*

will *voglia* [VOH-lyah]

win (to) *vincere* [VEEN-cheh-reh]

wind *vento* [VEHN-toh]

It's windy. *Tira vento.* [TEE-rah VEHN-toh]

window *finestra* [fee-NEH-strah]

wine *vino* [VEE-noh]

wine bar *enoteca* [eh-noh-TEH-kah]

winnings *vincite* [VEEN-chee-teh] *(f. pl.)*

winter *inverno* [een-VEHR-noh]

with *con* [kohn]

with it (coll.) *in gamba* [een GAHM-bah]

without *senza* [SEHN-tsah]

wolf *lupo* [LOO-poh]

wood *legno* [LEH-nyoh]

world *mondo* [MOHN-doh]

worry (to) *preoccuparsi* [preh-oh-koo-PAHR-see]

worse *peggio* [PEH-jjoh] *(adv.)*; *peggiore* [peh-JJOH-reh] *(adj.)*

worth (to be) *valere* [vah-LEH-reh]

It's (not) worth it. *(Non) vale la pena.* [nohn VAH-leh lah PEH-nah]

Wow!; Damn! *Accidenti!* [ah-chee-DEHN-tee]; *Cavolo!* [KAH-voh-loh]

wrap (to) *incartare* [een-kahr-TAH-reh]

write (to) *scrivere* [SKREE-veh-reh]

wrong *sbagliato* [zbah-LYAH-toh]

Y

yawn *sbadiglio* [zbah-DEE-lyoh]

year *anno* [AH-nnoh]

Happy New Year! *Buon anno!* [BWOHN ah-NNOH]

yellow *giallo* [JAH-lloh]

yes *sì* [SEE]

you *tu* [too] *(sing. fam.)*; *Lei* [LEH-ee] *(sing. fml.)*; *voi* [VOH-ee] *(pl.)*

young *giovane* [JOH-vah-neh]

younger *minore* [mee-NOH-reh]

your *tuo* [TOO-oh] *(infml. sing.)*; *Suo* [SOO-oh] *(fml. sing.)*; *vostro* [VOH-stroh] *(pl.)*

yourself *ti* [tee] *(infml.)*; *si* [see] *(fml.)*

Z

zero *zero* [TSEH-roh]

zone *zona* [TSOH-nah]

INDEX